The Life Of The Late Right Reverend John Henry Hopkins

First Bishop Of Vermont And Seventh Presiding Bishop

John Henry Hopkins

Alpha Editions

This Edition Published in 2021

ISBN: 9789354505645

Design and Setting By
Alpha Editions
www.alphaedis.com
Email – info@alphaedis.com

As per information held with us this book is in Public Domain.
This book is a reproduction of an important historical work. Alpha Editions uses the best technology to reproduce historical work in the same manner it was first published to preserve its original nature. Any marks or number seen are left intentionally to preserve its true form.

PREFACE.

Four years ago this day, my face was turned from New York to Rock Point, to undertake the work which is now laid before the reader. That it should have occupied me four years instead of one, has been far more of a disappointment and loss to me, than it can be to any of my Father's friends. But the task—easy as it seemed at first—was filled with difficulties which I did not anticipate, to say nothing of interruptions from other duties.

Most of our ecclesiastical biographies are written as flowers are pressed. Amiability excludes everything that may not be agreeable to others, until the result is perfectly dry, and quite flat. This result, it is hoped, has been avoided, on the whole. My Father's life was one of almost uninterrupted controversies: and to omit these would be like writing the life of a great General and omitting all the battles. To give a lifelike account of these controversies, however, in such a manner as at the same time to avoid injustice to others, required minute and painstaking caution. I cannot hope, in such delicate work, to avoid giving any dissatisfaction.

It will be enough if no real ground is afforded for serious blame.

In examining my Father's papers, I found that he had himself, a few years previous to his departure, gone patiently over the accumulated mass of letters received during his lifetime, and destroyed all except such as he thought would be of use to me in this work. For twenty years I had in vain besought him to write an *Autobiography*. A few brief fragments, and a sketch of his earlier years in verse (privately printed for his descendants at the time of the Golden Wedding in 1866), were all that I obtained: and his unfailing answer to fresh entreaties was, that I must do that work for him, if it was ever to be done at all. Knowing, therefore, that the letters left undestroyed by him were intended for my information in preparing this biography, I have used them perhaps more freely than I should have done under other circumstances.

In regard to the subject of Episcopal Trials, which touches some of the tenderest points herein alluded to, it must be remembered that we were in this country experimenting in a branch of Church discipline, where our Mother Church of England gave us no precedents for our guidance; nor was there anything in the Mediæval Church which could serve as a practical help. The Primitive Church alone could be of use: and yet even that only in a very general kind of way. Bishops, mostly without any professional legal training or experience, were compelled by the circumstances of their position to be

Judges in a Court from which there was no appeal. They were conscientiously most sensitive as to the doctrinal and moral bearings of what they were doing; but the very intensity of their feelings and convictions on these points tended to weaken or confuse such partial knowledge of the principles of justice and of law as they might have happened to acquire. The worst errors, as to confounding the offices of presenter and judge, in times of extreme excitement and alarm, were errors of the head, and should be very lightly passed over, since the intention was, evidently and most earnestly, to do what was right. I have detailed these things, not for the purpose of reflecting upon individuals, but rather as showing some parts of the process by which, as a National Church, we have obtained our education in this most difficult and disagreeable department of Ecclesiastical business; and as some assistance towards other National or Provincial Churches, whose work in this direction is as yet wholly or partially to be done. Our worst mistakes have been very slight, compared with such awful scenes as the Primitive Church witnessed at the Council of Tyre, or the Robber Synod of Ephesus, or many others that might be mentioned.

To a Catholic mind, when desponding or disheartened under some little annoyance of the present moment, there is nothing more consoling than to watch the gradual growth of the great Church Revival, as unfolded in the various steps of a life like this of the first Bishop of Vermont. The proof that GOD'S HOLY SPIRIT is at work in our American Branch of the Church,—that He is causing the "root out of a dry ground" to spring, and bud, and blossom, and to bring forth the ripe fruits of Catholic Unity and Beauty and Brotherly Love,—that He overrules errors, and brings good out of evil, and accomplishes results, through men, which those men never dreamed of: the proof of all this is a cumulative proof, and grows stronger with each year of our past history which is carefully examined.

My general rule of condensation in preparing this sketch of my Father's life, has been, to make as graphic a picture of the man himself as was in my power, under the limitations which must ever control the pen of a son; and as part of this, I have given some prominence to the characteristics of American society in the early part of the century, and to the peculiarly American commingling of nationalities,—English, Irish, French, and German, being here brought together in one family. Next, the chief stress has been laid on those parts of his thought and action which bore directly on the great Catholic Revival of our age, and the growth and hopes of the Future. And, lastly, I have paid the least attention to those things which belong to the fading and disappearing, the effete and dying, Past. This is the rule of choice which I know would have been most agreeable to him.

As a pledge of my fidelity to truth, I can only say, that every word of this work has been written in the room in which my Father breathed his last;—

has been written at the desk where he wrought, and from the very inkstand out of which he wrote, for years; and, as it were, with his presence in the very air about me all the while. And were it in my power, I would gladly lay the manuscript before him in Paradise, that it should receive his corrections before it is seen by any other eye.

Besides my personal consultations with the dear survivors at Home, who have expressed themselves as satisfied with the accuracy of every part of the completed work, I am indebted for valuable personal reminiscences of the Pennsylvania contest in 1827 to the Rev. Dr. William Cooper Mead; for similar services touching the Boston difficulty in 1832 to the Rev. Dr. Edson, of Lowell, and the Rev. Dr. Thomas W. Coit, of Troy; as well as to many others in other portions of my work. To the Rev. Dr. William Stevens Perry, of Geneva, Secretary of the House of Deputies, I owe most particular thanks, not only for the immense collection of books, pamphlets, and autograph letters concerning our American ecclesiastical history, which renders him a benefactor to the American Church as a whole: but also for the personal kindness which has placed his treasures so unreservedly at my disposal, and has so often supplemented my ignorance with his superior information concerning every part of our history.

But, notwithstanding my anxious care, if there are found in these pages errors which do injustice to others, I shall thank any one who may have the kindness to send me the proof of the truth, and will cheerfully make any correction and reparation that may be in my power.

J. H. H., Jr.

Rock Point, Burlington, Vt.,
Feast of S. Philip and S. James, 1872.

CONTENTS.

CHAPTER I.

FROM BIRTH TO MANHOOD.

The Hopkins family, English—Sketch of the Irish branch of it—Birth and Infancy—Education at Home—Character of Parents—Solitary—Precocious reading—Emigration to America—Trenton—School at Bordentown—Princeton—Removal to Philadelphia—Music—The Violoncello—S. Peter's Church—A year in a Counting-House—Wilson's Ornithology—The Philological Society—Separation of Parents—French and Scottish Friends—Spaniards and Germans—Temptations to Skepticism—Reads both sides—Attractions of Manufactures—Iron—Three years of Preparation—Twenty-one—Business begun at Bassenheim—Frequent Depression of Spirits—James O'Hara—New engagement in Ligonier Valley. . Pp. 21-36

CHAPTER II.

LIGONIER VALLEY.

Sketch of the Müller family—Caspar Otto—The Trance family—Hamburg and Lockstädt—Emigration—Baltimore, and the War of 1814—Melusina—Removal to the West—A Meeting on Laurel Hill—Courtship in a Log-cabin—Music and Poetry—Betrothal—Hermitage Furnace—Spiritual Conversion—Religious Services among the Workmen—Sympathy in the Change—Prospect of failure in Business—Peculiarities of Courtship—Study of Law begun—Marriage—Housekeeping in a Log-cabin—Medical Practice—Attachment of the Workmen—William Dobbin—Madam Hopkins—The Peace fatal to Iron manufacture—Failure and Debt—Generous Conduct of Mr. O'Hara—Closing up the Business at Hermitage—Literary Influence—Aquila M. Bolton—Francis B. Ogden—His new Steam-engine—Farewell to Ligonier Valley. . . . . . . Pp. 37-51

CHAPTER III.

THE LAWYER.

Teaching while studying Law—James R. Lambdin—Admission to the Bar—Suits against Lawyers—Compromising Suits without Litigation—No unjust Cause undertaken—Prompt payment of Moneys collected—First serious Case—Loss of Voice—A Jury case—Extemporary power—Sarcasm—Freemasonry — Failure of Health from Overwork—At the Head of the Pittsburgh Bar—Purchase of a Place in the Country—A Partner—Dr. Heron's Meeting-house — Organist in Trinity Church—The Rev. Abraham Carter—Family Prayer—Bible-reading, English and Greek—" I'll lend you a Sermon!"—Thoughts of the Ministry—In the Vestry—Death of Edward Müller—The Law and the Gospel—Elected Rector of Trinity Church—Admitted a Candidate for Orders—The Heirs of O'Hara—The Election accepted—Lay Reading—Law Business sold out—Candidacy of two Months—Diaconate of five Months—Ordained Priest—Reasons for these Anomalies. . . . . Pp. 52-68

Chapter IV.

FIRST-FRUITS OF THE PRIESTHOOD.

Sketch of previous Church History in Western Pennsylvania—Destitution and Decay—Dr. Doddridge—Efforts that came to Nothing—Trinity Church, Pittsburgh—Movement for a new Church—Brittan's Gothic Architecture—The Rector the Architect—Corner-stone laid by the Masons—Rector's Address—The Church a Success—The Rector furnishes all the Church Music—Bishop White's first Visitation — Labors in other places — Meadville—Greensburg—Journey to the East—Bishop Hobart—The Rector in the Diocesan Convention—Parochial Reports—In the General Conventions of 1826 and 1829—Opposes Bishop Hobart's plan for Altering the Prayer-Book—That plan defeated—Advocates the Consecration of the Rev. William Meade—His aid kindly remembered. . . . Pp. 69-83

Chapter V.

THE CONTESTED EPISCOPAL ELECTION.

Low-Church Irregularities—Bishop White openly and repeatedly denounces them—Elections in the Conventions of 1822, 1823, 1824, 1825—Low-Church Caucus—*Episcopal Recorder* started—High-Church Caucus and Triumph—Bishop White calls a Special Convention to Elect an Assistant Bishop—Pitched Battle begins—Low-Church inflammatory Pamphlets—Sharp Partisan electioneering — Bishop White's Address at the Special Convention—Bishop White insulted—A Tie defeats Mr. Meade's Election—Intense Excitement—Caucussing during the Convention—Permanent Organization of the Low-Church Party—Permanent Organization of the High-Church Party—"Confidential Circular" and "Private Letter"—Pamphlet War—The Laity rally to the support of Bishop White against Low-Church assaults—The Rev. Mr. Meade denouncing his own partisans—His honorable proposal of a Compromise—Rejected by his own Friends—He withdraws his Name—Pittsburgh holding the Balance of Power in the Diocese — The Rev. Mr. Hopkins talked of as the High-Church Candidate—He refuses to coöperate—Correspondence with Mr. Wallace—The Harrisburg Convention, 1827 — High-Church Caucus — Mr. Hopkins refuses to vote for himself—Dr. Henry U. Onderdonk the nominee—The full Story of his Election—The Remonstrance against his Consecration—More Pamphlets—Bishop Hobart's Sermon and Bishop White's Address at the Consecration—Low-Church rage against Bishop Hobart—Blind Blunders of human Passion—Moral of the Contest and its Consequences. . . . . Pp. 84-111

Chapter VI.

THE WORK DONE AT PITTSBURGH.

Reading both sides—Father McGuire—Patristic Studies begun—Eusebius—The Reformation an Appeal to the Primitive Church—Indexes and Latin Versions of the Fathers—The Mixed Chalice—Unleavened Bread—Ritualistic ideas—Christian Sisters—School for Girls and Boys—Oratory—Oil Painting—Seven men trained for the Ministry—Striking Influence of the System upon the Minds of various Persons—School Concerts and Festivals—Call to New York—Invitation to Maryland declined—Promoting Peace—Memorial in favor of a Theological Seminary at Pittsburgh—Site offered—New Constitution and Canons of Pennsylvania—Unfavorable Reports on the Memorial—The Proposal referred to the Trustees of the General Theological Seminary—Invitation to Boston declined—Visit to Boston—The Trustees of the General Theological Seminary decline to act on the Memorial—The Massachusetts Theological School—The renewed Call to Boston accepted—Parting from the Pittsburgh parish—The last Sunday—The Oratory—Farewell. . . . . Pp. 112-132

Chapter VII.

AT BOSTON.

Sketch of previous Church History in the Eastern Diocese—Bishop Griswold's Policy—The Rev. Mr. Doane—His dominant Influence—His promising Plan of a Seminary—Carried in the Convention of 1831—Arrival of the new Assistant Minister—Warm Reception from all—Too good to last—Differences of Temperament—The Low-Church take Advantage of the Occasion—Strife of Tongues—Rumors from Vermont—Bishop Griswold's reasons for persuading a continuance in Boston—The Theological School tested, and found wanting—Election as Bishop of Vermont—First Visit to Vermont—Acceptance—Canonical Difficulties—Climax of the Contest in Massachusetts—The Balance of Power in the Convention changes Hands—Desperate Effort to recover lost ground—The Manifesto—The Defence of the Convention—Popularity with the Low-Church—Silver Plate—Attempt to stop the Consecration of the Rev. Mr. Doane—Defeated—Ohio and New Jersey in the General Convention of 1832—Consecration of Four Bishops—Removal to Burlington—Moral of the Struggle and its Consequences. . . . Pp. 133-155

Chapter VIII.

BISHOP OF VERMONT.

Peculiarities of Vermont—Emigration to the West—Sketch of Church History in Vermont—Bishop Griswold's Administration—Church Lands—Appeals—Proportionate Representation of the Laity—The Bishop resides at Burlington—His House and Grounds—Enlargement for a School—Parochial Duty—Authorship begun—*Christianity Vindicated*—*The Primitive Creed*—" Father Irenæus "—Clergy to be provided within the Diocese—The Bishop a Judge—The Oratory highly adorned—Substitute for Stained Glass—Epidemic Typhoid—Death of a Daughter—Visit to Montreal and Quebec—*The Primitive Church*—His teaching concerning the Church, Baptismal Regeneration, Temperance Societies, the black Gown, Episcopacy, the Reünion of Christendom, the continued Validity of Primitive and Anglican Church Law, Appeals, Diocesan Codes of Canons, etc. . Pp. 156-173

Chapter IX.

THE STRUGGLE FOR DIOCESAN SCHOOLS.

Sale of Property in Pittsburgh—Proceeds invested in further Enlargement of Schools in Burlington—Rapid growth of the Schools—Extent of the new Buildings—Misgivings disregarded—Borrowed Money secured by Mortgage— Intention to devote all to the Church—*Essay on Gothic Architecture*—Denunciation of the Pew System—Visit of his aged Father—Parish School—Loss and Gain of Burlington Parish—Earnest pressure upon the Convention—The New Constitution and Canons of Vermont—Their salient Features—Defended in a Pamphlet on "The Episcopal Veto" so-called—An Ecclesiastical Trial—The enlarged Buildings occupied—The Hall of the Fine Arts—Concert-Festivals—The completed Oratory—The School System—*The Church of Rome*—Intense Pressure of varied Activities—Landscape Paintings—School Excursions—Boating, Bathing, Fishing, Music—Financial Revulsion of 1837—Festival to the Convention—Action of the Convention amounts to Nothing—The Hard Times—Decrease of Pupils—Canadian "Rebellion"—Withdrawal of Canadian Pupils—The Bishop in the Schoolroom—His proposal to the Convention of 1838—Cold reception—Finally carried—Excuses for the timidity of the Diocese—Determination to attempt the raising of Funds in England. . . . . Pp. 174-190

Chapter X.

EFFORT ABROAD, AND FAILURE AT HOME.

Life-Preserver—The good ship S. Andrew—Francis B. Ogden—Dublin—Archbishop Whately—Hurricane in Ireland—London—English reminiscences of Bishops McIlvaine, Hobart, and Philander Chase—Not permitted to preach in England—Speeches at public Meetings—High reputation of his work on *The Church of Rome* in England—An English Edition, with *Introduction* by the Rev. Henry Melvill—Bishop Copleston's Opinion of the Book—Oxford—The Guest of Mr. Newman—Dr. Pusey, Henry Wilberforce, Churton—Littlemore—Dublin Anniversaries—McNeile, McGhee—Oxford again—May Anniversaries in London—The Bible Society—At Court—His Songs—*Twelve Canzonets* published—Small pecuniary Results—Various Reasons for this Failure—Return Home—Discouraging Reception at Burlington—The Schools closed—Vain appeal to his Convention—Empty Efforts—Sheriff's sale of Personal Property—Meeting of Creditors—Enough for all, but they refuse to protect themselves—Foreclosure of Mortgage—House work at Home—The Oratory dismantled—Removal of the Dead—Present value of that Property—Similar Failures among our Bishops—Lesson to be learned from these Failures—Revival of the Religious Orders. . . . . Pp. 191-206

Chapter XI.

ROCK POINT.

Removal from the Old Place—Dilapidated House in Burlington—Pea-rods—Beautiful View from Hemlock Hill—A Lease of Rock Point obtained, with Right to purchase—Roughness subdued—The new House built for a Homestead—The first Winter—Description of the Point—Home Life there—Constant Gratitude—Poverty—Lectures—Fruits of the School—Arthur Carey—Discouragement as to the steady Decline in the Diocese—Desire to resign and labor elsewhere—Authorship and the General Institutions of the Church. . . . . Pp. 207-213

Chapter XII.

OXFORDISM—CANONICAL LEGISLATION.

The Oxford Tracts—Substantial Identity of Effort—Charge of 1842—Our new Missionary System—High Commendation of the Tracts—Mar Yohannan and Nestorianism—Efforts in General Convention for a Court of Appeals—The Three-Bishop Presenting Power—History of its Adoption—Attempted Revival of the Diaconate—Preference for Suffragan Bishops—Uniform System of Ecclesiastical Law—Progressive Legislation on the Trial of a Bishop—Proposed Canon "*Of Indefinite Suspension*"—General Denunciation of Tract No. 90—It drives Men out of the Church—*First Letter* to Bishop Kenrick—Invitation to Oral Discussion declined by Bishop Kenrick—*Second Letter* to Bishop Kenrick—The Carey Ordination—Anti-Papal Panic—Change of View as to Tract No. 90—*Letters on the Novelties that disturb our Peace*—Kindness of tone towards Arthur Carey and Bishop Benjamin T. Onderdonk—Delight of the Low-Church at the *Letters on the Novelties*—Challenged by the Bishop of New York to present him for Trial for False Doctrine—The Bishops of Illinois and Ohio willing to present—No such Presentment made—*Lectures on the British Reformation*—Proposed delivery of them in Philadelphia—Their Publication—The General Convention of 1844—Visitation of the General Theological Seminary by the Bishops—Debates on the Oxford Tracts and on the Character of Dr. Hawks—Case of Bishop Henry U. Onderdonk—Prospect of a similar attack on the Bishop of New York. . . Pp. 214–227

Chapter XIII.

THE ONDERDONK CASE.

Three Presenters undertake to act—Some of the Stories evaporate under Examination—The *animus* rested on only one Allegation—But for that, no Presentment would have been made—That Allegation Disproved on the Trial—Errors of Judgment by the Accused—The two-witness Rule—The Evidence substantially unimpeached—The vote for Deposition—Moral considerations influencing the Majority of the Bishops afterwards—The *Opinion* of the Bishop of Vermont—The two-witness Rule never heard of since—Anonymous Attacks—Lighting his Pipe—*The Protestant Churchman* started—The Bishop of Vermont a Contributor—He is treated as a Standard-bearer and Leader—The Low-Church sure of him—They hint their intentions against "New Jersey and Maryland"—Bishop McIlvaine desires united Action against Tractarianism—Letters Dimissory—Pamphlet against Dr. Seabury—Second Letter to Dr. Seabury—Low-Church Congratulations—Bishop McIlvaine wishes " to discipline some Puseyite distinctly for Puseyism "—How to punish a Parish—Friendly Visit from Dr. Seabury—Alarm of Dr. Anthon and his Friends—They find the Bishop of Vermont very intractable—He opposes their Notion about the Vacancy of the See—Their Reluctance to Print the Argument—Personal Motives urged upon him by them—Bishop Carlton Chase on the Argument—The Bishop of Vermont opposes any Increase of the Penalty inflicted on Bishop Onderdonk—Speech in the Board of Trustees—Sermon at the Consecration of Bishop Alonzo Potter—Attacked by the *Episcopal Recorder* as worse than all the Tenets of Oxford put together—Application for the Consecration of a Bishop for the Scottish Schismatics—How replied to—Bishop Daniel Wilson of Calcutta on Presbyterian Schisms—Disgust and Dissatisfaction of the High-Church—Their proposed Disintegration of the Church of America—Bishop De Lancey's scheme for rendering the General Theological Seminary merely Diocesan—Opposed by the Bishop of Vermont, and defeated—He writes the Onderdonk Reports of the

14   Contents.

House of Bishops in 1847 and 1850—The Special Meeting, called for in 1849, uncanonically postponed by the Presiding Bishop—The House of Bishops " in Council "—The case of Bishop Henry U. Onderdonk—Pamphlets by Mr. Horace Binney, Bishop Meade, and the Bishop of Vermont—*The True Principles of Restoration to the Episcopal Office*—Bishop Henry U. Onderdonk restored on those Principles in 1856—Those Principles disregarded in the case of Bishop Benjamin Onderdonk in 1859—Consequent Failure of the Effort—Last Declarations of Bishop Benjamin Onderdonk. . . . . Pp. 228-249

Chapter XIV.

THE NEW JERSEY CASE.

Proceedings against Bishop Doane contemplated for years—Ventured on after his Failure—All the Errors of Judgment made by the Presenters—Their first Blunder—The *Protest, Appeal, and Reply*—The New Jersey Investigation—The uncanonical Adjournment of the Court—The new Presentment—The Bishop of Vermont asks to be excused from sitting on the Trial—He is not excused—Is made President of the Court—The opening of the Court at Camden—The 35th Psalm—Bishop Doane his own Lawyer—The Court adjourns to Burlington—The New Jersey Committee is heard—How Bishop Doane " made the Trial of a Bishop hard "—The Bishop of Mississippi's *Opinion*—The Court decides not to proceed—The President one of the Minority—His *Opinion* concerning the Right of a Diocese to intervene—He labors to restore true Catholicity—Bishop Williams on that *Opinion*—Bishop Meade's Indignation at the Result—Third Presentment made—More Blunders—The Presenters have their Lawyers in a little Room adjoining—The Promise to produce the list of 130 Names is forfeited—The argument prepared by Counsel is read in Court—The Decision of the first Court overruled, and the *Opinion* of the Bishop of Vermont sustained, by the second Court—The " right " of the Diocese to intervene finally denied—Happy Compromise—Bishop Doane's frank and voluntary Acknowledgment—The Accused unanimously discharged without Trial—Results of all this Experience—Present Canon makes the Trial of a Bishop so " hard " as to be nearly impossible—The Constitutional Change wrought by these Trials in the position of the Episcopate as an Order—High-Church and Low-Church changing Parts in this Work—General Good-will when all was over. . . . . Pp. 250-267

Chapter XV.

BOOKS AND PAMPHLETS.

Parish Growth—Elected Rector in St. Alban's—Parsonage secured—Enlargement of the Church in 1851—Adorns the Chancel with his own Hands—Ecclesiological Society—Altar-Cloth—Choral Services—*Two Discourses on the Second Advent*—Completes his eighteen years' Work in reading the Fathers and Councils—Begins to translate the *Summa* of S. Thomas Aquinas—The *Vermont Drawing Books* of *Flowers* and *Figures*—Rock Point purchased, under Mortgage, by the aid of a Friend—Defections to Rome, in Vermont—Repeal of Church Law by *Non-user*—This Opinion changed soon afterwards—No Narrowness ever in Personal Relations with those of either Party—His Candidates free to attend any Parish in good standing—" Between Hawk and Buzzard "—Begins a *Commentary on the Whole Bible*—Plan, and Mode of Working—*The History of the Confessional*—Bishop McIlvaine in favor of presenting Bishop Ives for Trial—Intended Permission of private Confession and Absolution in the Church of England—Two Reasons for it—Letter from Bishop Ives—The First Book of Edward VI. gives the true Anglican position—*The Gorham Case considered*—The real Points of it not correctly understood—Popular Lectures—Slavery—Thanks from the Clergy of Buffalo—Approval of Henry Clay and Daniel Webster—Proposed Letter to Senator Phelps on Slavery, abandoned—*Milner's End of Controversy, Controverted*—*Friendly Remonstrance with the Editors of the Church Journal*—Importuned to write for the *Episcopal Recorder*. . . . . Pp. 268-285

Chapter XVI.

DIOCESAN AND GENERAL.

Double Depression of the Diocese—Decline in the number of Clergy—Repeating the General Confession—Clerical Changes in Vermont—Lowest Depression in 1848—Laity admitted to form part of the Standing Committee—Some signs of Improvement—Early Confirmation approved—Retrospective Summary in 1853—Convocation of Vermont—Opposition to the Consecration of the Rev. Dr. Upfold—Opposition to the Consecration of Bishops Meade, Burgess, Young, and Doane, all unsuccessful—Principle underlying the Failure—The *Digest* of the Canons—Sermons before the General Convention of 1847 and the Board of Missions in 1850—Adheres to our Mission System—Acting with the High-Church in 1850 on the Maryland Case—Plan for a Court of Appeals, involving the germ of the Provincial System—Bishop De Lancey's proposal for dividing into Provinces—Warm Reception on Passing through Pittsburgh—Deposition of Bishop Ives in 1853—Projects of new Canons for the Trial of a Bishop—Chairman of the Committee on Canons—One of the Committee on the Pastoral Letter—Canadian Hospitalities—Arrival of Bishop Fulford—Assistance in Synodical organization. . . . . . Pp. 286-294

Chapter XVII.

THE VERMONT EPISCOPAL INSTITUTE.

The Bishop of Vermont is arrested for debt in Boston in 1854—Bailed by two Friends—His silent Sorrow—Plan of Relief—Rock Point offered for Sale, to the Church the purchase money to extinguish the old Debts—Rock Point to become Church Property, for the Bishop's Residence and for Church Schools—The sad Silence broken in August—The Plan approved in Burlington—One subscriber of $5000—The Convention adopts the Plan—Charter obtained—Arrangement with Boston Creditor—Rock Point conveyed to the Trustees—Unexpected Opposition in Burlington—Exciting Interview—Easter afternoon Sermon—Protracted discussion at Easter Parish Meeting—Resignation both of Diocese and Parish threatened—The Parish unanimously vote to reject the Plan—The $5000 Subscription withdrawn—Apparent Hopelessness of canvassing the rest of the Diocese—The Willoughby bequest of $10,000—its Condition—The rest of the Diocese favorably disposed—The Clergy themselves subscribe—Even Burlington does better—The Parish Debt extinguished—Journey to St. Louis and New Orleans—Raising Funds in Philadelphia, Baltimore, Pittsburgh, and New York—Resignation of the Rectorship of S. Paul's—The *American Citizen*—The Pastoral Letter of 1856—Plan for the Seminary Building adopted—Duty of remembering God and the Church in every Last Will and Testament—Widow of Dr. Willoughby—The Building begun—Financial Revulsion of 1857—Subscriptions not paid—New Rector in Burlington—Episcopal Visitation in Pennsylvania for Bishop Alonzo Potter—New Episcopal Robes, different from the ordinary Pattern—Hospitality to the Convention, yearly, at Rock Point—Kind Feeling and Concord in the Diocese—Raising Funds in the Cities, harder than before—The General Convention of 1859—Consecration of Bishop Gregg of Texas—The *Digest*—Invitation to Sewanee—Rural life there—Winter's Cough cured—Religious Services—Meeting with Bishop Elliott and Bishop Polk—Artistic Work at Sewanee—The earnings there all given to finish the Chapel of the Institute—Description of the Building and Chapel—Consecration of the Chapel, 1860—Dr. Hicks elected Professor, and the Rev. Theodore A. Hopkins Principal of the Academic Department—Economy of Construction—Rectorship in Rutland earns more Money for the Institute—Similar Earnings in Brandon—Attempt to found a Girls' School also—The Effort Interrupted by the War—Never accomplished. . . . . Pp. 295-319

Chapter XVIII.

THE CIVIL WAR.

Request from Friends in New York in 1860—Pamphlet on *The Bible View of Slavery*—Same Views often published by him before—Pamphlet published in January, 1861—The "right to secede"—The Question of Treason to be submitted to the Supreme Court—Abolition of Slavery advisable, but to be done by the Southern States themselves—"American Society for Promoting National Unity"—Pamphlet reissued, omitting prefatory matter and the part touching Secession—Fall of Fort Sumter—Letter to Bishop Polk, opposing the Secession of his Diocese—Bishop Polk's reply—Similar Letter to Bishop Meade, and his Reply—Convention Address on Allegiance and political Preaching—No political Sermons or Resolutions in Vermont—Clergy and Relatives in the Army—Resists the attempt to stop the Stipend of Missionaries in Alabama—*Letter to the Bishops and Delegates at Montgomery*, against organizing "The Church in the Confederate States"—Special Forms of Prayer, non-committal—Thirty years' Retrospect of Diocesan Growth—The General Convention of 1862—Debate on the State of the Country—Democrats and Republicans combine to "do something"—Political pressure—Next to nothing done in the Lower House—The Bishop of Vermont presiding—Prestige of Bishop McIlvaine—His draft of a Pastoral Letter adopted—Its political Tone—The Bishops interpret the National Constitution "as official Expositors of the Word of God"—The Protest of the Bishop of Vermont—Published—He is absent from the Chancel while the political Pastoral is read—The Holy Eucharist offered on that Occasion—President Lincoln's Thanks for the Pastoral—The dropped "Memorial"—Resistance to the political Pastoral—Request in February, 1863, for the reissue of *The Bible View of Slavery*—The request granted—Reprinted at once—Larger Editions in June, in New York—Taken up by the Democratic Clubs in July—The political canvass in Pennsylvania that Year—The Democratic Candidate a Churchman—The Bishop of Pennsylvania drafts a Protest against *The Bible View of Slavery*—The Condition of his signing it—The Protest circulated for signatures to be given " immediately "—Invasion of Pennsylvania by Gen. Lee—Battle of Gettysburg—Intense political Excitement—Suspected collusion between the Democrats and the Enemy—Bishop Potter's "private" circular favoring peace and quietness—Perplexity of many of the Clergy—Reply to the Protest—A Book promised—Rejoinder by one of the Pennsylvania Clergy—Further Reply—Dissuasion attempted in vain—The Book on *The Bible View of Slavery* begun, and pushed with all Rapidity—The Feeling of Devotion to the Truth of God's Word with which it was written—Seven Editions—No evil

Consequences—His Diocese as attached as ever—"Declaration" in the *Essays and Reviews* Cases—Bitter local Controversies in Pennsylvania about the Protest—Bishop Stevens and other Clergymen attacked for not signing—The Diocesan Convention at Pittsburgh—Political Resolutions and Debate in Trinity Church—Dr. Washburn's speech—Proposed adoption of the Protest and Censure of Bishop Hopkins's Book—Hisses—The motion dropped—Judge Shaler's speech—Dr. Van Deusen's Resolution in Bishop Stevens's words adopted—Contrast in 1866—The Bishop of Vermont presiding in that same Church at the Consecration of the first Bishop of Pittsburgh—The First Lesson for the Day—Coincidence—Farewell to Pittsburgh. . . . . Pp. 320-342

CHAPTER XIX.

THE REÜNION OF THE CHURCH.

The Bishop of Vermont becomes Presiding Bishop—The Rule of Seniority unprimitive, absurd, and inconvenient—His Presidency favorable to Reünion—His ideas as to the War—His rejoicing at the prospect of Peace—Difficulties—The Low-Church as a War-party—Bloodthirsty Low-Church Editorial in Philadelphia—The Bishop of Vermont invited to New Orleans and Memphis before the War was over—Attempt to secure from the Northern Bishops a united Invitation to the Southern to return—Its Failure—The Presiding Bishop writes in his own Name—The General Convention of 1865—The Welcome given to the Bishop of North Carolina and Bishop Lay—Delegations from three Southern Dioceses—Consecration of Bishop Quintard—Triumphs at that General Convention—Reünion certain and speedy—No Pastoral Letter—Bishop McIlvaine's draft rejected—The Presiding Bishop's draft too late for Acceptance—"Suggestions for the General Convention of 1868"—Two of them already carried into Effect—Consecrations of Bishops at Chicago, Boston, Pittsburgh, New Orleans, Louisville—Singing of the *Veni, Creator Spiritus*—Ovation at the South—Thrown from the Railway Track on his Return—Uninjured—Letter from Bishop Cariton Chase—Disappointment in not meeting Bishop Elliott at New Orleans—His sudden Death—Last letter of Friendship from Bishop Elliott—Fears of a Schism laughed to Scorn. . . . . Pp. 342-367

CHAPTER XX.

THE GOLDEN WEDDING—POETRY—CANONICAL POINTS.

The Golden Wedding Festival in 1866—Presentation of a Pastoral Staff by the Clergy of the Diocese—The Evening Reception—The Family Dinner—*Autobiography in Verse*—The Rainbows—The Early Eucharist in the Chapel of the Institute—The Marriage in Cana of Galilee—Confirmations in Maryland—Meeting with Bishop Johns of Virginia—Hospitality of the Rev. Dr. Howe—Writing Poetry on the Railway—The Gospels Versified—*The History of the Church in Verse*—Temporary Rectorship of S. Paul's, Burlington—Pleasure of Returning to Parochial Work—Large Confirmation Class—Great Enlargement of the Church Building—Energetic lay co-operation—The Bishop once more the Architect—Plan of Enlargement—Two Canonical Points—A Candidate rejected without Statement of Cause or Accuser—Received and Ordained in Vermont—Arbitrary use of Power repugnant to his sense of Justice—The Election of Dr. Whittle as Assistant Bishop of Virginia—Uncanonical, because Bishop Johns was not "unable to discharge his Episcopal duties"—The Presiding Bishop's view of the case—Certificate of the Standing Committee of Virginia—Facts—Letter of Bishop Johns to the Standing Committee of Pittsburgh—The Presiding Bishop sends out the Notices to the other Bishops, but leaves on record his own Refusal to consent to the Consecration—The Consecration almost defeated—Excuses for the View of the Canon taken in Virginia. . . . . Pp. 358-374

CHAPTER XXI.

THEOLOGICAL OPINIONS—RITUALISM.

A Constant Reader—"Justification by Faith only"—"All Bosh!"—The Council of Trent—Dr. Pusey's *Eirenicon*—New Edition of Tract No. 90, with Dr. Pusey's *Historical Preface* and Keble's *Letter—Hail Mary* as a Scriptural Anthem—His Opinions on Ritualism—Request for them, in Print—*The Law of Ritualism*—Discussion of it in the House of Bishops—His sober second Thoughts—A "Mrs. Partington sort of Business"—The *Declaration* of the Twenty-eight Bishops—Its real Object the Bishop of Vermont's Book—Ignorance and Blunders in the *Declaration*—Covered with Ridicule—Tabled in the House of Bishops—The result of the Attempts in the General Conventions of 1868 and 1871 to legislate against Ritual, proves the Correctness of the Bishop of Vermont's "little book"—Four Editions sold—Approval of it at Home and Abroad—Bishop Coxe on *The Declaration*—*The Law of Ritualism* sent to the English Bishops by the English Church Union—Cited by Sir Robert Phillimore in the Mackonochie Judgment—The Real Objective Presence, and Eucharistical Adoration—In how far the Bishop of Vermont differed from Dr. Pusey and Keble—Their Doctrine is within the intended Comprehensiveness of the Church of England—Purple Stoles ordered for S. Paul's, Burlington—Two Lights on the Altar of S. Paul's, Burlington—Increased Richness of the Services at the Consecration of Bishops Neely and Tuttle—Processionals—Surpliced Choirs—Choral Services—Consecration of Bishop Young in Trinity Church, New York—The Pastoral Staff carried before the Presiding Bishop—Treatise on the Personal Reign of Christ—Retractation of an Error—*The Pope not the Antichrist*—Dr. Mahan's estimate of this Retractation—Sharp Criticism of the Homilies—Oppression about the Head—His sole trip in the Adirondacks—Drive through the Green Mountains—Failure of Eyesight—The right Eye blind—The left Eye beginning to sympathize.

Pp. 375-391

CHAPTER XXII.

PREPARATORY TO LAMBETH.

The Bishop of Vermont, in 1851, makes the first suggestion of the Conference of Lambeth—Testimony of the Bishop of Moray and Ross—The Bishop of Maryland—The Bishop of Montreal—The Church Journal—Request of the Canadian Bishops—Request from the Convocation of Canterbury—Request from informal Meeting of English, Irish, Colonial, and American Bishops—The Invitation issued—Its Terms—Accepted—The Question laid before the Vermont Convention—What the Bishop said concerning his Poverty and his Support—The Whining about the Starving of the Clergy—The Episcopal Endowment now required by the Constitution—Funds promptly raised for the Bishop's Expenses—Voyage to England—Mizen Head—Visits to The Cathedrals of Chester and Durham—Last Sketch from Nature made at Durham—York—Poetry on the State of the Church of Eng-

Contents.   19

land—Lincoln—Peterborough, Ely, Norwich, London—Westminster Palace Hotel—Sermon at S. Lawrence, Gresham Street—Kindness of Archdeacon Wordsworth—City Mission Work in the East of London—Private Confession and Absolution—Sisterhood of All Saints, Margaret Street—" The Religious "—A Guest at Addington Park—His Opinion asked and given on the Bishop of Salisbury's *Charge*—Meets Bishop Selwyn—About the Sermon at the Opening of the Conference—How the Bishop of Illinois was appointed—At his Request the Bishop of Vermont prepares a Sermon—Salient Points of it—The Greek Church has the best of the Argument about the *Filioque*—The Archbishop of Canterbury should be a Patriarch—" Lost Ground to be recovered, Catholic Usages to be restored "—Liturgical Revision so as to be more Primitive than even the First Book of Edward VI.—The Sermon read and approved by other American Bishops—Peremptory Refusal to Interfere with the published arrangement of the Archbishop—Preliminary Meeting of September 17—The Conference "invited," not "summoned "—The Limitation of the Session to four Days—The Right to preside—Previous Arrangement of a Programme of Business—Open to Amendment or Addition—Stenographic Report to be published—None but Bishops to be present—The Introduction of the Colenso business discussed, not decided—Three meetings of Colonial Bishops at the House of Archdeacon Wordsworth—Their Conclusion—Dr. Pusey's three Objections to the Programme—All three corrected. Pp. 392-412

Chapter XXIII.

THE LAMBETH CONFERENCE.

Opening Services, without Music—Indignation of those who were excluded—The Addington Park Hospitality declined—Order of Arrangement of Seats—First Day's Debate adjourned—Speech on the Fifth and Sixth General Councils—" The undisputed General Councils "—The Colenso Resolution—The Bishop of Vermont's Substitute offered—Opposed—The private Understanding between the Archbishop and the Bishop of S. David's and others—Acknowledged—The Substitute withdrawn—Asked for, to be used as a *Declaration*—The waiving of the private Understanding asked, and refused—A *Declaration* signed by fifty-six Bishops in the Conference Room—Appointment of a successor to Colenso—The Report of the Colenso Committee in December—Speech on Church and State—The Stenographic Report to be published with Omissions—Not to be published at all, nor seen except by Bishops—Transcript for the American Bishops voted under equally stringent Restrictions—Close of the Conference—Photographers—The *Conversazione* at S. James's Hall—Fulham—Closing Religious Services at S. Mary's, Lambeth—The Bishops of New York and Quebec on the part taken in the Conference by the Bishop of Vermont—Repose needed—Brighton—High Ritualistic Services at S. Michael's, Brighton—Purchase of a Present in Rouen—Quiet week in Paris—The Oriental Liturgy—Return Voyage—Welcome at Burlington by the Vermont Clergy.   .   .   .   . Pp. 413-423

Chapter XXIV.

AT HOME.

New Rector of S. Paul's, Burlington—Correspondence with Dean Stanley—Explanation of his Refusal of Westminster Abbey for the closing Service of the Lambeth Conference—Delay in the Receipt of Dean Stanley's Letter—The Reply—Winter

Visitation of the Diocese undertaken—Last Sermon in S. Paul's, Burlington—Conversation with him on the Way to his Work—Severe Cold—Christmas in the Chapel of the Institute—Last Words sent for Publication—Visitation resumed—Exposure—Visits Plattsburgh at the Request of the Bishop of New York—His last Eucharist, Confirmation, Sermon—Severe Exposure to intense Cold on his return—Last Illness—Departure—Expressions of Feeling—Burial—The Holy Eucharist at the Funeral—Last Resting-Place—Cemetery at Rock Point—Monument. . . . . Pp. 429-443

IN MEMORIAM. . . . . Pp. 443-445

APPENDIX.

I. Complete List of the Publications of Bishop Hopkins, . . . Pp. 449-452
II. "Conversation Comparisons" (1818), ... P. 453
 "The Bell of S. John's" (1825), ... Pp. 454, 455
III. Bishop Ravenscroft's Opposition to the Consecration of Bishop Meade, ... Pp. 456-458
IV. "O Peace, O heavenly Peace" (1845), ... P. 459
 "Oh! how the Spirit" (1854), ... P. 459
V. The Bishop of Vermont's Protest against the Political Tone of the Pastoral Letter of 1862, ... Pp. 461-465
VI. Reflections on the State of the Church of England (1867), . . Pp. 466-471
VII. The Westminster Abbey Correspondence, in full, . . . Pp. 472-481

Chapter I.

FROM BIRTH TO MANHOOD

AMONG the old families of Central England, the name of Hopkins has long occupied a respectable place, having been borne by members of the House of Commons from the city of Coventry as far back as the reign of Richard the Second. Isaac Hopkins—a scion of this stock—went over to Ireland with William the Third; where, soon after the conclusion of the Treaty of Limerick in October, 1691, he married Mary Fitzgerald, and established that branch of the family from which my Father was descended. About the middle of the eighteenth century—so says family tradition—John Gunning, of Castle Coote, in the county of Roscommon, had three daughters of famous loveliness and social charms: of whom the oldest married the Earl of Coventry, the second married first the Duke of Hamilton and afterwards the Duke of Argyll; while the third married a Roman Catholic and sturdy adherent of King James the Second. A daughter of this last marriage, by a union with the oldest son of Isaac Hopkins, recovered a large portion of the great landed estate of her ancestors, which had been confiscated by the Protestants, after the persuasive custom of those times. Their oldest son, John, married Elizabeth McDermot, a woman of remarkable beauty and ability, but whose extravagance and want of business management, after she was left a widow, grievously encumbered the family estates. This burden might have been cancelled by the heir, on an appeal to the Court of Chancery, as the estates were entailed: but her oldest son John, on coming of age, refused to take any action which might cast reproach upon his mother's administration of affairs; and abandoning the paternal estates in Roscommon to be devoured of their numerous mortgages, he went to Dublin to make his own way in the world, in the humbler line of merchandise. Thither he was soon followed by his younger brother, Thomas.

After some years of steady devotion to business, dealing both in flour and linen, Thomas Hopkins, in April, 1791, married Elizabeth Fitzakerly, a highly accomplished young bride of sixteen. Her father was a Fellow of Trinity College, Dublin, and had been tutor in the family of the Duke of Rutland while the latter was Lord Lieutenant of Ireland. These advantages had not been lost upon the daughter. The only child of Thomas and Elizabeth Hopkins, my Father, was born in the city of Dublin, on the 30th day of January, 1792; and when weaned was sent to reside for several years with his paternal grandmother, who was then living in the town of Athlone. My Father remembered her as a beautiful old lady, with long white hair, who, when she had washed and dressed him in the morning, or before his going to bed at night, made him kneel down by her side, and say some simple prayer. Little care was taken of him beside this: the constant succession of visitors, the coming and going of any number of uncles and aunts and cousins, the attractions of the military stationed in the neighborhood, and all the other elements of open-handed Irish hospitality, leaving but little leisure for the care of the young child, whose most faithful companions were the servants of the house. The lesson of daily private prayer, however, was so well learned, and the habit so firmly formed, that it never was forgotten or interrupted at any subsequent period of his life. And it was here, too, that he first learned to read, the big Bible being the volume which gave him the greatest and most constant delight.

It was not until he was about six years of age that his father came for him, and carried him to Dublin to live with his parents, who until that time were almost perfect strangers to him. His mother, whom he chiefly resembled, and to whom he was indebted for his intellectual powers, had not the tenderness of maternal instinct which makes the care of the helpless infant so sweet a task: but when that earliest period was well over, she began to take pride in her bright and beautiful son, and thenceforward his education was the leading labor of her life,—her chief joy. Possessed of remarkable personal beauty, and in the very prime of womanhood, she was not only an accomplished performer on the piano-forte, skilled in the use of the pencil, and an extraordinary adept in the now reviving art of embroidery: but she was yet more distinguished—especially among the women of those days—for her wide range of general reading, and her powers of argument and conversation. Her husband admired and loved her intensely, and in some points their tastes were in happy harmony. Exquisite was the wonder and delight of the little boy as he lay upon the carpet listening to Pleyel's Sonatas, his mother presiding at the piano-forte, while his father stood beside her, accompanying her on the flute. At other times Mozart or Haydn furnished still nobler themes, nor was the flute the only instrument upon which his father played.

But, unhappily, his parents were not, in other respects, so well suited to one another. Though the husband was the senior by eight years, yet the superiority of education and of talent was too great on the side of the wife; and she had too little experience and wisdom to hide her consciousness of it. There was a brilliancy about her which belonged to a different sphere, and was apt to produce, in all who approached her, and in her husband among the rest, a most uncomfortable sense of inferiority. Both were upright in their moral principles, well-meaning in their intentions, and cordial in their feelings towards one another; both abounded in good qualities, and both treated their son with the utmost affection: yet he was compelled to learn, before he was eight years old, the pains of matrimonial discord; and he already began to wonder whether married people were always so apt to differ from each other,—whether every home was as subject to contention as his own.

His parents were nominally members of the Irish Church, and it was a matter of course that he should be baptized in infancy: but religion had little or nothing to do with the tone of the household or the system of education laid out for the boy. An occasional attendance at Church—and the ancient tombs of Earl Strongbow and others in Christ Church Cathedral made an indelible impression on his imagination—could do but little. He received no regular instruction in the Christian Faith. He was taught no Catechism. He knew no clergyman of the Church.

Neither of his parents ever approached the Holy Communion. Neither of them ever said a word to him concerning the worth of the soul, or the great gift of salvation. Nor was it until many years after, when my Father was himself in Holy Orders, and mainly through his instrumentality, that his parents at last—though not together—became devout communicants in the Church.

It was natural that, with her fondness for society, his mother should frequently dilate upon the connection of the family—at the fourth or fifth remove—with the nobility: Ireland not being the only place where such connections are valued in the inverse ratio of their nearness. But even in his early childhood, her son derived impressions from her conversation on this subject, which were the opposite of what she wished to convey. It was very clear to him that those noble relatives did not think it worth their while to hold any intercourse with either his parents or himself; and he therefore regarded them with a goodly measure of contempt, mingled with a certain portion of resentment: while he inwardly resolved that he would attain a higher elevation by being the artificer of his own fortunes. This youthful feeling of proud self-reliance was rendered still stronger by the fact that he was entirely thrown in upon himself, so far as the heart was concerned. His mother did not know how to win his affectionate confidence. Among persons who were all so much older than himself, he became precociously thoughtful and reserved. He had no brother, or sister, or playmates; and the pride which his mother took in teaching him at home, prevented him from enjoying the usual companionships of schoolfellows. The habit of solitary and self-reliant action, thus early formed, moulded the character of his whole life, and shaped more or less the practical results of all its varied activities.

With so brilliant a teacher, and so apt a pupil, however, it is no wonder that rapid progress was made. Before his eighth year was completed, he had read Shakspere, Dryden, and Pope, besides any quantity of tales and romances. In music, he could take his part easily in Haydn's Symphonies. French was already familiar to his tongue; and in drawing he had made handsome progress. The want of companionship deprived him of any inducement to enjoy outdoor life; and he remained at home, devouring every kind of reading that he could lay his hands on.

His uncle John had meanwhile emigrated to the United States, and wrote thence such glowing accounts of that country and its openings for advancement in life, that it was determined to wind up business in Dublin, and sail for the New World. The passage was very long and stormy, and filled with all manner of discomforts and disgusts. But one incident is well worthy of mention.[1] During the height of a tremendous storm one day, when passengers and sailors were in great distress fearing total shipwreck, the little boy thought of One who seemed to be remembered by nobody else around him; and, retiring behind a pile of sails near the mainmast in order to be alone, he knelt down and prayed to God to deliver them out of their danger. One of the sailors happened to pass, and observed him; and, with the strong feeling so characteristic of his class, he went to the Captain at once, and told him what he had seen and heard: adding, that "the ship was safe; for it was impossible she should come to grief while such a little angel was on board of her."

It was in the month of August, 1800, while he was yet in his ninth year, that they landed at New York, and soon after went on to Philadelphia, where every effort made by his father to get into business failed. When all the money brought with him had been expended in these attempts, his mother came to the rescue, and provided for the support of the family by opening a girls' school at Trenton[2] in New Jersey. She was admirably qualified for this good work, not only by her own unusual variety of accomplishment and information, but by her contempt of false pretences and shams, the exactness and unflinching thoroughness of her instructions, and the high-toned manners which she knew how to impart to her pupils. These advantages gave her so strong a hold upon public esteem that for many years her school maintained a very high character, and a sufficient number of scholars, at good prices for those days.

---

[1] This was told us by my grandfather Hopkins himself, during the only visit he ever paid us, in 1836.
[2] The house in which they lived was a stone house, with brick front, or'ginally built by the British for a barrack, and commanding a good view of the river.

By the time my Father was eleven years old, he had learned all that his mother could teach him; and for Latin, Greek, and mathematics he must look elsewhere. He was therefore sent to a boarding-school at Bordentown, where he remained for nearly two years. The principal of this school was a Baptist minister,— a kind-hearted man and a good Latin scholar, with quite a library of books outside the usual studies of the school. The first contact of the high-strung, sensitive home-plant with the rough thorns and brambles of the highway, was painful enough. The rudeness, obscenity, and profanity that are commonly met with among schoolboys shocked him excessively. Their art of tormenting the delicate stranger was for some time kept in full play, until human nature could stand it no longer; and one day, under gross provocation, he defended himself against a bigger boy, and after a plucky and protracted contest, gave him a fair beating. After this he was treated very respectfully, and allowed to do pretty much as he pleased. In his Latin studies, the Colloquies of Corderius and the Dialogues of Erasmus occupied a prominent place, though they have long since disappeared from the *curriculum* of modern schools: and the large proportion of time then devoted to the writing of both Latin and Greek was more likely to produce accurate scholarship, than the easier slipshod modes which have since become fashionable. It was a matter of course for him to win his master's confidence by readiness and diligence in his studies. The good man was a widower, and possessed of sufficient accomplishment himself to be strongly drawn towards the precocious boy confided to his charge. He took him to sleep in his own chamber, and gave him the key to his extensive library, where the vacant hours, devoted by the other boys to outdoor amusement, were spent among far more congenial books. He did not avoid athletic exercises altogether, indeed: he took his fair share in these, from time to time. And he well remembered the natural beauties of the place: the broad, rippling current of the Delaware River, the varied foliage, the singing of the birds, the glorious sunsets, the wild flowers of the neighborhood, all left their impress upon his mind and heart. But his chief delight was in that library, where, all alone, he lived in a little world of his own. It afforded a range, it must be confessed, beyond the usual luck of Baptist ministers; for there he found *The British Drama*, complete; besides many of the Poets, the best Historians, and works on Art and on Medicine. Of novels there were not so many; and yet even here he found Fielding and Smollett, Miss Burney and Anna Radcliffe, besides "Don Quixote" and the "Arabian Nights," with not a few others. It is not often that so large an amount of general reading is mastered by one so young.

At that time there was no Church in Bordentown. On Sundays there was nothing to be done, therefore, but to attend the Baptist meeting, where my Father heard nothing that made any impression upon his memory. During the whole of his residence at that school, he could not remember that anything had been said to him personally on the subject of religion. But besides the remembrance of his master's partiality and kindness, he carried away with him vivid recollections of some of his schoolmates, one of whom—the son of a distinguished portrait painter—was a young fellow of infinite fun and drollery, and such "good company" that he turned out, at last, to be good for nothing else.

After nearly two years spent in this school at Bordentown, my Father was sent by his mother to Princeton, to reside in the family of a French refugee,—one of the old *noblesse*, who had fled penniless from the horrors of the Revolution in his native land, and was compelled to support himself in a strange country by giving lessons in dancing, fencing, and the Parisian pronunciation of his mother tongue. In less than a year these three accomplishments were sufficiently mastered; and meanwhile the passion for reading was further indulged among the books found on the shelves of the refugee, among which were Rousseau, Marmontel, Molière, and a considerable portion of Voltaire's works. The knowledge of French thus gained was of great value: but, in some points of view, that sort of reading did him more harm than good.

Meanwhile, his mother's school had succeeded so well in Trenton, that she was encouraged to transfer it to the larger sphere of Philadelphia. Here she was now joined by her son, who began to render active assistance in her labors, taking special charge of the drawing classes. The larger part of his time, however, was still devoted to the continuance of his own education, mathematics and Greek being his chief studies; while at the same time music occupied a portion of his leisure hours. He mastered the violin to a degree sufficient to enable him to take his part in the best amateur concerts which Philadelphia could then produce. A musical friend succeeded in organizing a society of these amateurs, and when they came together they found they had flutes, violins, clarionets, violas, bassoons, flageolets, and French horns; but there was no violoncello. What was to be done? No other solution of the problem presenting itself, my Father undertook to learn the indispensable instrument, and in one month's time bore his part to the satisfaction of all. This success encouraged him in his efforts, and he became so skilful that for years he was the only solo player on the violoncello in Philadelphia. A love for it remained with him during his whole life; and even when past his threescore years and ten, no winter passed by without two or three times, at least, drawing the bow across the strings of his old sonorous friend, and enjoying once more the melodies which were the favorites of his youth.

On removing to Philadelphia, he attended Church with his mother at old S. Peter's, then, with Christ Church, under the pastoral charge of Bishop White. The Rev. Dr. Abercrombie was one of the Assistant Ministers of the united parish at that time, and with his son my Father soon became quite intimate. But there seems to have been nothing in his Church associations, during these early years, that excited any real interest; he was conscious of no strong attraction, no living power which could influence or mould his youthful character. All the vivid forces of his opening life ran in far other channels than the quiet and prosy respectabilities of S. Peter's in those days. The idea of being confirmed never seems to have entered his head, or to have been suggested to him by others. But if religious helps were weak or lacking, it was to be expected that religious dangers should be strong and urgent. Many of his musical friends were Frenchmen, whose intimacy was too likely to lead to looseness both of tongue and morals. The open display of these tendencies, however, so disgusted the pure tastes of the home-bred youth, that he soon learned to evade the intimacy which he could not enjoy, and met such friends as these only on the evenings devoted to their music. As to general society, he was cordially welcomed in all the families which sent pupils to his mother's school, and these families formed a circle inferior to none in the city, whether for high position or refinement and intelligence.

It was about his fifteenth year that two of his worthiest friends, merchants, offered him a place in their counting-house, with the idea of training him to business. His mother consented, though with great reluctance, being anxious that he should devote himself to the Law : nor were his own desires by any means active in the direction of mercantile life. But the narrowness of his domestic circumstances, and the hope of soon doing something to relieve his mother of the burden of his support, induced him cheerfully to accept the offered place. A whole year's wasted weariness cured him. Jefferson's Embargo had put a stop to foreign commerce for a time ; and as his friends were in the foreign trade, their new *employé* found himself with little or nothing to do. What a year that must have been to one of such intense activities, already tasting the delights of vigorous exercise in so many different directions ! Long before the year was out, he was thoroughly satisfied that he could never be a merchant.

A much more congenial sort of drudgery was soon thrown in his way. Wilson the ornithologist had begun the publication of his *Birds of America ;* but, in the infancy of the arts among us at that time, he was unable to find any one competent to color the splendid plates of that great work from Nature. My Father was at length induced to attempt it. The price paid was lucrative, to him : and his proficiency in the art of painting,[1] his delicacy and accuracy of both eye and hand in observing and imitating the hues and the forms of Nature, ensured him a degree of success which delighted his employer, besides being, for a time, very agreeable to himself. Mr. Wilson always shot a fresh bird for his colorist, so that there should be no chance of the fading or changing of the brilliant tints of life. But constant repetition at length brought weariness, where the work had been begun with so much of zest and conscious self-improvement: and when other assistants had been sufficiently well trained, the task-work was willingly transferred to humbler hands.

[1] In water-colors, he had, at that day, no superior in this country ; and his love for this art, as for music, continued unabated during his whole life.

The first result of my Father's freedom from his counting-house experiment, was his joining a "Philological Society,"—an association in which quite a number of young men encouraged and aided each other in literary pursuits, by written essays and oral discussions on various subjects. To a mind and temperament like his, nothing could well have been more interesting or improving; and he devoted himself with the greatest zeal to the duties which this Society imposed. The question of his future profession was more or less a topic of frequent thought and conversation. His mother was still earnest that he should choose the Law, and his own prepossessions were very strong in that direction. An incident which happened in the Philological Society one evening greatly strengthened this prepossession in his own mind, and produced a very strong conviction to the same effect among his youthful associates. He had been appointed to open an oral debate on some point or other, and made quite an elaborate and convincing speech, as seemed to all. His opponent, instead of replying, only apologized for his failure to sustain the negative on that question, pleading that an inflammation of the eyes, much to his regret, had rendered it entirely impossible to read up and prepare himself on a subject of which he had no previous knowledge. The excuse was accepted as sufficient; but the Chairman, unwilling to mutilate so seriously the exercises of the evening, called on the members generally, hoping that some one of them might feel able and willing to fill the gap. Silence, however, was the only reply; and, after an awkward pause, the Chairman called on my Father to resume the discussion, hoping that a few words further from him might encourage the rest. He rose, therefore, and—taking the place of his opponent—argued the negative of the case himself, reviewing fluently all the points made in his former speech, and proving that they were all wrong! This unusual specimen of strength and skill struck them all with surprise and delight, and loud was the applause that rang through the room when he sat down. The story soon spread far and wide among their many friends, and all agreed that one who could so readily and cleverly argue both sides of the same question, "must be a lawyer."

It was not long after this, that the ever-increasing incompatibility of temper led to the permanent separation of his parents. It was only incompatibility; and, as in all such cases, both were more or less to blame. Neither had any fault to find with the son who was equally dutiful to both. Each—but especially his mother—regarded him with affection and growing pride. It was not for him, however, to take sides, or interfere between them; but often, with a silent tear, he retired to the solitude of his own chamber to escape the coming strife of bitter words. At length they parted. The husband remained, as a book-keeper, in Philadelphia: the wife transferred her school to Frederick, in Maryland, where for several years she kept it up with diminishing success. My Father remained in Philadelphia, supporting himself by his own exertions, and pleased that those who were so dear to him should cease the mutual irritation of a daily intercourse which neither could enjoy. He hoped that absence would not only suffer this irritation to cease, but would in time revive the affection of their earlier years. In this he was unhappily disappointed. They never met on earth again.

The growing circle of my Father's friends was not confined to the leading American families in Philadelphia. There were—as we have seen—some French families to whom he was attracted by their music and painting; there were Scotchmen, too—some literary men and some manufacturers—with whom he became quite intimate; and later still, Spaniards and Germans enlarged the sphere of his observation and the variety of his personal attachments. The tone of all these was irreligious, infidel, and loose on many subjects of morality: and that he should have moved among them, as he did, exposed to constant danger and temptation, and yet preserved from any gross or serious delinquency, my Father in after years regarded gratefully as one of the wonders of God's Providence. It was in the society of his Scottish friends, however, that he found his greatest danger. They were men of strong minds, much cultivated in a certain way, shrewd and ingenious; and as they were very partial to him, he soon found that the aggressiveness of their infidelity would be sure to affect him, if he did not make up his mind to a definite resistance. But so distant were the clergy from his sympathies, that it never once occurred to him to approach one of them, to ask the slightest question on the subject. He rushed into this new investigation himself, without shrinking; borrowed the books of the most noted infidels, Paine, Volney, Hume, Mirabeau, Voltaire, and Rousseau; and read them carefully, at intervals, during two years,[1] until he felt himself fully acquainted with all their arguments against Christianity.

But he was conscious that he had been reading only one side of a great question, and he was now resolved to know something of the other. He consulted a bookseller, not a clergyman, as to his choice of volumes, and procured without delay the work of Paley, the answer of Bishop Watson to Paine, and Leslie's *Short and Easy Method with the Deists.* The perusal of these, and especially the last, gave him his first clear and definite ideas upon the subject, convincing his intellect thoroughly of the truth of the Gospel. Thus armed and ready, it was not long before one of the most acute of his Scottish friends,—a young man some five years older than himself, the son of a wealthy manufacturer who had trained up his son in unbelief,—provoked an argument by calling the whole class of Christian ministers "a set of knaves and hypocrites, who gained an easy living by imposing a system of lies upon weak men, women, and children." He was at once met with a sturdy defence, and the two friends went into a protracted and—for men of their age and antecedents—a remarkably thorough controversy, covering the whole ground of the then coarse and popular infidelity. And the result was, that the younger champion was not worsted upon a single point, from beginning to end.

Meanwhile, though the inclination towards the Law was still dominant in my Father's desires, as it had been the constant object of his mother's ambition for him, his practical Scottish friends had succeeded in making more impression on him touching his career in life, than they could in their attempts to unsettle his faith as a Christian. Their first line of argument was indeed a failure. When they denounced the whole work of the noble profession of the Law, as simply selling the use of one's tongue

---

[1] From his seventeenth to his nineteenth year.

and brains to any purchaser who had money enough to pay the price—the furnishing of any amount of sophistry and lies needed for the service of any scoundrel: it was easy for my Father to refute them by enlarging upon that true ideal of the legal profession, which is embodied in its standard formulas of admission and obligation, and has led so many of the greatest human intellects to a rare height of usefulness in gaining and defending the liberties and rights of free men, as well as to the winning of that bright renown which deservedly rewards great services in shaping the history of great nations. They were more persuasive, however, when they enlarged upon the degree to which the Bar was overcrowded; the length of time that must elapse before he could be admitted to practice; and the still longer time that it would probably take to acquire a sufficient amount of reputation and business to ensure a decent living. On the other hand, they described in flattering colors the ease and certainty with which money was to be made in manufactures; and urged that here would be his best employment, at least for a few years. When he had made something to live on, they suggested, he could better afford to devote himself finally to the Law, if he should then still prefer it. These arguments at length convinced him that he ought not to permit his personal tastes and longings to prevent his acceptance of an opening which promised to be so speedily and certainly lucrative.

The manufacture of iron, it was generally agreed among his practical friends, was the surest of all enterprises, at that time. This country was then almost wholly dependent upon Europe for every variety of iron-ware: while yet the growing uneasiness of our relations with England (which had produced the Embargo, and went on from bad to worse until it resulted in open war) had produced a universal readiness to foster every attempt to naturalize the iron manufacture in America. With this great branch of national wants provided for at home, it would be easier to offer that armed resistance to "the insolence of England" which the national self-respect demanded. Every iron manufacturer, therefore, had not only the confident expectation of making money, but might well look upon himself in the comfortable light of a public benefactor at the same time.

His course once decided, his friends offered him every opportunity of preparation for this very different sphere of activity: and he plunged into the work with a determination only the more energetic, because he was jealous over himself lest his natural preference for a far different line of life should lead him to slight his duty in his new career. The leading mechanical genius and inventor of that day, Evans, took my Father as an inmate of his family, that he might have the best opportunity for acquiring full knowledge and skill in the art of iron-making. It was, to his accurate eye and facile fingers, an easy task to draw all the machinery he saw. *Emerson's Mechanics* he studied thoroughly. In Mineralogy he made rapid progress. In Chemistry he was equally successful. But book-learning and theory were only the foundation for practical work. Rising each morning before daylight, he took part, with his soft hands, in the roughest of the workmen's toil, and persevered until he satisfied them that he had completely mastered every detail of the tasks that were given them to do. The first year of his service closed with high commendation from all his friends.

A rich iron-master in New Jersey then sent him a friendly invitation to a residence for a while with him, where the process of smelting iron from the ore might be learned with the highest advantage. Here, too, books and labor divided his time, and the new friendships he made grew only stronger during every day of his sojourn. The year following was again passed in Philadelphia, at a good foundry. And there he came in contact with some Commissioners of rank and influence, from one of the South American States, sent hither in order to secure the establishment of the iron manufacture on a large scale in their own country, under the support of the Government. The headship of this South American enterprise was offered to him; and while he had it in contemplation, he devoted himself zealously to a mastery of the Spanish language, which his previous knowledge of Latin and French made easy work. But after six months the Commissioners had disappeared, and were heard of no more: some change of affairs at home having probably led to the quiet dropping of their scheme.

At length the three years of preparation—years which he

would so gladly have spent in College—were ended. The age of twenty-one was fully reached. The country was already engaged in war with Great Britain.[1] If money were ever to be made by the manufacture of iron, it was to be done at once. Mr. Basse, a German merchant, whose foreign commerce was broken up by the war, resolved to invest his capital in the iron business, with a partner, Mr. Gläser, who took an equal share of the risk. They undertook to build and run a furnace at Bassenheim, near Harmony, about twenty-five miles north of Pittsburgh, and engaged my Father to superintend the operation, offering him a salary of $1,000 a year, besides a percentage on the profits, if any. The terms were liberal, and the work was cheerfully undertaken. He left Philadelphia for the scene of his new labors in January, 1813, and the furnace was built and went into operation. The total severance from all that was dearest to him, both intellectually and socially, was very trying, and he suffered occasionally from severe depression of spirits, mind and body being overwearied, while yet he was conscious of no sufficient object for all this exertion. At such seasons he was a prey to a " miserable philosophy, which represents the world as a barren wilderness, and calls its business and its pleasures alike vanity and vexation of soul." These gloomy tempers sometimes held him for two days together; sometimes only for an hour or two. He looked forward hopefully to the happiness of having his mother live with him ere long; and his hope was partially realized before he left Bassenheim, which was towards the close of the year 1814: for the two partners, after more than a year's experiment, found that the expenses, in a business which neither of them understood, were much larger than they had counted on; misunderstandings arose between them; and at length the firm was dissolved, the business wound up, and my Father was left free to seek employment elsewhere.

But during this first experiment near Harmony, he had not failed to make new friends. Chief among these was James O'Hara, then the wealthiest man in Pittsburgh. A native of Ireland, he had made his entrance into Western Pennsylvania before

---

[1] War was declared in June, 1812.

the existence of wagon-roads, his trade being carried on, in a small way, in bags borne by horses over bridle-paths, which were the only means of threading the otherwise unbroken wildernesses. Through many years of the humblest and most indomitable struggle, he had risen to the head of that youthful community; and his acknowledged eminence was due to his high integrity, his great ability, and his warm and generous heart, far more than to his wealth. His wife was a noble helpmeet for such an husband. Her earlier difficulties were never forgotten. She could remember, she said, with what pride she looked up to the seven-foot ceiling of the first house she could call her own, having for so long before lived in a cabin whose accommodations were perceptibly lower. Both of these worthy people formed an attachment for my Father, which was cemented by innumerable acts of kindness, and not only remained unbroken during life, but has on both sides been continued down to the third generation. My Father could rarely speak of those dear old friends of his without visible emotion.

When it was certain that the winding up of the partnership in the business near Harmony would leave the young iron-master free, Mr. O'Hara proposed a new partnership, with himself. He owned a large property in Ligonier Valley, about forty miles southeast of Pittsburgh, on which there was an old furnace, much decayed. He would supply the capital needed: and the whole management should be in his young partner's hands. The proposal was at once thankfully accepted, and the work was undertaken promptly, with cheerful hope. And it was in one of the long horseback rides which were so frequent about the time of the closing up at Bassenheim and the new opening in Ligonier Valley, when slowly toiling along the miry roads, that something happened, which compels us to interrupt our story here, that we may take up another thread, to be interwoven with it unbrokenly from this point even unto the end.

Chapter II.

LIGONIER VALLEY.

THE Müller family—that branch of it, at least, which flourished in and near the Kingdom of Hanover—was almost wholly devoted to the German Lutheran ministry. From the time of Martin Luther himself, they had been *Pastoren*, or *Superintendenten*, or *General-Superintendenten*, generation after generation. Two thick volumes, bound in dark leather and closed with brazen clasps, have come down to us as heirlooms, and fair specimens of the learning and the piety that were then common in the family. One is by Dr. Martin Müller, who began his ministry in 1575, published his first book in 1593, and wrote another of such merit that it reached five subsequent editions.[1] The other is by Professor Heinrich Müller, who was born in 1631, was piously brought up by godly parents during the horrors of the Thirty Years' War, came to be Professor and Head of the Theological Faculty at Rostock, and dated in 1688 the preface of that big book, of which our copy was printed in 1698. The bold antique type, the yellow paper, the coarse and queer but significant woodcuts, and the sombre copperplate likenesses of these old worthies in their black gowns and white ruffs, will never be forgotten by any of us who made our first acquaintance with them in our childhood.

Caspar Otto Müller was the first of the name, in direct descent, who broke through this clerical tradition of the family: and his doing so was, in more senses than one, a mistake. His father, Heinrich Carl Wilhelm, was Pastor at Garlstorff, in the Jurisdiction of Blekede; and an elder brother, Heinrich August, was dutifully preparing to follow the ancestral calling. One morning, while Caspar Otto—yet a little boy of seven years old—

---

[1] In 1601, 1627, 1642, 1697, and 1733.

was quietly playing behind the door, he overheard his father very solemnly setting forth to that elder brother the tremendous responsibilities of the pastoral office. He understood him to say, that "a minister would have to answer at the bar of God for every soul that might be lost under his preaching." The dread of the sacred office produced in the boy's mind by this misapprehension was so great, that he instantly resolved to set himself against learning Latin and Greek, in order that he might never be qualified to take Orders. This determination he adhered to so firmly, that at fourteen years of age his father consented to apprentice him to a wholesale hardware merchant in Hamburg. Here he suffered keenly, being compelled to handle iron and steel without gloves during the cold winters, and without fire. After escaping from this bondage,—persuading his hard master to release him two years before the time, by the artifice of pretending to make love to his old and homely daughter,—he went to London, setting out from home with an ample wardrobe, of which every article of linen and cloth was spun and made up by his mother's own hands. The failure of his London employers, in the second year of his sojourn there, threw him out of place; and skeptical tendencies had meanwhile so far undermined the thorough Christian training he had received at home, that in his depression he at one time meditated suicide. But the chambermaid at his lodgings one day—by what men call mere accident—had taken down his long-neglected Bible, and, being hastily summoned elsewhere, left it open on the table, so that, on his return, with a lancet which he had just purchased in order to open his veins and bleed to death, he saw the well-known Book, and his eye caught these words on the open page: *We know that all things work together for good to them that love God.*[1] This recalled him to his former self, with a pungency and power which were never forgotten, and marked his whole after-life.

After seven years in London, favored with growing success, his father's death summoned him again to Germany. There, after a few years, he married Elizabeth Antoinette Trance[2]

---

[1] Rom. viii. 28.
[2] The great folio family Bible (in French) of Jean David Trance, who married Antoinette Marie Nicolas in 1755, is yet in our possession.

whose Huguenot family had fled from France in 1685 at the revocation of the Edict of Nantes, their hiding-place under the deck of the little vessel being searched by the thrusting of the swords of the soldiers between the planks, before they were allowed to set sail for Amsterdam. Caspar Otto, after his marriage, settled as a merchant in Hamburg, where for twenty years he continued, sometimes in great prosperity, and sometimes meeting with severe reverses. Here all his children were born,— four daughters and one son growing up afterwards to maturity. Great was the delight of the children, in this quaint old city, when, after the long, cold winter, they heard the loud clappering bills of the great storks on the housetops, announcing the return of spring; and well they remembered the joy of feeding the swans that floated all summer long on the placid bosom of the Binnen Alster. Their country residence at Lockstädt was far more full of pleasure than the eight storeys of their tall townhouse. There, in the copse of pine-trees under the window, the nightingales sang at night; and in the next cottage there lived a young lady who played the harp out-of-doors on the bright evenings, so that before long the third daughter, Melusina, must needs learn the harp also. Long walks were theirs in the summer months; and there was now and then a wedding at the village church, when flowers were strewed before the bride all the way from the west door to the altar rail.

But Napoleon's occupation of Hamburg in 1807, brought ruin upon Caspar Otto, as upon so many thousands of others. His children saw, from the rear windows of his house, the 18,000 men who marched in under Marshal Davoust, a seemingly endless column, to quarter themselves upon the peaceful citizens. The Bank of Hamburg was seized,—the jugular vein of all the commerce of the city. For seventeen months the fruitless struggle was made to recover from this disaster: but at length the effort was abandoned, and, gathering up the remnants of his shattered fortunes, the whole family, following the lead of some of their kindred, set sail from Töningen on the Eyder, for Baltimore, in the good ship *Perseverance*, Fisher, master, of Martha's Vineyard. This was the last ship from that port that arrived in the United States before the famous Embargo went into operation.

The weariness of the six weeks' voyage was enlivened by the piano and the guitar, on the former of which the "Battle of Prague" resounded in all its novelty, and the latter accompanied *Guter Mond*, and other songs,—for all the daughters were accomplished singers. As they drew towards the American coast, the delicious perfume of the Spring air was perceived three days before they saw the land. On their way up Chesapeake Bay they were becalmed, and landed for a few hours at Cox's Cliff on the Virginia shore, where the flowers, the strawberries and fresh milk, and the cherries, and the kindness of the people, made them feel—after the calamities in Hamburg and their long imprisonment on shipboard—as if the New World were verily a paradise.

They landed in Baltimore on the 4th of June, 1808, and were cordially received by relatives and friends. It was not long before a favorable establishment in business was made, and prosperity gilded the outlook of the future. The family formed one of a delightful circle in which high accomplishment, true refinement, and enthusiastic personal attachments, contributed to endear all to each and each to all.[1] A country residence reproduced the pleasures of Lockstädt at "Green Vale," four miles out of town on the Philadelphia road, with cottages of friends,—Loneys and Sterretts,—on either hand.

But war once more blighted the new-born blessings of peace. The financial convulsions that characterized the opening of the War of 1812 with Great Britain again prostrated the merchant: and while struggling to prevent total ruin, the British invasion brought the actual shock of the conflict to his very doors.

---

[1] The strength of this feeling may be illustrated by a little anecdote. About fifteen years ago, I was, for the first time, a guest under the hospitable roof of the late John G. Proud, Esq., of Baltimore,—then one of the few survivors of that happy circle. On entering the dining-room, and before taking our seats, he called my attention to the chairs about the table, which—as compared with the modern style—were rather an ordinary set of chairs. Those chairs, he said, had been purchased by him at the auction sale of the furniture of the Müller family, at the time when they left Baltimore for the West, nearly fifty years before; and they had been kept ever since, being seated and reseated, painted and varnished, time and again, but were still preserved and faithfully used as mementos of those happy days which would never come again.

The daughters and their friends the Loneys were escorted to a distance of twelve miles, and lay all night on the ground in a log-cabin, hearing and feeling the explosion of every bomb fired at Fort McHenry.[1] The death of General Ross [2] alone prevented a battle in Green Vale itself. The house and grounds of the Sterretts were partially ravaged by the British troops, and the American forces were equally attentive to Green Vale, leaving nothing that could be destroyed. All this was in September, 1814: and it was resolved to quit Baltimore, and once more seek peace and a livelihood further in the West. A German of wealth and intelligence—the same Mr. Basse who gave name to Bassenheim—had suggested that the war, which had proved a curse in destroying foreign commerce, might bring a blessing in fostering domestic production; and sheep-raising in Western Pennsylvania was resolved on. Caspar Otto, and his nephew George Henry, had already been on a prospecting tour, during which they met Mr. Hopkins and were much pleased with him. Mrs. Schroeder—one of that delightful Baltimore circle—had also met him, at Bedford Springs, and had spoken of him warmly to Melusina, who was at this time the oldest unmarried daughter. On a visit to Philadelphia, Melusina herself had been a guest of one who was an admiring friend of Mr. Hopkins—though he was then accidentally out of town; and friends on both sides had been sure that they were meant for each other, from their extraordinary love of music. But they had never met. His youth had been spent in the best society of Philadelphia, and hers amid the brightest attractions of Baltimore: and both went heart-free into the Western wilderness.

It was on the 28th of October, 1814, that the Müller family started from Baltimore for Harmony in Western Pennsylvania. All the little relics that had been preserved from the disasters of Hamburg and Baltimore,—a few pieces of family silver, and other mementos of happier times, especially including two pianos and Melusina's harp and guitar,—were packed in the big canvas-covered wagons which were then the sole reliance for such work, and they set out. The weather soon became rainy in the extreme, and the state of the roads among the mountains was frightful.

---

[1] September 14, 1814.   [2] September 12.

Three weeks this journey lasted. When they had passed about two-thirds of the way, and were on the descent of Laurel Hill, before reaching Youngstown, the wagons—which were up to the hub in clay mud—were abandoned by the passengers for a time, who preferred, in the transient sunshine, to try their fortune afoot. George Henry led the way, followed by his wife, then Melusina and the rest in Indian file, picking their steps along the side of the road, in and out of the angles of a Virginia rail fence, wherever they could find a chance of clean footing: when, some distance down the mountain road, a "solitary horseman" was seen approaching, equipped in Western fashion for just such roads and just such rainy weather. An oiled-cloth over his hat, saddlebags on either side, with an umbrella strapped on behind them, green baize leggings all splashed with mud, and his black mare Bess liberally covered with the same, completed the picture. George Henry, looking up, soon exclaimed: "It is Mr. Hopkins!" and so it was. As he drew near, his delight at meeting the pedestrian company may well be imagined; and when, with the ancient courtesy, he bared his head in honor of the ladies, his beautiful features and his white forehead shining in the sunlight, made an impression not easily forgotten by one who was, at the time, not altogether hidden behind the bushes that lined the roadside. After a few moments' conversation with the gentlemen concerning the closing up of his business at Bassenheim and his new engagement in Ligonier Valley, and a promise that he would soon return to Harmony and call on the ladies, he passed on up the mountain, and the weary journey was resumed for another week. It was only a few days after their arrival at Harmony that he kept his promise, and made his first call. He renewed it every day during the week of his sojourn there. Each subsequent return to that neighborhood strengthened the impression thus begun. The only son of the family, Edward, a youth of fifteen, went to Ligonier with him in the January following, to learn mineralogy; and in one of the letters written to Caspar Otto on this subject, Mr. Hopkins assured him that, "if he thought as much of his prayers as he did of that family in Harmony, he would be more of a saint than of an iron-master."

And certainly there was something in the circumstances

rather out of the common run. With as much of accomplishment and refinement as this country could then produce, familiar with the best society in two of her largest and wealthiest cities, these two young people first met on that dreary mountain road, and all their subsequent courtship was either in one of the three humble log-cabins occupied by the family (for Old Rapp[1] would not let them live in his village lest they should corrupt his people from his religion), or else in their rambles through the primeval forest that surrounded them. In those cabins, on the floor of earth, and while a curtain at one end was the partition which made it a bed-chamber: at the other end stood the piano, and in a neighboring corner the harp, while the guitar hung by its ribbon on its own peg: and piles of the best music of the day were at hand, among which were some of the choicest songs of Beethoven. Three languages were at her command,—her native German, the French which a French governess in early youth had made a second vernacular, and the English which she loved best of all: while besides the music of these three nations, with which he was also familiar, many of his favorites among the plaintive Irish and Scottish songs were added, Moore's *Irish Melodies* being then the rage. And before long he began writing new songs for her, and she learned to sing them for him, with a voice of rare richness, sweetness, and power. That voice, with perfect truth of intonation, combined the sympathetic quality of tone, and the sudden *crescendo* and *diminuendo*, which penetrates the heart before one is aware of it:—a voice that has retained all its sweetness, and nearly all its range and power, until far past the threescore years and ten. And so it was no wonder that while all the rest of the world was shut out from them, they soon became all the world to one another. Their betrothal, however, was not until the following May, 1815.

It was one night during this first winter of the abode in Ligonier Valley—he called the name of his place "Hermitage Furnace," from his loneliness there—that he sat, quite by himself, reading a work of Hannah More; when, as he often described it, a sudden beam of divine Truth shone into his inmost heart. Its force was pure and gentle; its nature he could not pretend

---

[1] A shrewd, long-headed old German fanatic, with some hundreds of unmarried followers of both sexes, whom he kept in abject but industrious slavery for many years.

to define: but from that hour the love of Christ Crucified—so far as his knowledge extended—was the guiding and ruling principle in his soul. The habit of private prayer had never been interrupted: and its guardian influence up to that time, its work of unnoticed preparation, who can overrate? But it was not until the hour of this great change that the full consciousness of deep repentance, sincere humility, and loving faith, wrought in him the maturity of Christian manhood: and it was so marked, both in time and in degree, as to satisfy all who knew of it that he had "experienced a sudden and genuine conversion of heart,"—to use the current language of that day.

He at once began to do his best in furnishing some spiritual help to his workmen. They were many miles from the nearest minister of any denomination. He therefore held a service in his own room on Sundays, to which they were all invited to come freely. He used the prayers furnished by the Church in the Prayer-Book, and read the Bible to them, with portions of "Scott's Commentary," and such sermons as he could obtain, to which were added some simple exhortations of his own. And this was continued until the winding up of Hermitage Furnace, producing no small amount of visible benefit among the workmen. But it must not be supposed that he had as yet any definite Churchmanship. His notions at this time touching the sacraments were very nearly those of the Quakers; for some time, subsequently, he inclined not a little towards Swedenborgianism; it was apparently a mere accident that decided his attaching himself to the Church rather than to the Presbyterians; and after becoming a practical Churchman, it was some time before he obtained anything like a clear view of fundamental Church principles.

Edward Müller, during that winter of 1815, frequently wrote home, and gave to his sister Melusina full and glowing accounts of all that was doing among the workmen, and of the deep change in their employer which brought it about. And she was well prepared to sympathize fully, and to follow lovingly such a guide. Her training in the old Lutheran system had been very thorough; and for some years the high sacramentarianism of that system was a preservative against the looser notions as yet held by her guide : but the practical energy of religion as the ruling principle of the whole life had not previously been felt ; nor was she the only member of her family who at this time learned the same great lesson of divine Love.

Meanwhile, the prospects of financial success at Hermitage began to look less and less promising. The ore was of a poor quality, and dear at that. The charcoal had to be brought from a considerable distance. The market for the iron was at Pittsburgh, fifty miles off, and the only mode of conveyance thither was by teaming over abominable roads. The river Conemaugh, indeed, could be reached by only fifteen miles of teaming; but it was too shallow for navigation, except during the brief Spring freshet, and even then, the delays from running aground and the danger of rapidly falling water, more than compensated for the gain in other ways. Only the high prices during the war could offer any chance of profit: and the approach of peace was no blessing to the manufacturers of iron. In the love-letters written during the latter part of the year 1815,[1] these gloomy prospects were plainly and honestly set forth, crowned by the possibility of coming bankruptcy; and a release from the betrothal was offered, if the risk of impending poverty were thought too great. But what true woman ever dreamed of deserting, for such a reason, the man whom she loved? The result was, a determination to cling only the more closely to one another. This straightforward honesty was shown also in another way. It was certainly not a very usual incident in courtship, that during his visits that winter, they never failed to spend a portion of their time together in reading the Bible, especially those portions of the New Testament which set forth the respective authority and duty of husbands and wives, pledging themselves to one another to accept that inspired guide as the rule of their future life. Moreover, he was most frank in mentioning to her all his faults of character and temper, that she should have no discoveries to make when it was too late. His pride, he assured her, was the worst of them all, and the hardest for him to conquer. He was the more conscientious in doing this, because, as he said, from the fewness of his visits and the little time they could spend together,

---

[1] The treaty of Ghent was signed December 24, 1814.

she could have no fair chance to find out his faults for herself.

It was clearly prudent to be looking out betimes for some other resource in case the fires of Hermitage Furnace should go out. Early in 1816 an enforced attendance for several days upon court in Greensburgh, as a witness, revived strongly the unsuccessful iron-master's early predilections in favor of the Law. He seldom made up his mind to do anything, without at the same moment putting forth some effort to begin; and as time was valuable, and a two years' preparation was required by law, he at once entered his name as a student with lawyer Foster of Greensburgh, who undertook to render him all requisite aid. This good friend also agreed to loan him books, and on his return to Hermitage he carried " Blackstone's Commentaries " tied across his saddle, fully determined to prosecute his legal studies in such moments of leisure as he could gain from his other duties. About the same time, in order to economize expenses, he dismissed the manager (or head overseer of the workmen), and undertook the duties of that post in addition to his own previous labors : but all was accomplished by rising so much earlier in the morning, and working the harder during the day.

At length he went to Harmony to claim his bride. Caspar Otto had by this time moved into a brick house of very modest pretensions; and there, on the 8th of May, 1816, in the presence of the family and a few friends, they were married by Mr. Coulson, a Lutheran minister. Among those present was Mr. John Loney, one of that happy Baltimore circle, who had ridden on horseback all the way from Baltimore to Harmony merely to see that marriage, and then returned in the same way : a proof of friendly devotion which it would be hard to match in these degenerate times of ours. The wedding was on a Wednesday; and for three days the new-married couple remained with the parents and family of the bride. On Saturday, accompanied by their younger sister, Amelia—the faithful and loving companion of almost the whole of their married life—they started for Hermitage. Arriving the first evening at Pittsburgh, they were the guests of their dear friends, the O'Haras; and on Sunday went to the Presbyterian meeting with them as a matter of course, Dr. Heron being then the leading preacher in all that region of country. On Monday they resumed their journey, the stage-coach taking them to Greensburgh, where they spent the night; and the next day carrying them to within two or three miles of Hermitage. This remaining distance they walked. It so chanced that a bridgeless brook which lay in their path was greatly swollen by rains. The bridegroom gallantly carried the bride across in his arms, and then her sister in like manner, neither of them wetting a shoe.

The house in which they began their married life was a log-cabin of the better sort. The logs were well squared, and neatly clapboarded on the outside. There was a wide hall in the middle running through, and a large room, twenty feet square, on either side, besides some smaller chambers. There was but one storey, with an unfinished attic above, which my Father used as his workroom; and there he would sit for long hours drawing designs for iron castings, while his young wife would sit by him and read aloud.

It may easily be imagined that this accession to the society of Hermitage Furnace enhanced in no small degree the interest of the Sunday services, sympathizing so deeply as the new-comers did in the more earnest religious life which brought forth such good fruits.

But this was not the only unusual source of influence for good, obtained by my Father over those among whom he then lived. His mother's school, in Maryland, had not proved permanently successful; and at his invitation she had taken up her residence with him while he was yet at Bassenheim. After Hermitage had been sufficiently prepared, she removed thither, having in the interim been, for some weeks, a guest in the Müller family. She had given great attention to medicine, since the closing of her school; and the activity of her mind found constant scope in this new sphere, especially since the nearest doctor lived twenty miles away. Her son, also, took part in the practice which such a rural neighborhood was sure to afford, and the books of Reese and Thomas—of high repute among the regular Faculty in those days—were his leading guides. He kept a stock of medicines on hand, and was ever ready, at the call of distress, to go any distance to relieve the sufferings of the poor country people; while, among his workmen, he was not merely the employer, but also the only physician of both soul and body within their reach.

The services he rendered in all these capacities gave him extraordinary influence among those uneducated people; and in some cases the manifestation of enthusiasm was irrepressible. One poor fellow, William Dobbin, who had been spiritually awakened under my Father's instructions, went to a neighboring camp-meeting, and came home in a state of no little excitement. Everything that my Father had done for him was magnified and glorified in his sight. While the family were at breakfast, he came to the house, entered the room, walked round and round the table, telling what great things my Father had done for him, and prophesying what blessings would come to the world from such a man, from his wife, and his children to the latest generation! It was with great difficulty he could be gotten out of the room and persuaded to go home. The same day, at dinner time, Dobbin's wife called and begged of my Father:—"Come, see my husband! he says that he will be sure to die at two o'clock this afternoon!" All went, of course, at once. They found Dobbin pacing to and fro before his house, singing with all his might, in an ecstasy of excitement, verse after verse of the Hymn, "Come, ye that love the Lord,"[1] and expecting surely, at two o'clock, to "reach the heavenly fields" and "walk the golden streets," in person. With no small persuasion my Father got him into the house, and coaxed him into taking a reasonable quantity of laudanum, by the aid of which he soon dozed comfortably, and thus passed the critical two o'clock without dying. There were many others who felt their obligations as deeply as William Dobbin, but were more quiet in the expression of their gratitude.

The summer passed delightfully,—the evening rambles through the picturesque neighborhood making all amends for the toil of the day; and the night work over Blackstone being sweetened

---

[1] No. 149, in our American collection; No. 462 in the New Hymnal.

by the help of the young wife who held the book and tested the fidelity of his memory. An autumnal visit to Harmony was made on horseback,—a ride of seventy-five miles, being what few young ladies of our days would like to undertake. Madam Hopkins continued her medical practice among the country folk: but though ever ready to ride twenty miles to doctor a poor sufferer, of whom she knew nothing except that he was in pain, she had not yet learned, with all her brilliance, how to render her society a pleasure to those whom she loved the most dearly, when living under the same roof with them. Thus the rural paradise had some drawbacks. Others were found in the steadily increasing losses incurred in carrying on the business. Ever since the peace, the importation of foreign iron had been bringing down the price of the domestic article, until the sum which it would command in market was only one-half what it cost to make it. Of course, further perseverance in the making of iron was not a virtue under such circumstances. In February, 1817, the experiment culminated in disaster, with a deficit of $20,000, the whole of which, for the time being, had to be borne by Mr. O'Hara, my Father having no capital.

Nothing could have been nobler than Mr. O'Hara's conduct, under a state of things which would have goaded most men into recrimination, if it did not produce permanent alienation or ill-will. He was not unprepared for the result, indeed, for my Father had been perfectly frank with him from the first, and he knew well all the causes to which the great loss was due. But few could have anticipated the open-handed cordiality, the undiminished confidence, the cheery and hearty encouragement, with which he faced the ugly balance-sheet, exonerating my Father from every shade of blame, and assuring him of the undiminished warmth of his friendship. My Father wrung his hand, with a heart too full of gratitude to be able to express more than a few broken words: but his sense of that man's generous kindness remained fresh so long as life lasted. It need hardly be added that the continued friendship thus pledged, was abundantly and repeatedly shown, in the most substantial manner.

A business of that kind, however, could not be closed all at once, with justice to the interests of others; and existing contracts must be fulfilled. The winding up ran through several months. During this period, letters received by him show to how great an extent his intellectual influence was beginning to be felt. He was looked to as the leader in a literary association just then forming in Pittsburgh, and epistles addressed to him both in prose and verse [1] witness to the admiration with which he was already looked up to by a growing circle of Western friends, who all anticipated for him a brilliant future.[2]

Another of these letters, in a tone of enthusiastic friendship, is written from Leeds, in England, by Mr. Francis B. Ogden, who had heard even there, from various sources, glowing accounts of his friend's marriage, and envied his good fortune [3]—not the only

[1] A short poem, "*Conversation Comparisons*," in the *Appendix*, p. 453, will serve as a specimen of my Father's style at about this time.

[2] No less than four of these poetic epistles—of no slight merit in their way—were written by Aquila M. Bolton, who had evidently a passion for literary exercises and societies not easily satiated. It was only the day after reading these that I took up the Rev. Dr. McVickar's "Early Years of Bishop Hobart," in which (pp. 15-19) a detailed account is given of the successful impeachment of Aquila M. Bolton, the President of "the Ciceronian Society," under the leadership of young Hobart, both being boys at the time (July, 1790) in the University of Pennsylvania. Bolton made a stout and very able defence. Dr. McVickar says of him:—"Even from his enemies' showing, Bolton played well the hero's part, and seems to have had hard measure dealt to him. . . . Whether this individual be living or dead, the editor knows not, nor even whether he grew up to man's estate; most probably not, since he certainly displayed, in the youthful contest, talent, that in life could not have been hid, and traits of character that must have made such talent not only respected, but feared." There is no doubt of the identity of the two. The unusual name, the age, the abilities, the tastes, all coincide. It was probably one of those cases in which a high order of literary or political ability is buried under a load of ordinary business, without sufficient clearness of sight or firmness of will to throw the burden off, and follow the stronger impulse, to a real success.

[3] An extract from this letter of Mr. Ogden's (dated Feb. 1, 1817) will be of some interest as bearing on the early history of ocean steam navigation. After alluding to a horseback ride through Ligonier Valley in 1815, he says :—" I was induced, contrary to the intention I had formed of returning to Pittsburgh, to enter upon an operation of some magnitude,—that of building a Steamboat, and of introducing by that means my improvement in the Engine. This business occupied my exclusive attention for a much longer period than I had anticipated, and was attended with many vexatious circumstances, from the difficulty I found in getting my work done as I wished it, and from the good-natured predictions and condolences of my friends, who all for forty miles round turned engineers on the occasion, and lamented my folly in persisting in a scheme that must terminate in my disgrace and ruin: for, 'what could Frank Ogden know of a steam engine?' The very engineer I employed to execute the work, saw with astonishment that in despite of all these predictions, and of his own misgivings, the engine *did go*, and Frank Ogden *did* know something of the matter. In short, my boat was completed in May (1816), and was to be transported from New Jersey to Norfolk. As no internal navigation had been yet established thus far, I again *outraged* the feelings of my *friends* by my temerity in venturing to sea in a steamboat. 'It was flying in

letter of the sort, by any means. Another shows that he still kept up his mineralogical studies, and exchanged specimens with scientific friends at the East. Others—evidently from poor and illiterate persons—in their crooked lines, pale ink, cramped handwriting, and awkward ill-spelt phrases on mere scraps of paper, are the most touching of all, for they thank my Father for being, "under God," the means of their recovery from the shadow of death.

The slow process of winding up affairs at Hermitage Furnace was not completed until October, 1817. Every liability of the concern was paid in full. There was great lamentation among the country people and the workmen, and not a few tears, at beholding the departure of those who had been such unselfish friends. And it was not without strong emotion on their own part that they left Ligonier Valley, where the first deep movements of their Christian course had been felt, the first work for Christ begun, and where the happiness of early married life had diffused a peculiar charm over every feature of the landscape. Neither of them ever saw the spot again.

the face of the Almighty,' said one old Lady, 'to make such machines to go against wind and tide; and no good could come out of it!' However, to sea I went; had the good fortune to encounter a gale of wind (which completely established my belief that it is perfectly practicable to navigate the ocean with steam-vessels); and arrived safe at my port of destination. The performance of the engine equalled my most sanguine expectation, but I was not satisfied with the execution of the work, and . . . I am now getting an engine executed on my plan at this place, that I think I may safely say will be the most complete one ever built. In this belief I am authorized by the opinions of the principal engineers I have had an opportunity to consult, Mr. Watt particularly, whose decided approbation of my plan was extremely gratifying. We shall likewise make a great saving in the price, at least 33⅓ *per cent.*,—a matter of some moment in so heavy a concern." Mr. Ogden's ocean trip to Norfolk doubtless was an encouragement to the Savannah, which, in the following year, 1817, was the first steamship that ever crossed the Atlantic.

Chapter III.

THE LAWYER.

ON their arrival in Pittsburgh, Mr. O'Hara—the head of the society of the place—insisted that for at least a week they should be his guests. My Father had returned from his experiment at iron manufacture, with a wife and child, ten thousand dollars of debt, and just the quarter of a dollar in his pocket: but his friends were warmer than ever. It was with reluctance that Mr. O'Hara would part with his guests at the end of the week; and he insisted that, as a regular thing, they should dine with him (baby included) every Saturday. Meanwhile, previous correspondence had secured temporary employment, to keep the wolf from the door. There was a girls' school in Pittsburgh, of high character, conducted by Mrs. Brévôst. A room in her house was assigned to my parents; they were to board with the family, and my Father was to be the instructor in drawing and painting, while my Mother gave lessons on the Piano, harp and guitar, and in singing, thus lending attractions to the school such as it had never known before. Mr. O'Hara also insisted that my Father should dine daily with him, should have a seat in his office, and "keep his books" for him,—a very slight labor; but it secured the use of a quiet room for studying Law when not engaged in the school.

My Father also taught a drawing class in the Academy, where one of his pupils was James R. Lambdin, who has won for himself no small name as a portrait painter.[1] The painting of occasional miniatures added still further to the art-earnings of this transition period.

But his main business was the study of Law. One of the two leading lawyers of Pittsburgh gladly recorded him as a

---

[1] Mr. Lambdin, in the year 1859, showed his kind feeling for his old drawing-master by painting a life-sized portrait of him, in his happiest style, and presenting it to the Vermont Episcopal Institute.

student, loaned him books, and gave any hints that might be needed in pursuing his studies,—a labor which was kept up with the most intense devotion, until the remaining six months of his probation were ended, and he was admitted to the Bar, in April, 1818. He took the lawyer's oath, not as a mere matter of form, but with deep Christian seriousness, and in full faith that he should keep it until death. In accordance with usual custom, the Court assigned to him at once his first client,—a friendless thief, who was too poor to pay a fee, and whose case was too clearly hopeless to be worth arguing. He was convicted: but my Father's effort in his behalf excited general commendation, and several of the lawyers present prophesied his rapid success: with which good news he went home to cheer his wife.

The school engagement was now soon over, though private pupils were still taught until the end of the year. My Father rented a small brick building just behind the Court-house, with one room in it set apart for an Office, and went to housekeeping. It is proverbially hard work for a young lawyer to get into business. Flattering promises had been made in certain quarters; but nothing came of them. There were twenty-four practising attorneys in Pittsburgh when he was admitted. Yet within a few months he was ranked as about the fifth, and earned enough the first year for the entire support of himself and his growing family. The joyous sense of exhilaration with which he launched into the career which had for so many years been the first choice of his heart, was enhanced by the real repulsiveness of his former occupation: and, comparing the two, he wrote to his mother that he felt as if he "had escaped from gaol." But the success which he achieved was not owing to this alone: and the means by which he obtained so rapid a start, and by which he continued to rise so steadily thereafter, were somewhat peculiar, and are well worthy of special mention.

I have alluded already to the deep seriousness with which he took the oath exacted on admission to the Bar. He had ever cherished a high ideal of the profession of the Law, as a characteristic outgrowth of Christianity, and originally supplied mainly from the ranks of the clergy. Its great object was, to facilitate the doing of justice between man and man, with the least practicable loss of time, temper and money. And this high ideal, which, in the eyes of many, would seem fatal to the prospect of getting into a run of business, worked in his favor to a charm, yet by no unworthy management of his own.

Hardly had he "put up his shingle," when a tradesman brought him a bill for collection, due by a brother-lawyer. This was rather an unpromising beginning, and with a very natural *esprit de corps* he declined to undertake it. Soon another and another came to him with similar proffers, and received similar answers: until at length he came to comprehend that nearly every lawyer and judge in the place was in debt to tradespeople, and that there was a sort of understanding among them that no one of them would take a case against another. When he saw that the members of a profession whose business was the doing of justice, were thus tacitly leagued together in the doing of injustice, his resolution was instantly taken. He accepted every case that was brought to him, and sued and recovered from so many of his brethren of the Law, that the profession thenceforth understood that it was as necessary for them to pay their honest debts as for other men. This course won the confidence of the general public —which furnishes the clients. "Take your case to Mr. Hopkins," one would say to another; "he is not in the league, and will see that justice is done you."

Another rule with him was, always to exert himself to the utmost to induce parties to come to an agreement, without litigation:—a poor way, one would think, to earn a living at the Law. But it was so manifestly disinterested, that—even where it did not succeed—it gained him the confidence and grateful esteem of both sides. No one whom he had thus saved from a lawsuit would be likely to place any other law business in any hands but his: and this result was equally sure to follow when his advice was disregarded, and the wilful parties went further and fared worse.

Another rule was, never to undertake any cause unless clearly convinced, in his own mind, that it was the cause of justice. Where there was any doubt on this score from his client's own statement, he made him bring his witnesses: and unless sure that the case was right, and could be proved right, he advised compromise rather than contest. Where this advice was not taken, they had his permission to try another lawyer. Whenever he carried a case into Court, it was one in which he had justice and full proofs on his side: and his contested cases were therefore almost invariably won. This uniform success of course increased his prestige, and he soon found that he gained much more in this way than he could have lost.

Moreover, he took care that there should be no delay in his clients' business by his neglect. His preparation was always promptly and thoroughly attended to; and money collected by him was paid over, punctually to the very hour, to the parties to whom it belonged. And this was a duty which he always discharged with real pleasure. His previous experience, too, was of great use to him. The knowledge of men and things, machinery and manufactures, enabled him to explain many points to a jury more readily and clearly than most other lawyers.

His first seriously contested case was one of peculiar interest. A Scotchman had left a young wife in his native land, and in America had become—in some twenty years—very wealthy, settling at Pittsburgh; but having all this while neglected utterly the wife he left behind him. She, after vain inquiries for years, and not knowing whether he was alive or dead, at length heard of his living in Pittsburgh; and receiving no answer to her letters, she came over in person, obtaining the funds with the greatest difficulty. He denied all knowledge of her, treating her as if she were an impostor. As the best means of testing the case, he was sued for her board-bill. He at once engaged all the leading lawyers in Pittsburgh in his defence. My Father was alone on the other side. When the case came to trial, my Father had spoken but a few moments, when he suddenly experienced a total loss of voice,—he could not tell why, for such a thing never happened to him before or since. In a scarcely audible whisper he asked for a continuance of the case to the next term, which was granted: the formidable array of opposing counsel smiling with triumphant incredulity, as if satisfied that the apparent loss of voice was a mere pretence, to avoid certain defeat. About a fortnight after, in looking over his case once more, he was utterly confounded at discovering that one important link in his chain of evidence—which could be supplied only from Scotland—had been omitted, and that, if he had gone to trial at first, he would certainly have lost his case. The link was supplied before the next term, and the case—after a tough fight—was won, carrying a strong public sympathy for the lady, of course, to say nothing of her lawyer, to whom it was no slight triumph to overcome, single-handed, such a combination of the ablest talent at the Bar.

Another case may be mentioned, as illustrating his ready tact in the management of a jury. A wealthy farmer living about fifty miles from Pittsburgh, and having a large family of grown-up children, had died intestate. Many years before his death, he had given to his oldest son a deed of the farm occupied and worked by him. The rest of the family denied the genuineness of this deed, and claimed that that farm was part of the estate to be equally divided among them all. My Father defended the integrity of the deed. When the case came to trial, the several opposing counsel made long and very learned speeches, piling up a mountain of authorities to prove that the different color of the ink in different parts of that deed, and the different size of the letters—some being much thicker and darker than others—were proofs that the whole was not written at one time, nor with the same pen and the same ink: in other words, that the deed had clearly been altered, or was a forgery outright. While the learned counsel were thus pouring out legal authorities by the hour, my Father, who noticed that the ink on the Clerk's desk was very pale, amused himself with a sheet of blank foolscap, slightly scratching the surface with his penknife in a few places. When it was his turn to reply, he alluded to this long argument, founded only on the ink and the writing; and sitting down he wrote a line or two before their eyes, and then passed the sheet to the jury for their inspection. "It was plain," he said, "that the ink was pale in some places and dark in others, and the letters were thicker in some words than in others, and yet they had seen with their own eyes that it was all done at the same time, and with the same ink and the same pen." This disposed of the whole mountain of legal learning in a moment. He then reminded them that the deed was executed many years before, in a rough part of the country, where stationery was scarce, and pens and ink not often used or kept in good order; and that these simple facts would satisfactorily account for the appearance of the deed: whereas, had it been a forgery, they might depend upon it, it would have been much more nicely gotten up. He did not speak ten minutes: but he won the case.

His natural fluency was a great advantage to him. The extemporary habit of thought was indeed so strong, that it fixed the order in which he arranged everything he had to say. During his whole life this peculiarity remained. He frequently attempted, by means of a written abstract or skeleton, to arrange beforehand the order in which the different parts of what he wished to say should be presented: but, when once on the floor, he never found himself able to adhere to it. His thoughts always spontaneously took an order of their own in the warmth of speaking; and he was generally satisfied, after all, that this spontaneous order was the best. But besides fluency, and the power of clear and vigorous thinking on his legs, he rapidly developed a rare mastery of sarcasm,—one of the most telling weapons of legal warfare: and, pitted as he often was against a superiority in numbers and experience, he made up for it by wielding this sword in such a style as to penetrate even the thickest professional epidermis. On one occasion the tricky practice of an opposing lawyer was shown up with such merciless irony, that the sufferer—having nothing else to say—forgot the respect due to the Court, and flung a law-book at the head of his tormentor. The degree of self-restraint needed in after-years in order to curb this dangerous power, and to learn the kindly and considerate courtesy of tone which so generally marks his controversial writings, can be imagined only by those who have had a similar battle to fight: but to the last, the power remained, and when there was a sufficient occasion for it, the flashes were as bright and strong after he had reached the age of threescore years and ten, as ever they were in the midst of his early contests in the Courts.

In the first year of his residence in Pittsburgh, and before he was admitted to the Bar, he became a Freemason, and proceeded as far as the third degree. He ever cherished a sincere regard for the Order, and could not see that it was in any wise opposed to Christianity. By its recognition of the Bible, and by reason of the many remains of the original working system, he regarded it as a worthy and estimable benevolent society, which impliedly required its members to become full and positive Christians, not to say Churchmen. And in after-years he often said that since the Romanists and some of the Protestant denominations had both run amuck at the Freemasons, the true policy of the Church was to meet them with open arms. So deeply was he interested in the Order, that he not only delivered an Address, which was printed, but he also began a Poem, entitled *Freemasonry*,—the longest and most elaborate work that he ever wrote in verse— and the object of it was to illustrate, in a tale of varied and striking incident, the beneficent workings of the Order, its close affiliation with pure and true Religion, and its incompatibility with Romanism. The hold which this theme had obtained upon him may be inferred from the fact that this poem was completed many long years after he had ceased all practical connection with the Order. He could not accept, however, the current traditions of Freemasons as to the immense antiquity of their Order, being satisfied that its origin was due to the times of the Crusades rather than to King Solomon, to Christianity rather than to Judaism. Moreover, a growing antipathy to the secrecy which is so characteristic of Masonry, aided in bringing him to the resolution to drop it altogether. He paid his farewell visit to the Lodge some time before closing his career at the Bar; but his kindly feeling continued strongly during his whole life.

The intense energy with which my Father had devoted himself to his legal studies and his rapidly extending practice,[1] taxed his physical powers to the utmost, and they soon showed signs of giving way under the pressure. Incessant brain-work all day long, and all night until one, two or even three o'clock in the morning, without any open-air exercise worth mentioning, no human constitution can long endure. In the summer of 1819 his physician promised him a speedy consumption if he did not amend his habits. He had grown very thin, had had an obstinate cough for more

---

[1] In August, 1818, he writes to his mother that his office is open at six o'clock in the morning, and not closed till sunset; that his conversation is all "law," and that even at night when he ought to be sleeping, he was "dreaming of law cases and arguments constantly." This was only four months after his admission to the Bar.

than six weeks, and was so weak that he could not go up a single flight of stairs without stopping on the landing to take breath. More exercise, and less of nerve-stimulus and study, with a glass of wine and a cracker at eleven o'clock in the forenoon, were the prescription: and he obeyed. His father-in-law lent him a hard-trotting horse, on which he rode every morning before breakfast. He gave up night reading, and the drinking of coffee and tea. He wrote cheerily to his mother: "I do not believe I am in any danger: but, however, I act as if I did, and I expect to grow fat —by and by." This change in his habits—only gradually established,—at length produced a restoration of health; and in March, 1820, he writes to his mother: "After innumerable failures, I think I have at last succeeded in keeping good hours. In bed at half-past ten, and up at daylight, has been my practice for the last month, instead of up till one, two, and sometimes three in the morning." But so jealous was he over himself in regard to the use of wine, that when he found that he missed his glass at eleven o'clock, he discontinued it at once, without waiting for a full recovery. He preferred the risk of consumption, rather than run the danger of becoming a slave to wine.

His business increased so rapidly, however, that before long the pressure again began to be threatening. In the second year of his practice, his income was so far improved that he moved into a rather better and more comfortable dwelling; and in the third year he could afford to hire a still better house, and had fairly risen to be at the head of the Pittsburgh bar, entering a larger number of new suits on the docket than any other lawyer, while scarcely one amongst them all was lost. From this time onward his superiority was so indisputable, that his legal brethren were at last beginning to talk of sending him to the Legislature or to Congress, in order to get him out of their way. His income rose to about $5000 a year,—a large sum for those days and in a city of the size and character of Pittsburgh:[1] and larger than he ever received during all his life after.

At length, overwork again gave a timely alarm, and rather more emphatically than before. After some slight premonitory

---

[1] The population was about 18,000 at the time when my Father settled there.

warnings, one night during the Winter of 1822, just as he was preparing to retire, a strange sensation affected his head. It was indescribable; but he felt that he should become insane if it continued: and he at once ran, late as it was, to the house of his kind and skilful physician, who had for years been warning him in vain. An opiate gave relief for the night: but the doctor's advice was despised no longer. The next day my Father bought ten acres of land[1] nearly two miles from town. It was on the crown of a gentle slope, on the north side of the Ohio River, commanding an extensive view. The smoky city, with the confluence of the Allegheny and Monongahela, the sweep of the Ohio River from that point for several miles of its westward course, and the range of high hills that forms its southern bank from above the city to many miles below, were all visible. In the sides of this long hill the coal miners were constantly busy, the loaded cars running by gravity down the parallel tramways, and dumping their dusky loads into the river barges. Its high and level outline was varied by only one break, just opposite, where the mingled white steam puffs and dark coal-smoke from the salt-works contributed another lively feature to the landscape. Towards the rear, the road from the city to Harmony and Zelienople was seen, at the distance of about a mile, to wind its way up a steep hill, disappearing at a nunnery near the top.

On the land thus purchased, a two-storey frame house was begun in the Spring, just beside an oak wood of venerable trees[2] covering four acres, which were a part of the purchase. The oversight of the building was a healthful interruption to the drudgery of the Law. A junior partner, moreover, was taken into the Office,—one who had for some time been a student under my Father, and an inmate of his family, and whose skilful energy soon lightened greatly the burden of legal labor. But while this decided change for the better was going on, other changes, of still more importance, were silently drawing nearer, day by day.

When the singular kindness of the O'Haras is remembered, and

---

[1] To which three adjoining lots of the same size were subsequently added.
[2] The trunks of the older oaks yet bore in their bark the tribe-mark of the Turtle Indians.

the absence of all definite Church principle, as yet, in my Father's mind is kept in view, it will not seem strange that, on his first coming to live in Pittsburgh, my parents went on Sundays, as a matter of course, to Dr. Heron's Presbyterian meeting, with seats in the O'Hara pew. And there they would probably have remained, had it not been for one of those trifling things which the world calls accidents.

The Presbyterian society was then, by all odds, the dominant one in Pittsburgh, whether for numbers, wealth, or social and intellectual weight and power. There was a Church parish, indeed; but it was a small affair in comparison. Few and feeble were the Church folk in Western Pennsylvania, in those days; and the worst step that a young man could take who wished to rise in the world as a lawyer, was, to quit the Presbyterians and "join the Episcopals." The Rev. Abraham Carter was then the Rector of Trinity Church,—a warm-hearted man, of good abilities, with a young and lovely wife: and an acquaintance with them soon ripened into something stronger. One day Mr. Carter told the young lawyer that he had succeeded in purchasing an organ for his Church, but had thus far sought in vain for an organist. He knew my Father's musical ability, and begged it of him, as a personal favor, to play the organ for them until some regular organist could be procured. His services would be gratuitous, of course, as the parish was thus far too poor to offer a salary to anybody but the clergyman—and hardly able to pay that. This request came to my Father simply as a religious man, not as a Churchman. He thought of all the time and labor that he had thus far, during his life, bestowed on acquiring musical skill, and in using it for his own enjoyment or the social pleasure of others: while as yet he had never, in any one thing, consecrated it to the service of his Master. This single thought decided him to undertake the task, which he did at once. He left his wife free to remain with her friends, or to come with him, as she preferred. At first she thought she would remain with her friends, who had been so kind, and whom it was certainly hard to leave. But the spending of one Sunday apart from her husband was enough. The second Sunday she was once more by his side, and her voice was as great a gain to the Church choir as his playing. Thenceforward, gradually and steadily, the Church system did its work; and within three months they knelt together before the Altar as communicants,—not being first confirmed, however, for in those days no Bishop had ever held Confirmation in Western Pennsylvania, and Bishop White's primary visit was yet eight years distant.

A sermon preached by Mr. Carter on the testimony borne by God Himself of Abraham: "I know him, that he will command his children and his household after him, and they shall keep the way of the LORD,"[1] soon induced my Father to begin family prayer in his household, never afterwards to be discontinued. Of all the lawyers at that time in Pittsburgh, he was the only one who "made a profession of religion," as the phrase was: and nearly all the rest—except some of the younger attorneys—were in the habit of taking it for granted that this profession of religion was only a politic piece of hypocrisy, with a view to a lucrative business among pious people. Could they have seen what was then the secret course of his daily life, they would not have been so uncharitable in their judgment. On the 2d of March, 1820, in reply to earnest inquiries from his mother, he writes:—"My exercise before breakfast is a little walk, and two pages of the Greek Testament, with half a dozen of the English Bible, which I am now perusing consecutively for the fourth time since I began to practise law. My calculation is, to read the Bible twice through from beginning to end, every year, and the Greek Testament as often, during the rest of my life.[2] I have no amusements, commonly so-called:—hardly ever leave home, but to Court, and on arbitrations, when business renders it indispensable: trying, with the blessing of God, to lead what many might consider a very dull life, but what I feel to be one of—not *happiness*, nor *wisdom*, nor *virtue*,—but perhaps the nearest approach to them within my weak and defective ability." And this was the measure of his daily devotion to the oracles of God at a time when he was just recovering from the consequences of severe over-

---
[1] Gen. xviii. 19.
[2] The Bishop of Connecticut, in a note to the Address delivered by him at my Father's funeral, says truly: "The Bishop of Vermont had read the Bible through, in English, more than fifty times; and when he was at home, read every day some part of it in the original tongues."

work, so that he would not have lacked for a good excuse to suspend or abridge his Biblical reading. But he preferred to change everything else sooner than that.

It was not many months before the Rev. Mr. Carter resigned and removed to Trenton in New Jersey. A long and painful vacancy followed, varied by fruitless efforts to procure the services of a new rector. Now one was obtained for a time, and now another; but of such moderate abilities that little growth could be expected under their leadership. One of them experienced great difficulty in the preparation of his sermons, and made no secret of it. He lived in a house the rear of which looked upon the rear of that occupied by the Rev. Mr. McElroy,[1] then a young Presbyterian minister of leading ability and a kind heart: and the gardens between them were narrow. Each had his study in the rear of the house. The story runs, that once upon a time, in the summer, our rector had found himself utterly unable during the week to write the dreaded sermon: and on Saturday, at about noon, despairing of success, bent down his head over his crossed arms upon his study-table, and wept audibly from sheer helplessness and mortification. The windows were all open: and the kind-hearted Presbyterian dominie, seeing his predicament and pitying him sincerely, called out loud enough to be heard across both gardens: "Don't cry, brother ——; I'll lend you a sermon!"

It was not strange that, during the weariness of such a rectorship, my Father should often wonder, that the service of the world never called in vain for the highest order of abilities, while such an one as *this* was the sole pillar of the Church throughout all Western Pennsylvania! Again and again the desire to devote himself to the work was felt: but was put aside by pleading the wants of a growing family and the claims of creditors—pleas which have often succeeded, in other cases, in drowning the still, small voice that called to the harder life, the higher duty. Then, again, he found the enjoyment of the noble strife of the Law to be more and more marred by the constant contact with that mass of falsehood, meanness, fraud and crime,

---

[1] Long known as the Rev. Dr. McElroy, of New York City.

which provides the work for so many lawyers: and the hunger for a purer element wherein to earn his daily bread, was ever growing stronger. His interest in parish affairs, meanwhile, was steadily increasing, and his attachment to the Church was now much more than mere accident or preference. He was elected one of the Vestry in 1822 and 1823, was generally present at the meetings, and by no means a silent or uninfluential member.

In the Spring of 1822, while busy furnishing his new house and preparing to occupy it, an incident occurred which was well adapted to deepen all his more religious feelings and convictions. His only brother-in-law, Edward Müller, who was in many ways specially endeared to him, was now an uncommonly attractive young man, and expecting within a week to be married to one of the choicest young ladies of Pittsburgh: when, in driving to attend the wedding of a friend, he was thrown out of his sulky, and broke his leg upon the only stone within sight. The place was on the banks of the Monongahela, twelve miles from the city; long delays occurred in procuring medical attendance, which was of a very unsatisfactory character when obtained: in short, mortification set in, and the young man died on the 23d of May, 1822,—the very day when he was to have been married. My Father was with him, broke to him the reality of his danger, and administered to him the only religious consolations which soothed his last hours. But in the grief which thus suddenly darkened a whole circle of friendships at the moment of brightest earthly anticipation, he saw a fresh proof of the vanity of laboring for anything except that which shall last throughout eternity. He even went so far as to write to the Standing Committee of the Diocese to ascertain whether he could be admitted as a Candidate for Holy Orders provisionally,—not yet seeing his way clear to the abandonment of his profession, and having some idea of trying to combine the two callings for a time.[1] But in August, they

---

[1] This idea seems to have presented itself to him as far back as in the latter part of the year 1818, shortly after Mr. Carter's leaving, and was the subject of some correspondence between them. Mr. Carter wrote him, very sensibly, from Trenton (January 4, 1819) against any such union of two professions: "I have tried two professions the year past," said he, "teaching and preaching; and have found it absolutely impossible to do my duty properly in either." A very common experience on the part of those who have made the experiment.

notified him that they could not feel at liberty to recommend him as a Candidate, until his own mind was first thoroughly made up on the subject.

It was with these feelings thus strengthening within him that he furnished and occupied his new house, during the summer of 1822. The current of his thoughts was one day casually mentioned in conversation, to a fellow-vestryman of the parish: and his words were remembered. Meanwhile his health was reëstablished, and the arrangement of the garden and grounds of his new purchase gave him abundant work for all the leisure which his legal partnership allowed.

The Rev. William Thompson[1] had now been the rector of the Parish from September, 1821, and several efforts were made towards fresh life and growth, but with small success. Even so late as December, 1822, the debt for the organ procured under Mr. Carter was not yet paid. Success seemed impossible, in any effort. At length, in July, 1823, Mr. Thompson's resignation was sent in, and on my Father's motion was accepted, to take effect at any time he pleased during the ensuing six months. Some little misunderstanding between him and the Vestry led to a total severance towards the end of August, during my Father's absence attending court in another county.

And now an unusual event formed the turning-point in my Father's life. The Vestryman to whom he had spoken, the year before, touching his thoughts of the Ministry, had resolved, without lisping a syllable to him on the subject, to act upon the information which he thus possessed; and to act at once, before my Father could return to town to prevent it.

On the day after Mr. Thompson received his *congé*, the Vestry " resolved" that a parish meeting should be convened " on business of importance " on the following Tuesday evening, at the Church, notice being twice given publicly on the intervening Sunday; and that, at the said meeting, " every Episcopalian who shall have for the last year, in any manner and degree, been a contributor towards the support of the Church and Minister, be

---

[1] On the minute-book of the Vestry he appears as the first Clergyman ever present at a Vestry meeting of that parish. One of the " By-Laws" adopted May 1, 1819, excluded the rector from a seat in that body!

entitled to a vote." The meeting was very fully attended. The Vestryman then brought forward his plan, which was, to elect Mr. Hopkins as their future Rector, if he would consent to give up the law, and proceed to ordination as soon as practicable, serving the parish as lay-reader, moreover, until duly ordained. The idea of electing as Rector a man who was not yet a Candidate for Orders drew out some opposition: but still greater was the reluctance to ask him to resign an income of some $5000 a year, with nothing laid up, and take instead of it a salary of $800 a year, on which to support and bring up a growing family. The discussion was long and animated. But the Vestryman—though acknowledging that he had no authority at all from my Father to say what he would do—yet so fully and earnestly enlarged upon his knowledge of those secret thoughts and longings, and the steadily increasing ardor of my Father's zeal in all Church matters, and the immense advantages to the Church in case he should accept the call thus strangely but strikingly made, that all opposition was at length overborne, and the singular call was *unanimously* given.[1]

On returning from the County court, my Father was startled with a strange surprise when the action of this meeting was formally laid before him. No prospects could be brighter than his in the profession of the Law. Politics, too, began to have some attractions, his principles then being those of the old Federal party. The income of the rectorship would not be enough to maintain his family; besides which, he contributed $300 a year towards his mother's support: and especially, he was yet heavily in debt to the estate of his friend O'Hara, for the advances made in settling the losses of their iron business. It seemed almost madness, in the face of these circumstances, to make the change proposed. And yet all these obstacles, one by one, were overcome. His wife—who, with her growing family, risked the most—was not only willing, but ardently desirous, to make the sacrifice, and urged him to accept. His last doubt was as to his large debt to the O'Hara estate: and he laid the case fully before the heirs, submitting it entirely to their decision whether he should or

---

[1] The Vestry minutes of Trinity parish have no record of my Father's Call. They only record the call for the parish meeting. It was this last that gave the call; and, not being a Vestry meeting, its action is not recorded in the Vestry book.

should not continue at the law until their claim were fully paid. But the noble spirit of O'Hara had descended with his blood : and they unanimously declared that they would put no pecuniary claim in the way of his obedience to so manifest a call from God.

His mind was now made up at once. The requisite formalities were complied with as speedily as possible. On the 6th of September he wrote to Bishop White, making his application in canonical form : and on the 2d of October he read to the Vestry the Bishop's reply, informing him of his admission as a Candidate, and licensing him to act as lay-reader until his ordination. His services in this capacity began the next Sunday, October 5th. At that same meeting of the Vestry, he was appointed one of a committee of three " to inquire into the expediency of making the necessary arrangements for the building of a new Church." The fresh leaven thus began to work at once.

The seat at the organ, which he had occupied for five years, was now taken by his wife, though with much fear and trembling. He wrote out for her the harmonies of the tunes, and composed all the voluntaries and interludes needed; and for four years, with more or less of aid from a young friend,[1] she continued to serve at one end of the Church while her husband was serving at the other.

His law business he sold out to the Hon. Henry Baldwin (who was returning from Congress to resume his preëminence at the Pittsburgh bar) and Mr. Fetterman, who had now for some time been his own junior partner. On the 8th of November he pleaded his last cause, and won it. And on the third Sunday in Advent, December 14, he was ordained Deacon by Bishop White, in Trinity Church, Philadelphia, preaching his first sermon the same afternoon in S. Peter's Church. On the Fourth Sunday in Advent, December 21, he entered upon his duties in Trinity Church, Pittsburgh. On Wednesday, the 12th of May following, before the Diocesan Convention then assembled in S. John's Church, Norristown, he was ordained Priest.

An election to the Rectorship before he was a Candidate for

---

[1] Mr. William Staunton, now for many years known as the Rev. William Staunton, D.D., who is more fully master of the science of music than any other of our American clergy.

Orders at all, a Candidacy of a little over two months before being ordained Deacon, and a Diaconate of scarce five months before being ordained Priest, form a combination, it is believed, without a parallel in our day and country. There were several reasons for this unusual haste. My Father's maturity of age and character was one element. Another was, the unusual amount of study which he had been able to give already to theology; for, besides his extraordinary industry in the study of the Scriptures, he had for more than a year been pursuing a steady course of theological reading, comprising the then standard works; and in compliance with what he supposed to be the requirements of the Canon, he brought with him, on asking for the Diaconate, a theological essay written in the Latin tongue. The high success in the Law, which he was leaving at so remarkable a pecuniary sacrifice, was an equitable claim against unnecessary delay before being permitted to begin the new work to which he was called. The singular confidence in him manifested by his election to the rectorship under such unprecedented circumstances, was felt to demand a prompt and emphatic response on the part of the Ecclesiastical Authority. And a due regard for the interests of the Church in the Western half of the Keystone State,—a vast region in which Trinity Church, Pittsburgh, was the only live parish and my Father was to be the only parish priest,—crowned the combination of reasons with an irresistible persuasiveness. But before we can properly understand his work there, we must glance for a few moments at the state of things previously.

Chapter IV.

FIRST-FRUITS OF THE PRIESTHOOD.

IN the year 1801, a meeting was held in Washington, Pennsylvania, at which a few clergymen of the Church in the western parts of Pennsylvania and Virginia discussed the prospects of Church growth west of the Allegheny Mountains. They resolved that the Rev. Joseph Doddridge, M.D., should correspond with Bishop White, requesting that, through him, the General Convention might permit that western country to be organized into a separate Diocese. But after waiting eighteen months for answer, he learned that nothing could be done. "Then," says Dr. Doddridge, "I lost all hope of ever witnessing any prosperity in our beloved Church in this part of America. Everything connected with it fell into a state of languor. The vestries were not reëlected, and our young people joined other societies. Could I prevent them, when I indulged no hope of a succession in the ministry? . . . I entertained no hope that even my own remains, after death, would be committed to the dust with the funeral services of my own Church."[1] He tells us that large portions of Western Pennsylvania and Virginia, as well as of Eastern Kentucky and Ohio, were settled by Church people, originally from Maryland, Carolina, or Virginia: and that they had had Methodist Bishops and Roman Bishops; but that they had never seen a Bishop of their own Church. In a letter written to Bishop Hobart in 1816, he says:[2]—"Had we imitated at an early period the example of other Christian communities, employed the same means for collecting our people into societies and building Churches with the same zeal, we should by this time have had four or five Bishops in this country (*i.e.*, west of the Alleghenies), surrounded by a numerous and respectable body of clergy, instead of having our

[1] See Bishop Stevens's Sermon at the Primary Convention of the Diocese of Pittsburgh.
[2] Ibid.

very name connected with a fallen Church. Instead of offering a rich and extensive plunder to every sectarian missionary, we should have occupied the first and highest station among the Christian societies of the West."

The dignified policy of doing nothing continued until 1808, when the General Convention passed resolutions authorizing the election and consecration of a Western Bishop: but nothing came of it. In 1811, the Bishops of Pennsylvania and Virginia were "requested to devise means for supplying the congregations of this Church, west of the Allegheny Mountains, with the ministrations and worship of the same, and for the organizing the Church in the Western States,—anything in the 37th Canon to the contrary notwithstanding." But Bishop Madison of Virginia died soon after, and nothing came of the resolution of 1811. In 1812, Bishop White stated the case to his Convention, and at his suggestion that body agreed to place the whole of the State west of the Alleghenies under any Bishop who should be consecrated for any State westward: but nothing came of it. No Bishop was sent forth for any part of the West until Bishop Philander Chase was consecrated for Ohio in 1819; and no Bishop was seen in Western Pennsylvania until Bishop White's first visit in 1825.

Meanwhile, the do-nothing policy was producing its usual fruits. At the last Convention held before my Father's ordination, the whole number of the Clergy in Pennsylvania was found to have increased from 16 in 1801 to only 34 in 1823: and there was but one candidate for orders admitted in 1823,—a colored man. All the growth, moreover, was in the eastern part of the Diocese: while, in regard to the western, we learn from the Journal of 1823 the results of the Rev. Mr. Thompson's missionary explorations:—" Some ten or fifteen years past, there were not less than five congregations belonging to the Church in the vicinity of Brownsville. . . . These congregations, through the want of clergymen to settle in this part of the country, are nearly all gone to other denominations; yet it is believed, if a Missionary could be sent amongst them, many of them would return to the

---

[1] " One at West's Church, six miles from Brownsville; one at Jackson's Church, seven miles; one at Muddy Creek, eleven miles; one at Red Stone, twelve miles from Brownsville; the name of the other I forget."

Church." And Bishop White himself, in giving the account of his first visitation in the West, admits that the Church, in that section, " had been for many years in a state of decline."

Trinity Church, Pittsburgh, was organized in September, 1805, under the Rev. John Taylor, who—under the familiar title of " Father Taylor "—continued to reside there for many years after, but with no parochial charge. At the time of my Father's ordination the number of communicants was about 40, and it was the only really living parish in the Diocese west of the Mountains. The Church building was a small octagon of brick, in the meeting-house style of architecture, and situated on a sort of triangular lot with streets on each of the three sides,[1] so that enlargement was out of the question. Of course it had never been consecrated, and there was no objection therefore to its sale or exchange for a better site, fronting on Sixth Street. The project had been under consideration for some time previous: but nothing had been done. Now, however, all was changed, and not a moment's time was lost.

During the first part of my Father's sojourn at Pittsburgh, while teaching and law studies and book-keeping all made their demands upon his attention, an English traveller had spent some months in the city, who had with him Brittan's work on Gothic Architecture,—the first thing of the sort my Father had ever seen. Unable to purchase so expensive a work, and knowing at any rate that it was not to be had in any American bookshop, he at once undertook the task of copying with his own hand the greater portion of the plates. These copies were executed in indian ink, with the greatest care and accuracy; and in this manner he became more thoroughly a master of that noble style than any professional architect who had as yet appeared in America. His skill was, of course, exceedingly imperfect when compared with the full revival of our times: but in that period of early twilight, his knowledge shone like the morning star, heralding the brighter day. He undertook to be the Architect of the new Church: and so rapid was the movement, that, within about six weeks after he took charge of the parish as a deacon, his plans

---

[1] The lot was bounded by Wood, Liberty, and Sixth Streets; and the Church was commonly known as "the Old Round Church."

and elevations for a church that would seat a thousand persons were completed, adopted by the Vestry without alteration, and put under contract.

On the feast of S. Philip and S. James, the corner-stone was laid by his old friends of the Masonic fraternity,[1] he delivering the Address. It was the first time that so much pomp and ceremony had marked the laying of any corner-stone in Western Pennsylvania; and the Address opened with a keen and unanswerable vindication of the use of a gorgeous ceremonial in the worship of God. Its being "uncommon" and "of no use to the building itself," he proved to be no objection. In regard to any such ceremony, he says: "Before we object to its introduction amongst ourselves, let us first ask, Can it do any harm? and if, to say the least of it, it is innocent, it may be as well, and certainly as charitable, to let it pass without any unfriendly observations." The real use of it all is, he says, "to show the interest which we feel in the subject of it, or, in other words, to express the emotions which ought to attend the establishment of everything connected with religion." The whole strain of the argument would just suit our own day, and lies really at the root of the last book published by him during his lifetime.[2]

The work was pushed forward with the utmost energy. The edifice was of brick, roughcast on the outside, the smoke of Pittsburgh aided by the rain soon giving it an air of antiquity which disguised the poorness of the material. The detail was of the latest period of Third Pointed or Perpendicular,—the revival of the art naturally beginning at that point where it disappeared, and working backwards towards the stronger and purer style of an earlier age. My Father's means for keeping up with the progress of the revival of Pointed architecture were, however, very slight; and his preference for the Perpendicular and for the four-centre arch remained during his whole life. The Church was wide, with galleries on three sides, supported by slender cluster

---

[1] My Father never cared to officiate at the laying of the corner-stone of a Church. He said that our branch of the Church had never provided an Office for the purpose; and he was of opinion that the custom of laying corner-stones ecclesiastically had sprung up in our day mainly out of prejudice against the Freemasons, to whom, from old traditionary use, that ceremony properly belonged.

[2] The *Law of Ritualism*, 1866.

shafts connected with spandrils at the top, the gallery front being panelled all round. The flat and plaistered ceiling was painted in imitation of fan-vaulting,—a style of work which the Pittsburgh house-painters were utterly ignorant of: my Father therefore—as he had done in many other parts of the building—set them the model with his own hands. An entire compartment of the ceiling he painted himself: and one of my earliest recollections is, the seeing my Father come home in the evening, utterly wearied with lying on his back all day, on the high scaffold, painting the ceiling of that Church. Moreover, it was a special enjoyment to him, so long as he remained in Pittsburgh, to tarry after night service watching the effect while the sexton put out the lamps one by one: for the increasing dimness of the light favored the more complete illusion, and just before the last was extinguished he could fancy that he was really looking upon one of those vaulted roofs of stone, which he regarded as the crowning glory of the art.

The success of this building—and it was a great thing for those days—brought him, for many years, a large number of applications for Church plans, from various parts of the country: architects being then very few, and no member of that honorable profession in America having as yet thought it worth while to pay any attention to the "Gothic style."

The kindred art of music offered an additional field for an activity which seemed to know no bounds. Church music was then in as wretched a condition as Church architecture: it could not well be worse. My Father believed that the songs of the House of the Lord should be written by the servants of the Lord, and not borrowed or stolen from the service of the world, the flesh, and the devil. As the architecture of the Church should be religious, and not in the style which was commonly used for State-houses and banks: so the music of the Psalms and Hymns should be religious, and free from all the associations of the concert-hall or the theatre, the parlor or the bar-room. He began to compose this music himself. The interludes and voluntaries written by him to aid my Mother in her work as organist, were gradually followed by chaunts, metrical tunes, and anthems; until, before he left Pittsburgh, the whole of the music used in public worship was his own. The style was not that which is strictly called ecclesiastical, for he had never had any opportunity to master it. Nor had he ever learned counterpoint, or the art of harmonizing and arranging music with scientific accuracy: and therefore he never published any music without first securing the oversight of some scientific friend. But his taste was formed in the school of Pleyel, Haydn and Mozart; and his natural gift was so strong that he produced, with easy profusion, melodies of striking beauty, which—whether tender or bold, plaintive or triumphant—were easily caught by all who had any ear for music. The simplicity of their structure, too, enabled many to sing an accompanying part without notes: so that, though the organ and choir were in the west-end gallery, the singing was general all over the Church; and, as is generally the case, the responses were as hearty as the singing.

In the year 1824—the first of my Father's priesthood—the venerable Bishop White made an attempt to visit the western part of his Diocese; but was thrown from his carriage on the way, near Lewistown, and with a broken arm returned to Philadelphia. The new church, opened and occupied this year, was still further advanced towards completion in the next: but with no small burden of debt, which, however, did not hinder the growth of the parish. The new church proved to be none too large: and when, at length, in June, 1825, the aged Bishop White, accompanied by the Rev. Mr. (afterwards Bishop) Kemper, made his *first* visitation of the West, the new church was consecrated on the Feast of S. Barnabas; and on that day (and the Friday previous) nearly 150[1] were confirmed. Thus, in a priesthood of hardly more than a year, the little one of about forty communicants had risen to between one and two hundred; and ranked as the *third* parish in the Diocese in point of numerical strength.

But my Father's energies had not been confined to his own parish. Being the only priest of the Church west of the mountains, he was ready to obey every call from the more destitute

---

[1] In Bishop White's Address to his Convention in 1826, the number is given as 135. In a memorandum prepared by my Father only two years before his death, it is 143. In a letter written to his mother within a few days after the Confirmation was held, he states the number as 150. This last is most probably correct.

parts of the State. In January, 1825, at the earnest request of his friend John B. Wallace, Esq.—one of the staunchest and noblest of the Church's laymen in those days—he "held a mission," as we should call it now, in the borough of Meadville, where, within twelve days, he preached eight times, baptized 75 persons (of whom 32 were adults and 43 were under 14 years of age), administered the Holy Communion, and a parish was duly organized before he left. Unhappily the Bishop's Visitation did not extend so far north as Meadville; and some vicissitudes were experienced before the parish, so auspiciously begun, ripened into strength. With similar results, about a fortnight before the Bishop's arrival, my Father, at his request, visited Greensburg, where, in four days, he preached or lectured seven times, baptized nineteen, and—when the Bishop arrived—eight more were baptized, and 62 were confirmed. By expeditions of this sort he was the means of establishing no less than seven new parishes during the seven years of his service in Pennsylvania, so that he was justly looked upon as the Father of the Church in the whole region which is now known as the Diocese of Pittsburgh.[1]

The debt incurred in erecting the new Church was not immediately discharged. Unused to such efforts, the congregation fancied that they were unable to bear the burden alone, and that the importance of the work done in Pittsburgh was sufficient to entitle them to help from the East. In this opinion their Rector did not coincide; but yielding to their desire he went, by their request and authority, to try what could be done.

His journey began in October, 1825, and the route he chose was by way of Niagara Falls and the Erie Canal, his dear friends Mr. and Mrs. John B. Wallace being his companions nearly all the way. At New York he was the guest of Bishop Hobart, and was so delighted at the opportunity of making his acquaintance and talking over many important subjects with him, that this

---

[1] The Bishop of Pittsburgh, in his first Address to his Convention, which sat in Trinity Church, Pittsburgh, and speaking of his first visitation, says: "It is only a ust recognition of valuable services done to the Church in our Diocese years ago, to say, that I was struck in this visitation of the Northern parts of it by the traces of the pioneer missionary work of the venerable Presiding Bishop of our Church, the rector, a generation ago, of the Church in which we are now assembled. Churches founded by his efforts still live on there, the centres of important and growing Church works."
—*Journal of Pittsburgh Convention*, 1866.

alone, he said, would have more than repaid him for the whole journey.[1] At Boston, too, as in New York, the personal reception given was flattering in a high degree: but the raising of the money was a very different question. A commercial panic then depressed both those cities. Not a few of the eastern parishes, moreover, were at that time heavily in debt themselves, some to a greater amount than the total cost of the Pittsburgh Church; and no eloquence in the world could induce such debt-burdened parishes to regard a congregation which had just enjoyed the confirmation of 150 persons, as a proper subject of pecuniary aid. Philadelphia was in a frame of mind equally admiring and equally economical; and so the Rector returned, after some three months' absence, with many sketches of the scenery he had beheld, with much new knowledge of the Church and its clergy and people, and having left an impression behind him which modified his whole subsequent career: but with no money towards the debt. The parish then came over to his opinion about it, and resolved that they were both able, and willing, to pay it themselves: and so they did in due time.

When my Father first took his seat as a member of the Diocesan Convention, in 1824, his only motion during the session was a resolution concurring with the venerable Bishop White in the interest which he had expressed in the General Theological Seminary, and heartily recommending that Institution to the zealous support and fostering care of Churchmen throughout the Diocese. In the parochial reports presented that year, some of the Low-Church Clergy had made no slight display of their peculiar views: all of which were judiciously omitted from the printed journal, by the direction of the Bishop. At this "liberty" taken with their documents great indignation was expressed, and a warm discussion took place in 1825. The common custom of handing in such reports at Convention time, had led to a forgetfulness of the fact that they are really reports made to the Bishop; and therefore are subject to his order. The Bishop's rights were vigorously maintained by my Father in a spirited debate; and he moved a

---

[1] In the *Appendix*, p. 454, will be found *The Bell of St. John's*, a poem written while in Bishop Hobart's house.

resolution which was carried, and settled the dispute in the Bishop's favor.

In 1826 and 1829—the only two General Conventions held during his priesthood—my Father sat in the Lower House as a clerical deputy from Pennsylvania: and in each of these Conventions he took a prominent part in the leading discussion of the session.

In 1826 there was a remarkable combination between High-Church and Low-Church for altering and shortening the Liturgy. Bishop Hobart led the movement, his object being twofold. One was, to render the use of the Ante-Communion Office obligatory on every Sunday and Holyday (which it was already, by Rubric, according to the clear words of it, and the unanimous declaration of the House of Bishops, though irregularly omitted in divers places); the other was, to tie the word *regeneration* to the Sacrament of Baptism, by changes in the Confirmation Office, so that there should no longer be any dispute about Baptismal Regeneration. To induce the Low-Church party to consent to this, the words which he proposed explained Baptismal Regeneration as only "giving *a title*" to all the blessings of the Covenant; or, as the Low-Church expressed it, it was an acknowledgment that Baptismal Regeneration was "only a *titular* regeneration": and he threw in the further inducement of permitting the minister, at discretion, to take any other psalm or psalms instead of the Psalter for the day, and to cut down the Lessons to fifteen verses; while, on other than Sundays and Holydays, he might ignore the Calendar altogether, and choose what Lessons he pleased.

Those who then opposed this movement were but dimly conscious of the greatness of the evil which they were preventing: for the proposed setting forth of a " titular " Regeneration would have been a calamity greater than any other which the American Church has yet had to deplore in connection with the alterations made in her standards: though it was that which least impressed itself upon the minds of Churchmen in those days. Bishop Hobart's overwhelming influence carried nearly the whole High-Church party, as a matter of course. The Low-Church party, by instinct, went for anything that would shorten the Liturgy. Those of them who objected, based their reluctance mainly upon the question of Baptismal Regeneration, being unwilling to concede *Baptismal* Regeneration in *any* shape, and preferring "the hypothetical theory." Each side seems, on this point, to have been judicially blinded: the High-Church in offering a "titular" Regeneration, and the Low-Church in refusing to accept it at once. But it was one of those crises which Providence overrules in a manner which a succeeding generation can appreciate much more correctly than the actors through whose exertions the issue is decided at the time.

The unusual combination at first threatened to carry all before it. The House of Bishops adopted Bishop Hobart's proposal unanimously, thus sending it down to the Lower House with a prestige likely to be similarly successful there. Speaker after speaker rose, of different parties, but each one of them earnestly advocated the adoption of the proposed changes. All opposition seemed to be cowed. My Father was a new member, and unwilling to speak: but his spirit began to boil within him. He was the guest of Mr. Meredith, one of the Lay Deputies from Pennsylvania, whom he found to be equally opposed to these sweeping innovations. Their conversation so stimulated them, that it was agreed, that Mr. Meredith[1]—being the older member—should move the indefinite postponement, with a speech; and that my Father should second the motion. The steady stream of approval from both sides of the House, however, so far overcame Mr. Meredith's courage, that when he at length rose to make the motion, his promised speech was by no means the important effort that the crisis demanded; and my Father, in seconding him, found that the whole brunt of the opposition—if it were to amount to anything—was left upon his own shoulders.

He at once rose to the full measure of the occasion, thus early in his career giving a significant proof of that quality which, perhaps, was the most prominent feature in his life-labor for the Church:—the power to stand forth alone, with perfectly conscientious convictions of truth, to battle with all his might against overwhelming majorities; and that, too, with a voice so firm and

---

[1] He had served in every General Convention from 1817.

First-Fruits of the Priesthood.

clear and fearless that it could not be utterly lost even amid the mad roar of popular passion excited to the utmost. On this first occasion there was not the slightest sign of hesitation. The unanimity of the Upper House, the strange yet powerful combination in the Lower, his own singular regard and esteem for Bishop Hobart as well as his reverence for Bishop White, all together could not weaken a particle the force of his attack, or dull the edge of merciless ridicule with which he dissected the arguments used in favor of the change proposed.

It was a curious circumstance that Vermont (his future Diocese) had furnished some of the most pointed and painful of the experiences which demanded the change. One clerical deputy had plaintively urged, that if the brethren were compelled to officiate, as had often been his luck in Vermont, in a church where several panes of glass had been knocked out of the windows, and where the wood in the stoves was often so green that the fires would not burn, while nevertheless the thermometer was 20° or 30° below zero, they would at once become satisfied that it was desirable to shorten the Liturgy. Such a style of advocacy afforded too tempting an opportunity to be let slip. "These reasons for altering the Prayer-Book," my Father said, "showed what wonders could be wrought by the exercise of a vivid imagination. My brother from the far North," said he, "tells us that in Vermont there are sometimes panes of glass missing from the windows in very cold weather. Now a plain, practical, common-sense man, like myself, would say that the shortest and best way to remedy this inconvenience, would be to get some panes of glass and a little putty, and stop up the holes in the usual way. But 'No!' says my imaginative brother: 'Shorten the Liturgy!' Will nothing answer in Vermont when the thermometer is 30° below zero, but to paste the broken church windows over with leaves torn from the Prayer-Book? Then, again, my brother tells us that sometimes the wood in the church stoves on cold Sundays is green and will not burn. A plain practical man, like myself, would say that the best cure for this would be to get some seasoned wood and dry kindlings, and thus make a fire that would burn. But 'No!' says my imaginative brother from Vermont: 'Shorten the Liturgy!' Will that cure the evil complained of? If my brother insists on taking enough out of the Prayer-Book to make the green wood burn merrily in mid-winter, pray how much of our incomparable Liturgy would be left?" With this keen raillery he analyzed all the arguments, and arrested the attention of every one present, to an unusual degree. Even the Bishops left their House and stole quietly into the church[1] to listen to the maiden speech of the new member: and when he had finished, Bishop Hobart rushed down to rebuke him, highly excited with indignation at such daring opposition to the pet project of the unanimous House of Bishops. "Sir," said he with great warmth to my Father, "you have this day done the Bishops more harm than you will ever live to do them good!" My Father answered, quietly and kindly, that in fighting for the Prayer-Book he was in reality fighting for the Bishops. The dashing brilliance which thus headed the opposition to the whole of the Upper House and an overwhelming combination of the Lower, gave courage to others; and the project was fought at every step of the way. Of course the combination triumphed, for the time being: but it was felt that the weight of the argument was heavily on the other side.

The Constitution wisely requires that a change of the Prayer-Book shall not take effect until it has been approved by two successive General Conventions, being sent down meanwhile to each Diocesan Convention[2] for further consideration by the sober second thoughts of the Clergy and Laity. When this process began, there soon became apparent a growing divergency among those who had been so harmonious in favor of the changes. Bishop Hobart struggled while there was any chance, and secured a strong approval from the Rev. William Meade of Virginia,[3] who was so sure that the service ought to be shortened, as to say

---

[1] S. Peter's, Philadelphia.

[2] In 1827 (May 25th, in a letter to Bishop Ravenscroft) Bishop Hobart already feared the turning of the tide against him:—"The Constitution requires that proposed alterations in the Liturgy should be laid before the several State Conventions, but does not require that they should be acted upon. Would it not be well for the State Conventions to express no opinion, but leave the result to the next General Convention?"

[3] Feb. 22, 1827. See correspondence in Bishop Johns's *Memoir of Bishop Meade*, pp. 158 et seqq.

that, if it be not done, "a heavy guilt will rest upon us. Nothing can prevent it," he added, " but pride, obstinacy, prejudice, and uncharitableness."[1] He was not quite so clear as to the alterations touching Regeneration, and would have preferred an alternative prayer in that Baptismal Office " which we must now use," he said, "but which I never do without pain, because its plain literal meaning contradicts my belief." This was written in 1827: yet Mr. Meade would probably have spared some of his hard words on the subject, could he have looked but two years ahead; for in 1829, the same Convention of Virginia which almost unanimously elected him Assistant Bishop,[2] voted *against* the proposed changes, in response to an earnest appeal from Bishop Moore.[3] Other Dioceses took a similar course. The Church papers were filled with unfriendly criticisms. And the minority of 1826 had so clearly become the irresistible majority in 1829, that on motion of Bishop Hobart himself, in that year, the House of Bishops "*Resolved*, That, under existing circumstances, it is not expedient to adopt the proposed" changes in the Prayer-Book, " and they are therefore hereby dismissed from the consideration of the Convention." And the Lower House, without any difficulty, "concurred in that resolution."

[1] He added further:—"If we continue to bite and devour one another, we must expect to be consumed [of] one another, and to be made a laughing-stock to our enemies which malign us." In the same letter, moreover, arguing for shorter Services, he showed that the opposition to the presence of non-communicants during the Holy Eucharist, about which some Low-Church people are now so zealous, was unknown even in Virginia in those days:—"I think, however, it would be very desirable to abridge the service on Communion days, by permitting the omission of the Litany on such occasions. This is more necessary in country congregations, because *all* persons, young and old, whether communicants or not, must remain in the Church during celebration, or else be tempted to spend the time of waiting for their friends improperly around the Church."

[2] He had every vote cast, of both orders, except two blank ballots of the clergy.

[3] Within two months of the date of the Rev. Wm. Meade's letter to Bishop Hobart, quoted above, Bishop Moore of Virginia wrote to Bishop Ravenscroft (April 21, 1827) on this subject:—"The unanimous declaration of the House of Bishops on the subject of the proposed alterations, I confess astonished me very much; and makes me tremble at the view of the prospect before us. In several conversations with Bishop Hobart, I expressed to him my great surprise; and assured him that, had I been present, I should have opposed that measure. . . . It is with pleasure I can say, that I have not met with any Clergyman since my return who has expressed a sentiment at variance with those I entertain. . . . When the subject was mentioned to me in Hartford, I inquired of the gentleman, what was the effect produced on the minds of the Clergy and Laity. He replied, that they were wrapt in amazement; and considered the resolutions as the result of great precipitancy, and want of reflection.

To Bishop Hobart's honor be it recorded, that his natural anger at my Father's course was but of short duration, and never interrupted for a moment their cordial personal relations. Nay, with a rare magnanimity, Bishop Hobart afterwards made repeated efforts to secure my Father's removal to the city of New York as rector of one or other of the leading city parishes.

Perhaps it is as well to mention here—though somewhat in anticipation of the course of our narrative—the other facts connected with my Father's action at that same General Convention of 1829 which crowned with quiet triumph the opposition begun by him in 1826. The most protracted and exciting debate of the session was about signing the testimonials of the Rev. Mr. Meade, who had been elected Assistant Bishop of Virginia, the Convention which elected him at the same time declaring that he was "not to be considered as entitled to the succession"; but that it should be "the right and duty of the Convention of the Diocese of Virginia, on the demise of their Bishop, to proceed to the election of a principal Bishop as a successor to the said deceased Bishop." There was, at the time, no Canon of our Church regulating the matter, our existing Canon [1]—the fruit of that contest—first appearing as Canon V. of 1829. The extreme impolicy of the plan proposed by Virginia was patent to all: and the prominence given during several years previous to Mr. Meade as a leader of the Low-Church party,—what was then looked upon as the extreme wing of it,—was a strong inducement to the leading High-Churchmen to make the most of the difficulty.

The distinguished Horace Binney was the leader of the opposition to Mr. Meade. My Father was satisfied that the decided expression of opinion on the part of General Convention would be sufficient to induce Virginia to reconsider her position of her own accord. Mr. Meade himself disapproved so strongly the denial of his right of succession, that he long hesitated whether he should accept the office. Moreover, the personal convictions expressed by the Deputies from Virginia, that their Diocesan Convention would without doubt promptly remove that

---

[1] Title I., Canon 13, § v. of the Digest.

restriction at the next session, were entitled to great weight, and were honorably vindicated by the event. My Father and Mr. Binney were both on the Committee to whom the subject was referred in the Lower House: and my Father, with the majority of the Committee, reported in favor of signing the Testimonials, though the Report contained a strong condemnation of the Virginia restriction. Mr. Binney presented a substitute, providing for a signing of the Testimonials with an exception attached; and even this document was not to be used until after the Diocese of Virginia had given to Mr. Meade the right of succession. He contended with all his great acumen and ability in favor of this course; while upon my Father devolved the chief labor of defending the report of the Committee. The Hon. E. F. Chambers, who in that session began his long career as one of the leading laymen in the House of Deputies, was very active in suggesting and bringing about a compromise which really secured to Virginia all she asked. Mr. Binney's proposal was defeated: while the Resolution to sign the Testimonials at once was carried, only embodying in it, first, that disapproval of the Virginia restriction as "highly inexpedient and wholly inadmissible," in regard to which there was a general agreement on all sides.

The course pursued on this point by my Father was one which Bishop Meade and many of his friends gratefully remembered ever after, showing him often such kindness as they never volunteered to any other person holding his opinions on test questions of Churchmanship.

It was certainly remarkable that two such triumphs should mark his career in the only two General Conventions in which he sat as a member of the Lower House.

Chapter V.

THE CONTESTED EPISCOPAL ELECTION.

BETWEEN the two General Conventions of which we have given some account in connection with one another, occurred an extraordinary excitement in the Diocese of Pennsylvania about the election of a Bishop to assist the aged Bishop White. It was, properly speaking, the first election of an Assistant Bishop among us: and the story will be given here with the greater minuteness, because my Father was very sensitive in regard to the injustice done to him by the formal record on the Pennsylvania Convention Journal, where he appears as the leading candidate of the Low-Church party, while in reality it was his vote which elected the nominee of the High-Church party. In order to understand the importance of these events, we must take somewhat of a retrospect.

When, not long before my Father was ordained, the almost fatal deadness which benumbed the Church for a generation after the conclusion of the Revolutionary war had begun to give way before the signs of returning life: that new life was found to be, in certain quarters, injured by a great disregard of some of the most important distinctive principles of the Church. A love for union prayer-meetings, a hankering after extemporary devotions in public, a desire to fraternize with the non-Episcopal bodies of Evangelical Christians which were so much stronger in this country than ourselves, a fondness for omitting the Ante-Communion service, and for taking other liberties with the Prayer-Book, were considered in many quarters as identified with the possession of vital piety; and the rapid and fervent growth of such sentiments and practices gave serious uneasiness to the steadier and wiser minds among Churchmen everywhere. We were then so feeble and so few, that a division on such points as these threatened great injury, if not total destruction.

No one was more alarmed than the venerable Bishop White;

and year after year, in his Conventional Address, he renewed his warnings with growing earnestness. In 1822 he declared that he had "resisted all endeavors for an intermixture of administrations in what concerns the faith, or the worship, or the discipline of the Church." The desire to fraternize, on the part of the denominations, he declared to be simply "the intolerance which in former ages pursued its designs by penal laws; but is now reduced to the necessity of making hollow professions of fraternity: the object being the same, with difference only in the means. . . . The question is, not whether we think correctly, but whether we are to be tolerated in what we think. If this be determined in the affirmative, we must, to be consistent, interdict all other than an episcopalian ministry within our bounds." It was "the fact," that "every proposal to the purpose" of fraternization, "when explained, amounts to the surrendering of one, or of another, of our institutions, without conformity to them in any instance." These were his views "of what the exigencies, and even the existence, of our Church require."

At that same Convention of 1822, the Rev. Dr. Abercrombie, one of the Bishop's friends, was dropped from the delegation to General Convention, and Mr. Boyd, one of the leading Low-Churchmen, was elected in his place.[1] In 1823, however, Mr. Boyd was dropped (being absent from Convention), and Abercrombie was restored: a course which the Low-Church regarded as an aggression.[2] The next year therefore, 1824, at Norristown (the Convention in which my Father first sat), the Low-Church held a caucus,[3] circulated written tickets among

[1] In the whole account of the partisan contest which culminated in the Consecration of Bishop H. U. Onderdonk, I have drawn upon a multiplicity of authorities, almost too numerous to be specified. I have read carefully every one of the numerous pamphlets and circulars which were issued on either side. Memoranda by my Father, letters written by him and to him at the time, and reminiscences written to him within a few years past by surviving participants in the struggle; together with oral communications made to me personally by others of them, of which notes were made at the time: all these, added to the Journals of Convention, have been employed more or less in weaving this narrative.

[2] "Three Letters," by Plain Truth.

[3] This caucus was held at the close of one of their extemporary prayer-meetings. When the combination of these two processes transpired, the Rev. Dr. Montgomery said:—"We were told that they were praying for us; but we soon found that they were preying upon us."

their friends, and succeeded in dropping Dr. Abercrombie and the Rev. Mr. Kemper, two of the Bishop's most intimate friends, electing in their place the Rev. Mr. Allen and the Rev. Mr. Boyd, two of his chief opponents. The High-Church party were not aware of the Low-Church organization, and in their simplicity were voting to place in other offices some of the very men who were engaged in it. It was this year that the Bishop omitted some very Evangelical superfluities from the Parochial Reports printed in the Journal, to the great indignation of the brethren concerned. The establishment of the General Theological Seminary, and the making of the Pennsylvania Education Society auxiliary to it, were two of the points on which Bishop White had set his heart, and which the Low-Church opposed with all their might: while the *Episcopal Recorder* was a great weapon in the hands of the opposition, and their chief instrument for exciting party feeling.[1]

In 1825, the Low-Church caucussed again, ran an exclusive ticket, and elected it. The High-Churchmen were not yet awake to this style of doing business, and did not run an exclusive ticket. But in that year the Bishop, in his Address, gave a further "caution" against "future danger of disorder"; denouncing strongly the prayer-meetings that were then coming into favor among the Low-Church. These meetings he declared to be really contrary to the Canons in "both the letter and the spirit": and he urged that "especial stress should be laid on the testimonies of clergymen, who, having unguardedly given countenance to the irregularity, and having had sorrowful experience of its effects, have left lasting records of their disappointments."[2] The discussion on the Parochial Reports, and the success of my Father's motion to leave full power over them to the Bishop, proved that, when their attention was fairly aroused, the Bishop's friends could carry the Convention.

[1] De Lancey, Montgomery and Kemper united in starting the *Recorder*, which was intended to be a "record" of Church news, not partisan: but after the Norristown Convention, 1824, Mr. Stavely became the printer, Mr. Bedell controlled the editorial columns, and it soon assumed its well-known party character.

[2] In a footnote he refers to the Rev. Devereux Jarratt, of Virginia; the Rev. Thomas Scott, the Commentator; the Rev. John Newton; and others: and the same are referred to by Bishop Hobart, in the *Notes* to his sermon preached at the consecration of Bishop H. U. Onderdonk, in 1827.

The Contested Episcopal Election.

In 1826, the Bishop's Address again returned to the charge, denouncing Prayer-meetings afresh as an "evasion" of the Canons of the Church, and declaring that he would refuse to ordain any Candidate for Orders who had taken part in them: adding that it was "from deliberate design" that he thus repeatedly "raised his warning voice," recording his sense of the subject on the Journal "that it may there survive him, and perhaps serve as a caution after his decease." His friends in the Convention had now, at length, learned the trick of their opponents' tactics. They caucussed carefully, ran an exclusive ticket, and made a clean sweep, carrying everything before them.[1]

It had long been in contemplation to elect an Assistant to Bishop White, who had by this time been for forty years in sole charge of the Diocese, and was nearly eighty years of age. With his friends in the majority, it was thought by him a safe time to move; and as an election previous to the General Convention (which met in the Autumn of the same year) would save time for the Diocese, he, of his own motion,[2] proposed the calling of a Special Convention for the purpose. The Standing Committee unanimously approving, the call was formally issued on the 1st of August, for a meeting on the 25th of October: and at once the war began,—beyond all question the most fiercely contested Episcopal election which the Church in our country has yet seen. It was the pitched battle between High-Church and Low-Church which really settled the question of future ascendancy in the Church of America;[3] and if both parties had fully

---

[1] Just after the Convention, the Rev. L. S. Ives wrote (May 13, 1826) to Bishop Hobart:—"Judging from appearances, Bedell, Allen, etc., were completely humbled. They uttered no complaints, however, as they doubtless felt that their own conduct amply justified the course we adopted. We evinced no signs of extraordinary joy till we found ourselves alone; and then, you may suppose, we indulged our feelings. It would do you good to witness the almost frenzied joy of Montgomery upon the occasion. He maintains that it is an evident and almost miraculous interposition of Providence. So full of gratitude to the Great Head of the Church was he, that we were no sooner alone than he returned *thanks* in a most animated *extemporaneous prayer!*"

[2] See *Candid Address, by Plain Truth*.

[3] So probable seemed the speedy ascendancy of the Low-Church party, and so painful was the apprehension excited by their sudden growth and aggressive temper, that even after this battle was won, Bishop Hobart—the most fearless of the champions of the Church—on the 25th of May, 1827, wrote concerning them to Bishop Ravens-

understood the magnitude of the issues ultimately involved, they could not have fought it out with greater energy or pertinacity.

Very soon after the call of the convention, two Low-Church circulars began the fiery work of inflaming passion. One of these was by "A fellow-Layman," and another by "Hooker"— a young deacon who had hardly been a month in the Diocese. The latter thought that the new Bishop should have "a private fortune of his own," and be "of good report among Methodists, Presbyterians, Baptists," etc., and should also have "connections" among them, to ensure his treating them kindly in controversy. In speaking of the High-Church doctrines, he said that they were defended "with a spirit that had its origin in hell." These sharp words were backed up by sharp deeds. Societies were set on foot in Philadelphia, and a missionary was employed there, with neither of which was the Bishop allowed to have any connection, direct or indirect. No effort was spared to bring in from other Dioceses Clergymen of their sort.[1] The organization of new parishes was pushed with the openly avowed object of increasing the lay vote. The *Recorder* had assumed such a tone towards Bishop White personally, that he refused to receive it into his

---

croft:—"But without doubt, the party hoped ultimately to succeed. It is said that a Southern Clergyman predicted, that after the present generation of Bishops were dead, all the Dioceses, except perhaps New York, would be filled with what he chooses to call Evangelical men. And Dr. Milnor, in his last speech before the American Bible Society, congratulated the friends of Evangelical principles that their number was increasing in the Episcopal Church, especially among the younger Clergy. I fear it is so. God give us wisdom and grace to defend His Church!" If the apprehensions that were so real then, seem to be so ridiculous now, there is no doubt that the fears about other things which drive some men nearly crazy now, will seem quite as absurd fifty years hence. A little more faith in the One Holy Catholic and Apostolic Church, and in its Divine Head and King in Heaven, would quiet our minds and strengthen our hearts wonderfully

[1] Bishop Kemp of Maryland wrote (August 30, 1826) to Bishop Hobart:—"Pennsylvania, I fear, has to encounter a fierce storm. Extremely sore at their defeat last Convention, the leaders of the Opposition are already at work with great diligence, and in a very insidious manner, to effect their purpose. They are trying to get as many of the Alexandria School into their Diocese as they can: and such is the unsuspicious character of our venerable Father [Bishop White], that I fear he will allow them to practise some unfairness. I have already had an instance of an attempt made to obtain a Letter of Dismission contrary to the Canons; but I have determined, and indeed I announced my determination at the last Convention, to check all irregularities respecting Clergymen moving from one Diocese to another. The Alexandrians have given me great trouble."

house.[1] The Low-Church leaders raised a fund to defray the expenses of delegates from the country who voted their ticket; and when this course was exposed, one of their pamphleteers gloried in it as " a most noble act of Gospel charity," calling that partisan fund " a consecrated treasury." One of their leading clergymen travelled through portions of the Diocese, dropping his word against the Rev. Dr. Bird Wilson, who was the first choice of Bishop White's friends. A missionary to Green Bay was induced to remain in Philadelphia, to the great injury of his mission, in order to get the benefit of his vote in October. Meanwhile, the Bishop's friends, secure in the remembrance of the victory they had won in May, were behindhand in activity, as a matter of course; and when the Convention met at S. Peter's, Philadelphia, and the fruits of the extraordinary and unscrupulous activity of the opposition were seen in the attendance of more than double the usual number of lay delegates, their feelings may better be imagined than described.

The Bishop's Address reiterated his devotion to the distinctive principles of the Church. With deeper forebodings he alluded to the possibility of there being a future Bishop of the Diocese who should " either openly oppose himself to the received properties of our Communion, or endeavor to undermine them insidiously and by degrees ": but prophesied that though such a Bishop " might distract and divide the Church, he would not consummate his work." Those who loved the old paths would " by a steady perseverance regain their rights, after experience of the result, and of a manifestation of the spirit which has produced it." His earnestness increased as he continued, speaking of himself, as was his wont, in the third person :—" Could he foresee that during his episcopacy, either now or at any future time, the stated points will be either dismissed or disregarded, he would make some such request as that of Hagar in the wilderness, in reference to what

---

[1] As early as October, 1825, Bishop Moore of Virginia wrote to Bishop Hobart :— " The most unwearied efforts to do good, united with the most honest intentions, and the most unassuming conduct, will not always secure a man from the malevolence of those with whom he is connected. Of this we have a shameful proof in the unkind attacks which have lately been made upon the feelings of our venerable and beloved Senior. When men can be so cruel as to attempt to embitter his life,—a life of so much virtue and so near its close,—who can expect to escape without unkind remarks ? "

has been so long an object of his anxieties, of his prayers, and of his exertions:—'Let me not see the death of the child!'" At these words the voice of the venerable prelate was almost choked with emotion. After a brief pause, he thus concluded:—"It is my desire and my prayer, that your deliberations may be conducted in such a spirit as would have borne to be laid open to the Searcher of Hearts during that celebration of the Eucharistic Sacrifice, in which we were occupied in the morning of yesterday."

There were protracted discussions on the right of members to seats; and to such an extent was partisan feeling carried that one of the leading Low-Church laymen insulted the venerable Bishop by insinuating, in open Convention, that, as President of the body, he could not be trusted to appoint a fair Committee.[1] At length, on the afternoon of the second day, the ballot was reached. The tellers reported that the Rev. Mr. Meade had 27 clerical votes, and the Rev. Bird Wilson 26 votes. With a hurried voice, and a countenance and manner betokening unusual excitement, Bishop White announced that the Clergy had nominated Mr. Meade; and he called on the Laity to prepare their ballots. But the keen eye of his young secretary, the Rev. Mr. (afterwards Bishop) De Lancey, was not so easily blinded. He leaned forward and whispered a few words to Mr. J. R. Ingersoll, who was in the square pew before him. Mr. Ingersoll immediately drew himself up to his full height, and with a very deliberate and impressive voice, said:—" Mr. President, may I be permitted, before further proceeding, to put a question to the Secretary?" "Certainly, certainly," was the nervous response. " Mr. Secretary," then continued Mr. Ingersoll, " will you be so good as to tell us how many of the Clergy have answered to their names?" The Secretary promptly replied:—"Yes, sir: *fifty-four.*" Mr. Ingersoll, with the cool precision of a man who is master of the position, then said:—" Mr. President, will you be kind enough to tell me by what kind of arithmetic *twenty-seven* is a *majority* of

---

[1] This imputation cut the mild yet dignified old man to the heart. It was one of the many things during this protracted contest which pained him so intensely, that Bishop Hobart (in his sermon at the consecration of Bishop Onderdonk) described it as " stretching him on the rack of moral martyrdom." The insult inflicted in public, was afterwards apologized for—in private.

fifty-four?" The venerable President saw the point at once, and altered his announcement accordingly: "There is *no* majority, gentlemen; no nomination is made."

The intense excitement that followed this decision may well be imagined. The tellers being then called upon, made a supplementary report, that one clergyman (it was the Rev. Dr. Wilson [1] himself) had declined to vote. The decision of the Chair was by no means acquiesced in. As Mr. Allen [2] himself says:—"It was, with violent gesticulation and vociferation, declared on the floor of the Convention that the decision of the Chair was incorrect." But notwithstanding this violence, no appeal to the House was made, for it was evident that any appeal would be tied by the clerical vote.[3] The High-Church, having escaped by the skin of their teeth, were only anxious to put off the next trial of the issue as long as possible. The Low-Church, having a large majority of the laity, and lacking only one to carry the clergy, felt sure that the victory was already within their grasp, and were determined to lose no time. They moved therefore to postpone all proceedings concerning the election of an Assistant Bishop, until the meeting of the next stated Convention. The High-Church tried to amend by postponing "indefinitely," and were defeated; they tried to adjourn *sine die*, and were defeated a second time. The original Low-Church motion was then carried. But before they adjourned, Bishop White made a closing Address, in which he once more reiterated his warnings, with a directness which induced him, for once, to use the first person singular:— "I purpose," said he, "with the aid of the Divine Grace, that

---

[1] Bishop Johns, in his Memoir of Bishop Meade (p. 143), says that Dr. Wilson, "though in attendance at the Convention, neither voted *nor was present* when the ballots were deposited." This is inconsistent with the supplementary report of the Tellers (of whom my Father was one), that "there were fifty-four clerical members *present*, and that *one* of them had *declined voting*." In fact, when his name was called, he openly said:—"I decline voting."

[2] First Letter to Bishop Hobart.

[3] It was only after the clerical vote was known to be a tie, that the Rev. Dr. Bedell moved the admission of the Rev. Mr. Ward—a colored clergyman, whose vote he was sure of; and that vote would have carried the day: but public opinion compelled the summary defeat of the proposal. And so totally was the effort destitute of any conscientious zeal for the advancement of the colored brethren, that it was Dr. Bedell himself who moved that all mention of the attempt to admit Mr. Ward be *expunged* from the Journal.—See *Candid Address, by Plain Truth*.

so long as my faculties shall be continued to me, my cares and my counsels shall not be wanting in any matter that may concern the integrity, the peace, and the prosperity of the Church ; and especially, by bearing my protest against whatever may be an inroad on her system in doctrine, or in discipline, or in ecclesiastical Constitution and government." And in these words he considered himself "as addressing not only you, but the members of the Church in the Diocese, when both myself and all you my juniors shall be laid in the dust."

The High-Church party—thus far sleepily behindhand again—now found that it was life or death with them to do their best. During the Convention, the Low-Church had held repeated caucuses at the lecture-room of S. Andrew's church, no one being admitted unless pledged to secresy. The High-Church held two meetings only, which were open, and gentlemen of both parties were present. Before the adjournment, the Low-Church appointed a Committee to sit *en permanence* until the next Convention: and the day after the adjournment the High-Church followed their example.[1] A "confidential" circular[2] was sent round by the Low-Church Committee: a "Private Letter" was copied out and forwarded by the High-Church Committee.

[1] The Rev. Mr. Kemper (Nov. 3, 1826) writes to Bishop Hobart:—"There is no ground for the rumor of *conciliation*. The Convention terminated on Friday night. On Saturday afternoon twenty-six of us met—not a whisper was breathed upon that subject. . . . We are indeed in a very sad state, but we do not despair. The excitement was prodigious, and we are not yet, I presume, capable of judging deliberately. For my own part, I am satisfied that Dr. Wilson must be relinquished, but depend upon it there will be no compromise of principle." Speaking of the Rev. Mr. Allen, he says:— " He, I greatly fear, is a deep intriguer, and is considered by us all as the author of all our troubles, and as somewhat deficient in the organ of conscientiousness." He adds concerning the beloved Bishop White:—" Half of our difficulties, even in the last Convention, we are compelled to place to the want of decision on the part of our venerable Bishop." This is the only confession of the fact which I have met in all the published or unpublished documents of those times: so great was the delicate reticence of the friends of Bishop White in regard to this his amiable but troublesome weakness.

[2] This was kept close for some time. It was not till the 16th of March, 1827, that Bishop Kemp wrote to Bishop Hobart:—" The *Confidential Circular* lately issued, or rather lately discovered, in the Diocese of Pennsylvania, is a proof that these gentlemen stop at nothing to secure success. . . . It grieves me to the heart to think that the evening of life, with such a man as Bishop White, should be rendered disquiet and comfortless by such men as Mr. Boyd and Bedell. Were there no other circumstances to evince the state of their principles and hearts, this with me would be sufficient."

Pamphlets and counter-pamphlets flew thick and fast from both sides, so that the literature of that one contest makes a thick volume of many hundreds of pages. But the High-Church, thus driven, developed that latent strength which they always have in reserve when the crisis needs it. De Lancey was a host in himself for keenness, prudence and knowledge of mankind; and he was the chief writer on that side, being as adroit in avoiding or covering the weak points of his friends, as he was unerring and unsparing in finding and exposing those of his foes. His coolness and courtesy of style seems always to have put the enemy into an additional passion.[1] He was now reinforced by the Rev. William Cooper Mead, who, in the power of manipulating deliberative bodies successfully, was not second even to De Lancey. These, with Montgomery and Kemper among the clergy, and the distinguished ability and high position of Horace Binney, aided by Meredith, Ingersoll, Lowber, and others among the laity, made a combination of singular brilliance and power. My Father, on every test division throughout the whole struggle, voted steadily with Bishop White and his friends, and was from the time of his ordination in close and confidential correspondence with De Lancey, Kemper, Abercrombie and Montgomery: but he took no part whatever in the management of the campaign. He lived three hundred miles from the scene of action. Besides, it was a sort of work for which he had no love, and no capacity. He could not do it: and he never attempted anything of the kind during his whole life.

The strong point to be pushed, was, the notorious hostility of the Low-Church to Bishop White, and the fact that the High-Church were his friends, and the only true friends he had.[2] The mild and venerable prelate, who had shepherded the Diocese for forty years, ought not, they said, to be insulted in his old age; nor ought an Assistant to be forced upon him who would bring down his gray hairs with sorrow to the grave. This was a power-

---

[1] In Allen's Second Letter to Bishop Hobart, De Lancey is credited with " a cunning equal to that of Machiavel."

[2] " This, as the Rev. Mr. Allen expressed it, was *the mystery of iniquity* which succeeded in deceiving so many of the lay members of the Church in the country."— *Second Letter to Bishop Hobart.*

ful position: and when it was fairly brought home to the laity, the changes were very great. Moreover, the representations thus made were entirely correct. Bishop White had for years been charging against Low-Church principles and practices; and in the *Recorder* as well as on the floor of Convention, to say nothing of private conversation, the Bishop was reflected upon to a degree that grieved the old man's soul. The fact of this hostility to him was palpable, notorious.

But when the Low-Church found how greatly it was damaging them, they tried—when too late—to put a different face upon the matter. After printing pamphlets in which Dr. Wilson's friends (of whom Bishop White was known to be one, if not the chief) were spoken of as opposed to "truth and piety," one of their writers had the—piety—to say, touching their alleged opposition to the Bishop:—"This is a refinement in electioneering which is as unworthy of the party, at it is disrespectful to Bishop White; and that must have been a most desperate cause which could have justified even a Jesuit in so desperate and dishonest an expedient. . . . No man can coolly look at it without disgust." Doubtless, they were themselves very much "disgusted" on finding how thoroughly their opposition to their venerable Bishop was turning the hearts of the laity against them. The Rev. Mr. Allen thus excitedly describes this result :—" High-Churchmen cunningly wrote the name, style, and title,—' *Rt. Rev. William White, D.D., Presiding Bishop, Father of the Church!*' in emblazoned characters, on their banner. They cried aloud with a voice which sounded o'er all the distant mountains, and echoed along the waters of the Susquehanna . . . ' *Bishop White is assailed! Ho, to the rescue!*' The appeal was heard, and . . . members of the Church came to vote as *they were told* would be grateful to Bishop White. The merits of the controversy they knew not. The difference between High and Low Churchmen they did not understand."[1]

Meanwhile, changes were quietly going on touching the important question of Candidates. The Rev. Mr. Meade, who had been pained by many acts of those who called themselves

---

[1] Allen's Second Letter to Bishop Hobart, p. 46.

his friends,[1] made an earnest effort to restore peace. He had no desire to be elected Assistant to a venerable Bishop who did not wish for him, and in a Diocese so fiercely and so equally divided. His course throughout the whole was delicate and high-toned, in a remarkable degree. Within a few weeks after the Special Convention, while in attendance on the General Convention then sitting in Philadelphia, he called on Bishop White, and proposed as a compromise that neither party should agitate the election of an Assistant during the life of Bishop White, unless after six months' notice, and at the call of Bishop White himself. Bishop White approved: and in his study on the 18th of November, these two met three of the leaders on each side (Kemper, De Lancey and Binney of the one, and Boyd, Bedell and Robbins of the other), and all agreed to support the compromise. Each of the permanent Committees was to send out a Circular to their own friends, asking their adherence; and another meeting was to be held on the 18th of December, at the same place, to learn the result. Mr. Meade, meanwhile, said freely that if his proposal was not accepted by his friends, he would withdraw from the contest altogether. The result on the 18th of December was, that the High-Churchmen almost unanimously agreed to the compromise, while the representatives of the other side " were then unable to express any such assent." Mr. Meade at once redeemed his pledge; and in a letter to Mr. Binney " absolutely and entirely withdrew from all future participation in this controversy," the earnest and even passionate appeals of his Philadelphia friends to the contrary notwithstanding.[2] His friends, however, had committed a serious error in their tactics. When a fair compromise had been accepted by their opponents, it was deliberately rejected by themselves, even though it originated with their own chosen standard-bearer: and when they afterwards came to the pinch, and cried out lustily for a compromise, it was bitterly remembered against them.

[1] Among these acts of his friends was the reprinting of an old sermon preached by him, for the purpose of circulating it as an electioneering document. He took it up, and read the title-page aloud, with a slight addition, thus:—"'A sermon preached by the Rev. William Meade, of Virginia,' and *published by the Devil*." This was rather hard on his friends: but it was spoken, of course, in only the conversational use of the word.—See *Candid Address, by Plain Truth*.

[2] See the correspondence in Bishop Johns's *Memoir of Bishop Meade*, pp. 138-154.

On the other side similar changes had been going on. The pure and gentle Dr. Wilson, weary of the strife and of the abuse heaped upon himself as being "essentially defective in his religious views and Church principles,"[1] early withdrew his name as a candidate. De Lancey, being only twenty-eight years of age, was too young to run. There was a general tendency to concentrate upon my Father, he being, after Dr. Wilson, the first choice of Bishop White. In fact, the extraordinary results of my Father's labors in the West were clear High-Church gain, the like of which was to be hoped for nowhere else: and the entreaties of his Philadelphia friends, as each successive Convention approached, to bring on his full strength clerical and lay, showed their consciousness that he held the balance of the Diocese in his hands.

But at length they overdid the matter. By the High-Church circular, they were pledged not to fix upon their Candidate until they met in caucus at Harrisburg, where the stated Convention was to be held. On the 17th of March, De Lancey, writing to my Father on the subject, said:—"My own mind is made up to vote for the Rev. J. H. Hopkins, and to push his claims. The matter, you know from the circular, is to be formally settled at Harrisburg. You must come down strong-handed, with a lay deputation from Pittsburgh and wherever else you can honestly collect them. You are the prominent man talked of (I might say almost the only one) among the sound part of the brethren in this quarter, as our candidate." On the 28th of March, the Rev. George Weller, Editor of the *Register*,—a High-Church paper then lately started as a make-weight for the *Recorder*—wrote him:—"I can assure you that your name is at present by far the most prominent in all conversations known to me, both among clergy and laymen, and there can be no doubt a serious effort will be made to procure your nomination. Efforts within your power would do much to secure this result, and I trust you will not hesitate to make them." Kemper and Montgomery also wrote him, to "bring a full delegation."

But they did not yet know their man. There was about him so sensitive a personal delicacy, that whenever there was or could

---

[1] See "An Answer to Plain Truth, by Plain Fact."

be the least appearance of self-seeking or personal intrigue, he stopped at once, and no earthly power could persuade him to budge an inch. Instead of stimulating him to increased exertion in procuring the attendance of the western Clergy and laity, he stood stock still, and never lifted a finger; but at the same time he replied to his friends candidly, and told them that after what they had written him his hands were tied. In vain they did their utmost to remove his scruples. His correspondence with his dear friend Mr. Wallace on this subject is a rare specimen of the ingenious obstinacy and modest independence with which he could resist triumphantly all that could be urged by personal friendship and Churchly zeal. The simple position which he took in regard to the Episcopate, and beyond question the right position, he thus expressed:—" If, without any effort of mine, the Great Head of the Church should put it upon me, I must look to Him for grace and strength to fulfil its arduous duties. But if I were to step one inch out of my parochial sphere in order to increase a favorable delegation, or to influence in the smallest degree the votes which are to decide the election, I should never feel satisfied that my appointment was so strictly Providential, as I must esteem it in order to be at peace in my own mind. This with me is a point of conscience, independently of all the minor motives of delicacy and propriety which dictate my being as quiescent as possible where I am aware that I may be myself concerned." Golden words!

The Convention met on Tuesday, May 8, 1827, in the Chamber of the House of Representatives, Harrisburg, and organized. In the evening, by previous appointment, the High-Church caucus met at Mrs. Elder's boarding-house, all the clergy being present except the Bishop, together with a large majority of the laity. As, in Convention, the Clergy nominated, and the laity then voted yea or nay on the nominee: so it was now decided that the selecting the candidate should be agreed upon first by the Clergy, and their choice should then be submitted to the laity. Accordingly, after an eloquent and stirring speech from Mr. Binney, the Clergy retired to ballot alone. Before beginning—as they had not a single vote to spare—it was resolved, on motion of the Rev. Mr. De Lancey, that no one should be the candidate who had not a unanimous vote. My Father had a large majority from the first, and on the third ballot had every vote cast but three.

At this stage of the proceedings the Rev. Mr. Montgomery—who, with a few others, was unwilling to vote for one who had opposed Bishop Hobart's plan for altering the Liturgy—rose and took a paper from his pocket, on the strength of which he announced that they had *one* majority of the Clergy and *fourteen* of the laity, so that they were sure of success: but that if their candidate were one of their own number, he could not be elected without his own vote. He asked, therefore, whether his Rev. Brother from Pittsburgh would consent to vote for himself. My Father, who had been standing with some others in a corner of the room, but taking no part in the voting, replied, that the brethren who had done him the honor to put him in nomination were well aware that he had given no countenance to the measure; that he regarded himself as being quite too young in the ministry for so high an office, having been scarce three years a priest; and that under no circumstances whatever would he consent to vote for himself. The Rev. Mr. Weller then rose and said, that he was not going to argue the general principle; but that he desired to inform his Brother of a fact probably unknown to him, namely, that there were at that time in the House of Bishops *two* prelates who had been elected by their own votes;[1] and he added that no reasonable and candid man could find fault, if, for

---

[1] A careful search of the records of the election of all the Bishops then forming the House—White, Hobart, Griswold, Kemp, Croes, Bowen, Chase, Brownell, and Ravenscroft—satisfies me that the two referred to were Bishops White and Philander Chase.

As to Bishop White, only four Clergymen were present and took part in his election,—the Rev. Messrs White (President), Magaw, Pilmore and Blackwell: and Mr. White " was *unanimously* chosen," which involves his voting for himself. See Journals of First Six Conventions of Pennsylvania, pp. 17, 18.

As to Bishop Philander Chase, he himself states in his *Reminiscences* (p. 148):— " The writer was *unanimously* elected to fill that elevated but most responsible office." This is again an acknowledgment that he voted for himself: for there were only four Clergymen present, and four votes were cast. The record—the printed *Journal*—says indeed that *three* of those votes were given to Mr. Chase and *one* to the Rev. Joseph Doddridge, M.D. If Mr. Chase had thrown the one vote for Dr. Doddridge, he would never have forgotten it so completely as to call the election " unanimous." He evidently voted for himself, and forgot the one vote for Dr. Doddridge.

There is not a syllable of evidence that I know of, pointing to any other than these two, as the only two referred to by Mr. Weller.

the sake of the peace of the Church, his brother from Pittsburgh should, under such pressure of circumstances, do the same. My Father answered, that he had never known this before, and was sorry to hear it now; but that he should be still more sorry to follow what he could not but regard as a very dangerous precedent. He then asked leave to withdraw, pledging himself to give his vote for any man whom they might select, and who was at the same time agreeable to Bishop White. Leave was given, and he withdrew.

The balloting was resumed, and was continued patiently until late in the night, my Father's vote gradually falling, and Dr. Henry U. Onderdonk's gradually but slowly rising, until he had a majority of one. It was then late, and everybody was tired and worn out. On motion of the Rev. Mr. De Lancey it was decided that the name having a majority at the next ensuing ballot should be the candidate; and of course Dr. Onderdonk was the man. The laity—who had all this while been patiently waiting for the action of the clergy,—though grievously surprised and disappointed, yet promptly, under the vigorous leadership of Mr. Binney, pledged their concurrence: and the High-Church party were ready for the struggle.

The Low-Church party, unable to agree on a new candidate of their own, (Dr. Milnor had declined to permit the use of his name) went to Harrisburg determined to adhere to Mr. Meade,[1] although he had, in writing,—when his proposed compromise was rejected by his own friends,—declared his final resolve "not to accept the office, even if offered under the most flattering circumstances."[2] They knew they were in a minority in both orders, unless the Rev. Mr. Carter's admission should enable them to tie the clerical vote. They had some hopes however, that two absent brethren might arrive in time for the critical moment.[3]

---

[1] See Allen's *First Letter to Bishop Hobart*
[2] Bp. Johns's Memoir of Bp. Meade, p. 154.
[3] It may seem surprising that, with all the sharp tactics and pressure of both parties, the number of clergy present (51) should be less than at the Special Convention in the October previous (54). But the contest was so hot, that some quiet men were more anxious to keep out of it than to take part in it, knowing that if they voted with one party it would never be forgotten by the other. Harrisburg, too, was a less convenient rendezvous than Philadelphia. One Low-Church absentee knew that, if he came, the Rev. Mr. Kemper was likely to show him up as a liar, by letters in his own handwriting: and he therefore wisely stopped at home.

They were thoroughly organized, anyhow, and determined to do the best they could to embarrass and defeat their opponents, if they were not strong enough to win themselves.

The next day, Wednesday, in the afternoon—Divine Service and the Eucharistic Sacrifice having occupied the morning—the Bishop delivered his Address, and once more the trumpet gave no uncertain sound. In unmistakable language he denounced the American Sunday-School Union as "invading the worship and the ministry" of the Church "under the specious pretence of liberality." He desired to record his view as opposed to any Institution "when a part of the professed design is, to be silent, in the instructions given and in the books distributed, on any points coming under the head of Gospel truth." He could not "concur in a profession to explain the Word of Truth, under a stipulated silence as to any part of its contents." And he added, that the stipulations that nothing would be published in disparagement of the principles of the Church had "not been punctually regarded by any Institutions of that description, coming under his observation." As to the appointment of an Assistant, he declined to press further for it owing to "the excitement of feeling" which had been produced, and occurrences which his mind "could not reconcile to the integrity of ecclesiastical proceedings; such," he added, "as I had never before witnessed in our Church, and concerning which I was resolved, that if there should be a continuance of them, no act of mine should contribute to it." He gave an account of the abortive effort at compromise made by Mr. Meade; and then, after a brief retrospect of the past growth of the Diocese, under him, "from a state bordering on annihilation," and all, until lately, in brotherly peace and amity, the venerable octogenarian pathetically added:—
"This state of amity has been always considered as one of the best of the blessings which a gracious Providence has bestowed on me. From present appearances, I perceive reason to fear, that trials, hitherto unknown, are reserved for the small remainder of my days. I have painfully witnessed the progress of ecclesiastical transactions, in contrariety to the clearest dictates of religious and moral obligation,—not without the accompaniment of indignities personally wounding to my feelings, such as I think

unmerited, and certainly such as I have been a stranger to in my earlier years. The subject is mentioned with the view of pledging my assurance to those who seek the integrity of our Zion, that during my continuance in life, and looking to Divine aid for support, I will bear my testimony in favor of the truths of our holy religion, as exhibited by the institutions of our Church, and against all endeavors directed to their destruction or to their deterioration." From such mild lips as his, this was a severe condemnation of the course pursued by the Low-Churchmen thus far.

After the Address, the Low-Church made a desperate effort to secure the admission of the Rev. Lucius Carter to a seat. His only business in Pennsylvania was as Agent of the American Sunday-School Union,—a concern which the Bishop had just expressed his opinion of: and he had never been canonically received into the Diocese at all. The Bishop considered his papers insufficient,[1] and had repeatedly refused to receive him. Every vote was known. There were twenty-six High-Church clergymen present, and twenty-five Low-Church. Unless the latter could get Mr. Carter in, they were done for. It was in this hot debate, that the patience of Bishop White was tried beyond endurance. The Rev. Mr. Ridgeley—after all that had happened—had the hardihood, in a speech, to allude to the Bishop himself as being a Low-Churchman,—one of *their* party! The gentle old man showed that, like flint, if struck hard enough, he could flash fire. He rose at once, apologizing for such an unusual thing on his part as interrupting a debate; but the personal allusion to himself must be his excuse. As the word was used in England, and a hundred years ago, perhaps it might not be altogether incorrect to call him a Low-Churchman. "But," continued he, with an emphasis rare indeed as coming from his lips, "as the word is understood in this country, and among us now, you might as well call me a Turk or a Jew!" The House refused to admit Carter, by a strict party vote: 26 to 25 of the Clergy. The lay majority was large enough to make everything safe, being 72 to 58.

[1] He was a Deacon, and had only a general letter to any Bishop who might be willing to receive him, instead of one addressed to Bishop White himself.

The Low-Church passed an uncomfortable night. They had learned during that Wednesday that Dr. Onderdonk was the High-Church nominee:—one whom they regarded as a New York High-Church bigot, the incarnation of every evil which they detested or deplored. They learned that my Father was the first choice of a great majority of the Clergy and laity, but had been dropped because he would not vote for nimself. With the prospect of having one of the terrible Bishop Hobart's lieutenants forced upon them by a majority of one, my Father began to look lovelier in their eyes than he had ever been before. He was known to be a High-Churchman, always voting with his party; and they knew, by public and private evidence, that in most of the salient points of Low-Churchmanship, he did not agree with them at all. But he had not been one of the active leaders of the party, and was therefore less obnoxious. In precept and in practice, too, he sympathized rather more with the strictness of the Low-Church in regard to worldly amusements, than with the then prevailing laxity of their opponents : and this, together with the unusual pecuniary sacrifices he had made in entering the ministry, the great success he had achieved in his work, and his constant willingness to exchange with or preach for his Low-Church brethren, induced them to believe that he was "a truly converted man," which was more than they were willing to allow concerning most of those who voted with him. They resolved, therefore, to try for a compromise on my Father, rather than have that detested New Yorker.

The High-Church likewise spent a very uneasy night, but for a very different reason. The Rev. Mr. Hutchins, one of their number—and not one could be spared—was seized that night with a violent attack of bilious colic. No poor clergyman was ever the object of a more intense sympathy in his sufferings. All the doctors in the place were gotten together around his bed; and what with their efforts, and good nursing, and vigorous prayer for him all night, and a carriage in the morning, he was brought to the House in good time, and strong enough to hand in a written ballot when he was called on.

Thursday was a rainy day. As the venerable Bishop White was on his way to the Capitol, and drew near the steps,—the

Rev. Mr. Montgomery walking with him and holding the umbrella over his head,—the modest Carter made a final attempt to secure his seat. Running round, in the rain, in front of the Bishop, he held out a paper document, and begged him to receive it. The Bishop asked him if it was the same that he had seen before (and which he had refused to accept as a Letter Dimissory). On learning that it was, the old man answered hurriedly, but very decidedly:—" I will not receive it, sir; I will not receive it ": and waving him away, the Bishop ascended the steps, and entered the House of Representatives, where the business of the day soon began.

When Mr. Hutchins was brought in and helped to a seat, it was understood that not a moment was to be lost.

The report of the Standing Committee was then being read: but the reading was, on motion, suspended. A Low-Church motion to admit *four* additional lay delegations, was lost. A Low-Church motion to adjourn till 3 o'clock in the afternoon, was lost. The Rev. Mr. Sheets[1] then moved to go "*forthwith*" into the election of an Assistant Bishop, who should be Bishop of the Diocese after the decease of Bishop White: and it was carried. Meanwhile busy talk was going on privately. One clergyman of the majority assured some of his opponents that they would change their candidate back to their first choice, if the minority would engage to give Mr. Hopkins six votes. A lay member of the majority said, that if the minority would give Mr. Hopkins " a respectable vote," the laity would negative the nomination of Dr. Onderdonk, and thus bring about a concentration on Mr. Hopkins. But the trouble was, that both parties—thanks to the Low-Church example—were well drilled in caucus, and pledged, to a man, to vote as agreed. It was now past 11 o'clock, and a Low-Church motion to adjourn until 12 o'clock was ruled to be

---

[1] This was poetic justice. The Rev. George Sheets, of Frankford, had formerly been inclined to go with the Low-Church: but when Mr. Ridgeley called on him and avowed his determination to start a new parish at Frankford (where at that time it was utterly uncalled for), for the mere purpose of getting another lay vote in the election for Assistant Bishop, Mr. Sheets was utterly disgusted, and replied:— " Brother Ridgeley, I'm ashamed of you! If that is the way you are going to elect a Bishop, I want to have nothing more to do with you!" From that moment he acted with the Bishop's friends. The motion was seconded by the Rev. Mr. (afterwards Bishop) Bowman, long considered " doubtful " in those days.

"out of order," as inconsistent with the vote just taken to go into the election "forthwith." Excitement was reaching a painful pitch. A motion to adjourn *sine die* was threatened, but not actually made. A motion to reconsider the "forthwith" in Mr. Sheets's resolution, though moved and seconded by members of the majority, was ruled to be "out of order," as inconsistent with the said "forthwith." The Rev. Mr. Allen then rose, being authorized by a number of his friends (though not by the action of the caucus), and made a formal proposition, to avoid the apparent certainty of the choice of a very obnoxious person by a majority of *one* vote. He said that he was satisfied that a union *could* be made, sufficient to give to some one a large majority of votes. Though certainly preferring one of their own friends, they would surrender their choice, and unite upon some member of the other party, if, only, they were permitted to unite with their opponents in selecting him. If an adjournment were granted, merely long enough for a conference with their brethren, he doubted not that such a result would take place.[1]

But it was too late. If they had really been so anxious, they would, some time or other during the whole of Wednesday, have acted on it in their caucus, and thus made the proposal in definite form, instead of only suggesting it informally at the last scratch. It was suspected that they hoped to see one of their absent clergy arrive by the stage-coach which was due at noon. In fact, the sincerity of the offer was not trusted at all by the leaders of the High-Church party: and it was no wonder. Besides, they remembered how the compromise proposed by Mr. Meade and accepted by them, had been deliberately rejected by those very men who were now earnestly begging for compromise in their turn. They remembered also, the precarious condition of Mr. Hutchins's health. The only response, therefore, made to the Low-Church appeal was from Mr. Binney, who coolly said to the President of the Convention:—"I hope, sir, the election will proceed." And it proceeded: the Rev. Mr. Bedell saying, just before the balloting began:—"We shall now show you, by our votes, that when it was in your power, by one slight act of fraternal courtesy, to give

---

[1] *Second Letter to Bishop Hobart.*

peace to this distracted Diocese, you have preferred to continue our dissensions, God only knows how long!"

As the voting began, one or more of the Low-Churchmen had taken my Father aside, and were energetically talking to him in a low voice, in the recess behind the Speaker's chair.[1] The leaders, at and around the Secretary's table, were exceedingly uneasy at this. They knew the straightforward simplicity of my Father's character; and when they saw with what a flushed and troubled countenance, and downcast eye, he was listening to their earnest persuasions, their hearts almost failed them. His name was called aloud, as it was reached on the clerical roll; but he did not hear. It was called again; but still he did not hear, so preoccupied was he by the zeal of his new friends. One of the tellers at last touched him on the shoulder, and asked him if he wished to vote. At once he sprang up, with a face clear as the day, and an eye bright as a sunbeam, and held out an open ballot with the name of the Rev. Dr. Onderdonk on it, so that the teller should read it before it was dropped into the box. The leaders then breathed freely once more: they knew that *he* was true as steel. The clerical vote was carried for Dr. Onderdonk by that ballot, 26 out of 51. The minority, meanwhile, so far proved their sincerity, that, of their twenty-five votes, *eighteen* were given to my Father: thus making it appear, by the record, as if he had been the leading Low-Church candidate.

The nomination thus made then went to the Laity, who could only vote *yea* or *nay*. The talked-of plan of rejection by them was impracticable. How could honorable men, pledged up to the eyes in caucus, change their front, without any opportunity for further consultation and fresh resolves? No doubt the great majority of them would have preferred a different result: but they kept their word manfully, and completed the election of Dr. Onderdonk by a vote of 72 to 58. The event thus realized the exact majority, in each order, which was pre-announced by the Rev. Mr. Montgomery on Tuesday evening; and which had been

---

[1] They were doing their utmost to persuade him to secure the desired conference, assuring him that "if it were obtained he would surely be Bishop." He told them he thought it would be the proper and fraternal course to grant the conference: but that the reason given by them for his exerting himself to obtain it, was precisely the thing which made it impossible for *him* to say a word in favor of it.

shown on *every* vote without exception, from the rejection of Mr. Carter down to the consummation.[1]

The testimonials were signed by the 26 clergy and 78 laymen who voted for Dr. Onderdonk, and by not a single other member of the Convention. Nor was this all. A formal written *Remonstrance* against his Consecration, was drawn up, under ten distinct heads, part of which consisted of a publication of private correspondence and a retailing of private conversations. This document was signed by every one of the 25 clergy[2] and 58 lay delegates who did not vote for Dr. Onderdonk, and by 20 other laymen who had been members of the Special Convention: so that the Consecrators, when assembled, found themselves called to act on Testimonials and a Remonstrance, the former having by only *one* clerical signature the advantage over the other. How the Church at large regarded the dispute—for every document had been sent diligently to every Diocese—may be judged from the fact that every Standing Committee at first signed Dr. Onderdonk's testimonials: but four members of the Virginia Standing Committee[3] (a majority), and two members of that of Maryland[4] (not a majority), withdrew their signatures before the Consecration. Of the Bishops, *all* gave their consent, except Bishop Philander Chase, then of Ohio. The five Bishops who took part

---

[1] There was once or twice an unimportant variation of one or two on the part of the laity: but the clergy were firm as a rock.

[2] The Rev. Dr. Tyng, in his Memoir of the Rev. Dr. Bedell, quotes from editorial articles in the *Episcopal Recorder* just before and just after this Convention, as proof of "the unvarying kindness and disposition for peace, by which the subject of the present memoir [Dr. Bedell] was distinguished, even in this most exciting and trying season, in all his ecclesiastical relations." And Dr. Tyng adds, after stating that the result of this Convention was adverse to the views and wishes of Dr. Bedell:—" His meek and Christian spirit, however, immediately accorded with the manifest will of God, and entered upon a course of conciliating conduct, from which he was never known subsequently to swerve." It is for Dr. Tyng, not for me, to reconcile these statements with the *facts*, that Dr. Bedell did *not* sign Dr. Onderdonk's testimonials, that he *did* sign the Remonstrance against his Consecration, and that he continued—conscientiously, no doubt—in unbroken solidarity with his party friends in all their measures of factious opposition, until after the Consecration of the new Bishop had taken place. The first decided *action* of Dr. Bedell towards a conciliatory course, so far as appears from Dr. Tyng's Memoir, was about two years afterwards, in 1829: but from other sources we know that his amiable heart had taken the kindlier course, and had brought over the greater part of his parish besides, previous to the Convention of 1828. See Dr. Tyng's Memoir of the Rev. Dr. Bedell, pp. 291-296.

[3] Three clergymen and one layman.

[4] Both clergymen.

in the Consecration (Bishops White, Hobart, Kemp,[1] Croes and Bowen) received the *Remonstrance* on the 23d of October; performed the Consecration on the 25th, and on the 3d of November published an elaborate *Decision* on every point of the *Remonstrance*.

The Consecration itself was like the celebration of a triumph after a victory. No Low-Church Bishop or clergyman took part in the services. Bishop Hobart's sermon on the occasion rang loud and clear as the blast of a trumpet. It was specially devoted to the crisis of which this Consecration was the turning-point. In alluding to Bishop White, whose piety, he said, was " as pure as it was lovely and engaging," he added, that this " had not disarmed that rage of faction which had stretched even him on the rack of moral martyrdom." And he continued, with words far more true than conciliatory:—" The scenes which have been witnessed in this Diocese, well might we wish that they should for ever pass from memory. But duty to God, to His Truth, and His Church, forbids. I would indelibly engrave them, and raise aloft the record, an awful beacon, to mark the region of wild uproar and of storms; to warn the friends of genuine piety against those who, in her fairest garb, and with her highest professions, employ arts that dishonor her sacred name ; to admonish Churchmen to the latest generations to shun those principles and practices which will inevitably distract, disgrace, degrade their Church, and, but that she is founded on the Rock of Ages, ruin her."

After the act of Consecration of the new Bishop was complete, and before going on with the Holy Communion, Bishop White read an address, in which, after testifying that his Assistant

---

[1] A few days previous (October 10, 1827) Bishop Kemp wrote to Bishop Ravenscroft:—" It is true we are threatened with consequences ; but in my judgment the Opposition only have to dread consequences. I have had a pretty severe experience in such cases. Mr. Dashiell and his adherents pursued me to the very verge of the Altar. And when they were defeated, they still made a bold attempt to obtain Consecration in an irregular manner for him. What has been the result? Their head and a majority of the members have become nothing better than mere vagabonds. I do not apprehend that these poor, infatuated men intend to disavow the Church. Their object is, to model it to their taste ; and they once thought there was a fair chance of advancing so far as to obtain another Bishop who would suit their views. Should Bishop C.[hase] attempt an irregular Consecration, he would forfeit the esteem and assistance of his English friends, which of all things he would dread the most."

had *all* the qualifications which he had deemed desirable, he added that he " had been always jealous of opinions which ground the Episcopacy on such principles as would render the government of our Church not that of laws, but of human will. There ought not to be entertained a doubt that the like views of the subject will be those of his Assistant and Successor; and so long as he shall walk in this line of conduct . . .' any invasion of his just rights will have a tendency to the placing of power in the hands of persons whose 'little finger' of unauthorized authority will be heavier than 'the loins' of an authority made legal by the Constitution and the Canons of the Church." After personal allusions,—especially referring to the pew near by, where he had worshipped when a boy, and to the pulpit from which he heard the Gospel then, and from which he had himself now preached for fifty-five years,—he thus concluded:—" There remains of the duties of the occasion, the celebration of the great Sacrifice for sin, which was prefigured in animal sacrifices from the time of the expulsion from Paradise; and will be commemorated to the end of time in the spiritual Sacrifice which is to follow."

On finding that their *Remonstrance* was of no avail, but that the note of victory, from the lips of the detested Hobart himself, rang louder than ever over their double defeat: the Low-Church party boiled over with even greater indignation than before.[1] Within seventeen days after the appearance of the Bishops' Decision on the *Remonstrance*, the minority were out with another thick pamphlet, attempting to bolster up all their positions: and so the war went on. They separated themselves entirely from their High-Church brethren in Philadelphia. There was no communication except bowing in the street, and not always that. Bishop Hobart was the especial object of attack.[2] Stale

---

[1] The sudden death of Bishop Kemp on returning from the Consecration of Bishop Onderdonk, was by some of the Low-Church interpreted as a judgment of God upon the wickedness of the High-Church.

[2] In the Rev. Benjamin Allen's First Letter to Bishop Hobart, he thus expresses the amiable feelings of his party:—" In my inmost soul, I do honestly believe you to be the worst enemy of the Liturgy, the greatest opponent to the spread of Episcopacy, and the certain author of entire ruin to our Church, if your policy prevail. In every portion of the Church of these United States, I have seen and heard discontent and dissatisfaction concerning you. You are entitled 'the Talleyrand, the would-be Archbishop,' and every other name that can indicate the existence of a feeling which

old slanders against him which had been refuted and silenced sixteen years before, were revived and reprinted without a hint as to their ever having been disposed of in any way : so that Bishop White, speaking of Bishop Hobart in his next Convention Address, said :—" I hold myself bound to declare *my abhorrence* of the calumnies to which he became subject, by his compliance with my request." [1] And he actually refused clean Letters Dimissory to some of those Low-Churchmen, considering their conduct in these affairs to be " inconsistent with integrity." [2] It was only slowly and sullenly that the storm of bitter and fiery disappointment died away into something like the ordinary state of feeling.

From this distance of time, and knowing what we know, one can hardly help smiling, in not unkindly mockery, at the blind blunders of human passion. It was because they thought Dr. Onderdonk to be Bishop Hobart's special friend and nominee, that the Low-Church were so bitterly opposed to him : [3] and yet, on arriving at Harrisburg, my Father received a letter from Dr.

---

regards you as ambitious, as grasping, imperious, intermeddling, and determined to attain power. Hardly a Diocese is there that does not expect it must ask your permission as to who shall be its Bishop : scarcely a religious institution but beholds you with dread. . . . Are you to . . . introduce Jacobite notions of Church Government, and claim to be no schismatic ? " Great allowance must be made for men who were unquestionably sincere in believing, with all their heart, such frenzied nonsense.

[1] He refers to his requesting that Bishop Hobart should preach the sermon at the Consecration of Bishop H. U. Onderdonk.

[2] In a letter to Bishop Ravenscroft of North Carolina (Nov. 2, 1827), Bishop White says, speaking of the Consecration of his Assistant :—" To have postponed the Measure when possessed of unrevoked Testimonials of 16 out of the whole 17 of the Committees, and of the unrevoked Consent of all the Bishops, except of one who had not been heard from ; was what we could not answer for to the Church generally, and to that of Pennsylvania in particular ; especially as it would have furnished an opportunity for the continuance of Measures which you must perceive to have been marked by utter Disregard of moral Obligation. What will be the Result, God only knows ; and I hope and pray that He will overrule to good, the Operation of a Spirit, which I perceive, with you, to be radically bent on Mischief ; but which, I trust, has contemplated more than it will be able to accomplish." Bishop Ravenscroft regarded the election of Dr. Onderdonk " as an additional proof of the superintending care of the Divine Head of the Church, and that the Almighty can make the machinations as well as the wrath of man to praise him."

[3] The young Mr. (afterwards Bishop) G. W. Doane wrote to Bishop Hobart (May 31, 1827) on the election of Dr. H. U. Onderdonk :—" I do not doubt, my dear Sir, that if you had been planting potatoes at Short Hills [his country place near Summit, New Jersey], the credit of that result would in a good degree have fallen to your share."

Onderdonk, which showed clearly that there had been no love lost between him and Bishop Hobart for several years; that Bishop Hobart would not recommend Dr. Onderdonk for any promotion; and that one reason of it was, Dr. Onderdonk's having omitted the Ante-Communion service at Canandaigua, like a Low-Churchman! Through another source it appears that when Bishop Hobart was sounded by one of the Pennsylvania clergy as to the fitness of Dr. Onderdonk for the office of Assistant Bishop, he replied:—"Take Meade of Virginia a hundred times rather than H. U. Onderdonk!" Moreover, before the Bishops consecrated Dr. Onderdonk, they insisted, and under the leadership of Hobart carried their point, that Dr. Onderdonk should sign a written pledge that he would do nothing, as Assistant Bishop, without the knowledge and consent of Bishop White: an exaction which Dr. Onderdonk felt very deeply, and with anything rather than gratitude.[1] Then again, Dr. Montgomery was disinclined to favor my Father's election, owing to his opposition to Bishop Hobart's proposed changes; and Dr. Montgomery was therefore one of the first to push Dr. Onderdonk's name: never dreaming that Dr. Onderdonk, on that point, agreed most heartily with my Father, and had just written to him assuring him of his high appreciation of "the firmness and independence" of his "speeches last November," in the General Convention of 1826. After further remarks in this strain, Dr. Onderdonk writes to my Father:—"I beg pardon for troubling you with my poor thoughts . . . but you are the leader in this battle, and it is but proper that your subalterns make their reports to you. . . . I hope the Prayer-Book will never be touched till the *whole* is reviewed; and that, I hope, will not be in our day." Moreover, Dr. Onderdonk so little desired the office himself, that, understanding his name might be proposed, he sent a message peremptorily refusing to permit such a use of it: but—whether accidentally or not—the message never was delivered.

On the whole, viewed as a purely party contest, there is no

---

[1] The Canonical requirement that the Assistant Bishop "shall perform such Episcopal duties, and exercise such Episcopal authority in the Diocese, as the Bishop shall assign to him," was not then in existence. It was first enacted at the ensuing General Convention of 1829.

fault to be found with the High-Churchmen for refusing the compromise which was asked for only at the last gasp. The Low-Church had no just cause of complaint when their own inventions returned to plague the inventors. The complete severance of parties, the military precision of caucus drill, have never been brought to such marvellous perfection on any other occasion among us. The battle was fought through with splendid ability and pertinacity; and the stern driving the enemy to the wall in spite of all his pleadings for compromise, was not inconsistent with the laws of party warfare. But it was not wise; it was not statesmanlike; it was not in the higher spirit of Christianity. And this harsh policy brought its own punishment. By allowing an almost unanimous vote upon such a man as my Father, the Low-Church party in Pennsylvania would, in a few years, have shown itself in the fair way to die a natural death. As it was, the rankling bitterness of disappointed rage bred in that party a concentrated virus of vitality, the fruits of which are felt among us, for evil, unto this day.

There was one man, however, who went home still a simple priest, but with his mind relieved from a great weight of apprehension and anxiety;—one who had performed his whole duty to his own conscience as well as to his party and his friends, and who yet found no man of either party maligning or abusing him. It was he who had, virtually, received the vote of nearly every member of that fiercely divided Convention except his own, and yet was not elected Bishop.

Chapter VI.

THE WORK DONE AT PITTSBURGH.

WE must now retrace our steps, to take up some threads which it was best to drop for a time, in order to obtain a more continuous narrative of that great Diocesan struggle.

One would think that what with planning and superintending the erection of his new Church, and gathering his numerous candidates for confirmation, and composing all the music used in his parish, and founding so many other parishes in Western Pennsylvania, and attending faithfully all the councils of the Church in which he had a seat, my Father's attention would have been very fully occupied. But there was yet room for more.

Though well prepared—as things went—for Holy Orders, at the time when he was ordained, he was by no means satisfied with his own attainments, and at once began to read up, for his own satisfaction. He had taken Hooker as his general standard, until he could inquire further for himself. It was not long before he became satisfied that the points at issue between the Church and the Protestant denominations around her are so simple and clear, and so easily settled, that they demand no protracted study. Our only controversy worthy of the name is with the Church of Rome; and that includes not only a difference as to the Canonical Books of Holy Scripture, but an appeal to the whole history of the Christian Church in every age. Now his experience of the Law, and of the methods which the matured wisdom of centuries has provided for the ascertainment of truth, taught him that, as a mere matter of justice, each party should be allowed a fair chance to tell his own story, and plead his own side of the case. He therefore went to Father McGuire, then the Romish priest settled in Pittsburgh, told him what he wanted, and borrowed of him a number of the standard controversial works of Romanists against Protestantism. The amiable and sanguine Father McGuire lent them gladly, and expressed the entire conviction that his visitor would soon become "a good Catholic," as he called it.

On reading them carefully, my Father found that they professed to be simple appeals to the testimony of the Primitive Church, based on the common-sense ground that those ancient Christians who lived nearest the Apostles, were most likely to know the true meaning of the New Testament, written by Apostles and their immediate disciples. Quotations from the Fathers were also given, which seemed to prove all that was claimed for them. But a lawyer is well versed in the art of quotation: and so my Father determined to procure and read the old Fathers for himself, to see if the quotations were fairly made. He went again to Father McGuire on this errand; and was kindly permitted to carry away with him such of the Fathers as the good priest possessed, who was now more sure than ever that his visitor was on the high-road to Rome. But the full perusal of the context, in every instance where he could find the original of a quotation, soon satisfied him that a case which required such constant and careful cooking, lacked the better ground of honesty and justice. The studies here referred to were begun by him immediately after his ordination: and so anxious was he to communicate to others the benefit of such studies, that before he had been for two months a deacon, he contemplated a translation of Eusebius for the press. This design he abandoned, on finding that recent translations were already extant, though not then very accessible.

He resolved, however, to continue his patristic studies: and he did so with a perseverance and a thoroughness of which, at that time, our American Church had given no example. He recognized the simple fact, that the Anglican Reformation was neither more nor less than an appeal to the Primitive Church. He understood that the Reformers, as such, had no power to originate anything. They could only restore. They were of no authority whatever, unless they restored correctly. He therefore paid little comparative attention to the Reformation, accepting—much too easily—the representations of Burnet and other authorities current in those days. He knew that the *real* battle must be fought within the lines drawn by the Undivided Church at the beginning: and *there* he expended his chief strength. One by one, as his narrow purse would permit, he purchased the works of the old Fathers, sometimes picking them up at a secondhand bookstall, sometimes importing them to order; and to the Fathers adding collections of the Councils. The few that he failed to buy, he managed to borrow and peruse carefully, making extracts, before he returned them.

Thus during *eighteen years* his chief studies turned in this direction, until he had himself perused *the whole* of the ancient Fathers in the original, down to and including S. Bernard; besides carefully plodding through the whole of Hardouin's immense collection of the Councils, which he supplemented by going over the ground again with Mansi. Throughout the whole of this eighteen years of study, his method was the same. He made notes with pen and ink, not in the book itself, but on half-quires of foolscap paper, as he read: so that he could at any time turn to what he wanted. He found himself compelled to this course by two discoveries, which he soon made. Nearly all of the best editions of the Fathers, in those days, were from Romish presses and under the learned care of Romish editors, by whom elaborate indexes were prepared. In these indexes, every passage capable of being twisted in support of Romish claims, was prominently given: but those which were strongest against Rome were omitted from the indexes altogether, and the whole body of the work had to be read carefully before they could be found. The other discovery was, a similar bias in the translations. The Greek Fathers were usually published by these Romish editors with a Latin version in parallel columns; which being the more familiar language, would naturally be depended upon, by ordinary readers, who would seldom look at the Greek,—crabbed as it was with all manner of old-fashioned crooked-looking abbreviations. In passages bearing on the Roman controversy, my Father found that the translation had felt the same bias which was so perceptible in the indexes, being strengthened or weakened, expanded or condensed, as would be most favorable to Roman views. This made him careful always to go to the original, instead of glancing—as too many do—over the translation only. When he came to write his controversial works, *all* his quotations from the Fathers—which are commonly their main substance—were made from these results of his own reading, as drawn from his own notes: and never is *any* quotation taken at secondhand, except where it is so stated in the margin.

Nor did he hesitate to change his practice in various respects, in accordance with patristic teachings, without waiting for the sanction of general usage or the enactment of Canons or the changing of Rubrics by the General Convention. His reading of S. Cyprian showed him the meaning of the Mixed Chalice: and this primitive and beautiful custom of mixing a little pure water with the wine, in consecrating the Eucharistic Cup, my Father practised for several years in Pittsburgh, and throughout his whole life subsequently, whenever he was Rector of a parish. S. Cyprian, he said, taught him to do it; and he thought S. Cyprian was very good authority. He also began, in Pittsburgh, the custom of having the bread for the Holy Eucharist made carefully in his own house, and unleavened, in thin cakes, deeply indented so as to be easily broken. He also reached, at that early day, the firm conviction, that in the terrible battle of the Reformation, some innocent, beautiful, Scriptural and edifying things had been lost, which it would have been much better to retain: and among these he reckoned the rich colored and embroidered vestments, and lights, and incense. And this, be it remembered, all took place in Western Pennsylvania before even the first edition of *The Christian Year* had appeared in England. He had then no idea that he should ever see those things actually restored, however; any more than he could then suppose that he should ever live to wear his full beard. His convictions, nevertheless, on these subjects were clear and strong, for several years before the first of the Tracts for the Times was ever thought of. As to practical measures, too, he had succeeded, before he left Pittsburgh, in organizing a band of *Christian Sisters*, peculiarly devoted to good works among the poor and sick: no indistinct foreshadowing of the Sisterhoods which have since arisen, with such glorious promise of an abundant harvest of good works, in both portions of our Anglican Communion.

Although his salary was increased first to $1000 and afterwards to $1200 a year in Pittsburgh, his rapidly growing family made it necessary that an addition to his income should be made from some other source. At the suggestion of a friend therefore, in the spring of 1826, he took half a dozen young girls into his house, to be educated along with his own daughters; and the number was gradually more than doubled. Afterwards, as his sons became also old enough to need a similar provision, another department was added for boys. The modest frame house was twice enlarged to meet these growing needs, the front, of brick, being last added, and having a slight touch in its style of the collegiate Gothic, with buttresses, pinnacles, and Tudor arches over doors, and hood mouldings over windows.

When it was first found needful to erect this part of the house, it was resolved that the best room in it,—what in other houses would have been set apart as the drawing-room,—should be devoted to God. It was known as "The Oratory," and was used only for the daily Morning and Evening worship. Between the windows stood a parlor organ of good tone and six stops, its case rising up to the ceiling. Along the sides of the room, at certain intervals, were little cluster shafts at some distance from the wall, connected by spandrils above, while ribs crossed the flat ceiling diagonally, with pendants at the intersection in the centre. Singing always formed a portion of family worship; and there, as the number of voices was so great, there was always at least one Canticle chaunted, besides a metrical psalm or hymn: and all the music was composed by my Father, who, when at home, was usually the organist as well: my Mother taking his place whenever he was away from home. It was for the suitable adornment of this Oratory that my Father made his first attempt in oil painting. A copy of Raffaele's famous Madonna della Seggiola was, for a few weeks, in Pittsburgh, and he obtained permission to duplicate it. In about six weeks of such leisure as he could command, it was finished, and in a style really superior to that of the professional artist from whose work it was taken. It was then hung upon the wall of the Oratory, in the place of honor: and in all the subsequent removals of the family, that picture has always hung in the room used for family prayer.

As the boys' department of the school grew upon his hands, it enabled him to give maintenance to one or more theological students, whom he trained, adding the direction of their studies to all his other avocations. Their work in the school, their daily participation in the service of the Oratory, their aid in the Sunday-School in town, all contributed to leaven their characters, and prepare them in various ways for their future work. Seven young men were thus ordained in Western Pennsylvania, trained by my Father, during the seven years of his priesthood there; besides others who, beginning under his influence, completed their studies elsewhere.[1]

It is beautiful to see, in the letters written by some of these young men, the powerful impression made upon them by my Father's influence. The Gothic architecture, the Oratory, the music, the family worship,—all so different from what was commonly known elsewhere in those days,—combined with other things in attracting them, and in producing feelings which were too strong for utterance. They all address their pastor, guide, and friend by the endearing title of "Father." One of those letters, now before me, gives an interesting account of a young man's struggles of mind and heart before forsaking the law for the ministry,—fasting as well as praying being among the means by which Divine guidance was sought: until at last, repairing to the Church in the silence of its weekday solitude, he kneeled down before the Altar, and devoted himself to God and His Ministry, yet asking to be punished if he were too presumptuous in offering himself for so great a work. Another, writing of one of the Hymn-tunes composed by my Father, says:—"You know where *my* thoughts fly when those tunes are played, that used to thrill our hearts in the dear Oratory." Another, when far away, kept a little woodcut of Trinity Church, Pittsburgh, over his mantel-shelf, and says that he and his young wife sit and look at it on Sundays, and are "not ashamed to find tears filling their eyes," while thinking of all that it recalls in their past experience.[2]

---

[1] The seven were, John W. James, John T. Adderly, William Hilton, F. H. L. Laird, Sanson K. Brunot, Lyman N. Freeman, and Samuel W. Selden. Of these, Messrs. James, Freeman and Selden were, for a time, engaged in the school.

[2] After further personal reminiscences, that writer adds:—"And the Oratory, too;—the murmur of voices to 'Our Father who art in Heaven'; the simple impressive petition of a single modulated voice; the 'Catholic *Amen*'; the rapturous peal of the organ, and the full swell of those dear voices: all, and everything else that is

One letter is strange, from its curious evidence of the effect produced by the striking difference of the tone of that household from that of other households. A young man who, under my Father's influence, had thought of entering the ministry, afterwards visited the family, and in consequence of that visit withdrew from his resolution to be a Candidate for Orders. He wrote to my Father:—" I had not sufficiently examined myself. Whether it was the piety of your conversation, the sanctity that breathed around your hallowed mansion, or some more hidden and mysterious agency that operated on me, I know not; but I felt as if I had entered upon forbidden ground. The more I reflected on the step I had taken and the prospect that lay before me, the more hopeless I became." Indeed, it would appear as if the impression produced upon most persons, was very much that which was produced in ancient times among ordinary Christians by a visit to a Monastery while it yet preserved the early fervor of that intense personal piety and glowing devotion which gave birth to each Monastic Order in its turn.

But it must not be supposed that there was any air of gloom about the house. Though dancing was not taught and novel-reading not allowed, and even the usual games of children were mostly dispensed with, and there were no vacations, yet there was no gloom. Each department had a garden of its own, and to each pupil was assigned the care of some specific portion of that garden; and the old oak grove near the house was a shadowy delight. Then music and drawing and painting diversified the more serious branches of study. There was no competition, and public examinations were not held. But twice in each year an evening concert was given in the large schoolroom, to which parents and friends from town were invited; and joyous festivals they were! All the performers were teachers or pupils of the school, and every particle of the music used— overtures, marches, waltzes, solo songs, duetts, vocal choruses, and what not—was composed and arranged by my Father himself: our little orchestra including piano-forte, harp, violins, violoncello, clarinets, flutes, and French horn. On a table in the

there, I have *here* in chambers of the heart;—I can enter them, and look upon you unseen, like a spirit of the other world."

middle of the hall were placed, for the inspection of the invited guests, specimens of the work of each pupil,—drawings, maps, paintings, or pieces of ornamental writing,—the name and age of the doer being placed in the lower corner. At these concerts, and in the daily morning and evening worship in the Oratory, and at meals, all the pupils—boys and girls—came together: but on the two last-mentioned occasions the intercourse was only ocular, as they sat on opposite sides of the Oratory, and ate at different tables. At all other times during the week, the two departments were kept entirely separate. It was certainly a very peculiar school; but it won the love of the pupils to a degree excelled by no other school which I have ever seen.[1]

Meanwhile, there were not wanting efforts to draw my Father to New York. In November, 1827, on a rumor that he had been invited to the rectorship of S. Thomas's church in that city, Bishop H. U. Onderdonk wrote at once, strongly dissuading him from accepting it. "Your zeal," said he, "in the cause of the Church, and particularly of the western part of it, is every way delightful; and it is a subject of gratitude that the West has in you one who is able as well as willing. We must not lose you from among us." That rumor was premature.

About a year afterwards, however, he was unanimously elected rector of S. Stephen's church, New York, then one of the more prominent and influential parishes of that city: and the Rev. Dr. B. T. Onderdonk—who seems to have been one of the leading movers in the matter—wrote to assure him that his removal to New York "would be a high personal gratification to Bishop Hobart," as well as to the other city clergy. A special messenger went to Pittsburgh to convey the formal call; and letters from the Rev. Dr. Lyell, the Rev. Drs. Wainwright and Berrian, the Rev. L. S. Ives, and others of the New York clergy, urged his acceptance in strong, and sometimes enthusiastic, language. Bishops White and Onderdonk both advised him against

---

[1] At first my Father thought of giving to his school the name of "Cranmer Hall," as a mark of affectionate devotion to the principles of the English Reformation; and for some time the title was used conversationally. But eventually he dropped it, being satisfied, on further examination, that Cranmer was hardly worthy even of this inferior and nominal sort of canonization.

the change, however: and when he laid the matter before his vestry, they unanimously resolved, "that, considering the situation of the congregation of this Church, and the interest and welfare of the Church in this section of the country, it is decidedly the opinion of this vestry, that the removal of the Rev. Mr. Hopkins would be the means of *dissolving* a Congregation and Church, which has been built up by his zeal and exertions, and that it would therefore be inexpedient in him to accept said call." It was therefore at once declined: though the kind magnanimity of Bishop Hobart—to whose exertions it was largely if not mainly due—was ever warmly remembered by my Father.[1] As to S. Thomas's church, New York, he was more than once sounded; and at one time (October, 1831), with an assurance from the Vestry that he should be at once elected if he would intimate his willingness to accept: but that intimation was never given.

Towards the close of the long contest in Maryland between the friends of Dr. Wyatt and Dr. Johns, there were some who were looking towards my Father as one on whom both parties could unite. The Low-Church party—since so many of their friends had voted for him in Pennsylvania—were kindly disposed. The Rev. Mr. H. V. D. Johns, brother of the Low-Church candidate, said to a friend that my Father's High-Churchmanship would be no difficulty with him; and that he would be most happy to

[1] In his letter to Bishop Hobart (December 29, 1828) declining the call, my Father writes:—"And now, my dear Sir, allow me to thank you from my heart for the expression of confidence and esteem conveyed to me by your letter. The idea of being near to you and to your family, and of being considered one of those whom you felt disposed to admit to an intimate and friendly intercourse with you, did, I frankly acknowledge, incline me powerfully to accept the opportunity afforded me by this call. For, however warm my attachment to you became while I enjoyed the hospitality of your house, I yet supposed it was not likely that you could tolerate as a near friend, any one troubled with so much awkward obstinacy of opinion as, then and since, I have manifested on some subjects. The magnanimity and kindness with which your letter convinced me that, in this respect, I had undervalued your character, almost upset all my prudence, and well-nigh persuaded me to leave Pittsburgh on this personal ground alone. In reference to the subject of our difference of sentiment in the late General Convention, I recollect nothing said by you which either did excite at the time, or ought to have excited, any unpleasant feelings on my part, save only the impression that my own blunt freedom of opinion had perhaps lost me a highly valued friend. That I was mistaken in this fear, I rejoice to discover; and if for no other reason than this, I should prize the circumstances of my call to S. Stephen's as amongst the most gratifying of my life."

see him Bishop of Maryland. But my Father was personally known but to few in that State; and when he was invited to visit that Diocese and preach, that he might thus help on the movement, the invitation was "promptly declined."

His influence with his Low-Church brethren—such as it was—he always used in a way likely to promote peace. The Rev. B. B. Smith, then the newly appointed editor of the *Episcopal Recorder*, wrote (in August, 1830) showing that my Father had not only taken an interest in the establishment of the Greek Mission, but had prevented controversy touching some misunderstanding between Bishop Hobart and the Rev. Dr. Milnor:—"To your most wise, most Christian, most fraternal admonitions is it owing, that the *Recorder* did not agitate the Church with that controversy." Under his management, the *Recorder* was making a transient effort "in the pacific line": but so gentle an influence was not long suffered to prevail; and in a little more than two years, the Rev. Mr. Smith had not only removed to Kentucky, but had been twice elected, and at length consecrated, Bishop of that new Diocese.

The pressure for more ministers in Western Pennsylvania, the difficulty—not to say impossibility—of sending all candidates for orders to the General Theological Seminary in New York; and the probability that those who spent three years there would not return, or would soon after their return be called elsewhere, early satisfied my Father that, if Western Pennsylvania were to be won, it must be by Clergymen trained on the ground. He had already made a promising beginning. At the Diocesan Convention of 1829 the Episcopal Address contains the names of *four* of his students as among those ordained deacons during the year by Bishop Onderdonk, while the names of *four* others appear on the list of Candidates for Orders. At that same Convention, then,—and surely no better time could have been chosen,—he presented a *Memorial* to the two Bishops and the Convention, signed by himself and 68 other persons "members and friends of the Church in Pittsburgh and vicinity," praying for the establishment of a Theological Seminary near Pittsburgh.

This *Memorial* states the insufficient supply of Ministers in the Church; that, in the sixteen years before the Revolutionary

War, 250 Ministers had been ordained for the Atlantic States (then Colonies), when the population did not amount to three millions, and that to supply the increased population at the same rate would now require a thousand ministers, whereas the Church had actually only about five hundred and twenty-seven, thus showing that the supply was only *half* of what it had been sixty years before; that in the colonial times the principal part of our clergy were in Virginia and Maryland, both of which Dioceses put together did not now number clergy enough to supply the ruins of the churches built before the Revolution; while in every quarter of the land there were Church families left year after year looking in vain for a ministry, and at length abandoning in despair the Church of their fathers. As to Pennsylvania, the *Memorial* stated that more than an hundred towns, each large enough to support a parish, were yet totally untouched by the Church; that no supply could be hoped from the General Theological Seminary, which only numbered 24 students in all, or from Alexandria and Gambier: the united supply of all three being called for by the whole Church; and that if this state of things continued, the gradual decay of the Church was all that could be expected. Without at all impugning the importance of the General Theological Seminary, the *Memorial* suggested the necessity of organizing a Diocesan Seminary for Pennsylvania, recommending the neighborhood of Pittsburgh as the best site, since Philadelphia was near enough to be supplied from New York, and Pittsburgh was the next city in importance in the State of Pennsylvania, and the most remote from the General Theological Seminary, which could not be injured thereby, nor indeed by there being a seminary in every Diocese for the better supply of local needs. And, moreover, it was added that a highly commanding and beautiful site, together with several large subscriptions, were already provided for this object by the Rector and congregation of Trinity Church, Pittsburgh, in the hope of laying a good foundation for so laudable a work. The site here spoken of was three acres of land, offered by my Father, just on the opposite side of the road from his own house, and commanding the same beautiful view of city, hill, and river.

This *Memorial* was referred to a Committee, of which my

Father was chairman, and the Rev. Messrs. De Lancey and Rutledge, Mr. Binney and Judge Reed, were the other members.

The chief debates of the session were on the adoption of the revised Constitution and Canons, prepared by a Committee appointed immediately on the election of Dr. Onderdonk (Mr. Binney being the leading mind in the work), and the chief object of which was to consolidate power firmly in the hands of the High-Churchmen who were now triumphant. The unseemly violence of the Low-Church had left them not only defeated, but with a disadvantageous flavor hanging about them, which did not disappear for some time : and the High-Church were minded to make the best of their opportunity. That Committee reported in 1828, and were continued to perfect their work. In the course of this last year, Mr. Binney wrote to my Father, asking for such suggestions as he might wish to make, and saying :—" Your knowledge and experience in two professions, both of which must contribute something to a good ecclesiastical code, entitle your opinions to great weight ; and I think it of importance that the Committee shall have the benefit of them before the Canons are again presented to the Convention." While the Canons were under discussion, my Father took a prominent part in the moving of amendments, several of which he carried over the Committee : and at the close of the work he moved and carried a resolution of thanks to the Committee " for the ability, assiduity and zeal " with which they had " performed the arduous and important task confided to them."

The Committee on the Pittsburgh *Memorial* at length reported, at a late hour in the session, that " in their opinion, it was highly expedient to organize a Theological Seminary in the neighborhood of Pittsburgh, for the supply of ministers to that portion of the Diocese which lies West of the Allegheny mountains ; and that, in their judgment, such an institution cannot justly be considered as interfering with the connection at present existing between this Diocese and the General Theological Seminary " : but as the organization of such a Seminary required more time and consideration than could then be given, they recommended the subject to the early consideration of the next annual Convention. Two resolutions were passed accordingly, one declaring that "*it is expedient to establish a Theological Seminary in the neighborhood of Pittsburgh*"; and the other recommending the subject to the early consideration of the next Convention.

The parochial report of Trinity Church in that year, 1829, showed the entire completion of the arrangements of the New Church, with a town clock and an excellent bell in the tower, only $1000 of the Church debt yet unpaid, and many more applicants for seats than could possibly be accommodated.

In the Convention of 1830 the subject of the Western Theological Seminary was early referred to another Committee, consisting of the same persons as before, except that the Rev. Mr. Boyd was placed on it instead of Judge Reed. The next day, Ascension Day,[1] the Committee reported two resolutions, the first " fully concurring" in the opinion expressed the year previous, in regard to the expediency of establishing such a Seminary in the vicinity of Pittsburgh; but the second declared that " the organization of such a seminary as a *Diocesan institution* was not, at the present time, of such urgency as to require immediate legislation"; though it was " highly desirable that such organization should be effected as soon as the circumstances of the case may warrant the proceeding." The tone of the Committee was so evidently unfavorable, that my Father would not preside over it, and the Rev. Mr. DeLancey signs the report as Chairman. There was, in Philadelphia, no real favor for the enterprise at all. The sympathies of the High-Church there were with the General Theological Seminary;[2] those of the Low-Church were with Alexandria. The only desire was to smother the Western project as unobtrusively and as inoffensively as possible. In the committee of five, twice appointed, my Father was the only Western man; and each time *four* members from the East (which cared nothing about it) were put with him, to ensure the Convention against rash action. When the resolutions reported by the Committee came up for discussion, on motion of Mr. Meredith a substitute was adopted which showed the *animus* of the opposition, and at the same time gave one more chance

---

[1] It was observed by the assembled Convention only with "Morning Prayers."

[2] And the Kohne legacy, then lately announced, promised to increase largely Pennsylvania's representation in the Board of Trustees.

of life before the project was killed altogether. The substitute was, that "the expediency of establishing in the Diocese of Pennsylvania a branch or branches of the General Theological Seminary, one of which to be located at Pittsburgh, be respectfully recommended to the consideration of the Trustees of that Seminary"; and the Pennsylvania Trustees were requested to present the subject at the next meeting of the Board. It was pretty evident that this was only a more roundabout way of reaching the tomb of the Capulets: but so long as there was any chance, however remote, my Father was content to wait patiently.

Meanwhile, in January, 1831, the Rev. Mr. (afterwards Bishop) Doane, Rector of Trinity Church, Boston, wrote to sound my Father in regard to the possibility of inducing him to become the Assistant Minister of that parish, on the Greene Foundation. Mr. Doane had only lately become Rector, on the demise of Dr. Gardiner; and the glowing energy and impetuous zeal with which he threw himself into the work breathed in every line of the eloquent and persuasive letters which he wrote on the subject. The formal call followed, on the 20th of February. My Father advised with his best friends, and their opinion was not unanimous. Mr. Wallace, though at great self-sacrifice, advised him to go, as Boston was the more important field. Philadelphia— the Bishops included—was against it. My Father laid the matter before his Vestry: and they unanimously acknowledged the disinterestedness with which he submitted the decision of the question to them, expressed the opinion that he would be more usefully employed, and his sphere of usefulness be greater, in Pittsburgh than in Boston, and that he would therefore serve the Church more effectually by remaining than by removing. They added:—" The Vestry have the greater confidence in the opinion thus expressed, from the fact, that there is not among themselves, or in the congregation, *a single voice* opposed to the sentiment of this Resolution": and they therefore tender their thankfulness for the course pursued by their Rector, and respectfully solicit him to decline the call to Boston. It was declined accordingly.

But his enthusiastic friend in Boston was not minded to take *No* for an answer; and the Trustees of the Greene Foundation renewed their call, begging my Father to visit Boston, at their expense, before giving his final answer. That visit was made early in May: and in the interviews with the Rector and his friends, the many young men brought into the Ministry already, and the idea of the Western Theological Seminary, were prominently urged as reasons for remaining at Pittsburgh. But the Bishop of the Eastern Diocese had often urged the establishment of a Seminary near Boston, the want of clergy being as severely felt in New England as in Pennsylvania or elsewhere: and the enthusiastic Rector had no doubt that Massachusetts would rejoice to establish the Seminary which Pennsylvania seemed disposed to reject. My Father at once admitted that if a Theological Seminary were to be started, and this project were coupled with a renewal of the call, it would make an entirely different case from that which he had already considered and refused. Measures were taken at once,[1] which proved it to be morally certain that the Massachusetts Convention would gladly approve the plan. With this conviction, my Father left Boston, giving his friends there reason to believe that he would take the matter into favorable consideration, *provided* that nothing were done at the approaching Pennsylvania Convention in regard to accepting the proposals made for establishing the Western Theological Seminary at Pittsburgh.

An accident to one of the steamers on Long Island Sound detained him at Providence on his return from Boston, so that on his arrival in Philadelphia he found the Pennsylvania Convention already adjourned, after an unusually brief session. As to his proposed Seminary, the Philadelphia Trustees reported that they had laid before the Board the resolutions passed at the last Convention, and the Board had responded, " that it is inexpedient, at present, to establish in any Diocese a branch or branches of the General Theological Seminary." And having heard this report, the Convention of the Diocese of Pennsylvania had done—nothing.

The icy coldness with which his plan for promoting to the utmost the growth of the Church in Western Pennsylvania was killed, cut my Father to the heart, and satisfied him that it would

[1] See page 136.

be better to attempt the realization of his convictions elsewhere, under more favorable auspices. He had so thoroughly convinced his Vestry of the importance of an institution for Theological training, and they so cordially sustained his effort for Pittsburgh, that now, when that plan had proved to be impossible, they could not refuse him the chance to try that better policy elsewhere. The case was put to them, as before, simply for their judgment in regard to the comparative usefulness of the two positions: and they replied unanimously:—" That, under the existing circumstances of the Eastern Diocese, with the prospect of the establishment of a Theological Seminary in that Diocese, this Vestry are of the opinion that it is the duty of the Rev. Mr. Hopkins to accept the call to Boston, firmly believing that the sphere of his usefulness will be enlarged and extended by his acceptance of the same."

This decided the question. All needed preparations were made as speedily as possible. The school was broken up; the house and gardens were sold; the books and a few other things were packed and forwarded; the rest went under the auctioneer's hammer. The last visits and farewells were paid to Benvenue and the dear relatives there; and on the 17th of July his formal resignation was sent in to the Vestry, and accepted unanimously: but both documents were such as seldom pass on such occasions. My Father began by assuring them, in the warmest terms, that his resignation was from no want of affection and support on their part:—

All my calculations on your concord and attachment have been surpassed; and in declining, for your sake, the many calls to other places with which I have been honored, I have felt that I had no merit, since no prospect of congregational usefulness abroad could hold out stronger inducements for my going, than the actual experience of our success afforded for my stay. The cause therefore, and the single cause, which has determined me to leave you, is the claim advanced upon my services by the great interests of Theological Education. You know my sentiments on that subject. They have been declared, publicly and privately, from the pulpit of your church and on the floor of the Convention. You know the efforts made by me more than two years ago, to induce our own Diocese to foster the establishment of a Theological Seminary in our own immediate neighborhood. You know the fate of my application. And although alone, without any aid or public countenance, we have seen seven young men enter the field of ministerial labor out of our congregation within four years, some of whom may rank with the best of any Seminary; and, besides these seven, the names of three other candidates have, within the current year, been added to the list;—although the young and flourishing churches of Western Pennsylvania bear no doubtful evidence to the zeal and influence of Pittsburgh, and to her just claims to have had her opinions and exertions regarded with some little more than common feeling: yet you know that, up to this hour, the product of these last four years has been unnoticed, and unmarked by any official or public token of recognition. And therefore when, in the good Providence of God, the Bishop and Clergy of Massachusetts thought fit to offer me an important agency in the establishment of a Theological Seminary in conjunction with the office of Assistant Minister of Trinity Church at Boston, I had no recollections of the past nor expectations of the future support of Pennsylvania, which could justify me in withholding my best services to the all-controlling interests of Ministerial Education. I do not mention these facts for any other purpose than to present to you, in my last address, the real motive for my resignation, as a standing record in behalf of the uniform satisfaction which has marked our intercourse together; and to free your minds from all idea that any disappointment from the hands of the congregation, or from yours, has influenced me. I desire to find no fault with the course of the Convention of the Diocese, or the opinions of any of those who preside over their counsels. Towards the venerable Prelate, by whom I have been twice ordained, I have never had any other than feelings of the deepest respect and attachment, nor do I think that between him and me there ever has been, or ever could be, any serious misunderstanding; and towards others, in whose policy and judgment I have not always been able to confide with the same degree of satisfaction, I bear the kindest sentiments of personal good-will, and in leaving them the same prayer will continue to be offered up, which ought to make a part of every Minister's devotions, that the blessings of the Most High may prosper their efforts for good, and His Spirit guide and direct them.

He then closed his letter, with renewed expressions of personal tenderness and affection, asking their forgiveness of all the infirmities and defects of his ministry among them, and invoking on them the choicest blessings of God. The Wardens and Vestry, in their reply, say :—

They would do injustice to their own feelings, and to those of the congregation, if they omitted to express the unfeigned sense they entertain of the high and important services of which, under the providence of God, you have been the agent and chief Instrument. In recurring to the period at which your labors commenced, they well remember the dark cloud which hung in gloom over the prospects of our branch of Christ's

Church ; they remember that in Western Pennsylvania . . . the members of our Communion were scattered and divided among the other denominations, or attached to none ; that in our own church there were less than fifty communicants ; that in many of our largest and most flourishing villages the voice of an Episcopal clergyman never had been heard. But we now turn with pleasure to our present situation. In this place there has been erected a splendid church, an ornament and honor of the West, and the number of worshippers and members of the Communion have increased nearly tenfold. Butler, Mercer, Meadville, Erie, Greensburgh, and Blairsville,[1] will all remember the spirit and zeal which were infused by your visits to those places, and most of them have responded to your efforts by the erection of churches not surpassed in the elegance and taste of their workmanship by any in those places ; and those churches, except one, are all supplied by clergymen who have been prepared for the Ministry under your special care and direction, all of them holding the first rank for piety and usefulness where they are stationed, and some of them destined to be shining lights of the Gospel. Thus have we seen the light bursting through that gloom, and the cloud and darkness have given way to the broad glare of mid-day which surrounds us.

Their letter closed with their testimony to the " uninterrupted unanimity and harmony which had always existed " between him and them ; to his "zeal, fervency and ability in preaching the whole truth, and to his life as a practical and laudable commentary and example of the doctrines " he had preached. They "know that nothing but a deep conviction of duty could induce the change "; and in yielding, themselves, to that conviction, they fervently wish all success upon his future labors, and a happy reünion with him in the Kingdom of Heaven.

At first, he intended to write a " farewell sermon ": but as the

---

[1] Kittanning should be added to the above. The affection with which he was regarded in nearly all these places was very touching. Mr. Wallace, from Meadville, writes in 1828 an account of the consecration of the new little Church there, and adds: —" Little did I think, when you were here, that the little seed which you then planted was so soon to vegetate and grow up to a tree in which the birds of the air might lodge " : and the year previous, when my Father found it difficult to comply with a request to be present at the laying of the corner-stone, the clergyman, the Rev. C. Smith, wrote :—" Destitute as we are of clergy in this section, on such an occasion it requires every man, and especially the presence of *one* so peculiarly styled by his brethren *an host in himself*. . . . I would rather come to Pittsburgh on foot, than that you should be absent." From Blairsville formal thanks were sent by a vestry " anxious to testify their gratitude for his last visit, and for the important service rendered to the Church in that place by his zeal in her behalf." The clergyman at Greensburgh writes to him :—" The Greensburgh people look upon you as a kind of Father,"—one who had " built up their Church." And so of others: but why multiply details ?

time approached he shrank from it, and thought it not kind to his successor to do anything which might excite personal feelings to a still more painful degree. He could not trust himself to say even a few words extemporaneously. His last Sunday there was the Seventh after Trinity; and in the hurry of preparations for departure he had not noticed that the latter part of the Second Lesson for the morning service (the 20th Chapter of the Acts of the Apostles) narrates that most tender farewell of S. Paul to his beloved flock at Ephesus. After proceeding with some difficulty as far as the seventeenth verse, he made a sudden pause, as if to measure his ability to continue;—his eye glancing in silence over the rest of the chapter: but the surprise of the coïncidence was too much for him. Closing the Book, he gave way to an emotion he could not control; and the singing of the Canticle that followed scarcely enabled him to recover his composure sufficiently to lead the people in the Creed. The sermons he preached were both old written sermons, with no allusion to the approaching departure: yet many times his voice faltered, as if other thoughts and feelings were scarce hidden beneath the surface. The closing benediction in the afternoon was almost inarticulate. The deep hush that followed it was broken by the sobs and sighs of many in the congregation.[1] On attempting to leave the Church, he was beset on all sides, the poor—of whom not a few had cause to remember him and his—being foremost among his many friends, all begging for some kind token of farewell. But he could not utter a word. He wept like a woman, pressing their hands in solemn silence as he passed slowly through the crowd.

Even after the sale, and the dismantling of the whole house, the family continued to assemble in the dear Oratory at their Morning and Evening Prayers, down to the very last evening, although nothing was left in it but the Organ. Nor was the customary music omitted: though there were some voices that could not maintain their firm clear tone throughout, and many tears were mingled with their service of song. On the evening

---

[1] Seventeen infants were baptized that afternoon,—all who had unbaptized children seeming to be anxious for their Pastor's blessing upon the little ones, before he should leave them.

of Monday, my Father's last act was to take up one of the cedars that grew near the house, and plant it, with his own hands, at the foot of the grave of the infant son, whose dust he had himself committed to the earth in that well-loved Churchyard, near the Chancel wall.¹ The next morning, as they passed through the City towards the East, the whole family stopped at the Churchyard, to visit once more that little grave: and there they found a number of their warmest friends assembled, waiting to bid them a last farewell.

It was, indeed, a painful parting, the like of which my Father never knew again. His early manhood had, in various ways, struck its roots like a vigorous plant, through that Western soil. His influence was felt throughout all the Ohio valley,² and as far as St. Louis. His previous reputation as a lawyer, his remarkable accomplishments and successes in the work of the Ministry, —*every* part of his career thus far, was to him a proof of the hold he had upon the sympathies of the people,—an element of living and growing strength, and full of hope for the future.³ In all his after-life, he never again took such deep root in any other soil: and there was an ever fresh tenderness and warmth about his

---

[1] On the Sunday after the funeral (the Eighteenth after Trinity) it so happened that the First Lesson in the Morning Prayer was the touching account of the death of David's child :—" I shall go to him, but he shall not return to me."

[2] His friendly visits and strengthening services were long remembered gratefully at Wheeling, Va.

[3] In those days of primitive simplicity, there was an almost total absence of that personal laudation,—or, as some would call it, that generous recognition of good service well done,—which is now so prominent a feature in the Addresses of our Bishops to their Conventions. What my Father's work was, has been somewhat shown. On his leaving the Diocese, Bishop White made no allusion to it, except that in the list of the Clergymen to whom Letters Dimissory had been given during the year, we find the "Rev. John H. Hopkins, to Massachusetts." Bishop Onderdonk, though recording the ordination of one of my Father's candidates, in Trinity Church, Pittsburgh, and though *five* out of the thirteen Missionaries whom he reports as at work in the Diocese were brought into the ministry by my Father, never mentions or alludes to him in the slightest manner. So, also, when describing the Consecration of the four Bishops in 1832, the mention of my Father's name is the sole tribute paid to him by Bishop White; while Bishop Onderdonk says, of the whole four undistinguishingly :—"All these prelates are eminent in the Church, and enter on their high functions with every reason for the confidence that they will strengthen, extend, and adorn both their Dioceses respectively, and our whole Communion." His only separate allusion to any one of the four, is to Bishop McIlvaine's "high reputation and talents." This silence is mentioned, not as blaming it, but simply as illustrating the different customs of that day in such things.

recollections of his work in Pennsylvania, which clung to no part of his subsequent career in equal degree. It was while his heart was wrung with the multiplied griefs of this great change, that he thus wrote his *Farewell* :—

> Farewell, ye pinnacles and buttressed towers!
>   Ye Gothic lights, and arch-crowned pillars high!
> Fruits of a zealous hand, though humble powers,
>   We cannot leave you now, without a sigh.
>
> Farewell, dear church! No more thy Sabbath bell
>   Calls us to worship in thy place of prayer;
> No more we hear thy organ's solemn swell,
>   Or mark the full response which rises there.
>
> Farewell, thou grassy mound, where peaceful sleeps,
>   In its cold bed, our precious infant's clay!
> But faith can triumph, even while Nature weeps;
>   The Lord had given: 't was His to take away.
>
> Farewell, our Home, embosomed deep in trees,
>   And decked with all the garden's choicest pride!
> No more we breathe thy woodbine-scented breeze,
>   Or tread thy flowery alleys side by side.
>
> But why art thou so heavy, O my soul?
>   Why so disquieted, my murmuring heart?
> Art thou not led by duty's high control?
>   Has not thy Master called thee to depart?
>
> Farewell, then, *all!* Though homeless now we go,
>   A better, brighter home to us is given;
> Nor may we mourn to leave a Church below,
>   While Christ secures to us a Church in Heaven.
>
> There, in that paradise of joy above,
>   Partings and griefs and pains shall all be o'er;
> There shall we meet again with all we love,
>   And sighs shall breathe, and tears shall fall, no more.

Chapter VII.

AT BOSTON.

IT was a singular coincidence that, after having been through the fierce Pennsylvania contest of 1827, acting entirely with one party while retaining the good-will and esteem of both, my Father should have come to Massachusetts to take a prominent part in the most excited period of the history of that Diocese, culminating in 1832. And in this new conflict, entering upon the field as an acknowledged High-Churchman, he closed the campaign apparently as the Low-Church champion : and thus reaped a storm of obloquy which fully atoned for his exemption on the former occasion.

During the twenty years of the Episcopate which had then elapsed, the Church in the Eastern Diocese had slowly but steadily risen from almost nothing, whether we consider the numbers of her children, or the tone and quality of their Churchmanship : and the growth and improvement, in both these departments, was largely due to the meek wisdom, the gentle firmness, the unobtrusive yet indomitable energy and perseverance, of good old Bishop Griswold. As he said once in a letter to my Father in the midst of the troubles of which we shall speak presently:—

I am well aware that I am generally thought to be deficient in energy and decision, perhaps justly. But very few, if any, of those who so judge know the difficulties of the situation in which I have been placed. To unite in one body, and keep at peace and in harmony, our churches and clergy, thinly scattered over five States, has been a work which required more prudence, study and care, than is generally supposed. There is always some danger of doing too much, unless a man were perfectly wise and good. It is perhaps better to neglect doing ten good things, than to do one which is injurious and wrong. Had Bishop Hobart pursued in this Diocese the same course as in New York, the result, in my belief, would have been very different; and they who attempt to introduce his policy here, may at length be convinced of it.

This quiet policy—certainly the best for a New England

atmosphere in those days—had preserved the peace, and avoided all partisan conflicts. When the purely personal difficulty which led to Dr. Jarvis's resignation of S. Paul's church, Boston, was settled, and the Rev. Dr. Alonzo Potter, of the Diocese of New York, was elected Rector in his place, the Institution Office was not only used—an uncommon event in Bishop Griswold's experience[1]—but, at the suggestion of the Senior Warden of the parish, Bishop Hobart was invited to preach the Institution sermon: a request which he complied with, and that day was "an high day" for Boston. This was in 1826. For some years, the discussions about prayer-meetings and other Low-Church peculiarities on the one side, and the spreading of the more Churchly leaven from New York on the other side, had been charging the ecclesiastical atmosphere with more and more of electricity, so that the inevitable breaking of the storm was daily drawing nearer. In 1828 the Rev. Mr. Doane came to Boston, as Assistant Minister in Trinity Church; the age and infirmities of Dr. Gardiner throwing upon the Assistant almost the entire control: and in the same year[2] Bishop Griswold first proposed a Theological School for the Eastern Diocese. In 1829 the new edifice of Trinity Church was completed and consecrated: and in the same year, Bishop Griswold removed his residence from Bristol, Rhode Island, to Salem, Massachusetts, thus quickening the pulses of Church life in and near Boston. In 1830, on the death of Dr. Gardiner, Mr. Doane became Rector of Trinity Church, and was instituted, Bishop Griswold preaching on the occasion from the words: "He must increase, but I must decrease," and modestly applying the words to the new Rector and himself. In this same year, he again urged upon his Convention the need of a Theological School in the Eastern Diocese.

[1] Dr. Stone, in his Memoir of Bishop Griswold, p. 338, says, of this occasion: "Bishop Griswold, for the first time in his life, performed the Institution Office." This is an error. In Bishop Griswold's Address to the Biennial Convention of 1818, at Greenfield, Massachusetts, describing his visitation of Fairfield, Vermont, on the 20th of September that same year, he says of the Rev. Mr. Beach, rector of the parish there: "Mr. Beach was then by me instituted." Address, p. 13. He also instituted the Rev. Thomas Carlile, in Salem, some years before the Institution of the Rev. Dr. Potter.

[2] In his Address to the Convention of the Eastern Diocese, which that year met in Bellow's Falls, Vermont.

It need hardly be said, that Mr. Doane, then in the flush of early manhood, and overflowing with poetic enthusiasm, personal magnetism, indefatigable activity, and singular practical adroitness in the management of men as well as in the conduct of business, had already made his influence felt in every part of Church work. He had instinctively ascertained with whom he could act harmoniously, and with whom he could not. He was the centre and rallying point of a far more thorough and earnest Church life,—something very different from the quiet reign of Bishop Griswold during the previous twenty years. He controlled the Standing Committee: and, being at the head of the oldest and most powerful parish in Boston, while the Bishop was somewhat out of the way at Salem, it is not to be wondered at that his influence seemed to be greater, in some eyes, than that of the Bishop himself. Outside of his circle of devoted friends, co-workers and admirers, he was looked upon as the one who was attempting to introduce " Bishop Hobart's policy " into the uncongenial latitude and longitude of Boston: and suspicion and antagonism were developed afresh, by each successive proof of activity and zeal.

In procuring my Father's removal to Boston—for it was wholly his work—he had displayed consummate ability, crowned at first, apparently, with perfect success. My Father's unusual eminence as a preacher and debater was universally acknowledged; and the Bostonians, with the pride they take in intellectual power, were ready to give him a general and hearty welcome. Bishops White, Hobart and Onderdonk were known to give him their full confidence as a Churchman, so that Mr. Doane felt sure of his substantial support in building up the High-Church party in Massachusetts and throughout the Eastern Diocese. Moreover, the circumstances of the Pennsylvania Episcopal election of 1827 were still fresh in men's minds, and ensured my Father a more kindly confidence from the Low-Church side of the house than any other prominent High-Churchman could have obtained. My Father's coming, therefore, seemed sure to be, not only a great gain to the right side in itself, but also an irresistible power of leverage over the Low-Church party, quieting their suspicions, calming their hostility, and even drawing from them a considerable portion of the funds which would be needed in building up and endowing the new Theological Seminary: while this Institution—conducted on the thoroughly Patristic principles to which my Father was devoted—might be depended on to pour forth a stream of young clergymen all trained in the right way. It was a most tempting prospect: and, with the materials then at disposal in the Church of America, no more effective combination could easily have been made.

There were additional attractions in the mode of carrying it into effect. If there was any leader of the Low-Church party at that time in the Diocese, it was the Bishop. He did not mean to be a party Bishop, and was annoyed at being called a Low-Churchman: yet both parties agreed substantially as to his real position when any party battle was going on. Now it was the Bishop who had once and again urged the idea of establishing a Theological Seminary for the Eastern Diocese: and if he could have established such an Institution, there can be no doubt that the tone of it would have been decidedly different from that of the General Theological Seminary in New York. The Bishop, indeed, had no talent for organizing such an Institution, or raising money for it; and, therefore, nothing had been done: but he was committed to the idea, as his own original suggestion. What could be more delightful, then, than to take up the Bishop's own idea, with his own consent and approval (for how could he refuse it?), and with an honored place assigned him both on the Board of Trustees and in the Faculty, and yet so arrange the whole affair that every solid advantage of the entire enterprise should redound to the other side?

This is precisely what Mr. Doane did. And the ingenuity of the combination was surpassed, if possible, by his rapidity and success in executing the plan. It seems to have taken full shape in his mind during the conversation which he had with my Father on his visit to Boston in May, 1831, when he first learned the full depth and earnestness of my Father's convictions and desires touching Ministerial education, and its true basis in the study of the Fathers; and saw that a Theological Seminary would probably bring him to Boston, when nothing else could. Instantly, Mr. Doane wrote letters to Bishop

Griswold and several others of the prominent Clergy of the Diocese, and five favorable replies were placed in my Father's hands before that visit to Boston was ended. As for the Clergy then in the city, they were invited to meet my Father at the Rector's hospitable dinner table, where the idea was received with unanimous favor.

With this happy beginning, Mr. Doane felt no hesitation in promising the favorable action of the Convention. Not many days after, while in company with the amiable Bishop on one of his Visitations, he secured a cordial understanding with him. A day or two before the annual Convention met, Dr. Potter was called on, but was not at home; and a note was left requesting him to call : but this he did not do, and therefore was not made fully aware of what was contemplated until the morning of Convention (June 15th), when it was entirely too late to organize a successful resistance. The resolutions were already drawn by Mr. Doane, the scheme of organization completed, and the Board of Trustees judiciously selected. Dr. Potter opposed the movement with all his might, as an interference with the General Seminary in New York,[1] as trusting too great a responsibility upon one man (my Father), and because Cambridge, where it was to be established, had not a suitable atmosphere for a Church school of Theology. On every vote the Rector carried the House by seven or eight to one.[2] The list of Trustees prepared by Mr.

[1] Not two years before, on the 21st of August, 1829, Dr. Potter himself had written to Bishop Hobart that the Eastern Diocese was suffering greatly from the paucity of suitable ministers. "If," continued he, "we would have a competent number of ministers, and would retain them whenever they were ordained, they must be *educated at Home*. On this point I have thought long and anxiously, and the conclusion to which I have arrived is that we *must have* some provision for this purpose. It is not improbable that some attempts will be made to this end, but we are exceedingly anxious that they should not be misunderstood by the friends of the General Seminary, and especially by yourself; and that, if possible, they should be taken with your concurrence."

[2] The same Convention, by about the same vote, decided *in favor* of Massachusetts separating from the rest of the Eastern Diocese, retaining Bishop Griswold as her Bishop ; and *against* the adoption of Resolutions advocating the newly risen Temperance Reformation. Nearly the same men voted together on all these questions. The defeat of the Temperance Resolutions could hardly have been pleasant to the Bishop, who in his Episcopal Address that year had just lauded "the wonderful effects of Temperance Societies," adding : " The good already effected seems almost incredible ; and daily on our knees should we thank God for the success he has given to their labors."

Doane was decorously placed before the House by a well-arranged Committee of nomination, and was elected of course. They soon met, and when the organization was completed, there was found to be a recognition, indeed, of the other side, and all honor had been shown to the Bishop: but the preponderance, in the Board, the Standing Committee, the Faculty, and everything else of real importance, was in High-Church hands. The Rector and his friends were complete masters of the situation; and within a few days even the show of opposition disappeared in Dr. Potter's writing a letter of very cordial welcome to my Father, explaining his opposition in Convention as meaning nothing unkind either to him or to the substance of the measure as carried.

On my Father's arrival in Boston, on Thursday, the 28th of July, 1831, after a ten days' journey with his whole family, his welcome was one of overwhelming kindness from all. Nothing could exceed the hospitable enthusiasm of the Rector and his friends; and the other side were anxious not to be behindhand. Crowds attended upon the preaching of the new comer. The newspapers gave flattering notices of his eloquence and argumentative power. When, after the lapse of a few weeks, he had succeeded in purchasing a house near Cambridge, about a quarter of a mile from Harvard College on the high road to Boston, and had there settled his family (September 20th), the Seminary work began, and four students attended their recitations in his department, Systematic Theology: while the Rev. Thomas W. Coit was the Professor of Biblical Learning, the Rev. Dr. Eaton of Ecclesiastical History and Church Polity, and the Bishop himself was responsible for the Rhetorical and Pastoral instruction.

In other points of view the prospect was equally pleasing. My Father had a few private pupils whom he was bringing up with his own sons; and the Rector showed his personal confidence by placing one of his step-sons among the number. The *Banner of the Church* was started by the Rector, and my Father immediately became a contributor, furnishing a series of papers on " Christian Education," which embodied the substance of the principles and practice of his own exertions in that noble cause during so many years. It was a cause, too, equally dear to Mr. Doane, as he proved by the labors and sacrifices of his whole life thereafter.

But such a state of general cordiality and enthusiastic good-feeling was too good to last. It was artificial, not natural: and it was easy to see the rocks and sandbars at no great depth below the smooth surface of the transparent water. My Father and Mr. Doane were both men of such remarkable emphasis in their individuality of character, that it was impossible they should long continue to work harmoniously in a scheme so complicated in its delicate equilibrium. Each was destined to be grievously disappointed in the other. My Father was as simple-hearted as a child, and could often be greatly influenced by what seemed to him to be spontaneous affection, admiration, or zeal: but if he began to think that he was being managed, his spirit of independence was in arms at once, and all the rest of the world put together could do nothing with him. He was, moreover, quite as averse to the business of managing other people, as to being managed himself.

Within two or three months, Mr. Doane began to discover several things which he had not before suspected. One was, that my Father's course in Pennsylvania was largely due to his conviction that it was his duty to sustain his Bishop; that when neither Bishop White nor Bishop Onderdonk approved heartily of his plan for a Pittsburgh Seminary, he gave it up; and that he felt himself, on principle, bound to show as much regard to Bishop Griswold in Massachusetts as to Bishop White in Pennsylvania, —a course for which there was a great deal to be said, and in which my Father was immovable. Another was, that the events of the past few years had produced a degree of real personal kindness and confidence between my Father and Low-Churchmen generally, which had no conscious effect on my Father's principles or theological teachings, indeed, but which made him anything but a reliable party man in the practical measures of the day; and as this relation between him and his Low-Church brethren was well known, and was one of the leading inducements to placing him in the position which he held, he thought it only fair that they should have some solid benefit from it.

Another was, that my Father was utterly useless in helping to manage anybody. And last of all, Mr. Doane—being then young, and never predisposed to extreme caution—was so outspoken on several occasions that my Father began, rightly or wrongly, to feel that he was himself *being managed*, for the accomplishment of purposes which certainly were not those for which he had parted with his beloved flock in Pittsburgh : and from that moment his personal independence of party and party management,—a feeling irresistible in him, when once roused,—began to assert itself more and more, as occasion arose.

On the other hand, Mr. Doane's power to mould the wills of ordinary men and combine their efforts wherever combination was necessary, was a special gift of character, which he could by no means neglect to use; and his conviction that the true life of the Church is in her Catholicity, and that it was his paramount duty to labor by all lawful means to promote that Catholicity, was so strong, and so glowing in its strength, that he did not feel bound to restrain his energies within that series of hesitating and halfhearted measures in which alone—if even there—he could look to Bishop Griswold as a leader among men. He could not understand my Father's deference to the Bishop, unless as a pretext for lukewarmness in the cause of Catholicity. My Father could not sympathize with a High-Churchmanship too impetuous to pay what seemed to him the proper deference due to an aged and venerable Bishop : and Mr. Doane could not see, in the personal peculiarities of a Bishop, any sufficient reason to let slip an extraordinary opportunity for the advancement of those great Catholic principles, without which the whole order of Bishops is, after all, a useless incumbrance.

The divergence at first was rather in tone than in substance : but began to be felt by both before three months of the new relation had elapsed. Within two or three months more, from some phrases dropped by the one or the other, or both, the impression began to make its way among others. With the succession of the Rev. John S. Stone to the Rectorship of S. Paul's—which took place soon after my Father's removal to Boston—the rivalry between that parish and old Trinity (which had previously been rather social and sympathetic) began to take a stronger partisan hue, Trinity being High and S. Paul's Low. And in the peculiar state of affairs—the Low-Church feeling that the generalship of Mr. Doane had gotten an undue advantage over them—the slightest appearance of a divergence between him and my Father was sure to be seized upon, magnified to the utmost, and used as a means of regaining what had been lost.

Never acting from party motives himself, my Father was always slow to suspect others of it: and in his vigilance over himself, his susceptibility was always the most delicate in regard to the High-Church party, with which he substantially agreed in principle, from the first. As to the Low-Church party, knowing that he did not agree with them in principle, he seems to have had little fears, being conscious that nothing but a sense of duty could ever induce him to act with them at all.

It was not long before rumors of a disagreement between Mr. Doane and his Assistant began to get abroad, in a very exaggerated shape. When brought to my Father's notice by one of the Vestry of Trinity Church, towards the end of March, 1832, he promptly replied:—

> The intercourse of Mr. Doane and myself is as courteous and as friendly as need be expected or desired in this imperfect world; and as to "hostility of feeling" on the part of either towards the other, I can confidently say that I have never entertained it for a moment, and I have no ground whatever to impute it to Mr. Doane, but the contrary. Indeed I have no hesitation in saying, that our mutual relations are such, at this moment, as I should be content to continue to the end of my life, if undisturbed by extraneous causes of dissatisfaction. . . . Let them [the Vestry of Trinity Church] be assured that if ever we should disagree so as to make it worth talking seriously about, I shall not leave them to gather the information from any other quarter, but shall remove the difficulty by a speedy resignation.

But while my Father thought that the few points of slight divergency between them were not "worth talking about," it may easily be understood that the strategic importance of such things was much more correctly weighed by Mr. Doane. Accustomed to entire independence of thought and action, my Father did not expect to find himself in entire agreement with any body; and as the manifestation of such little discrepancies made no difference in his feelings towards others, he took it for granted that it made none in the feeling with which others regarded him. As to becoming an active or passive means whereby the balance of power in the Diocese should be changed from High-Church to Low-Church hands, he never dreamed of it for an instant. Mr. Doane, however, soon saw that my Father's "impracticability"—as he regarded it—was imperilling the interests of that truth which they both had equally at heart. To him, the rapid development of the admiration and attention shown to my Father by the Low-Church, was very intelligible: while my Father's simple-heartedness never suspected any partisan bearing in it, or else thought it a proof that his new friends were rising to a healthier and truer position as to Churchmanship.

In this state of things, it is easy to see how well-meaning friends, and deliberate mischief makers, on both sides, had an excellent chance to show what can be done by the strife of tongues: and how each of the two leading figures should seem, to the other, to be responsible for many things of which he was entirely innocent and ignorant. To Mr. Doane the change must have been specially annoying: for he seemed to be on the point of a grievous defeat, not only for himself personally but for the cause which was so dear to him, and that by means of the very man whom he had himself brought into the Diocese through such remarkable efforts of influence and skill. His own most brilliant victory was about being stolen from him, to inure wholly to the benefit of the enemy. It was certainly a hard thing to bear with equanimity: and all the harder because, in case of an open division of action, my Father would be sure to carry a considerable portion of the High-Church party with him, together with the whole of their opponents, thus commanding a clear majority in the Diocese which Mr. Doane himself had previously ruled with such easy sway.

Meanwhile, another complication was beginning to entangle itself with the progress of affairs in Boston. As early as November 11th, one of the leading clergy in Vermont wrote to sound the Assistant Minister of Trinity touching the probability of his acceptance of the Episcopate of that new Diocese, the Rev. Mr. McIlvaine being then the other candidate chiefly spoken of.

My Father gave no encouragement to the idea, being loth to think of another removal of his large family so soon; and naturally very reluctant to leave a growing circle of new and enthusiastic friends in one of the most intellectual and refined communities in the land, for a State which was supposed to be comparatively rural, and in which he knew not a single soul, clerical or lay. The prominence with which his name was brought forward in Vermont, however, soon compelled him to advise with his friends. Bishop Griswold's opinion was first sought: and in February, a Clergyman wrote him the results of a serious conversation with Bishop Griswold:—

Taking into consideration the peculiar situation of this Diocese, and the need that would soon exist here of a new Bishop, with the probability and propriety of your being called to that station, he [Bishop Griswold] thought that the Church at large would lose more than it would gain by your accepting Vermont : and that, to our fondest hopes and prospects *here* [the writer was a Low-Churchman], such a step would prove—to report the very unusual expression he made use of—a ruinous one.

They mistook their man. He was not in the slightest danger, for a moment, of guiding his course with a view to become the future Bishop of Massachusetts, or to avert the ruin of the Low-Church party in that Diocese: and his final decision showed it. Meanwhile the urgency from Vermont became more and more pressing: and, owing to the newness and feebleness of that Diocese, and the discouragement of a refusal after election (involving the trouble and delay and expense of a Special Convention in that case, for a new choice), my Father felt it his duty to place the question of his accepting it or not, upon its true basis of solution. And that was, to test the actual solidity and sincerity of the scheme for the newly formed Theological School, which and which alone had drawn him thither from Pittsburgh. If there were reasonable zeal and liberality shown in that cause, he would say *No* to Vermont. If there were really no heartiness in sustaining that work, he would be satisfied that the only consideration for which he had come had proved a failure, and could not conscientiously refuse the call to Vermont, if it should be offered.

He therefore laid the matter before the Vestry of Trinity

Church, and, in conference with a Committee of that body, specified the sum of $10,000 as the lowest (and certainly his reluctance to leave Boston was clear in his fixing so small a sum) which he could regard as proof of a serious determination to make the Seminary a reality. He requested their answer by the 19th of May, so that the Vermont Convention, which was to meet on the 30th, might be informed of the result in time to guide their action accordingly. A circular was at once printed, and a form of pledge for subscriptions circulated, neither of which was shown to my Father beforehand, as it ought to have been. Just before the day named, he was informed of the result, which was, the raising of several thousand dollars as a trust fund, the income of which should be paid to the Professor of Systematic Theology, so long as my Father should fill that chair. The terms in which the papers were drawn were meant to be highly complimentary, the Committee hoping that this would be regarded as "a sufficient pledge to induce Mr. Hopkins to decline the Vermont invitation, in connection with the evidence they have had of an universal expression of high gratification derived from the preaching of that Reverend gentleman, and of the sincere regret the Congregation would feel at being deprived of his religious instruction, besides the disadvantages that would ensue to the Theological School by his removal from this place."

But this was touching my Father in perhaps his tenderest point. The idea that a few hundred dollars of income, more or less, could decide his doubts as to his sphere of usefulness in the Church to which the Providence of God was really calling him, was a fatal mistake to make with one who had already left an income of thousands at the Law, for one of hundreds in preaching the Gospel. It was a special blunder in this case, because my Father's income was sufficient for all his wants, and he had expressly undertaken to serve as Professor without fee or reward. He was indignant that he should now appear to be anxious, in so crooked a way, to secure merely an increase of salary. Restraining his indignation for awhile, however, he made one more effort to induce his pecuniary friends to change the form of their liberality, so that it should be a direct gift to the Seminary, for the purchase of land or the erection of a building: but in vain. For his own emolument they were willing to act, but for the Seminary they cared nothing and would do nothing. And so dead was all idea of the Seminary, that at the ensuing Diocesan Convention the Board of Trustees did not even think it worth while to make the "Report," which it was their duty to present. This entire apathy settled the question. The result was communicated to his friends in Vermont, and the issue left with them.

The Vermont Convention met in S. Stephen's Church, Middlebury, on Wednesday, May 30. On the following morning they reached the business of the election of a Bishop. In accordance with the mode prescribed in the Constitution of the Diocese, the Clergy first retired, to nominate some suitable person to the laity. They were thirteen in number: of whom *seven* voted for my Father, and *six* for the Rev. John S. Stone, Rector of S. Paul's Church, Boston. On making the nomination of my Father, accordingly, the Clergy again retired, in order to allow the free action of the Laity in electing or refusing to elect. There were forty Lay Delegates present, of whom, at the first ballot, *thirty-one* voted for my Father, and *nine* against him. There was very little of partisan feeling. The minority expressed their entire willingness to sign the Testimonial, provided the real state of the vote were allowed to appear on the Journal, and every member of the Convention, clerical and lay, signed the Testimonial accordingly.[1] The leading members of the minority wrote letters to their Bishop-elect, assuring him of the cordial unanimity with which he would be received; and stating that their vote for Mr. Stone was only from a slight personal preference for him, but

---

[1] This statement gives the impression left upon my Father's mind, as I repeatedly heard it from him. But the *Biographical Sketch* of the late Rt. Rev. Carlton Chase, D.D., first Bishop of New Hampshire, gives further light on the subject. Dr. Chase was the leading clergyman in Vermont at the time, for influence and weight of character. Speaking of the Convention of 1832, the *Biographical Sketch* says:—"The Clergy were almost equally divided in their choice of a new Bishop, and the feeling was at first so strong that it threatened to break out in opposition to the result of the ballot. A lay member of that Convention, a man of excellent memory, attributes much of the fraternal acquiescence which followed, to the 'conciliatory course of Mr. Chase . . . his manner of meeting the opposition, cool, quiet, dignified, at the same time firm; not once losing the Christian deportment which followed him through life.'" Pp. 51-52.

must *not* be understood as implying any opposition to my Father.

Before deciding upon his answer—he had refused the most pressing invitations to be present at the Convention and give his answer at once—he visited Vermont for the first time in his life, going as far North as Burlington, and stopping in several of the leading parishes. He was agreeably surprised with all he saw of the beauties of Nature, of the sturdy intelligence of the people, and of the hearty zeal and cordiality of Clergy and Laity. The Rectorship of S. Paul's Church, Burlington,—vacant by the resignation of the Rev. Dr. G. T. Chapman,—was tendered to him. And not long after his return to Boston from his ten days' excursion among the Green Mountains, he sent his formal acceptance of the Episcopate of Vermont.

There were canonical difficulties in the way, however, which caused some discussion and correspondence during the ensuing months. Both the Bishops Onderdonk were inclined to the opinion that the subdivision of the Eastern Diocese, so as to allow the election of a Diocesan Bishop by Vermont alone, was not regular or proper until after additional legislation by the General Convention. Bishop Griswold had indeed "resigned" his jurisdiction in Vermont: but there was no Canon allowing a Bishop to resign part of his jurisdiction while retaining the rest: and Bishop H. U. Onderdonk reiterated his conviction "that both resignations and translations are contrary to sound views."

This question of resignations was then very prominently before the Church, Bishop Philander Chase having resigned his Episcopal jurisdiction in Ohio on the 9th of September, 1831. In the absence of legislation on the subject, there was no small difference of opinion as to whether Ohio was actually vacant or not: and this difference could not be settled until the meeting of General Convention in October, 1832. The certainty that a decided Low-Churchman would be elected in Ohio (Bishop McIlvaine was elected on the 5th of September), caused the lines to be drawn very sharply on this subject. The good sense of Bishop White, with whom Mr. Binney entirely coincided, saw the wide difference between the cases of Vermont and Ohio; and the difficulty, as applying to Vermont, had almost entirely disappeared from men's minds before the meeting of the General Convention.

But my Father had as yet by no means ended his troubles in Massachusetts. A difference of opinion between the Bishop and the Standing Committee was like a spark upon the tow, and kindled quite a conflagration in the Diocese. There were six vacant parishes in Massachusetts alone, at that time, desiring the services of clergymen. There were two candidates for Orders, graduates of Harvard, who had been on the Bishop's list for more than two years, and had stood all their examinations to the satisfaction of the Bishop and the Presbyters appointed by him. He was willing to dispense with the remainder of the time of their candidateship, and applied to the Standing Committee for their consent: which they refused, as they had a canonical right to do. It was injudicious, however, for it gave to those who were dissatisfied a chance to say, that they must have a Standing Committee that would act in harmony with the Bishop. What made their refusal still more unfortunate, was the fact, that these two young men had both spent the previous scholastic year as Students of the new Massachusetts Theological School: and this was the first welcome given to its pupils by the Standing Committee of the Diocese.[1] This was a powerful element of agitation, added to all that we have previously mentioned, and giving tangible direction to much of it, when the time came.

In about two months after this, and before my Father's first visit to Vermont, the Massachusetts Convention met, on Wednesday, the 20th of June. The Rev. Mr. Doane seems to have been unaware of the extent of dissatisfaction; and supposed that an easy and informal coöperation on the part of himself and his friends would suffice to reëlect the old ticket as usual, with a couple of vacancies supplied by themselves. There does not seem to have been any thorough organization on the other side: but there was a sort of a general understanding which partially answered the purpose. On the first ballot, Mr. Doane was the

---

[1] Doubtless, since the regular course of study was fixed at three years, as in the General Theological Seminary, they wished to discourage the students from seeking ordination until they had gone through the whole course: a policy for which many and strong reasons may easily be urged.

only clerical member of the Standing Committee elected; and on the second, the Rev. Messrs. Stone and Edson were added: which placed the balance of power in the Bishop's hands. As Deputies to General Convention, the Rev. Messrs. West and Baury were chosen instead of the Rev. Messrs. Morss and Doane, the Rev. Messrs. Edson and Stone being on both tickets. In the latter case my Father voted for Messrs. Morss and Doane; in the former he had voted for those who were elected.

Mr. Doane was not a little surprised by finding the whole balance of the Diocese thus suddenly turned over to the other side; and he made a desperate effort to restore the previous *régime*. Not a few having gone home—as usual—supposing that the main business of Convention was over, and finding next day that he could rely upon a decided majority of the clergy who were left, it was moved to declare all the elections of the previous day null and void, the vote not having been taken "by orders," as required in the Constitution. The simple fact was, that the Constitution, as interpreted by the constant usage of the thirty or forty years during which it had been in existence, gave the vote by orders whenever it was called for; but when not called for by any person before the vote was taken, the distinction was not made. It had never been called for in the annual elections: and in this year 1832 they were conducted precisely as in all those years previous, no one calling for any vote "by orders." Besides which, an amendment of the Constitution, inserting the words that the vote was to be by orders "when a division is called for," had already been approved in 1831, and became law within a few hours after this attempt to nullify the elections was made. It was very bold, very brilliant, and very ingenious, considered as a piece of parliamentary tactics: and that a decided majority of the clergy could be brought to support such a course in solid phalanx, was a striking proof of the remarkable power of Mr. Doane in influencing and controlling bodies of men. But the attempt, if successful, would have pronounced invalid *all* the action of the Diocese of Massachusetts for thirty or forty years: and that was by far too heavy a price to pay for carrying the elections at one session. It was not wise to try it. The making of the attempt, however, proves the excitement of the occasion, and the feeling of desperation with which any chance of averting the impending consequences was seized upon.

This was not all. The excitement and surprise had so far overmastered the imagination and feelings of Mr. Doane, that he published a "Manifesto" in the *Banner of the Church*[1] giving an account of the proceedings which was so strongly colored by his own views, surmises and fears, that the Bishop and his friends were wounded deeply by a sense of injustice. Yet even this would have been borne in silence, also, but for one provocation more. A zealous lay friend of Mr. Doane procured the signatures of fourteen clergymen to a document addressed to the chosen deputies to General Convention, advising three of them to resign in favor of three others who were not elected, but who it was said ought to have been: and intimating that, if this were not done, there would be trouble in subsequent meetings of the Convention.

This was too much. It was the general conviction of those concerned that an answer to the Manifesto must be prepared; and the work was strongly urged upon my Father. He was extremely reluctant to undertake it, for many reasons, but especially because of the personal and official ties which had connected him so closely with Mr. Doane, and the power of which he still felt so strongly in many respects. But when the Bishop also added his advice and request to that of all the others, he felt it to be a duty, however disagreeable. His "Defence of the Convention"[2] was not only signed by himself, but was supported also by the added certificates of the Bishop and a large number of the Clergy and Laity of the Convention,—the Rev. Dr. Edson being one of the clerical signers. That pamphlet settled the business. There was no rejoinder.

Meanwhile, my Father's independent course in the Convention had brought upon him a more pointed manifestation of favor from his Low-Church brethren than ever before. In July, at the

---

[1] My Father had for some time ceased his contributions to the columns of this paper. Indeed, I believe he sent to it little or nothing besides his series of fifteen articles on "Christian Education," signed "THEOPHILUS."

[2] A pamphlet of forty-four pages; Stimpson & Clapp, Boston. 1832.

formal request of the Rector, Churchwardens and Vestrymen of S. Paul's Church, he repeated to them, on Sunday evenings (when Trinity Church was closed), the series of sermons on *The Evidences of Christianity* and on *The Apostles' Creed* which he had already delivered in Trinity; and the congregations which crowded to hear them (hundreds being unable to enter), and the notices in the daily papers, were all complimentary to an enthusiastic degree. After the conclusion of them, the present of a modest service of silver plate [1]—the only thing of the sort my Father ever received in his life—gave solid proof of the satisfaction of his hearers. The Rector, Wardens and Vestry of S. Paul's formally requested the publication of both those courses of sermons: and to this was afterwards added a *Testimonial* of grateful affection and admiration, signed by a large number of the leading members of both parishes.

Owing to the delay in undertaking the *Defence of the Convention*, and in getting the signatures of so many parties, it did not appear until late in August. If the position in which Mr. Doane had been left by the action of the Convention itself was uncomfortable, the appearance of the *Defence* certainly diminished any probability of a speedy return to his previous position of controlling influence in the Diocese; and it unintentionally stimulated the tongues of those who had groaned in secret under the yoke of an influence which they had neither wit nor strength enough to break; but now that it was broken, they buzzed their slanders loudly through the air. The impetus in this direction was brought to its climax by the unexpected election of Mr. Doane to the Episcopate of New Jersey,[2] on the 3rd of October, only a fortnight before the meeting of the General Convention. The time was short; but an attempt was at once organized with the intent to defeat Mr. Doane's consecration, if possible, by charges against his integrity of character.[3]

---

[1] The silver of which this was made was once a part of the plate of the King of France, confiscated during the French Revolution.

[2] His testimonials, like those of my Father, were signed by *all* the clerical and lay members of Convention present: though he was elected only on the sixth ballot. Of the others voted for, *four* became Bishops subsequently.

[3] See Memoir of Bishop Doane, by his Son:—" Every effort was made to blast his character in Boston, and prevent his Consecration. The courage of the Presiding

It must not be supposed, however, that all the talk was on one side. In times of high excitement there is great injustice done by bitter tongues on both sides. And in all cases, the most of it is done by the third and fourth rate hangers-on,—the weak and enthusiastic friends of leaders who have too much of coolness and manliness and high-toned character to take any share in the dirty work themselves, but upon whom the whole of the responsibility is apt to be charged by their aggrieved opponents. A clerical friend of my Father's wrote him in November:—" I have been . . . an indignant and always a disgusted hearer of the calumnies not whispered but almost shouted against your integrity, during the crisis through which we have been struggling "; and with a refinement of malice these charges were set to circulating in Pittsburgh among my Father's old friends there, who wrote to him in amazement to ask what it all could mean. Among other things it was said that he had himself circulated stories against Mr. Doane, of which he had in fact only been an unwilling and utterly incredulous hearer. When he was approached for the purpose of asking his coöperation in preventing Mr. Doane's consecration, he utterly and indignantly refused to have anything to do with it.

The charges brought against Mr. Doane were a foreshadowing of the sort of thing which long afterwards came upon him in its maturity, in the two attempts to put him upon his trial: and at both periods they were simply the tribute which meanness, cowardice, fear and hatred are wont to pay to those who display unusual power as leaders of men, in pushing forward principles that are unpopular. My Father had no fault to find with Mr. Doane, beyond that slight difference of views and action which had already found full expression in print, and which did not necessarily imply any loss of personal esteem or confidence on the part of either in the other. It had but a transient influence on the feelings of both, passing away entirely with the curious crisis which gave it birth. Both were substantially agreed in Church principles. Both were devoted to Church Education,

Bishop, the firm rallying of the leading men in Boston, the perfect consciousness of truth, and the power of Almighty God, prevailed here, as so often again."—Note, p. 191.

and willingly sacrificed in that cause all they had to lose. And the story of 1832 is recorded in humble imitation of the candor which has told us of the difference between S. Paul and S. Barnabas, to show, that a temporary disagreement about persons and things should not be understood to the prejudice of either party, where lifelong devotion and zeal prove them to be faithful servants of the Church.

The General Convention of 1832 was one of extraordinary importance and interest. The Ohio case—whether the resignation of Bishop Philander Chase should be regarded as valid, and the Rev. Mr. McIlvaine be consecrated—was the leading topic in debate: and as Mr. McIlvaine was not only a leading Low-Churchman, but one to whom great prominence had been given in the anti-Onderdonk campaign of 1827, men's party position naturally went far to influence the relative importance of those considerations which governed their votes. Sound Church principles were unquestionably hostile to Episcopal resignations: and of course hostile to one which would add another Low-Church Bishop to the House. The Low-Church had no principles which would oppose any Episcopal resignation by which they could gain an additional vote. Parties were very evenly divided: and the Low-Church were not only very much excited, but were so sure that nothing but partizanship could oppose Mr. McIlvaine's consecration, that, in case it were refused, there was every prospect of a schism, or at least an irregular and schismatical consecration. On the other hand, Mr. Doane was as obnoxious to the Low-Church as Mr. McIlvaine was to the High-Church, though the warfare against the two was carried on in a very different manner, the objections in the Ohio case being made in open Convention and fought by daylight, while those against Mr. Doane were made in secret and fought in the dark. But that there was a correlation of the two forces is evident.

There was no objection or difficulty in the cases of Vermont and Kentucky. The Bishops-elect of those Dioceses might have been consecrated early in the session, and thereupon have taken their seats in the House: and my Father thought it rather unfair that this was not done until the very close of the session.

But the two who had no opponents were made to await the end of the contest in regard to those who had. The session opened on the 17th of October. On the 18th, the Vermont, Kentucky and Ohio papers were referred, and on the 19th those of New Jersey. On the 23d, the Committee reported in favor of signing the Testimonials of Vermont and Kentucky; but they " had not opened" the papers of Ohio, and as to New Jersey they said nothing. But meanwhile, for days together, the Ohio debate had been raging. At last, in the Lower House, a majority and a minority report were both defeated, as was also a form of resolutions which came down from the House of Bishops: and a compromise was carried by so close a vote, that, had the delegation from Massachusetts been what Mr. Doane tried to make it, the compromise would have been lost, and we should have had a schism or something very like it. Little did either party dream of such serious consequences hinging upon the result of the little Massachusetts squabble in June! It is not the only case where a temporary check to the High-Church party has been the means of securing in the long run the steadier and more solid growth of High-Church principles.

This result was not reached until the same day on which the Ohio and New Jersey papers were first reported, together, as being " all right." And the Testimonials were actually signed in the order of prominence given to each in the contest: Ohio first, then New Jersey; and after these, those of Vermont and Kentucky, in regard to which there had been no question. This was done late on Saturday, the 27th of October. On Monday, the House of Bishops laid the Ohio papers on the table, until they should see what the Lower House would do with the Canon *Of Episcopal Resignations:* which, on that same Monday, passed by the narrow majority of one clerical and one lay vote. On Tuesday, therefore, the House of Bishops sent down notice that the Consecration of the four Bishops would be on Wednesday: adding " that they were induced to agree to the consecration of a Bishop for the Diocese of Ohio in consequence of the passage of the Canon *Of Episcopal Resignations,* a measure deemed essential by them in order to prevent future injury from the precedent of the resignation which has led to the consecration."

On Wednesday, October 31st, accordingly, in S. Paul's Chapel, New York, the whole four were consecrated,—a larger number than were ever in this country, before or since, consecrated on the same day and in the same Church. The sermon was preached by Bishop H. U. Onderdonk. My Father's election having preceded that of the other three, he was the first of the four to be consecrated. The venerable Bishop White was assisted in the laying on of hands, in his case, by Bishop Griswold, and Bishop Bowen of South Carolina.

That day was the 46th anniversary of the day on which Bishop White—then a simple priest—had sailed from the harbor of New York, to seek for the Church of America, from the Mother Church of England, the vital gift of the Apostolic Succession: and his heart was filled with gratitude at beholding the fulness of the measure with which the Head of the Church had blessed the gift then received.[1] On the evening of the same day, all the new Bishops took their seats in the House of Bishops at its closing session.

It had been my Father's intention, at first, to postpone the removal of his family until the Spring. But his energy of character made him now prefer to act at once. His resignation as Assistant Minister of Trinity Church was accepted,[2] the Trustees paying him the whole of the current quarter to the 1st of January, as they had begun by a similar act of liberality in antedating his connection with the parish. A warm testimonial of admiration and gratitude was forwarded to him, signed by the leading parishioners of Trinity and S. Paul's, thanking him especially for his sermons on the Creed and on Baptism. Two trips to Vermont were made; the whole family of fifteen souls were removed to Burlington; a house was bought, with thirteen acres of ground attached: and all this was completed within three weeks after my Father's consecration in New York.

Bishop Doane's removal to New Jersey took place not long

---

[1] Bishop White's Address to his Convention, 1833.

[2] In order to enable the Trustees to go into an immediate election of a successor to him in the Assistant Ministership of Trinity Church, he had, on the 10th of July, sent in his resignation, to take effect unconditionally on the 10th of November. But the Trustees, in very handsome terms, then declined to accept it, "until the course of events should render it absolutely necessary."

afterwards. The high excitement that had marked the year[1] died away, and left long years of dead inactivity behind it. But they were years in which the Low-Church party were in full control, and they have continued so to be until within a very few years past.

Pennsylvania and Massachusetts both teach us the lesson that moderation in the exercise of a party majority is true wisdom. Each of these Dioceses was at one time under the control of the High-Church party. In each the same mistake was made, of overloading a small majority with too great a burden of sharp and hard-pushed party action. In each case there was an outburst of excitement and personalities which alone did more mischief than any such narrow party triumph was worth. In each case the reaction carried the Diocese for a long series of years over to the opposite side in Church politics: in Massachusetts, where it came at once, it has only lately passed away; in Pennsylvania, where it came more slowly, it has not disappeared even yet. The kingdom of God cometh not with observation. It is only in the quiet growth of opinion and true faith that the strength of Churchmanship is found. In the Eastern Diocese, where there was once neither Bishop nor Convention that was not Low-Church, there are now five Bishops and five Conventions; and of these, the Low-Church retain not a single Bishop, and not a single Convention: but that Bishop and that Convention which they retained the longest, were both due to the erroneous policy of 1832.

[1] Dr. Stone, in his Memoir of Bishop Griswold, speaks of it as a "sudden, volcanic explosion." The action in the Convention, he says, "was sufficient to uncap a laboring volcano, and to kindle the flames of disunion into their fiercest glow. All the other States in the [Eastern] Diocese were heated by them. They flashed up through the weekly-religious, and through the daily-secular, papers; and scorching, even in their descent, were the mixed elements which they cast abroad through the air. Other and more distant Dioceses felt the shock of the commotion from the Trimountain City. Its waving and heaving agitations rolled troublously through even the General Convention, which assembled the ensuing October."—P. 369. Again he speaks of 1832 as "that acme in the troubles of the Eastern Diocese, whose history, it is not likely, will ever be fully written, save on the pages of memory."—P. 376. It was the most exciting and troubled year of Bishop Griswold's long Episcopate.

Chapter VIII.

BISHOP OF VERMONT.

IT is not possible to do justice to the first Bishop of Vermont, without considering the peculiarities of his field of labor. The population of that State increased rapidly for twenty years after her admission to the Union: but then the first attack of the emigration fever—Western New York and Ohio being the chief attractions—suddenly pulled down the increase in a decade from 62,000 to 18,000. During the period immediately preceding my Father's election there had been a rally of strength, and the increase of the decade rose to nearly 45,000. But the Erie Canal was finished in 1825, opening up the wonders of the farther West, which by the year 1832 had begun to bear the fruit of desolation in Vermont, so that in 1840 it was found that the total increase of the whole State population in ten years was only 11,145; and five of the Counties—including nearly all those in which the Church had been started—had actually *decreased*, by over 4000 souls. Hardly had there been a slight recovery from this, when the completion of the chief Vermont railways, combining with the marvellous extension of the railway system in the West, enabled the population of Vermont to leave their native State faster than ever: so that the last census taken during my Father's episcopate (1860) showed a total increase during ten years of only 996 souls:—a smaller increase than that of any other part of the United States. And even this dead level has only been maintained by the large influx of Irish and French Roman Catholics from Canada. Without this immigration, the properly American population of the State—which alone is accessible to our Church—would have shown a positive decrease of many thousands.

The Western emigration, too, told more heavily upon the Church than upon any other body of Christians in the State.

Not being largely represented in the original settlement of the towns, the chief growth of the Church must needs be by making converts from the Protestant denominations around her, which were already in possession of the ground. Her success, here, would naturally be among the younger people, with whom the prejudices of a lifetime had the least weight: and these were, of all others, the first to emigrate,—a business in which youth commonly takes the lead. Whole parishes, numbering from 50 to 100 communicants, have thus, in a few years' time, been so broken down in numbers and strength as to be unable, for a long while, to support a minister: and some have become practically defunct. More than one flourishing parish had already come to this condition during Bishop Griswold's Episcopate.[1] And what made this disastrous change the easier, was, the sparseness of the population, and the agricultural employment which has from the first been almost their sole dependence. It is notorious that a population of small farmers is more economical in its notions of what is due towards Church support and Church extension, than any other: and at least nine-tenths of the population of Vermont are of this class. The towns are properly townships of about six miles square: and even now, the average population of a township is only about 1500. Scatter this small number over a territory of 36 square miles, and few will be found to cluster in the hamlets. Give each hamlet a Congregationalist, a Methodist, and a Baptist or Universalist society to begin with, and it will be easy to see what chance there would be for the successful planting of the Church. Moreover, so equal is the distribution of the population, that when my Father was elected, there were only five townships in the State that had as many as 3000 inhabitants, and the highest of these was only 3468. During his Episcopate many of the towns greatly decreased in population, only a few increasing. Thirty years of change showed, in 1860, only two

---

[1] He complains of the grievous effects of this emigration as early as 1818. In that year he speaks of the parish at Vergennes as "declining," and Shelburne as being only "the remnant of a Church." And in 1830, just as his connection with Vermont was drawing towards an end, he says: "In many parts of the Diocese we have scarce been able to maintain the ground which we before possessed. A considerable number of our parishes, from being so long either wholly vacant or destitute of any permanent ministrations, are, we fear, declining."—See Dr. Stone's Memoir, p. 259.

places in the State with over 7000 inhabitants,[1] while hardly any others even reached 4000. There is no large city, and never has been, in the State of Vermont. Her rate of increase in population, and in wealth, has been by far the lowest of all the States in the Union: while, as to the ratio in which her native population has deserted her, she has surpassed all the rest except South Carolina. Vermont Churchmen have done good service in building up the Church in Northern and Western New York, and all over the Great West, but they have left desolate parishes, and feeble hands, and often fainting hearts, behind them in their native valleys.

Nor was the original Churchmanship of Vermont marked by that clear and conscientious grasp of fundamental principle which alone could give any chance of growth, or even of steady continuance, in the midst of circumstances so shifting. Bishop Griswold[2] speaks of the prevailing tone throughout the whole Eastern Diocese as showing little regard for "true Church principles"; and adds, that "the authority of the Church and our General Convention were held in much less estimation." Even under his own administration, which he justly appeals to as producing a great improvement, he narrates some things which would hardly be considered now as exactly in accordance with true Church principles:[3] and the cases in which apparently flourishing parishes of nearly an hundred communicants, with large confirmations of from 20 to 47 persons, began speedily to break and disappear, showed rather a sympathy with the weaknesses of the religion of the day, than the ripe fruit of Church culture.[4] But, with all these drawbacks, Vermont was spoken of

---

[1] Burlington, the largest, had only 7713 at the census of 1860. The census of 1870, made since my Father's departure, shows rather more improvement, and it is greater in Burlington than in any other part of the State, it being now a city of over 14,000 inhabitants, and rapidly growing.

[2] Convention Address, 1828, see Dr. Stone's Memoir, p. 343.

[3] In 1820 he says, "We know that many of our people contribute to the propagation of the Gospel by other [sic] sects." And in 1821, at the Consecration of Zion Church, Manchester, the good Bishop relates, with evident satisfaction, that "with the exception of one denomination, all the communicants of various Churches present, including several Congregational Ministers, received with us the Lord's Supper."

[4] Over some of the defunct parishes of Vermont, as elsewhere, the truthful epitaph might well be set up: "Died of a Union Meeting-House." Such a "union" is enough to kill any parish.

by Bishop Griswold in 1826 as apparently the most flourishing part of the Eastern Diocese. Very interesting incidents of visitation are narrated by him in his Addresses and letters. On one occasion [1] he confirmed thirty-five persons in a grove of young maples, in the midst of the most picturesque scenery, as no building large enough for the congregation could be found. The Church soon rose on the same ground, and some of the timbers for it, already lying by, were used in these preliminary services. He speaks of the visible improvement in the State, and in the tone and character of the people.[2] It was owing to this decided growth,[3] together with the fact that no marked development of party spirit on either side had yet taken place, that Vermont was the first to be separated from the Eastern Diocese: and that this separation took place without opposition from any quarter. Bishop Griswold, as early as 1822,[4] had put himself on record as in favor of the separation of "Vermont especially"; and he went further to declare that "it requires no great wisdom to foresee" that the States themselves must soon be subdivided into two or more Dioceses, for the size of many of the Dioceses would otherwise "be very pernicious to the cause of true godliness, and the best interest of the churches." He reiterated his opinions from time to time, down to the year of the separation. And in closing his connection [5] with a part of his charge which had cost him so much of labor, and given him so much of pleasure, he thus [6] summed up the results of the past:—

As I have resigned the jurisdiction of Vermont, and that State is now become a separate Diocese, it will be sufficient to state, and I am happy to have it in my power truly to state, that I leave it in great prosperity. Eighteen years ago they had but one, or at most two officiating clergy-

---

[1] In 1821, at Berkshire. See Dr. Stone's Memoir, pp. 275, 276.

[2] Ib. pp. 274-276.

[3] Bishop Griswold confirmed a larger number in his last year's service, than my Father did in his first, or in any one year after.

[4] Convention Address of 1822.

[5] The Vermont Convention of 1832 unanimously adopted a grateful and affectionate Address of Farewell to Bishop Griswold, every word of which he had richly earned. This address was drawn by the Rev. Dr. Carlton Chase, afterwards the first Bishop of New Hampshire.

[6] Dr. Stone's Memoir, p. 374.

men: now they have twelve or more. They then had not one Church edifice properly their own; now they have twelve new ones, which are consecrated, and five or six more, which are built, or in building. Then, if I recollect aright, they had three organized parishes: in their late Convention, twenty-four were represented.[1] Thousands of dollars they have in that time expended in obtaining possession of the lands, which belong to this Church: now, as we hope, the business is settled, and those expensive litigations at an end.

The litigation here referred to resulted in recovering possession of a large amount of lands which the State had unjustly confiscated. The result was, a small and stationary income, which enabled the Diocese to pay the Bishop a salary of $500 (eventually raised to $1200) a year, without calling on any person to put his hand in his own pocket; and supplying besides a pittance of $50 or $75 each, to the poorer parishes, to aid them in sustaining a clergyman. There have been some benefits, doubtless, from the recovery of these lands: but they have not been a tithe of what was anticipated. On the other hand, the litigation increased the bitterness of the prejudice with which the Church was already regarded: and the consciousness that there was a fund to draw on tended rather to deaden than to stimulate the liberality of the Churchmen of the Diocese. If there is any class of Churchmen not easy to be roused to personal exertion, it is a rural community, with a small endowment.

All these things united have certainly made Vermont without exception the hardest and least remunerative part of the vineyard, in these United States. There are three features, however, of this early history of the Diocese which are worthy of special mention. In the first Canon ever adopted in Vermont for the trial of a clergyman (1811), it was provided that if a degraded clergyman considered himself aggrieved, " he shall be allowed an *appeal to the House of Bishops*"; and in the amended Constitution of 1820, they adopted the principle of the *proportionate representation of the laity*, the number of lay delegates being regulated by the number of actual Communicants. And that same Constitution provided that no person should be eligible on the Standing Committee or as a representative of the Diocese in either the

---

[1] The whole number of Communicants was then about 1100.

General or the Diocesan Convention, unless he were a regular communicant of the Church. We do not know whether of the two is worthy of the greater wonder: that three such sound and thorough principles should have been enacted so early in Vermont; or that no one of the three should have worked its way to general acceptance throughout the Church of America even at this late day.

On the 21st of November, three weeks from the day of his consecration, my Father began his permanent residence at Burlington. His family were at once settled in the brick house which he had bought at the southern end of the village. His first Episcopal act was the consecration of the stone church then just finished at Burlington, under the brief but efficient rectorship of Dr. Chapman. Before the close of the year he confirmed twenty-nine persons, and in the March following sixteen more, making forty-five for his first year's work in his parish. On the 30th of December he set out on his first visitation of the Diocese, in the course of which 165 persons were confirmed (besides the 45 at Burlington), and three other new Churches were consecrated. He was twice upset, once between Brattleborough and Bennington, when he was uninjured, though one of his companions was severely shaken; and the second time at Enosburgh, when he was somewhat bruised, but happily no serious harm was done. His reception everywhere was cordial in the extreme: and the Low-Church parishes were particularly pleased with his preaching extemporaneously for them,—a mode which they preferred, and in which his readiness of mind and tongue made him perfectly at home. But the result of his personal acquaintance with the needs of his Diocese made him only more enthusiastic in the cause of education than he was before. If Western Pennsylvania—towards which the movement of the population was bringing constant increase—needed it; if Massachusetts, with all her wealth and numbers, yet needed it as imbued with Church principles: it was more than doubly needful in Vermont, which had no Church wealth or strength to begin with, and was losing instead of gaining, by every fresh movement of the people towards the West. Moreover, it was evident that the only chance of keeping or supporting the theological students while preparing for Orders, was by employing them as teachers in an academic department, conducted upon a remunerative scale. And no time was lost in making a beginning.

The house, as bought, was an ordinary two-storey, brick edifice, fronting the Lake, at the distance of less than quarter of a mile. The view of that loveliest of American lakes was then unimpeded. Its ten miles of width diversified with islands, the four promontories that bounded the bays on the eastern side, and the whole range of the Adirondacs that guard the western shore, were a constant feast. The varied beauty of the sunsets behind those ranges of lofty mountains, and the golden glories reflected in the tranquil bosom of the lake, no pen can describe. But the house was not only utterly commonplace itself, but there were hardly any trees near it except the large orchard in the rear; and not far below it, in front, was the nuisance and eyesore of a great open brickyard, in full operation. That winter, young pines were removed from the forests a few miles distant, and planted with their frozen balls of earth in the frozen soil. Not one failed: and they are now much higher than the roof of the house,—the chief ornament of all that part of the city. It was not long before the brickyard was bought out, laid down in grass, and skirted with shade trees also. Three pupils had accompanied my Father from Boston: and plans were at once drawn for an enlargement of the building which would furnish accommodations for twelve or more. A wing was added at each end of the house. The southern was for the school-room, with dormitory above: and the lower room in the north wing was devoted to the Oratory, which was larger and more beautifully finished, by far, than the first one in Pittsburgh. The workmen began before the first of May; and before the first of July the southern wing was occupied, and all its accommodations were filled with pupils at once. Two teachers—both candidates for Orders—were at work: and there was every prospect that a still further addition would soon be needed. The north wing was finished and occupied before October.

The parish work was not neglected, as the number of confirmations shows. A full series of carefully prepared Confirmation Lectures preceded each administration of the laying on of hands. There were services, with sermon or lecture, on Wednesday and Friday as well as Sunday: and twice a day during Holy Week, with daily sermons.

But besides all, my Father—having reached his fortieth year—began his career as author by issuing, under the title of *Christianity Vindicated*, the shorter of the two series of Sermons which had now been delivered once in Pittsburgh, twice in Boston, and once in Burlington, and on each occasion had elicited many requests for their publication. The other series, on *The Primitive Creed*, appeared in the following year, 1834. Both these works were prepared originally for the pulpit, and for popular effect among persons of ordinary education. They were not designed for the controversialist or the scholar. Clearness, vigor, and a forcible and impressive mode of placing the whole subject before the mind of the honest inquirer, are the leading characteristics of my Father's style in all his works. There is never an ambiguous sentence;—never a period which needs to be read over twice before one can understand exactly what was meant to be conveyed. But in preparing these sermons for the press, there was added, to each volume, a *Dissertation*, in which was contained such further examination of various points as would have been unsuitable in a popular discourse. Each of these works bore abundant testimony to that which was the fundamental principle of all my Father's publications, the primary authority of the Primitive and Undivided Church in deciding all questions of controversy among Christians. In the summer of 1833, he delivered the Commencement Address to the students of the General Theological Seminary; the burden of which was, the necessity of the study of the Fathers as the basis of all sound theology, and illustrating the general principle by a special consideration of the value of S. Irenæus. A copy of the Address, on the motion of the Bishop of New York, was indeed requested for publication:[1] but the prevailing tone of that noble Institution was then so little in accord with Patristic lore, that for some time the author of the address was currently spoken of in the Seminary under the *sobriquet* of "Father Irenæus." In the

---

[1] The request was declined.

Dissertation appended to *The Primitive Creed*, a large portion of the space was devoted to the Socinian difficulties which were then so rife in New England, and which had not been always satisfactorily treated by their so-called "orthodox" opponents among the Congregationalists. In his quotations from the Fathers, the original was always added at the foot of the page, so that the correctness of his translation might be verified by scholars at once, without the trouble of referring to volumes which were then accessible in but few American libraries, public or private. This custom was continued in nearly all his subsequent works.

On meeting his first Convention, in 1833, my Father earnestly set forth the great needs of the Diocese, the constant losses by emigration, and the impossibility of obtaining any aid from without. Local effort was their only hope: and he specially urged that parents should piously devote their sons to the work of the ministry, bringing them up to regard that holy office as the highest on earth, and with the hope that the Spirit of God would call them to it when they came to man's estate. And he added: —"I wish it to be understood that, until better arrangements for the purpose can be made, I shall cheerfully give a portion of my house, my time, and my library, to those whose hearts are led to honor their Redeemer by devoting their lives to the ministry of His Word." In response to his Address, resolutions were adopted, in general terms, favoring the formation of a Diocesan fund for the education of young men for the ministry: but nothing came of it.

On the 10th of August, in this first year of his Episcopate, his mother very suddenly yet peacefully departed this life, in Philadelphia, and was buried in S. Andrew's Church-yard. Only three months before her death, he had received from her a large and beautiful historical painting, supposed to be by Parmegiano; and the letter which she wrote to accompany it gives characteristic proof both of his ready and filial self-sacrifice, and of his mother's romantic intensity of affection for him. She tells him that she sends the picture, "which I beg my son's acceptance of, as a slight memorial of his mother's love, and some equivalent for the beautiful mirror and timepiece he on one occasion so promptly sacrificed to his mother's service:—a sacrifice so repugnant to my feelings that I have ever since hated the sight of the handsome carpets that were the original cause of my sudden demand on your financial resources at the time. In consequence of which the carpets remain as good as ever, carefully sewed up in a bale, and excluded at once from sight and use; ever since your departure from this city, when, on one of your clerical visits, they had been laid down for your reception."

In 1834 his Address very strongly and clearly took the ground so long maintained by Bishop White,[1] that there should be no official mingling with the ministry of the denominations: and this drew upon him some sharp criticism from Low-Church quarters. He also strongly affirmed that it belonged properly to the office of a Bishop that he should be recognized as the Judge, by whose construction of the laws and rules of the Church his diocese is to be governed: but he never held this in the absolute sense, as excluding an appeal to the rest of the Episcopate.

Towards the latter part of the year, the Oratory was still further adorned. An Altar, raised on several steps, stood at one end, under a wide window, with the lectern on one side and the pulpit on the other. Cluster shafts, at a slight distance from the walls, formed spaces which were filled with bookshelves, where rested the heavy tomes of the old Fathers, covered from sight by doors of panelled woodwork. The floor was painted after the pattern of a tessellated pavement: and muslin transparencies, painted in well-meant imitation of stained glass—the reality being then unknown in this country—gave the "dim religious light."[2] Tablets of illuminated texts appeared upon the walls. Works of somewhat similar kind were wrought for the parish Church also, thus relieving a little the white bareness of the walls as

[1] Bishop White, in his semi-centennial Charge entitled "*The Past and Future*," expresses the hope that the Clergy "may consistently sustain this point of the divine institution of the Episcopacy, not accommodating, in the least degree, to the contrary opinion. When this characteristic of our Communion is lost sight of, under any specious plea of accommodation to popular prejudice, instead of being conciliatory, as is imagined, it brings conflicting opinions into view, to the loss of Christian charity; or, if this be not the consequence, to the sacrifice of a truth of Scripture." See Dr. McVickar's *Early Life and Professional Years of Bishop Hobart*.

[2] The window immediately over the Altar bore a Chalice, with a legend which seemed prophetic of the troubles and disappointments yet to come: *The Cup which My Father hath given me, shall I not drink it?*

they stood at first. In all these things he was not only the architect, but he also began the work and framed the models with his own hands, and then made his oldest son the chief workman, thus training him to love every part of the labor of adorning the sanctuary of the Lord.

On the first day of December in that year (1834) he started on a visitation, leaving his whole family in their usual good health. On the ninth day of that same month he returned to find that an epidemic typhoid fever had invaded his household, that seven of his own children were down with it, besides six of the pupils, and one of the servants. The thoroughness of his unselfish devotion to the cause of Education was now brought to a sharp test. There never was a more affectionate father: yet on thus finding his home become an hospital, he at once said to the attending physician that if it should please Providence that any should die, he trusted that one of his own flock might be called, rather than one of the pupils: that no shade of doubt might be thrown upon the entire integrity with which he received and treated the children of strangers, as if they were his own. It pleased God to take him at his word: and the only one who died during that grievous season was his third daughter, Melusina, in her eleventh year,—the loving, merry-hearted, beaming sunshine of the house. Delirium prevailed during almost the whole of her illness; and her Father, writing of its close on Saturday afternoon, said:—" We knelt around her bedside twice, once before and once after the final moment, committing that precious soul to the God who gave it." Already, in a sequestered part of the ground purchased by my Father, a lot had been marked out and set apart for a cemetery, and planted round about with evergreens; and there, a few months previous, his venerable mother-in-law had been laid, in the fulness of a ripe old age. The young now followed the old. The Church part of the service was performed in the Oratory, and my Father, though now and then with a trembling voice, standing upon the snow, himself committed his darling to the frozen earth. The whole family stood round that open grave: and my Father's help-meet was one who could thus reply, not long after, to the condolence of a dear friend:—

I assure you that I have never felt so great peace and happy enjoyment in my religion, as during this strange season of sickness and death, that visited our late so happy and so healthy family. I felt that it must be the will of the Most High to remind us that this is not our abiding place; and to teach us to look still more diligently and more watchfully for that change which sooner or later we are all to experience. Oh! there is nothing on this earth so sure to draw our souls nearer to the Fountain of Life, and to bring us into closer communion with the unseen world, as to watch the last moments of a beloved relative; and if that relative be an own child, so lovely, so holy and so pure, that no doubt can possibly be entertained of her removal to the blessed company of the redeemed, the transports of love and gratitude that fill the soul of the doting mother almost amount to a foretaste of that joy which the immediate presence of our adorable Redeemer alone can inspire.

On the day after the funeral, my oldest sister, with her husband and child, left us for a temporary sojourn in Vergennes,—her husband being rector of the parish there; and thus more room was made in the crowded house for the proper care of the sick. At the time of their leaving, *nine* were still unable to move, and the services of six watchers were needed every night. But all, in due time, by the blessing of God, recovered. It was the only epidemic visitation the family ever knew: and was fatally prevalent at the time through the whole region round about.

In the Convention of 1835 the Bishop again assured his Clergy that "in these days of emigration" the Church in Vermont could not increase, or even be sustained much longer, unless some zealous effort were made to encourage and support students of theology. Thirteen towns were wanting clergymen; and he found it "painful and distressing beyond expression to know of these wants, to be applied to for their supply, and to have nothing in his power to relieve them." He urged immediate and decisive action, for the raising of a fund for the aid of students and the support of Diocesan Missions.[1] Resolutions were accordingly adopted, favoring both objects more emphatically than before: but nothing came of it.

Thrice during the course of the year 1835 my Father accepted kind invitations to visit Montreal and Quebec, and two of the sermons preached by him in Quebec, *On the Religious Education*

---

[1] Vermont has never asked or received a dollar from the Domestic Committee.

of the Poor, were printed by request. The important assistance of the Rev. Mr. Stewart[1] in securing the benefits of the Church lands in Vermont, had begun the cordial intercourse between Vermont and Canada. It was fostered by Bishop Griswold's visit to Montreal and Quebec in 1826. And this invitation to my Father was only the first of many occasions during his Episcopate, which strengthened the feeling of brotherhood between the two Churches by acts of mutual kindness and high esteem. His residence being nearer to Canada than that of any other of our Bishops then, the interchange of courtesies between the two Churches fell naturally, on our side, chiefly to the share of the Bishop of Vermont: and this pleasant tradition of the see has already descended to his successor. The popularity resulting from these visits to the Canadas opened fresh sources of supply for the school at Burlington: and friends in Quebec were so enthusiastic as to say that that city alone would fill all the accommodations that the Bishop of Vermont should provide.

My Father's third volume, *The Primitive Church*, appeared about the same time, and attracted far more attention than his previous works. In his book on the Creed, he had passed lightly over the article concerning the Holy Catholic Church, intending to enlarge upon that in this treatise. Nor is its form such as the abstract proportions of theology would suggest, but rather such as a free and popular handling of the current issues of the day would require. It opens with an allusion to the Church on the day of Pentecost, and adds:—

That Church still exists, to attest the truth and power of its divine Master. . . . And still, those who would be saved must be added unto it, must profess the same repentance and faith, and receive the same ordinances, and hold communion with its ministry, for there is no other mode revealed whereby we may enter the Kingdom of Heaven.

With the keynote thus sounded on the first page, there could be little doubt as to the general bearing of the rest. In the *Second* and *Third* Lectures the doctrine of Baptism was considered, and the usual quotations from the Prayer Book and the Articles were made and thus summed up :—

Now these various passages concur in the doctrine, that regeneration,

---

[1] Afterwards the Lord Bishop of Quebec.

or the new birth, is granted in baptism. I know that much ingenuity and labor have been spent in the effort to extract some other meaning from them, but, in my mind, with no other effect than to show how good men may waste their strength in support of any favorite theological error. For myself, I consider the doctrine of the Church too plain for equivocation.

Describing the yet unbaptized penitent, he says:—

What should we say of such an one? That he is regenerate? No. That he is born of God? No. But that he is penitent, contrite, converted, and changed by the power of divine grace, in order that he *may become* regenerate, in order that he *may be* born again in the way appointed by Christ,—of water and of the Spirit.

And then describing the act of baptizing such an one, he says:—

The Minister of Christ, by the authority of his Divine Master, pours upon his head the water of baptism. His name is forthwith registered in the book of Life, the Grace of Adoption descends upon him, and he is received into the family of the heavenly King, the child of God, born of water and the Spirit—regenerate—forgiven—washed—sanctified—the heir of glory.

And in regard to the baptism of infants, he says:—

The Spirit of God, in receiving the infant consecrated to Christ by baptism, not only adopts him as an heir of immortality, not only grants him the remission of sins, not only registers his name in the book of Life, but also gives him a *Spiritual blessing*, which blessing I am willing to understand as the first pulse of spiritual life in his soul,—the earnest, if I may so express myself, of all the future influences of divine grace—the dawning ray of that heavenly light which is in due time to arise upon his heart as the Sun of righteousness—the germ of sanctification.

This doctrine was abundantly proved from Holy Scripture, the Fathers, and the Reformers, both English and Continental.

The *Fourth* Lecture taught "the giving of the Holy Ghost" through the laying on of the Bishop's hands in Confirmation. The *Fifth* defended the Church for showing no sympathy with the modern Revival System.

The *Sixth* made more noise than all the rest of the book put together. It was the first printed proof given by my Father of that rare gift, the power to stand out, solitary and alone, in the midst of the whirlwind of a widespread popular excitement, not only perfectly free from any sympathy with it, but daring, with equal coolness and clearness, to lay bare the fatal error that formed the root of it, to demonstrate without passion or exaggeration the certain failure of it, and then to maintain an unwavering calmness and quietness of spirit under all the rage and froth of popular abuse. The "Temperance Reformation" was then in the height of its first triumphant popularity.[1] My Father was the first to prove, publicly, that the triumph of such a Reform, on its own methods and principles, would be the triumph of infidelity: and that true Christians could not have anything to do with new-fangled modes of recovering men from the power of any sin, without thereby confessing and condemning the failure of Christ and His Church, and proclaiming to all the world that they had now invented a better plan. It is not easy, at this date, to realize the bitterness of the fanatical wrath outpoured upon my Father for this brave and unanswerable Lecture. Charges of personal devotion to the bottle were freely made, as a matter of course, and for many years were devoutly believed in many quarters. Hardly a single issue of any leading Temperance periodical appeared, during more than a year, without some labored article, or vituperative fling, at the abominable Bishop of Vermont. As to his personal habits, it would have been hard in those days to find any one more abstemious. His usual dinner on Fridays was only a cup of tea and a piece of dry toast. His only beverage, besides tea and cold water, was sometimes a little very weak wine and water, making a slightly acidulated drink, shortly before going to bed at night. But at the time of writing the Temperance Lecture, he stopped even that, and became practically a teetotaler. If in company where wine was used, he filled his glass, and perhaps would touch it once to his lips: and would then leave it full beside his plate. Even in his old age, and when it was prescribed, in small quantity, by his physician, it was almost impossible to get him to take anything of the sort. But the advocates of "Temperance" manufactured their slanders, and thousands believed them, all the same notwithstanding.

The seventh Lecture of *The Primitive Church*, on Vestments

---

[1] In the February previous (1834) he had received a joint invitation from the Unitarian, Congregationalist and Methodist ministers of Burlington to unite with them in preaching a series of Temperance Sermons; and had declined, with reasons.

and Liturgical worship, is remarkable for its condemnation of the black gown, then universally worn among us in preaching. My Father says of it:—

> I am ignorant of any authority for its use, either in Scripture or in Primitive Antiquity, and must acknowledge it to be one of the few points in which the Church has yielded to a practice no older than the era of the Reformation.[1]

In the next three Lectures, the subject of Church Government was considered; and the Temple, not the Synagogue, was shown to be the true model of the Church. Episcopacy was proved to be of Divine Authority; and the proper power of Bishops was set forth as being partly patriarchal in its nature, partly judicial, and partly legislative. The closing lecture was devoted to the only possible basis of the Reunion of Christendom, namely, "the Bible and Apostolical Tradition": with the understanding that "the earlier Fathers and Councils must be taken as the best evidence of Apostolical Tradition, because they were nearest to the Apostolic day." He drew a picture—in fanciful reverie—of a great universal Council, representing all who profess and call themselves Christians, meeting to settle their differences by that great standard, and persevering in their labors for years, while all parts of Christendom were fasting and praying for the restoration of Unity, until that prayer at length should be answered. And so glorious was the thought, so entire was the rapture of his spirit in dwelling on so bright a consummation, that ere he finished he found the tears running down his face as he wrote. It was the only time in his life that any such emotion overcame him while engaged in his labors as an author.

A *Dissertation* was added, in which my Father showed his preference for using the word Church rather as coëxtensive with the *Ecclesia credens* than the *Ecclesia docens*. With Hooker he considered that all sorts of sectarians, heretics, and schismatics, are in some measure a part of the Church: but at the same time he adhered to the old maxim that *Out of the Church there is no salvation*. The former part of his opinion on this subject has often been quoted by persons who are careful to omit all refer-

---

[1] It is, in fact, due to the Preaching Friars, the black gown being the purest "rag of Popery" to be found among us.

ence to the latter part of it. Though defending the validity of lay baptism, he maintained that " a commission by ordination is as essential to the regular administration of the one sacrament, as it is to that of the other"; and that " a wanton or a needless departure from the Apostolic order of sacramental administration involves a sin of the nature of sacrilege." The idea " that the frame of our ecclesiastical polity, and the measure of Episcopal powers, must be taken from the Constitution and Canons of the American Church ; and that Bishops and Clergy have no inherent and official rights until some express provision of our own code bestows them": he regarded as an error so monstrous that he would have thought it inconceivable among Church people, had he not himself heard some persons avow it. While maintaining the inherent right of a Bishop to be the Judge in his own Diocese, he added that "in precise accordance with primitive practice, . . . an appeal should lie from the judgment of any single Bishop, to the House of Bishops, . . . whose judgment, of course, would be final. Nothing short of this provision," he added, " can be a full security for the rights of the clergy on the one hand, and for unity of principle throughout the various Dioceses, on the other." He doubted, also, the necessity or the wisdom of having a separate Constitution and Code of Canons for each Diocese. " The Diocesan Conventions," he thought, " would still have enough to do, if they were relieved of the burthen of canonical regulations." It would be well that this suggestion should not be forgotten in arranging the Provincial System of our American Church.

The attention awakened by this volume was so great, that it passed to a second edition within six months. Very complimentary notices appeared in various quarters, as some offset for the abundance of the opposite sort. The " Church Press," in New York, which at first had refused to keep my Father's books on sale, ordered a whole case of the second edition of *The Primitive Church*, and offered to sell all of his previous books, and anything that he might print thenceforward. An order for a number of copies came all the way from Scotland. Harper and Brothers, about this time, volunteered to become his publishers, issuing at their own risk anything that he might wish to print, and giving him a percentage on all sales. It would have been well had he accepted this offer. But what to do with a work after it was published, was one of the mysteries which he never learned. He seemed to think that when a book was fairly out, it would take care of itself: nor did the frequent change of publishers produce much improvement.

Chapter IX.

THE STRUGGLE FOR DIOCESAN SCHOOLS.

JUST before the General Convention met in 1835, my Father had paid a business visit to Pittsburgh, where he was most enthusiastically received by his old friends, and where he effected a sale of nearly all his remaining real estate in that vicinity, at very favorable prices. The whole was to be expended in still further enlargements of the establishment at Burlington. The demands from all quarters, especially from Canada, were steadily and rapidly increasing. The buildings, intended for twenty pupils at the outside, were compelled to receive twenty-six. Before the close of the year 1835, the number was thirty-eight: and before any increase of the buildings could be made, there were fifty-two. To meet this steady and rapid demand, the accommodations of the family had been encroached on to the utmost. Rear buildings and attics had been fitted up with additional rooms, which were filled to overflowing: and yet there were more than twenty applications which had to be refused because there was no place for another bed. The increase of the Academic department involved that of the Theological department also, as the only support thus far provided for the students was their employment as assistant teachers in the school.

Before the Spring of 1836, therefore, the Bishop had prepared complete plans for a vast enlargement of his buildings, symmetrically, in both directions. The then main building was to stand, as the central portion. Two wings (each finished, towards the Lake, with an Ionic portico of four columns) stood at the distance of about forty feet from the central portion, and not so far advanced as its front line. The south wing was for the school, and its three storeys and basement would provide for about an hundred boys. The north wing, of the same size, but of different internal arrangement, had accommodations for several married professors and their families, besides some twenty theological students. In this wing my Father had his own library and work-room. Immediately in the rear of the central portion was the Hall of the Fine Arts, eighty feet long and twenty-one feet high, with a platform at one end for the domestic orchestra, and a gallery running all round it. Smaller chambers, in two storeys, united the centre and the two wings; and behind these and the Hall one straight corridor an hundred and twenty feet long connected all the three parts of the building. The Oratory, too, was to be further enlarged. As the chambers above it were no longer needed, the floor was to be removed, and the height of that storey to be added, with a proportionate increase of adornment.

When the plans for this enormous enlargement,—the front alone extending for two hundred and forty feet,—were shown to my Mother, her heart misgave her: and, as events turned out, the instinct of the woman would have been a safer practical guide than the vigorous reason of the man. She begged and implored my Father to be content as he was, or to enlarge on a much more moderate scale; for those vast buildings would not only absorb every dollar of available means, but would certainly call for some ten thousand dollars of borrowed money, to be secured on a mortgage of all his real estate in and near Burlington. But my Father's convictions, both of duty and of the happy results, were too strong to be thus shaken. Those who remember the tremendous inflation of everything for the few years culminating in 1836, will not be surprised that one whose position and avocations could not teach him any wise foresight as to probable financial revulsions, should not dream of that which came only too soon. He already had over fifty boys, and six candidates for Orders: and the applications for pupils were such as to leave no doubt on his mind that, in two or three years, his new buildings would be filled. He was now possessed of forty acres of land in one plot, with his buildings; and about two miles north of the village had purchased over four hundred acres more: the whole worth —at a moderate estimate—forty thousand dollars. He felt confident that ten thousand was not too heavy an incumbrance for that property to bear for a few years, until the increased numbers of pupils and the rise of part of his real estate in value, would enable him to pay it off. Heavy as was the burden of care upon himself, and upon every other member of his own family who was old enough to bear any part of the pressure, he yet saw no other ray of hope for supplying the great and growing wants of his diocese; and therefore he went on. The money was borrowed at bank on a note, and the endorser was protected by a mortgage on every foot of land then owned by my Father in Vermont. He was not only willing, but anxious, that the endorser should feel abundantly protected, and for himself entertained no doubt that, in a few years, all would be free again.

It was at this time,—when he thought himself worth about $40,000 above the world,—that he constantly told his numerous and growing family, that he would give them the best education in his power, specially qualifying his boys for the Ministry,—if it should please God to call them to it: but that every dollar of property he might own when he came to die, he intended to leave to the Church.

As soon as the frost was out of the ground in the spring of 1836, a little army of workmen began on the enormous scheme, the whole of which was pushed through in one season.

And as the by-play of this busy Spring, his *Essay on Gothic Architecture* was issued,—the pioneer publication on that subject, on this side of the water. He had begun the preparation for it while at Cambridge, there mastering the art of drawing on stone, and completing a number of the drawings with his own hand. At times, after removing to Burlington, a new box of prepared lithographic stones would come by stage-coach from Boston, and after some weeks would return in the same manner with fresh drawings: and thus all the lithography of that book was done by his own hands, including the ornamental title page.[1] It did a good work in its day, though pretending to nothing higher than what might fairly be aimed at by a pioneer, and an amateur at that. But it deserves mention for its earnestness in advocating costly Churches,—that " they should be the most precious of all earthly edifices"; and that everything about them should " answer to the sublime and glorious end for which they are erected." The strong denunciation of the pew system is also worthy of note, and

---

[1] As to the typography and general appearance, it was the handsomest book, up to that time, ever published in Vermont.

is made in terms wonderfully sharp and crisp for those days:—

The right to occupy a place in the House of God, and that, too, the best place, is in our day a pure matter of merchandise. It is a right sold at auction to the highest bidder. Religion has nothing to do with it. Personal piety has nothing to do with it. The seats next to the Altar, and in the immediate eye of the ministers of Christ, may be occupied by men who . . . exhibit, in the gaze of the whole congregation, a constant example of ungodliness. Still, they pay for their seats, and the omnipotence of gold covers the glaring inconsistency.

The evils of driving away the poor; of keeping vacant space unoccupied, "as if men thought it was sufficient to pay their minister, without being obliged to listen to him"; of luxuries and ostentatious upholstering; of making the pews so narrow that nobody could kneel (then almost universal): were all boldly rebuked. Many good principles were inculcated in the book, and a *Glossary* of architectural terms did much to familiarize many minds with the language of improvements which were soon to become general. The chief labor on this slender quarto had been finished long previous, and the mere seeing it through the press was a scarcely perceptible addition to the new toils of the Spring.

A very pleasant incident of the earlier part of the year 1836 was the visit paid him by his father,—the last time they ever met on earth. He spent three months with us, and it was a delight to us children to get him comfortably seated in a corner, telling us stories of our Father's early childhood. He was greatly surprised at seeing all that his son had done, and admired him intensely. "You may look all over the United States," he would say, "and may be all over the world, but you will not find one man like my John!" Not long after his return to Philadelphia, he departed in peace, after a brief illness, and was buried in Trinity Churchyard, Southwark.

My Father's interest had not been monopolized by those children whose parents were able to pay for their education. He had by this time established, and was maintaining out of his own means, a parish school in which about fifty children were taught by a worthy communicant of the Church, being faithfully instructed in the Catechism, and attending regularly on the Church services.

The number confirmed had naturally increased in Burlington until, this year, it was fifty-seven,—more than one third of the whole number confirmed in the Diocese. During these four years, however, Burlington had lost, mainly by removals, *seventy-nine* of those whom my Father had gathered in.

At the Diocesan Convention of 1836, he informed the Clergy and Laity of the building which he was erecting, and again pressed upon them the absolute necessity of training their Clergy at home in Vermont :—" If," said he, " we compel them to leave their native State in pursuit of theological education, and thus promote that spirit of emigration by which both the Church and the Commonwealth of Vermont have already suffered so severely, we certainly cannot evade the painful conviction that we have been accessories to the fault, and therefore deserve the consequences."

At this Convention the revised Constitution and Canons, which had been under consideration ever since my Father came to the see, were after discussion and some slight amendment unanimously adopted. They were mainly my Father's work, and their unanimous adoption was a high proof of the confidence felt in him, and of his great influence over his Clergy and Laity. Some features of this code have given rise to more extended discussion than that of any other Diocese in our land; and the salient points of that Constitution are therefore mentioned here.

In Article II., *Of the Church*, the Laity are defined to be " all who are admitted to the Covenant of Grace, by Christian Baptism."

In Article III., *Of the Ministry*, we read :—

The Bishop, being successor to the Apostolic Order, has the sole right to ordain, to confirm, to consecrate, to pronounce sentence on offenders, to preside over the Church in his Diocese or district, and to govern the same according to the Scriptures and the Canons. The Priests or Presbyters, nevertheless, are bound to counsel and advise him; and he does not act in any important matter without consulting with a portion of them, elected for that purpose by the rest, and called the Standing Committee or Council of Advice; neither does he exercise any legislative power, except in concurrence with the Clergy and the Laity, duly assembled in Convention.

In Article V., *Of the Convention*, we read:—

Every act of legislation requires the concurrence of the Bishop. The Clergy and the Laity may elect officers and pass resolutions of advice or recommendation, without a Diocesan; but they cannot, without Episcopal concurrence, enact, alter, or abrogate any law, or Canon.

In Article VII., of the Provision to be made for the General Fund, we read:—

At every Convention the lay delegates shall report to the Bishop the temporal condition of their respective parishes; stating their income, their debts, and the amount of their Minister's salary. When these reports are laid before the Convention, the laity shall proceed to fix the quota which each parish shall pay to the General Fund of the Diocese at the next Convention, according to the circumstances of each parish respectively. A failure to pay this quota may be accounted for satisfactorily, . . . but if it be not paid, and no sufficient excuse be offered, the parish in default shall be admonished; and if it continue in default for two successive Conventions, it may be, on motion, stricken from the list of the Diocese, until due satisfaction be made

In Article VIII., *Of the Administration of Ecclesiastical Justice*, we read:—

All cases of presentment of Clergy or Laymen . . . are tried before the Bishop, as Ecclesiastical Judge, assisted by his Council of Advice, or by other Presbyters appointed for the purpose. etc.

And in Article X., *Of Alterations*, it is provided that if an amendment be approved at one session, it shall lie over until the next annual Convention, "and if then approved by the Bishop, and by two-thirds of the Clergy, and by two-thirds of the Laity present, voting by Orders," it shall become law.

Nor were the peculiarities confined to the Constitution. In Canon 1, it is provided that whenever a vacancy of the see occurs, it shall be the duty of the President of the Council of Advice "to call a meeting forthwith," and "summon a special Convention of the Diocese to elect a successor with all convenient speed." Wardens and Vestrymen are to be chosen from among those who are "of pious and sober life and conversation." The annual Convention "shall be holden in the Church of the Bishop," unless for some special cause, the previous Convention have directed otherwise. The lay deputation of the parishes is proportional, each parish sending from one to seven delegates, according to the number of male communicants. As to the Bishop's position, we read:—

> The Bishop presides, as Bishop, in the Convention, being expected to express his opinion, from his seat, on every subject, as freely as the Judge upon the bench, or the father in his family.

The proceedings of each Convention were to be published by the Secretary, "under the supervision of the Bishop": and the sessions of the Convention were not open to the public. It is declared to be the duty of all members of Convention "to attend its sessions punctually, unless hindered by some Providential obstacle"; and Clergymen absenting themselves "may be presented for ecclesiastical censure," and parishes neglecting for two successive Conventions to send delegates, "may, on motion, be stricken from the list until they make a suitable acknowledgment. The Canon 22, *Of the Administration of Ecclesiastical Justice*, is almost identical with the one reported by the Joint-Committee of which my Father was Chairman, and passed by the Upper House, in the General Convention of 1835. The Bishop is not only recognized as, *ex officio*, the Judge in every trial, but he is not bound to decide according to the finding of his clerical assessors:—"On the verdict of these assessors, or a majority of them, the Bishop *may* rest his judgment in the case, and the sentence which he pronounces shall be recorded before the rising of the court."

These are some of the peculiar features of the Vermont Code. There is no other Diocese in the land, no matter how "High-Church" may be its reputation, which has ever acknowledged so fully, or could now secure the adoption of a Constitution and Canons so plainly embodying, the ancient inherent rights of Catholic Bishops. What has been incorrectly called the "Episcopal Veto" has been especially the subject of attack:[1] and in later years, when the Colonial Dioceses of Canada were organizing their synodical system, my Father defended this

---

[1] The Diocese of Albany has substantially adopted it in Article X. of her Constitution, in the year 1870:—"No alteration of the Constitution or Canons shall be valid without the concurrence of the Bishop, . . . and the Bishop's concurrence shall be presumed unless the contrary be openly expressed by him to the Convention after the vote of the Clergy and Laity, and before the adjournment *sine die*.

feature of the Vermont Code in a vigorous pamphlet,[1] which was not without good effect. In this pamphlet he declares that he himself was the responsible party in regard to the Constitution and Canons:—" It was my hand which prepared the report of the large Committee to whom the new Constitution and Canons of 1836 had been entrusted." He repudiates the idea that this system gives the Bishop absolute legislative power over the Clergy and Laity:—

> The Bishop has no more power over the Clergy, than they have over him. And the Laity have the very same power against Bishop and Clergy together. By what logic, then, can it be proved that such a Constitution makes the Bishop "absolute"? For if the fact that the Bishop's concurrence is necessary makes him absolute, it is evident that the Clergy and the Laity must each be equally absolute for the very same reason: so that here we should have *three absolute powers* in the same government!

The Constitution and Canons of Vermont underwent revision in 1851, at the Bishop's suggestion, but with no change in principles. The only Ecclesiastical trial ever conducted during my Father's Episcopate, took place in the November after the adoption of these Canons of 1836; and resulted in the condemnation of a priest, for certain irregularities of conduct. He was sentenced to a suspension from the ministry, until he should present to the Bishop his written declaration of sincere regret that he had given occasion for that presentment; and that, for the time to come, he would conform himself to the laws and canons of the Church, as a faithful minister thereof, according as the same might be delivered to him by the Bishop under whom he should reside. This written declaration was made within an hour, with many tears; and the suspension was at an end. One of the offences of which he was found guilty, was the unrubrical mutilation of the Baptismal service. During the more than thirty years that followed, there was no occasion for any further ecclesiastical trial in Vermont. Irregularity steadily diminished, and at length disappeared.

In the Autumn of 1836 the central part of the new buildings

---

[1] It appeared in January, 1854, in answer to a fresh assault in the *Episcopal Recorder*, and noticed at the same time some sharp points of censure that had formerly been made in the *New York Review*.

and the southern wing were ready for use, and the number of pupils rose at once to nearly eighty. Six schoolrooms were occupied with the various classes. In the dining hall, seventy feet long, over an hundred persons sate down to meat together. The Hall of the Fine Arts soon began to show the purpose of its name. A large number of engravings—among them the colored plates of Wilson's Ornithology, and the spoils of a number of other works on Natural History—were framed and hung upon the long stretch of the walls, a certain portion of space being given to cases of minerals and shells, carefully arranged and classified.

When Christmas came, the feast was kept with more animation than ever before in Burlington. For some years, there had been a gradual approximation towards the old Pittsburgh ideal of school-festivals with orchestral and vocal music, and other proofs of proficiency. The time was now ripe for far more than the Pittsburgh measure of success. A Christmas concert was given in the Hall of Fine Arts, all the music, vocal and instrumental, being (as of old) composed by my Father, besides all the words of the songs as well: and each pupil was represented on the tables in the midst of the Hall, by drawings, or paintings, or maps, or specimens of ornamental writing, or some other proof of artistic skill, the name and age of the doer being inscribed on one of the lower corners.

During the course of a few months more, the north wing was also finished, and occupied by the large number of teachers, among whom were his oldest daughter and her husband. Last and best of all, the Oratory was at length completed, with nearly double its original height. The cluster shafts now ran up to the ceiling above, connected by pierced spandrils laterally, while others crossed the ceiling, with intersecting ribs, and with a carved pendant at each intersection. The whole of the ceiling was elaborately painted in imitation of fan-vaulting, while similar panelling adorned the walls, and rich open woodwork formed the front of the narrow gallery that ran round three sides, and was entered from the second storey of the house. The picture of the Holy Family (after Raffaele) hung upon the walls in the place of honor; and even the backs of the wooden benches were painted with a fair imitation of Gothic carving. Every visitor could feel, at once, that this room was the chief joy and crown of the whole house. The daily Morning Prayer, which was always before breakfast, and the daily Evening Prayer, which was always just before retiring for the night, were brief but very impressive services. At the close of each, all remained in their places until my Father had taken his seat by the door of exit; and then, from the least to the greatest, in regular order, each boy as he passed made to him the morning or the evening salutation. On the occasion of the festivals, the whole of the invited guests went with the rest of the family into the Oratory, and the usual Evening Worship gave to all our friends their parting benediction.

The finishing touch of the exterior of the building, was the setting up of my Father's favorite motto, "*Pro Ecclesia Dei*," in large raised letters, above the eaves, high over the central doorway. It was adorned with wreaths and festoons of flowers, which were not only designed, but actually carved in the wood, by my Father's own hands, as an act of love.

Perhaps nothing can give a clearer idea of the extraordinary activity of my Father's mind, and his marvellous capacity for endurance and variety of work, than the fact that, during the year which produced all that we have spoken of, he was,—at such hours as he could snatch from Diocese, and parish, and family, and school, and theological students, and carpenters, and builders,—engaged in writing a book which far exceeded his previous volumes in its labor of learned research. It was *The Church of Rome in her Primitive Purity, compared with the Church of Rome at the Present Day*, and was confined to the one subject of the Papal Supremacy. It was thus far the best of the ripe fruits of the Patristic studies which he had now been steadily prosecuting for more than ten years, and was still to continue for nearly ten years to come. Its plan was very simple. It was an appeal to Primitive Antiquity: the examination, one by one, of all the Fathers and Councils of the early Church, down to Isidore of Pelusium; adding a summary not only of the Primitive fact and doctrine thus set forth, but also of all that has since occurred to change it into modern Roman doctrine. This book appeared early in the summer of 1837.

The opening part of that year was indeed the highest measure of success which my Father was to experience in his great educational work,—the passion of his ministerial life. With his new buildings almost filled as soon as they were opened, with his three oldest children and two sons-in-law hard at work among the numerous corps of teachers, and six or seven Candidates for Orders earning their support in the same labor, while continuing their studies and learning their duties practically[1] as well as theoretically,—the whole household numbering over an hundred,—it is no wonder that one of those thus employed, wrote, at the time:—"Busy, busy, we all are; and are likewise the happiest set of people, I believe, in the world."

But the weight that pressed on the heads of the great establishment could not be properly appreciated by the younger ones. My Father's nervous headaches came oftener than ever, and were more severe; and my Mother was oftener completely overdone with fatigue. There was one refreshment, however, which he permitted himself. He had brought home with him from Philadelphia, in 1835, a choice case of prepared colors for painting in oils, with a small stock of canvas. And occasionally, in summer time, he would take a walk of a few miles, accompanied by a son or a daughter, and spend the part of an afternoon in transferring to canvas some features of river, or rock, or lake, or mountain, from among the innumerable natural beauties lavished on the region surrounding Lake Champlain: while his companion would sit silent beside him, reading, or sewing, or knitting, and now and then glancing over his shoulder to see the progress of the picture. A quiet afternoon thus spent refreshed him for his work for many days after: and thus was slowly produced the collection of paintings by his hand which were the chief ornament of the walls of his house during the whole remainder of his life.

Often these little excursions were connected with a regular part of the school routine in summer. My Father's school had no vacations. He asked no vacations for himself; and never could understand how any one else should need them. He was

---

[1] Every Friday evening, the full Evening Service was used in the Oratory, as in Church, the students officiating, and preaching by turns: while afterwards they met for mutual criticism, and for the closing remarks by my Father.

sure that the boys, coming back at the end of a couple of months' interruption of study, had forgotten something of what they knew before, and must first make up lost ground before they could go on to fresh advances. The winter festivals, which we have already mentioned, gave a break to the usual routine which—as he thought—had, for the boys, a great part of the advantages of a vacation, without the drawbacks. And during the summer, there was not only the bathing in the lake, but Wednesday afternoon was generally appropriated to boating, fishing and rambling in the woods and over the rocks. Part of the domestic orchestra was usually on board on these occasions; and at the setting out, as well as at the return in the early twilight, the measured dipping of the oars of the three or four large boats would be accompanied by the horn, trombone and bugle heard from afar over the glassy bosom of the lake: or by some song, with a full and frequent chorus.

But the changing circumstances of the country soon began to alter all this. No one familiar with the story of those days needs to be reminded that 1836 was the climax of inflation and artificial prosperity; and that in 1837 the revulsion began. The total breakdown of the United States Bank helped to aggravate every difficulty, so that failures occurred on every side, and panic seized the minds of nearly all who were engaged in business operations. Had the brilliant promise of 1836 gone on unchanged for only a few years, all would probably have been safe. But when the revulsion came immediately, with not even one full year of respite, the financial consequences may easily be imagined.

The pressure was soon felt so plainly in Vermont, that my Father was compelled to increase his urgency with his Convention. It had been his custom, at every meeting of the Convention in Burlington, to invite all the Clergy and Laity in attendance to either a dinner or a supper at the Bishop's house. In 1837 this custom was kept up, but with better facilities than ever. The tables were spread in the Hall of the Fine Arts, and a full musical festival followed, the evening being closed as usual in the Oratory. In his Address, he renewed his pressure upon the Clergy and Laity to provide for the training of their own clergy. He alluded to the policy adopted in Ohio, Virginia and other

Dioceses; " and if," said he, " this plan is adopted by those parts of the Church to which the tide of emigration carries such large accessions, how much more necessary is it for us, from whom the same tide of emigration takes so many away." He called attention to the enlargement of his buildings, and the number of candidates then living with him, and begged them to provide a moderate salary for a resident Professor of Theology.[1] He did not, as yet, doubt his ability to carry his chief burden alone. A Committee was appointed, and its report was unanimously adopted, accepting such part of the Bishop's house for the accommodation of theological students as he could spare for the purpose, and providing for the election of a Theological Professor, whose salary of $600 a year was to be assessed on the parishes. An acceptable clergyman of the Diocese was elected Professor. The Laity, as a separate order, voted the assessment of the $600, and provision was made for a Board of Trustees, with full powers to make regulations and statutes, and procure an Incorporation for the Theological Seminary. But the new Professor shortly after accepted a call to the Diocese of Delaware: and the resolutions adopted came to nothing.

One disappointment now trode close upon the heels of another. The " hard times " had compelled the parents of nearly half the boys to remove them, while others could not meet their bills. Then the Canadian troubles broke out, and, with the " sympathizing " all along our frontier line, the " rebels " were able to protract their exertions so far as to lead to no little embitterment of the public mind in Canada. The pupils sent from there were all from the loyal portion of the people : and in the then excited state of the public mind, it was impossible for loyal people to keep their sons at school in the United States. They were all, therefore, called home; thus reducing the pupils to about one-third of their former full number. This change compelled the discharge of as many of the teachers as possible : and

---

[1] In that same Address, my Father very forcibly enlarges upon the practical loss of the Diaconate among us, and rightly infers that the odium of not being the Church of the poor arises mainly from insisting on full literary qualifications for all our Clergy. He advocates strongly the ordination of Deacons with no knowledge of any language but English ; and states that this was Bishop White's idea also. The Canons have, since then, rendered this possible.

(on emerging from the sick-chamber to which a severe dislocation of the left shoulder had confined him for some weeks) my Father transferred his own desk into the schoolroom, and heard recitations himself in Latin, Greek and French. In the intervals between recitations he began and made good progress in lithographing the plates for the *Vermont Drawing Book of Landscapes:*[1] and he meditated the preparation of a complete series of Church school books. Meanwhile, no exertion was spared by him to put off the coming crisis, by loans obtained from kind friends in Troy, New York and Philadelphia, in the hope that some change in the financial and political condition of the country would permit the revived success of the school, and the completion of the original plans.

But the financial condition of the country would not improve; and the prospect began to grow darker. In his Address in 1838, my Father reminded his Convention that in less than six years the number of Clergy in the Diocese had increased from eleven to twenty-four, of whom no less than *eighteen* had been instructed and ordained among themselves:—

> For my own part, so earnest have I been on the subject of education, that I have devoted myself, and my family and my whole property, as most of you know, to an establishment for that purpose, on a scale which cannot be called discreditable either to our Church or to our State.

Finding the burden too heavy for his own shoulders, however, he now proposed to transfer it to the Diocese at cost. " It was my intention," said he, " to have left this property to the Church as a legacy, should it please God to prosper my labors so as to put it in my power. But I have been led to believe that the object designed would be much better accomplished if the establishment should immediately present the aspect of a public institution." He proposed to give his own services in the attempt to raise funds for the transfer, both abroad and at home: and as there was need for the execution of fresh papers by the Society for the Propagation of the Gospel, in regard to their lands in Vermont, he offered to attend to that business for the Diocese also, while he should be in London.

[1] See page 270 *post.*

The desired resolution concerning the lands was easily passed. But touching the Vermont Episcopal Institute, a Committee appointed on that part of the Bishop's Address reported that, for various reasons, they " did not feel themselves able, with their present limited opportunities for consultation and reflection, to recommend a definite plan for the action of the Convention at that time, and therefore begged to be discharged from the further consideration of the subject." After all that their Bishop had said and done, this was a marvellously cool way of showing their appreciation! But in the afternoon of the same day they thought a little better of it, and embodied their excuses more formally in other resolutions, recommending the consideration of the important question to the next Convention, and adding " that this Convention highly appreciates the very energetic and self-sacrificing efforts of its Bishop in the great cause of Education; and recommends his noble enterprise to the Christian favor and liberal aid of the Sister Dioceses in this country, and of the Mother Church in England; provided he shall see fit to present his plans and make his appeal either to one or both of them." Even this conditional permission to apply for aid from abroad was only carried after a sharp debate, in which my Father was left to bear the brunt of the battle all by himself.

The weakness of the Diocese, the absence of any experience which could then have given them enlarged ideas or sympathies on any subject, and the fact that this phase of mind and feeling was paralyzed into panic by the then condition of the country, must plead some excuse for an apathy which would otherwise be hard to comprehend. From Burlington itself,—not only the strongest parish in the Diocese then, but the one where the most had been done, and was then doing, to increase the strength—the stream of emigration was so great, that the list of Communicants lengthened but slowly. Had the large numbers confirmed been retained, the 55 Communicants whom my Father found on the list in 1832 would have increased to 300 in 1838. But one hundred and seventy-five had disappeared in those six years, and only one hundred and twenty-five remained. What could keep up the hope and courage of the other parishes in the Diocese, when such was the condition of the strongest and most flourishing among them? Just after the Convention, one of his leading laymen very correctly stated the case in a letter to him:—

> I am well aware of the greatness of the undertaking to plant the Church among a people ignorant of her principles, hostile to her practices, and whose prejudices are stubborn and unyielding as their own mountains. But most disheartening of all is it, to have those who should cordially and kindly coöperate with us, freeze the weak with chilling doubts, and alarm the timid with unmanly fears. And yet so it is, in all human affairs. The eye that looks ahead with a wide and piercing gaze, and realizes the future by a keen perception of the present and the past, must ever be tormented by the faltering steps of those to whom much is doubtless dark, because much is beyond their reach of vision. Still, I indulge the hope that you will not be discouraged, as I know you will not be dismayed, for we know that the most brilliant gem must be wrought with incredible labor from the hardest stone; and I doubt not, in times that are to come, when the stream of emigration is checked, and wealth and population are accumulated, the towers of our churches will rise above every village, and the deep resounding melody of our organs be heard throughout the land.

Of the hardness of the stone there could be no doubt: it remained to be seen whether it could be wrought into a gem.

The Convention was held about the middle of October, and all needed preparations for a long absence were speedily made. The work to be attempted was a great work: but still heavier upon my Father's heart weighed the burden which he was leaving upon her who remained behind. The chief authority and responsibility of the whole establishment had always been left in my Mother's hands during all previous absences, which had seldom exceeded a month at a time: and never had her willingness, her hope or her courage, failed to carry her through the ordeal, although those absences were the heaviest trial of her life. To ask her now to bear the burden for four or five months (it proved to be eight) in one stretch, was hard: but as it was the only chance for saving all that had thus far been done, the consent was given and the responsibility undertaken, with a ready courage and loving cheerful face, though with a trembling and an aching heart. After their parting, and before sailing, my Father wrote her:—"The fear that I have imposed too great a task on your affection and your magnanimity, grieves me more than I can tell you."

He knew that, in the then state of business, and for an object so remote from the popular sympathies of the great cities as Vermont, it would be useless to attempt to raise money in the United States; and England was his only hope.

Chapter X.

EFFORT ABROAD, AND FAILURE AT HOME.

WHILE making his little purchases before going on board the packet-ship in New York, my Father bought among other things a life-preserver. This was contrary to his usual principle. He never insured his life or any property of his own, and never placed a lightning-rod on his house. He said that, to him, these acts would appear to show a want of full faith and trust in God, by whom even the hairs of our head are numbered. He had not gone more than a few steps from the door of the shop where he bought the life-preserver, when his heart smote him, as if he had distrusted his God: and immediately returning, he begged, and obtained, permission to exchange the life-preserver for an umbrella, being willing to use a human defence against rain if not against lightning or storm.[1] This done, he went his way, happy once more. The good ship S. Andrew, sailing from New York on Friday, the 16th of November, carried him rapidly and safely, though somewhat roughly, to Liverpool, where he landed on Sunday, the 2d of December. They had passed on the outer edge of a tremendous storm, which drove twenty-seven sail on the coast of Ireland; while another packet-ship being compelled to put to sea to avoid the same fate, had all her canvas blown to tatters. On her return voyage, the good ship S. Andrew foundered, and was seen no more.

The first person upon whom he called, in Liverpool, was the American Consul,—no other than his old friend Francis B. Ogden,[2] whose welcome was all that he could have expected. One of his earliest visits, of course, was to the neighboring Cathedral of Chester, and after divine service he spent some time

---

[1] My Father never taught this as a duty: it was a matter simply of personal feeling in himself as an individual. He blamed no one for insuring, or for using lightning-rods or life-preservers.

[2] See *ante*, pp. 50, 51.

"walking through the venerable pile, not without some regret that the Reformation had failed to cherish those peculiar customs which made the Cathedrals of former days so attractive and imposing." His first attempt at raising money for the Vermont Episcopal Institute was in his native city of Dublin, the season not being yet sufficiently advanced for operations in London. He was very kindly received, and gained many warm friends. The Archbishop of Dublin, Dr. Whately, gave him the largest subscription made by any one abroad (£50), and his conversational powers were a rich treat to my Father. As to the two parties in the Church, he found that "the Archbishop seemed to enjoy the advantage of belonging to neither, if it can be called one;[1] although he did not appear to be a connecting bond between them." And it was well that my Father states this advantage in the hypothetical form. It may be desirable for some purposes; but the raising of money for Church objects is not one of them. And this was one of my Father's chief difficulties. He did not appear as a partisan committed to either side. He moved among the leaders on both sides, and both received him kindly, and gave very moderately: but neither made any great exertion in his behalf. He preached and lectured several times in Dublin, and presided at a Clerical meeting for the comparing of their views on the prophecies. He was just beginning to reap some tangible fruits for the Vermont Episcopal Institute, when the terrible hurricane of the night of January 7th —the worst known for many years—produced such distress and so many urgent claims for sufferers on the spot, that it was hardly worth while to persevere then and there.

On the 18th of January he arrived in London, and was very kindly received by the Archbishop of Canterbury (Dr. Howley)

---

[1] Further acquaintance with Archbishop Whately's writings did not increase my Father's admiration for him. In answer to a letter of mine, two or three years later, about Whately's treatment of the Apostolic Succession, my Father wrote:—" As to the Archbishop's book, it is, just as you have characterized it, pure Erastianism, altogether inconsistent with his position as a scholar, and still more as a divine. Many great names among the Presbyterian ranks have said much more in favor of Episcopacy than he. But in truth no Churchman now cares a farthing about his opinions, nor has he had much weight amongst thoroughbred theologians at any time. His case is one of a very common class, where the load of theology is so light, that literature and politics run away with it."

and the Bishop of London (Dr. Blomfield), who both subscribed; indeed he had on his list not only the four Archbishops but fourteen Bishops besides, together with a large number of leading names among the nobility and gentry: but all for moderate sums.

It is pleasing to find on his brief and fragmentary diary while abroad, notices of the kindly estimation in which other American Bishops were then held. In one family, where he was a guest, he says:—"They had a great deal to say of our excellent Bishop McIlvaine, who was chiefly their guest during his last visit to England, and was a prodigious favorite with them, and every one else who knew him." The only thing he records of Bunsen, whom he met at a dinner party, is that he was "the particular admirer of Bishop Hobart, with whom he had a great deal of intercourse in 1824, while the Bishop was at Rome for his health." And after dining with Mr. Gilbert (of the publishing house of Gilbert and Rivingtons), he records:—"He told me that Bishop Hobart used to spend the greater part of his Sundays with him, reading in his study, and loving to be retired, quiet, and alone." He records also the impression produced by Bishop Chase at his first visit,—an impression of primitive sanctity so profound that on one occasion a Clergyman at one of the Universities was so overcome by it, that, being alone with the Bishop, he fell on his knees and begged his blessing.

At that time, the Act of Parliament prohibiting our American Bishops and Clergy from preaching or ministering in the churches of England had not yet been altered: though, during my Father's visit, and in some measure owing to its influence, the amendment was prepared, and put upon its passage. It did not become law, however, until after he left: and it was another point of the singular coincidences that linked my Father and Bishop Doane, that the liberty which my Father had helped to procure, Bishop Doane should be the first to enjoy, preaching the Sermon at the consecration of the new parish church in Leeds on the 2d of September, 1841. Not being able to preach in England (in Ireland the law was different), my Father was willing to avail himself of any other modes of gaining publicity that might be open to him. In February, at the Freemasons' Hall in London, there was a great meeting presided over by Lord Ashley (now the Earl of Shaftesbury), at which, after three hours of speaking, and at the close of a popular harangue by the Rev. Hugh McNeile, my Father was unexpectedly called on. That he should have been able, ever so briefly, to hold the attention of a wearied crowd, would have been no slight proof of power: but yet he actually made a speech, under such circumstances, declared by the Chairman to be "invaluable," and by others to be "one of the most important speeches of the meeting," while the interest of the crowded audience was enthusiastically kept up to the very last. At a meeting subsequently held in aid of the Society for the Propagation of the Gospel he offered the first resolution, sustaining it in a vigorous speech.

The arrangements which he desired to be made touching the Church lands in Vermont were cordially approved, in substance; and were gradually passing through all the forms needful for their legal validity.

My Father had brought with him a number of copies of his books, hoping that the judicious presenting of them in certain quarters might aid him in his chief work. He was very agreeably surprised to find that the latest of them—that on *The Church of Rome*—was already well known, and highly commended by those whose good opinion was best worth having. The Archbishop of Canterbury had read the work, and expressed himself in very handsome terms in regard to it; as did so many others that it would be difficult here to give even the names of them all. The suggestion was often made to the author that he should publish an English edition of the work,—the American being a very provincial looking volume; and at length he became satisfied that it could not hinder, and would be much more likely to help, the main object which he had in view. The Rev. Henry Melvill—then the most popular preacher in London—had expressed so high an opinion of the treatise,[1] that he at once accepted the proposal to be the English sponsor, and wrote a very complimentary *Introduction*, with which the Rivingtons

---

[1] Before seeing my Father, he had read the whole volume twice, parts of it three times, and had declared his intention to read it yet again.

undertook to publish at their own risk. The first proof was read on the 16th of March, and sixteen days finished the volume. Many gratifying notices appeared in newspapers and reviews; and the Bishop of Llandaff (the Dr. Copleston who was Provost of Oriel College during the first years of Mr. Newman's residence there), in publishing a couple of sermons, named that work as the third in a list of five which he "most recommended to those who desired to acquaint themselves more thoroughly with the subject" of Romanism. Moreover, in a *Pastoral Address* on Roman Catholic Errors (1841) the same prelate, on the point of the Supremacy of the Pope, again names the Bishop of Vermont's book to his readers, as a work which, alone, would be found sufficient to satisfy their minds. He quotes a large portion of Mr. Melvill's commendation, and adds:—"I would willingly transcribe the whole of Mr. Melvill's *Introduction*, if anything more were requisite to induce you to peruse the admirable treatise which it recommends."[1] And the Bishop then goes on to defend his old friend Mr. Newman, in his "latest publication":—"He has been, I think, unjustly accused of leaning towards Popery,— for his language has been strong and unequivocal in condemning the usurpation, and the corrupt, unscriptural tenets, of that Church:" and the defence is with equal warmth extended to Dr. Pusey.

Immediately after correcting the last proofsheet of his book, my Father paid a three days' visit to Oxford. He had had some previous correspondence with Mr. Newman, through whom a set of his books had been presented to one of the Oxford Libraries,[2] and who had kindly offered to be his host. On his arrival he found his rooms in Oriel College ready for him, cheerful with a pleasant coal fire, and every possible attention rendered his brief stay not only pleasant, but somewhat profitable also. Beside others then prominent in the University, he met Dr. Pusey, Henry W. Wilberforce, and Churton: but Keble was not then at Oxford. He went out to Littlemore, and carefully sketched and

---

[1] The fact that this strong commendation appeared more than two years after my Father had returned home, proves that it was not due to that politeness which sometimes says handsome things of a person only because he is present to hear them.

[2] That of Oriel College.

noted all the chancel arrangements at the new and then famous S. Mary's. And on leaving, he thus sums up his impression of the Oxford men : "Certainly I was greatly pleased with them."

Immediately on leaving Oxford he once more visited Dublin, to attend the Anniversaries there : which was darting at once to the opposite theological pole from Oxford. On the 9th of April and the three following days he was fully occupied, having one or more speeches to make each day, and being called on to preside at two or three of the meetings. Dr. Hugh McNeile, he found, was the *magnus Apollo* of these meetings, being "looked up to as a kind of oracle, with extraordinary confidence and admiration." The Rev. R. J. McGhee—one of the bitterest and most unmeasured assailants of Rome—divided the honors with Dr. McNeile. At one of the clerical meetings there was some disorderly debating, which was afterwards commented on in the papers : the gentlemen being too much excited against the Oxford divinity to be able to exercise due control over themselves. On one occasion, finding that he was expected to take part with dissenting ministers at the Bible Society meeting, the Bishop of Vermont declined the invitation to offer one of the resolutions. He declined also to officiate at an early Evangelical prayer-meeting. He offered one of the resolutions, however, at a public Missionary meeting, and was very warmly applauded. The anti-Papal tone of the whole affair, however, was too violent and bitter for his taste. He noted it as "being, on the whole, a sort of thing which I did not relish, though it was interesting to see so many good men, engaged so zealously in trying to do good, however little I might like some things about the *modus operandi*."

On his way back to London, two days, far more pleasant, were spent at Oxford with Mr. Newman and his friends : and thence he went to Town to take some share in the May anniversaries, which many of his friends thought to be the best way of forwarding his chief work. He spoke on a number of occasions, and in company with many distinguished men. Probably the most noticeable was his moving the second Resolution at the anniversary of the Bible Society, when, on the subject of Tradition, he gave them an amount of sound Church teaching such as had seldom been heard at a meeting of that Society. The

Bishops of Winchester and Chester both told him that in this he had done what a *native* could not have ventured to attempt, in those days of controversial agitation. At a meeting of the British Reformation Society he found that the Hall was not half filled, nor the platform either. He had undertaken—by request—to move the printing of the Report, with a speech :—" a duty rather embarrassing," he writes, " because I found its language more *ultra* than suited my sentiments with regard to the Roman Catholic question. I got through it as well as I could, and retired immediately afterwards." At the meeting for the Jews, he moved the second resolution, being followed by the Chevalier Bunsen. And not long afterwards he spoke at a meeting for aiding the instruction of the Irish in their native tongue, and at another in support of the Colonial Church Society. He was a guest at one of the Archbishop of Canterbury's state dinners; and was presented at Court, attending both a *levée* and a Drawing-room: but he did not attend her Majesty's Grand Ball, though he was invited, and was accordingly published in the *Times* as present on that occasion.[1]

Every means of making himself and his object known among those who were influential and wealthy, was thus turned to account. His book was most handsomely noticed and spoken of, and sold fairly. His speeches at public meetings made him known to many thousands whom he would otherwise never have seen. The impression produced by him in social intercourse, as is evident from letters, was happy in the extreme, a more than usual charm being found in the songs of his own composition, words and music, which he sang with great sweetness, accompanying himself on the piano.[2] The array of distinguished names on his subscription list was remarkable for its comprehensiveness. His diligence in turning every opportunity to advantage for his main object was indefatigable. The hope of ultimate success induced him to prolong his stay further and further, until the

---

[1] It is taken for granted that all who are invited are present, and their names are published accordingly.

[2] Twelve of these "*Canzonets*" were printed shortly before he left London; and were afterwards reprinted in New York. In 1867, while in England, I met several persons who vividly remembered the impression produced upon them by my Father's songs nearly thirty years before.

expected four or five months' absence proved, in reality, to be eight. And yet he did not succeed. The total amount realized, over his expenses, was less than $4000.

There was more than one reason for this unsatisfactory result. In the first place, the cream of the enthusiasm for America had too recently been skimmed by Bishop Chase first and Bishop McIlvaine afterwards, and the third reaper in such a field could hardly expect much beside gleanings. Then they had the exciting theme of the Great West, and its marvellous growth, to stimulate the imaginations of their English friends: but who could expect to kindle equal enthusiasm by a tale of gradual dwindling, and an apathy so great that nothing at all had as yet been done for Vermont in the United States? The proximity of the Canadas—a main part of my Father's claim for English assistance—was rather a hindrance than a help just then; for the American sympathy with Canadian "rebels," and the boundary quarrel in Maine, had provoked at the time no little public excitement against America, in the English mind. The English Church, moreover, was at that time preöccupied, to an extraordinary degree, with efforts for Colonial extension such as had never been known before: and the necessity of doing something to resist the advance of Romanism in England itself, was, with many, a sufficient reason for taking no real interest in anything abroad. These obstacles met my Father at every turn. Then, in the practical management of his campaign (it being his first experience in that business), there was an error of judgment in laying out the ground too largely in his circulars. The plan looked so vast, that practical men could not easily feel the desired confidence in its realization. Nor was it possible for my Father to remain in England long enough to gather the full fruits of the favorable personal impression which he made in many quarters.

But more than all these put together, his sensitive and conscientious determination not to be identified with either party in the Church, was fatal to his success in raising any large sums of money for Church Institutions under his control. Heavy subscriptions in such matters flow only from the fullest personal sympathy: and that will not be felt where there is not the fullest concord in theological tone. Now just at that time the Oxford controversy ran very high, and was the one prominent theme of discourse at all gatherings of Church people. The Low-Church orators and organs were as fierce and furious as they well could be, though as yet Tract No. 90 had not appeared, and no important secessions to Rome had frightened timid men from their propriety. My Father had, up to that time, seen no point of serious weight in which he differed from the Oxford Tracts, and he certainly sympathized with the writers of them incomparably more than with their opponents. Yet he was jealous over himself, for fear that he might, from this very sympathy, become a partisan on their side; and, as a matter of obligation, made his advances to the Evangelicals as fully and freely as to their opponents.

Nor is it to be supposed for an instant, that this was done, as it is by a trimmer, in order that his own barque might be helped forward by breezes from both quarters. On the contrary, while at Oxford, he brought up for conversational discussion the few minor points in which he did *not* quite agree with the Tracts: and at Dublin and elsewhere he labored, amiably but earnestly, to convince the great Protestant platform orators that their language against Rome was far too sweeping and too bitter, whether measured by the standard of truth or of Christian charity. The leaders on each side were thus speedily satisfied that my Father could not be depended upon as thoroughgoing for them: and the pecuniary consequences were what might have been expected.

Early in May he received a letter from his most active Oxford friend, Mr. Newman, complaining pointedly of the Bishop of Vermont's being mixed up so largely in the anti-Oxford Dublin meetings. "All men," said Mr. Newman, "and ourselves in the number, naturally feel less drawn to those who take an active part in proceedings which are avowedly levelled against them, than to those who abstain from them." And within a few days he received another letter, from a prominent Low-Church clergyman, remonstrating in the opposite direction:—

I trust you will excuse the expression of regret at remarking in the list of books you have received for the use of your Students' Library the works of the Rev. J. H. Newman, which are regarded by the most orthodox and pious amongst our clergy and laity as being of a highly dangerous tendency. . . . I venture to offer this suggestion from apprehension that the circumstance may seriously interfere with the success of your cause by the impression it is calculated to make on the minds of others.

On that list of books there appeared donations not only from Keble and Newman and Pusey, but also from Henry and Robert Wilberforce and others of their friends, all of which did "seriously interfere," as anticipated. And in private conversation the impression was deepened, as he freely defended High Churchmen, when attacked in his presence. In his journal, for instance, he speaks of one clerical party, to which he was invited, and where there was "a good deal of kindly discussion of High Churchmanship, in which I stood almost alone, the party being quite exclusive in their views." The course which he pursued in England was the same which he had always pursued at home. It won high respect, often expressions of warm personal admiration, and he met with only one positive refusal while he was abroad: but he received no large donations from any quarter. With three exceptions (one £50, one £30 and one £25), no subscription was over £20, while some donations were as low as ten shillings. The delicate and high-toned sensitiveness with which he always kept himself free from partisan entanglements was not the short road to success in raising money. When the inspection of his list of donors showed that Mr. Newman had given exactly the same as the editor of the London *Record*, and that Dr. Pusey's subscription was for the same amount as that of Lord Ashley, the case was settled. What he received was given as a personal compliment to the man, and indicated little or no real interest in his cause.

One other reason of his failure in this peculiar field of operations, I cannot but mention. He was practically too thorough a Republican to feel the requisite zest in the pursuit of the titled personages whose favor, in an aristocratic form of society, so often gives prestige, and then success, to similar efforts for the raising of money. When, time after time, in the height of the London season, one can come away from great gatherings of great people, and mention in his diary that he met such and such people, "and several others of the gentry of title, whose names, as usual, I cannot remember": what else can be expected but a return home with a light balance at his banker's?

It was with a heavy heart, though with many bright memories of personal kindnesses shown him in England and Ireland, and much valuable knowledge and experience, that he turned his face homeward: and yet—though disappointed in the results of his journey—it was an intense happiness to see once more that dear Home from which he had never been so long an exile before. He sailed from Liverpool on the 13th of June, arriving in Burlington on the 3d of July; and then, for the first time, he learned that his youngest child had been born during his absence, his heroic wife having carefully concealed from him all knowledge of her condition lest it should disturb or hinder him in making the only effort which seemed to promise a chance of saving the fruits of so many years of hard labor.

On the third day after his return, a meeting of the leading Churchmen in Burlington was held, at which it was resolved that $10,000 could be raised in Burlington to relieve the Bishop from pecuniary embarrassment, on a pledge of his property, provided $20,000 could be raised elsewhere on the like pledge: but that his plan of a School, to be supported and conducted either by the Diocese or by individual or associated effort, was, under all the circumstances, impracticable. They furthermore thought that the interest of the Diocese required his entire Episcopal services, and that his salary should be $2000 on condition of devoting himself to his Episcopal and parochial duties.

This was not a very promising beginning, so far as the Institution was concerned. The next day a hurried visitation of the Diocese was begun, the notices for which had been sent out by his direction while he was yet in England. The School, though with diminished numbers, had been regularly kept up during his absence, in spite of extraordinary difficulties. But satisfied, on this visitation, of the impossibility of its being maintained any longer under his control, in face of the pecuniary embarrassments and the total absence of support on the part of the Diocese, he now closed it, and the remaining pupils were sent home. He still hoped that, in other hands, it might be preserved to the Church: and therefore, at his Convention in September, after sketching his foreign tour, and stating and accounting for its meagre results, he once more urged the great work upon his Clergy and Laity:—

To establish such an Institution for this Diocese, I have devoted all my means, and best efforts, for several years; until I can truly say that I have spent and am spent in the service. Thus far, it has been a doubtful, solitary, unaided labor, without any adequate response or sympathy from the Diocese, under the prevailing impression that I had undertaken what was too great either for our ability, or for our wants, and what therefore must fail. But I trust the time is at hand for the diffusion of a far better opinion, notwithstanding the discouraging opposition of such as may have heretofore thought me guilty of the sin of attempting too much,— too sanguine in forming my plans, and too weak in their execution.

No one who can appreciate all that he had done and suffered in the cause will wonder that his voice was almost choked with emotion as he read these words, and that many who heard them were moved to tears. He went on to declare that it was his intention to withdraw from any future connection with the Institution, except that which was inseparable from his Episcopal office: and offered the Diocese the full benefit of what he had raised in England, not deducting his travelling expenses. Of the reduced amount thus needed, he had secured pledges in Burlington, Highgate and St. Alban's for nearly half, provided the rest were raised. Resolutions were adopted, as usual; and a Committee was appointed, and the Clergy and Vestries were requested, with the least practicable delay, to ascertain the amount of subscriptions that could be raised. But the responses from the parishes were so few, and for such trifling amounts, that the effort came to nothing. The unexampled distress which yet so fearfully paralyzed the great cities and the whole country, made it useless to attempt anything elsewhere.

Before the close of the year, a sheriff's sale was held on the premises, at which all the furniture needed in the school, and which had cost some six or seven thousand dollars, together with the Library and other chattels, were sold, of course at the usual low price which prevails on such occasions. The Library and sundry other articles of family comfort were bought in by personal friends for my Father's use: and the Library eventually became the property of the Diocese. It fell to my lot not only to make the preparations for that day's work, but also to accompany the auctioneer from the beginning to the end, and give such information as might be needed:—a day's work which I shall never forget. My Father spent the day in another part of the great empty house, quietly painting some fresh adornments for the parish Church: but his outward quietness covered thoughts and feelings which he never would express, and I never could.

In the following January a meeting of his creditors was held in Burlington, and my Father most earnestly begged them to take the whole of his property in Burlington, which would be found abundantly sufficient to satisfy all their claims. But they could not agree among themselves as to the best course to be pursued, the fear of fresh entanglements in the then prostrate condition of business making some of them prefer the loss of their whole debt, rather than face the risk of further outlay. During the year requisite for completing the foreclosure of the mortgage, two other attempts were made to save the buildings and four or six acres immediately around them: but these failed also. And at length the twelve months came to an end,[1] and all was over. The fruit of so many years of the most intense labor, the purest enthusiasm, the noblest self-sacrifice, was swept away for ever.

From the day when the School was closed, the domestic expenses had been governed by the most rigid economy. Except the aid of a washerwoman on Mondays and Tuesdays, there was no servant in the house. For many months, my Mother's health was seriously impaired: and that of my Aunt was still more infirm. Among all the children at home there was only one daughter, and she was but three years old. We boys, therefore, divided all the household work among ourselves; and to encourage us in this new line of activity, my Father insisted on taking his share also, and for a few mornings came down early, with a handkerchief tied over his head, and swept and dusted the two principal rooms occupied by the family. His word was always law under his roof, and we children at first did not know

---

[1] January 15, 1841.

what to do about it. To contradict, disobey or overrule him seemed absolutely contrary to nature; and this was a matter about which he was evidently minded to be obstinate. But after privately conspiring together for a few days, we finally flatly rebelled, captured the broom, and being in the majority successfully established our little revolution, the "minority of one" at length accepting our *ultimatum*, which was, that he should not make his appearance in the morning until the usual hour for prayers, and that he should let the house-work alone.

It was a dreary time, living thus, a little company, in the midst of that vast and empty house. But when it became finally and completely the property of others, a home had to be sought elsewhere in the village. The new owners had no use for the Oratory or its beautiful work: and therefore the Altar and the rest of the Church furniture, the cluster shafts and the pierced spandrils, the windows and seats and panel-work, were reverently removed. The *Pro Ecclesia Dei* was taken down from over the central doorway, though the wooden flowers were suffered to remain: and there, for more than the quarter of a century, a female seminary under Congregationalist influences has been kept up, in the very building which my Father had erected, and so earnestly labored to preserve, for the Church. Last of all, the little enclosure, surrounded with evergreens, where slept our dead, must be disturbed. It also, like all the rest, was covered by the mortgage: and therefore the bodies of those loved ones were taken up and removed to the public cemetery of the village.

The property, which passed into the hands of five gentlemen of the parish in Burlington, eventually fulfilled all my Father's anticipations of its value. At first they were as much puzzled what to do with that enormous building, as was the proverbial person who won an elephant in a raffle. But finally they removed entirely the connection between the centre and the two wings, thus making three houses out of one: which enabled them at length to find purchasers. But the rest of the land— some forty acres in all—was what my Father had always relied upon as the chief source of profit. He had planned the running of new streets, and the laying it out in town lots: and his plans were substantially followed, to good advantage. That property

—which was swept away from him in those dark and disastrous days by a mortgage for ten thousand dollars—has now long since been covered with houses, and the land alone would bring to-day over two hundred thousand dollars.

My father was not alone among our Bishops, either in his effort to establish a noble Institution for Church education, or in his failure. His old friend Bishop Doane, in another Burlington, was going through very much the same experience, but with a happier result. He, indeed, like my Father, lost his all in the work: but he succeeded in sustaining his Institutions, partly because he had more to lose, and could therefore keep up the struggle much longer; and partly, too, because his position in the neighborhood of our two greatest cities, and his personal relationships, enabled him eventually to command sources of supply which were beyond my Father's reach. Georgia, also, before many years, saw similar sacrifices followed by disastrous failure, on the part of her noble Bishop Elliott. And North Carolina, and Tennessee, and other Dioceses, could tell similar tales.

And if all these heavy losses only teach the right lesson to the Church of America, they will prove to be well worth all they have cost. That lesson is, that our usual plan of building up such institutions, on a scale which requires heavy endowments to give competent salaries to a large number of married officials; or relying mainly on the services of those who teach only for a few years as a stepping-stone to something else; or expecting to charge such prices for tuition as will pay a handsome profit to those who take the risk and do the work; or trusting entirely to family or individual interest as the chief sustaining power of a good school: is all a mistake. Small beginnings and gradual growth; under the charge of those who give themselves up to the life-work of teaching for the love of God and His Church, associated from choice and long training in the work, and—being without families and without salaries except a bare support—able to offer the best education at the most moderate price: in other words, the *revival of the Religious Orders among us*, is the only true road to success in this branch of Church work, as well as in some others; and the sooner we find it out, the better.

It is true that my Father did not, for a long while, draw this conclusion from his experience; though in his latter years he had begun to suspect it. The life of the Church, however, is a long life, even until the end of the world. We are no competent judges either of the successes or of the failures of our own day. And the fact that the full teachings of our failures are not learned except by succeeding generations, is only an additional proof that the lesson thus slowly learned is the truth.

Chapter XI.

ROCK POINT.

ON removing from the old place in May, 1841, after two years spent in vain efforts to retain a part of it for the Church, the depression of business in general and of S. Paul's parish in particular was so great, that there was no effort made to procure a parsonage, and my Father was left to find a house for himself where he could. The only building in the village then available at a rent within his means, was an aged frame-house in Pearl street, so dilapidated that we were the last tenants it could find, and after our departure it was at length turned into a carriage-maker's shop. The whole family were exceedingly incommoded in this wretched building.

Meanwhile, in setting the garden to rights, we children found occasion to go some distance for pea-rods; and as we heard that the choppers had been put into the wood-lots lately owned by my Father about two miles and a half north of the village, we went thither for what we wanted. We found that the choppers, by rare good luck, had felled all the timber on the southern exposure of a hill near the Lake, leaving the whole northern portion still covered with its native growth of evergreen, mainly hemlock; and therefore we gave the spot the name of Hemlock Hill. The view thus opened towards the south was remarkably beautiful. A large extent of the Green Mountain range, with intervening hills, formed the distance; while, near by, the village of Burlington, from the college on the top of the hill to the wharves on the lake shore, was spread out before us, together with the whole breadth of Burlington Bay. To the right, we looked down the deep recess of Shelburne Bay, guarded by its promontories and islands, and then far southward through the narrowing Lake to Split-rock mountain, with a glimpse of the Adirondacks beyond. An undulating valley immediately below Hemlock Hill was filled with an unbroken growth of young pines. Through an opening in the forest, another vista towards the northwest showed Appletree Bay with its low, sharp, wooded Point, and the broad Lake as far as Port Kent and Plattsburgh, with the northern spurs of the Adirondacks. We returned to the dingy Pearl street house in raptures with that exquisite view, and glowing with the idea that perhaps means might be contrived to secure the rough-looking spot of rocky ground, and build some sort of a homestead there.

For the sake of his numerous and growing family of boys, my Father thought it his duty to make the attempt; and after several disappointments, it proved successful. Kind friends combined to purchase the lot of an hundred acres ("be the same more or less"), which includes nearly the whole of Rock Point,—the picturesque and precipitous promontory which forms the northern boundary of Burlington Bay: besides which, that lot comprised also the valley of young pines already mentioned, and a large meadow, through which Hemlock Hill is approached from the public road. The terms were, that my Father should have a lease of the land for ten years, paying legal interest on the purchase money as rent, with the right to fell the timber to pay for permanent improvements, and also, to purchase the fee at cost, at any time before the expiration of the lease.

This secured,—the papers were executed on the 17th of July— the work began at once. Most of the good people in the village thought we were crazy to build on such a hill of solid rock, surrounded by rough boulders, and stumps, and brush heaps, and scraggy bushes, and piles of cordwood. But stumps were dug up, rocks were blasted and prepared for building, the surrounding roughnesses were gradually overcome, and in August the walls began to rise. The materials for the stone foundation were quarried on the spot. Economy reluctantly compelled the using of brick for the rest of the edifice. The plan was, of course, prepared by my Father. One long, large room—the family room— ran through the house, the two rear windows (with an open fireplace between them) looking out upon the evergreen wood which was our shelter from all northern storms; and the glazed door at the other end opening upon the broad porch commanding that finest Lake view which first captivated us. On each side were two smaller rooms, separated by an entry, with outer door and staircase. The plan of the upper story was similar, the long room above being in due time finished as the library, adorned with the cluster shafts and spandrils and pendants and painted panels which had been removed from the dear old Oratory, and the front window being adorned with Gothic tracery. The smaller rooms at the sides were low, needing the slant of the roof to give standing room. All the sons then at home and old enough to do anything, helped in every part of the work with all their might; and on the first of December it was occupied, though the walls were yet very damp, and the finishing and furnishing quite incomplete.

It was dreary, at times, to see the snow-storms roll over the tops of the young pine forest below the hill; and to find our communications with the village shut off by snow-drifts for days together; but the logs were piled only the more cheerily upon the open fireplace, and hard labor and affectionate good-humor turned all hardships into happiness. My Father's desk was fixed in one corner of that large room, near the fireplace; and there it remained for more than fifteen years. He was never disturbed by the ordinary noises of a large family, or by the musical practisings (the piano and the harp had their places in the same room): but before many years the visits of children and grandchildren and other summer friends filled the house during the warmer months to overflowing. When thus driven out, he first set up a tent in the woods, where he wrote his sermons; but soon afterwards he erected for himself a slight octagonal summer house, with sides of trellis-work, at a little distance, near some great hemlocks, and with full command of the view towards Appletree Bay and Plattsburgh. This was his favorite summer working-place during the whole remainder of his life.

Slowly, year by year, the rough place began to put on the beauties of cultivation. The old stumps were rolled up and made the foundation of the terrace around the porch. The hollows and some of the bare rocks were covered with earth brought up from below the hill. Barns were erected, and the garden made, and a young orchard planted. The first winter, the choppers were sent in to the unbroken forest that then covered the whole Point, and levelled enough wood to help pay the mason's bills, and providing in course of time plentiful pasture for cattle. The wood of young pines below the hill gave place to undulating fields of varied green. First one and then another of the sons, as they grew up and until they went to College, took the management of the farm, aided more or less by a hired man who, with his family, occupied a small house on the place. Paths were opened through the forest, winding among the moss-covered rocks, and round the whole Point, with its precipices of from eighty to one hundred and twenty feet in height; and another path, to the rear of the house, across a meadow and down through a shady dell, led to Eagle Bay,—so named by us, because an eagle for years had his nest on one of its crags. This bay is of small extent, indeed, but of singular beauty. Its beach of shelving sand is flanked on one side by a smooth flat rock, and the bay itself is formed by two high cliffs rising out of the foliage, and crested with cedars and pines, while the eye passes over the broad lake towards the west and northwest, commanding nearly the entire range of the Adirondacks, with their northern sloping line, falling away gently towards the level plains of Canada.

The singular combination of natural beauties in and about this place proved a constant source of enjoyment to my Father during the whole of his remaining life. Clad in a long cassock-like coat of domestic make, his erect and vigorous form might be seen pruning the trees in the orchard, or superintending or directing the operations of the farm; or else seated in his open arbor, hard at work with his papers and books. In moments of leisure he transferred not a few of the special beauties of the landscape to canvas, for the adornment of the walls of the house, which we all looked upon as the permanent Homestead of the family. Every return thither from visitations or other journeyings was to him a fresh feast. And many a time and oft, when, walking home with him from the village towards the close of the afternoon, we have stopped for a few moments on the gentle hill that leads down westwards into the meadow; and there, gazing upon the brilliant green lit up by the sun's rays shining through it, and the skirting wood beyond in deep shadow, and the house embosomed in the dark verdure that crowns Hemlock Hill, and the picturesque clumps of foliage towards the lake, through which its broad waters, its bays and headlands and islands, are seen, with the distant ranges of the Adirondacks on the further shore: many a time and oft have I heard him utter his wonder and gratitude that, after all his losses and disappointments, a kind Providence should have given him a far more beautiful place of abode than had fallen to the lot of any of his Episcopal brethren.

But poverty pressed him sorely, from this time on, and through all his remaining years. More than once, he accepted an invitation to deliver the Price Lectures in Boston, or to render some similar service, by which an addition to his scanty salary might be procured. And before many years passed, he found that lectures in various places helped in the same direction. Yet notwithstanding the claims of his large and growing family,[1] his rigid economy was such that, every year, he managed to squeeze together several hundred dollars to apply on the old debts left unprovided for by the sacrifice of the Institute. And this was steadily continued, year by year, until their entire extinguishment in 1856.

Meanwhile, although the school had failed, he was not left without the consolation of seeing, occasionally, some good fruits in his old pupils. When attending the Commencement of the General Theological Seminary in 1842, he was the guest of Bishop Onderdonk of New York, together with his old colleague Bishop Doane, and in writing to my Mother an account of the Commencement day, he says:—

> Our dear Arthur Carey was one of those who received the Testimonials. He read a very masterly essay, and is most highly esteemed by all who know him. After the services I was not a little affected by the warm expressions of Mr. Carey, attributing to me, under God, all the good that was in his son, and assuring me that Arthur regarded me as more than a father. Assuredly, dear wife, if our enemies exaggerate the defect of our services, our friends exaggerate quite as much their value. But it is a privilege worth more than all my losses and trouble to be instrumental in the formation of one such mind as Arthur Carey's.

---

[1] Five of his eight sons graduated at the University of Vermont; and the other three had the same opportunity, but preferred a different career.

In regard to his own Diocese, my Father for many years felt the deepest discouragement. He had lost his all in the attempt to render it the service which it needed most: and not a hand had been stretched out to help him, or to save a plank from the wreck. In the attempt to procure an assistant in his parish, so that he might devote more time to the Diocese, he found no active sympathy in Burlington, and no aid elsewhere. Again and again, in his addresses to his Convention, he raised his despairing cry in regard to this state of things: and then settled down in the conviction that these "numerous and serious disadvantages to the interests of the Diocese and the usefulness of the Episcopal office must be quietly endured, along with the host of evils which the penurious and grudging spirit of our day inflicts upon the whole administration of the Gospel system."

Now and then some circumstance kindled his hopes afresh for a little while,—some sign of reviving life and energy among a native population steadily diminishing: but on the whole the discouragements preponderated so strongly, that during many years he would have been glad to leave Vermont for some other field where he could feel that he was doing more of active service for his Master. He believed that, among a people with such a keen eye for business as the Vermonters, his pecuniary failure and position of permanent indebtedness must have gone far to destroy his power of usefulness: and that the work which he evidently could not do, might prosper much better in the hands of another. This feeling was so strong at times, that he long meditated the resignation of his see, and at one time even went so far as to draw up the paper in which that decision should be announced to the Diocese: but he took counsel with his friends, and finding that not one of them, whether in the Diocese or out of it, approved of the idea, he let it drop. Once, indeed, so late as the year 1849, he wrote confidentially to the Domestic Committee offering to go as Missionary Bishop to California; but, as they saw mountains of canonical difficulties in the way, he withdrew the application, and rested thenceforward contented in the conviction that it was the will of Providence that he should remain for life where he was.

But the extent to which his activities were restrained in Vermont naturally induced him to look more and more abroad: and authorship and the general institutions of the Church offered him the best fields in which he could perform effective service.

Chapter XII.

OXFORDISM—CANONICAL LEGISLATION.

FOR some time, the Oxford Tracts had been rising rapidly into notice, as the chief object of controversy throughout the length and breadth of the Anglican Communion; and each successive year showed more clearly that the dividing lines in this country were almost as sharp and as hotly contested as in the Mother Church of England. They had now come to be the touchstone of every man's position: and the one question asked of every Bishop or clergyman was, " Does he agree with the Oxford Tracts ?"

My Father's prepossessions and general theological position were almost wholly in accord with those of the writers of these Tracts. In his remote position, he had been, singly and independently, engaged in the same work which they had pursued conjointly in one of the greatest Universities of Europe. He had begun his patristic studies several years before the rise of the Oxford movement in England :[1] and his object was precisely the same as theirs, —to bring back our own communion into more thorough harmony with the opinions and practices of the Primitive and Undivided Church as the paramount authority over a now divided Christendom. Moreover, his practical sympathy with the Church Movement was abundantly visible in many points which to the general public are more intelligible than abstract statements of doctrine. His adoption of the mixed chalice and unleavened bread in Pittsburgh has already been mentioned. His efforts to promote the growth of Church architecture and adornment were well known throughout all the Church of America. He had sanctioned the use of pictures in Churches by painting with his own hand a figure of Faith holding up the Cross, which was placed over the Chancel arch of his own Church in Burlington. Ever since his return from England in 1839, he had preached in the

[1] In 1833.

surplice,—a practice which he recommended to his clergy also, though he did not require them to comply with his suggestion. The central position of the Altar,—the pulpit and prayer-desk being removed to either side,—had long before been adopted by him in Burlington, and was commended to his Convention whenever he found it elsewhere. "Nothing," said he, "is more certain than the fact, that the modern custom of making the pulpit the principal object in the Church, instead of the Altar, is altogether unsupported by any authority in Scripture, in antiquity, or in the Mother Church of England."[1] Still later,[2] he commended the zeal of the Rector of one of his most important parishes, who had introduced the Gregorian Chants, and the whole portion of the daily Psalms were sung by his choir with great correctness: "a result," said my Father, "which I never supposed likely to be accomplished beyond the sphere of Cathedral, collegiate, and large city churches."

But while there was so much in common, the independent character of my Father's mind, and his jealous suspicion of himself for fear he should be influenced by friends whom he admired, had made him scrupulous in noting down and insisting on every point, however minute, in which he differed from the writers of the Tracts for the Times. In the year 1842 he delivered his first *Charge* to his Clergy. The chief part of it was devoted to an attack on some of the principles embodied in the new Missionary Constitution of 1835; and many of the objections which he made are unanswerable. But the process of time showed that practically some of these objectionable phrases were only rhetorical rather than legislative; the evils have not been what he anticipated: and in after years he waived his objections, warmly advocating an adhesion to the existing system, which on the whole has worked so well.[3] He next touched on the Oxford Tracts, whose authors, he said, had secured a large measure of his admiration and esteem:—

I hold the Oxford Tracts in high estimation, as writings of a most useful tendency in some respects, particularly adapted to the present

---

[1] See Convention Journal 1840. [2] In 1843.
[3] See p. 291, *post;* and the Sermon preached by the Bishop of Vermont before the Board of Missions in Cincinnati, 1850.

circumstances of our venerated Mother Church of England. With some of the distinguished authors I have held a personal intercourse, marked on their part with the kindest liberality and most friendly attention. And I have never doubted, for a moment, the purity of their motives, their attachment to the Church, the ardor of their piety, their deep reverence for sacred things, their exalted standard of Christian effort, their learning, and their spirit of rare meekness and humility.

He then goes on to specify in detail a number of points in which he could not quite subscribe to the opinions expressed in the Tracts, calling marked attention to Tract No. 90, though even in regard to that, he says that "its ground-work may be admitted." After concluding his mention of the points of difference, he adds:—

Let me not be here supposed to charge the authors of the Tracts with setting forth anything which had not been substantially asserted long before their time, by writers of unquestioned orthodoxy. . . . I am quite persuaded that the effects of these writings, in many important respects, have been eminently conservative and beneficial. Clearer notions of Church principles and a far higher estimate of their value, a more elevated standard of clerical character, an humbler temper, a more zealous effort to do good, a more sacred regard for divine services, and a plainer line of ecclesiastical subordination, may be traced, under divine Providence, to their influence, . . . so that, on the whole, it may be doubted whether they will not stand before the judgment of an impartial posterity, as eminent benefactors to their age and country, however men of piety and learning may differ about their merits at the present day.

The only other point treated in the *Charge* was as to the Nestorian Bishop, Mar Yohannan, who was then in this country, making no small sensation, and who had been received with the right hand of fellowship, publicly, by Bishop Griswold and some others of our Clergy. My Father, on the other hand, reässerted, in the strongest terms, the binding authority of the Council of Ephesus; and summed up his proofs of this by saying:—

To the Church of England and to us, therefore, as well as to the universal Church throughout the world, the Nestorian is a heretic; and it results, however I might be disposed to have it otherwise, that I could not feel myself at liberty to hold Christian communion with such an one, unless I were ready to break the wholesome bonds of Catholic unity, for the perilous irresponsibility of heretical freedom.

After alluding to the Congregationalist and Presbyterian

auspices under which the Nestorian Bishop came to this country as aggravating the difficulty, my Father adds:—" It is not, perhaps, very strange in itself, that those who have no strict ideas about heresy, should be indifferent to schism": and he concludes, that any official recognition of Mar Yohannan would involve " a total dereliction of our principles."

This was the only *Charge*, technically so called, that my Father ever delivered. His frequent publication of his opinions in other forms, seemed to him to render the issuing of further *Charges* unnecessary.

The time was now approaching when the events of the day were to give form and substance to some of the objects for which my Father had long been striving in his place in General Convention.

No one estimated more highly the importance of that body, or its power for good: and he was never absent from any session of it during his life; nor ever absent even for a day or part of a day during any session, unless from temporary indisposition, or for the better performance of his individual duty on his return. In 1835,—his first attendance after the day of his Consecration,—on the morning of the third day of the session, he moved the appointment of a Joint Committee to consider the best system for a uniform administration of ecclesiastical justice throughout the several Dioceses, together with a provision for a Court of Appeals; and also, to consider whether it be expedient to grant to any one or more Bishops the right to prefer charges against any one of their own Order, to the House of Bishops. There was a curious coincidence in the fact that the three appointed on this Committee were Bishops Hopkins, Meade, and Benjamin T. Onderdonk. The result of their labors was a Report in which the evils of the existing want of system in regard to the matter were clearly set forth: and two Canons were proposed, embodying several of the leading points for which my Father had contended so earnestly. Others were modified or wholly omitted: and among these last was the much needed right of appeal. The second of the two proposed Canons provided for the presentment of a Bishop either by his own Convention,—two thirds of each Order concurring,—or by any three Bishops.

These two Canons passed the Upper House, but fell through for want of time for their consideration in the Lower.

So much of odium and personal bitterness has resulted from the subsequent adoption of this provision giving the presenting power to any three Bishops, that the original intention of it is very likely to escape notice. Until the year 1841, the 6th Article of the Constitution read:—" In every State, the mode of trying Clergymen shall be instituted by the Convention of the Church therein. At every trial of a Bishop there shall be one or more of the Episcopal Order present; and none but a Bishop shall pronounce sentence," etc.: so that, up to the year 1841, as my Father expressed it,[1] " The Dioceses, each in its own way, had the entire control of our most important branch of discipline; and, with the single exception of Vermont, a Canon for the trial of the Bishop stood at the head of every system of Diocesan legislation." This proposal of my Father's was the first step taken towards restoring the universal Catholic principle that each Bishop is amenable only to his own Order, instead of being amenable only to his own Diocesan Convention. The change was too great to be brought about suddenly. Although, as my Father says, it "was hailed by all intelligent and reflecting Churchmen as a most important step in the right direction," it took nine years to reach the stage of the Canon of 1844; and " during the whole of those nine years there was no opposition upon the subject, and no doubt expressed as to the wisdom and propriety of the alteration. It was undeniable that our former system of confining the presentment [and trial] of a Bishop to his own Diocese, was a pure American novelty, which had not the slightest pretence of primitive authority, and which could be found in no other regularly constituted Church throughout the world."[2] He showed, however, that it was due to the peculiarities of our position at the period of the first organization of the Church of America.

Another subject proposed by him, in 1835, but so unfavorably received that he did not embody it in a formal motion, was the practical revival of the Diaconate as a separate Order in

---

[1] Opinion, Proceedings of the Court of Bishops, 1852, p. 75.
[2] *Ibid.*

the Church, by reducing the intellectual qualifications for it very decidedly below the canonical standard required of priests. The idea was followed up, however, session after session, until, through the successful manipulation of its increasingly numerous friends, our present canonical distinction between the requisites for the two Orders was firmly established.

In 1838, on the third day, my Father introduced another favorite idea of his, for which he long struggled in vain. It was, that the increase in our Episcopate,—which he foresaw would be needed, and which he strongly advocated himself,—should be accomplished by the appointment of Suffragan Bishops, who should not sit in the House of Bishops. In this way he thought the evil of dividing large States into many disconnected Dioceses, and the other evil of making the House of Bishops unwieldy through its great numbers, would both be avoided. He obtained a committee on the subject, but its three members, rather significantly, found themselves so entirely unable to agree, that their request to be discharged was made and granted on the next day after their appointment. He made many subsequent efforts in the same cause, and his hope of final success induced him on more than one occasion to vote against the removal of obstructions in the way of erecting new Sees. But at length he became convinced that one of the two objects he had in view could better be reached by the Provincial System, which would unite sufficiently all the Sees erected in any one State; and that the other object, —preventing the numerical increase of the House of Bishops,— was entirely unattainable.

Early in that same session of 1838 he again moved for a Joint Committee on a uniform system of Ecclesiastical Law regarding the trials of Bishops and Clergymen, and obtained his committee: but so little interest was yet felt in the subject that all his efforts to get the Committee together for action failed. They were continued, to sit during the recess; but in 1841 the only report made was that they had never been able to get a quorum together. The foundation for action, however, was laid in 1838, in the alteration of Article 6 of the Constitution, which was finally adopted in 1841, on my Father's motion.

In 1841 he again returned to the charge, and the resolutions of 1835 and 1838 were referred to a new Committee, Bishops Benjamin Onderdonk and De Lancey being appointed his colleagues. They reported three Canons, all of which passed their own House, but only the first of them passed the Lower and became law; the other two falling through for want of time. The one that passed was the first (and very imperfect) Canon for the trial of a Bishop; which, however, agrees with the Canon passed by the Bishops in 1835, in giving the presenting power to any three Bishops, as well as to the Convention of the Diocese concerned. The enlarged Canon of 1844 originated in the Lower House, which consented to all the amendments made by the House of Bishops. It is easy to see from the proofs of this continuous effort running through nine years, how idle is the idea that the legislation on that subject was solely gotten up with a view to a particular case.[1]

Meanwhile, during all these years, the excitements growing out of the great Church Revival were on the increase; and since the appearance of Tract No. 90, had waxed so hot as to threaten

---

[1] Further proof of this may be found in a Canon passed by the Bishops, which provided that a sentence of "indefinite suspension" should void jurisdiction, and took order for a supply of Episcopal services during a "limited suspension." This has been supposed, by some imaginative persons, to have been started by the enemies of Bishop Onderdonk, to make sure that his subsequent suspension should void his jurisdiction. Those who might be thought capable of such malicious forethought, it so happened, all voted for his deposition, not for his suspension: which alone should be sufficient to disprove the idea. But besides that, this very Canon was originally offered in the Upper House, on the *eighth* day of the session, by Bishop Ives, one of Bishop Onderdonk's friends; it was referred to the Committee on Canons on motion of Bishop Doane, another of Bishop Onderdonk's friends, seconded by Bishop McCoskry. These being the facts, it was hardly fair for Dr. Seabury to begin his consideration of the Canon with its being reported back by Bishop McIlvaine, Chairman of the Committee on Canons, as if it had originated with him instead of with Bishop Ives. (See *Obsequies and Obituary Notices* of the late Rt. Rev. B. T. Onderdonk, etc., p. 93.) On being reported back, it was passed on motion of Bishop Ives, seconded by Bishop Doane: and this was on the *tenth* day of the session, while the first introduction of the New York business to the House, by Bishop P. Chase, was not until the *eleventh* day. The Lower House struck out the 1st and 3d sections, and took out the word "limited" from the only section left: that is to say, they would not hear to it that indefinite suspension should void jurisdiction, and evidently thought that the word "limited" before "suspension" was superfluous. When this Canon again came up to the House of Bishops, it was *Bishop Onderdonk of New York himself* who moved "that this House non-concur" in those amendments, and "request a conference": and Bishop Gadsden, another friend of Bishop Onderdonk, seconded the final motion for dropping the Canon altogether, rather than accept the fatal amendments which the Lower House insisted on.

mischief. There was no perversion to Rome worth mentioning, until the systematic denunciation of that particular Tract began. The object of that Tract was, to show that the Catholic party (so-called) had a rightful and honest place within the intended comprehensiveness of the Church of England. The result of the almost universal denunciation heaped upon that Tract, was, to create the impression that the Catholic party had no honest or rightful standing ground within the Church of England, and that, if they were honest men, they should leave her communion, and " go over to Rome where they belonged."

It was no wonder that language like this, used by so many of the Bishops in one concerted chorus, and with not one Bishop on either side of the water speaking out loud in the opposite sense, broke the hope and heart of many of the more ardent and sensitive leaders in the Church movement. From the end of 1841, Newman was "on his death-bed as an Anglican," although—so hard was it to sunder the marvellous ties that bound him to his old home—it required nearly four years more of anguish, conflict, doubt, and the outpouring of popular wrath, before the work of alienation was complete. The younger and more excited men were beginning to go over, in advance of him, and in spite of all that he could do to keep them back.

Under these circumstances, it was but natural that my Father's views as to the dangerous character of some portions of Oxford teaching, should steadily gain in sharpness and strength for some years. In 1842 he repudiated the idea of "charging the authors of the Tracts with setting forth anything which had not been substantially asserted long before their time, by writers of unquestioned orthodoxy." When the Roman Bishop, Dr. Francis Patrick Kenrick, appealed to our Bishops to return at once to the Church of Rome, on the professed ground that the Tracts "had yielded, one by one, almost every ground of dispute, and had proposed to reconcile the Articles with the Council of Trent": my Father indignantly repudiated the accusation, declaring in his *First Letter* to Bishop Kenrick that "those very Tracts themselves bear a clear and decided testimony against the innovations and corruptions of Rome's modern system." He invited Bishop Kenrick to an oral discussion, which the latter preferred to decline, while still attempting to maintain his position in regard to the Tracts. My Father thereupon wrote him a *Second Letter*, in which the Roman prelate was met with a spirit and vigor which did not a little to comfort the hearts and lift up the heads of some timid Churchmen who were then trembling at the signs of the times. In that *Second Letter*, the Bishop of Vermont defended the Tracts at no small length, with extracts from Dr. Pusey, Newman, Froude, and Tract No. 90 itself; and thus summed up the case: "If you are willing to accept such declarations as the voice of praise, it passes my ingenuity to imagine what you would call the voice of censure." He still mentions, indeed, that he "dissents from several of the opinions which they maintain, and should be obliged, in a variety of instances, to modify, before he could adopt, their statements of doctrine," while nevertheless making light of "the fears entertained of their soundness among Protestants."[1] This was in the Spring of 1843.

But in less than three months the Carey Ordination had brought the question close to our own doors. New York was in a ferment. The excitement was spreading throughout the whole country like wildfire. The uneasiness which had for so many years been increasing, crystallized at once, like a saturated solution, into all the forms of an anti-papal panic. Fresh impulse was given by the refusal, in the New York Convention that September, to entertain the resolutions growing out of that Ordination; and echoes of the New York conflict soon reverberated loudly through the Conventions of other Dioceses.

Towards the close of the year, therefore, my Father began to

---

[1] In a *Postscript* to this *Second Letter*, my Father went into an elaborate disproof of the Roman interpretation of that famous passage of S. Irenæus, speaking of the Church in the City of Rome:—"Ad hanc enim ecclesiam, proper potiorem principalitatem, necesse est omnem convenire ecclesiam, hoc est, eos qui sunt undique fideles," etc.,—a passage which some, who ought to know better, have been willing to concede as properly bearing the Roman sense, in spite of its being as incompatible with good Latinity as it is with History. It is some consolation to find that the brother of his then opponent,—now the Roman Archbishop of St. Louis,—in his honest and admirable speech prepared for delivery at the Vatican Council, candidly gives up that passage of S. Irenæus:—"Inter testimonia ex traditione desumpta, nonnulla *rejicienda censui; ut in commate Irenæi de potiore principalitate, quam Ecclesiæ Romanæ vindicasse communiter creditur:* sed id præstiti, adductis rationum momentis; quibus, non contumeliis, sed rationibus, occurri debeat."—*See* Documenta ad Illustrandum Concilium Vaticanum anni 1870; I. Abtheilung, p. 200.

issue, in rapid succession, four *Letters on the Novelties that disturb our Peace*, in which he argued at some length against the repetition of Lay-Baptism, and some other points in which he thought the Tracts had gone too far, closing the series with an examination of the Carey Ordination. The substance of the objection to Arthur Carey was, that he held the position of Tract No. 90, of which, though not himself altogether approving it, my Father had said in 1842 that "its ground-work may be admitted," and that the authors of it "had said nothing more than had been substantially asserted, long before their time, by writers of unquestioned orthodoxy." By the end of 1843, however, seeing the increasing defections to Romanism in England, and the furious tempest awakened by the first known attempt to introduce that sort of "unquestioned orthodoxy" among ourselves, my Father naturally began to look upon it in a more serious light. His relations with Bishop Benjamin Onderdonk had always been of the most kindly description, having been more than once a guest at his house, and never having had the slightest personal disagreement with him. Arthur Carey had been his pupil, like a son under his own roof for years, and he regarded him with the tenderest love as well as with admiration for his high character and brilliant powers. All this was freely and cordially expressed in that *Letter*, together with his confidence in the "ultimate soundness" of Mr. Carey's theological principles. Yet still, he clearly stated his own conviction that Drs. Smith and Anthon had a right to protest as they did; and that the ordination ought to have been postponed until a further and more formal trial should have been had; and that the opinions then professed by Mr. Carey should have been regarded as a disqualification for the Diaconate.

These *Letters on the Novelties* created no small sensation, and rapidly passed through two Editions. The Low-Churchmen were all highly delighted. Bishop Meade, in a public letter addressed to my Father, said:—"I render thanks to the Giver of all grace, that he has granted to you the talents, the learning, the opportunity, and above all the spirit, to perform the task you have undertaken in so able, so learned, so judicious, temperate and courteous a manner as must ensure the respect of the candid, the wise, and pious, even though some of them may not in every thing agree with you. You have set an example to those who write on disputed points, of a candor which enters into the feelings and prejudices of both parties, and makes all due allowance for their influence over their judgment, while at the same time you are entirely free from the weakness of indecorous reserve or ambiguity,—prevailing errors of our day." Bishops Smith, McIlvaine and others wrote in a similar strain. So great was the joy of all who were hostile to the Tracts, at gaining so powerful and unexpected an ally, that they swallowed without a wry face many declarations of sound doctrine in various parts of those *Letters*, which under other circumstances they would have objected to as being nothing less than Tractarianism itself.

The displeasure on the other side was almost as great: but it was hardly fair in the Bishop of New York to respond by publicly challenging the Bishop of Vermont (together with the Bishops of Illinois and Ohio) to present him for trial for false doctrine, when, in the very *Letter* complained of, my Father had demonstrated the impossibility of making a case for presentment or trial out of the Carey Ordination. It was, as he contended, merely an error of judgment, such as the best men are liable to; and he had suggested such an array of motives leading to the course resolved on by the Bishop of New York,—motives so strong, so kindly and so generous,—that my Father candidly confessed he could not feel sure that his own decision would have been different, if placed in the same position. There was no thought or feeling of unkindness towards either the Bishop or Mr. Carey; and no phrase in regard to either that was not sheathed in the most affectionate and considerate delicacy of expression: nor was any doctrinal statement made by the Bishop himself impugned by my Father. But, in those times of high excitement, all this did not hinder some strong partisans from reiterating again and again for years thereafter, that the Bishop of Vermont was one of those who was both " doctrinally and personally opposed to the Bishop of New York."

There was more justice in considering the Bishops of Illinois and Ohio among doctrinal opponents: for, after the Bishop of New York's challenge, the Bishop of Ohio wrote to my Father, expressing his readiness to be one of the presenters;[1] and though the Bishop of Illinois, in his published reply, declared that he felt no other sentiments but those of regard and friendship for the Bishop of New York personally: yet it was that peculiar sort of personal regard and friendship which permitted him at the same time to write to my Father asking him to be one of the presenters of the Bishop of New York, and requesting him to write to any two others he might choose, to take part in the work. My Father's answer soon convinced them of their mistake. Bishop Meade was more clear-sighted, and took the same ground with my Father, that there was no case for a presentment in any thing connected with the Carey Ordination.

Early in 1840, just after the failure of the school, my Father had prepared and delivered in Burlington a course of *Lectures on the British Reformation;* and on his going to Philadelphia for a few weeks to put the *Letters on the Novelties* to press, it was thought seasonable, after conference with several of the Clergy of that city, to arrange for the delivery of those Lectures there. Five of the leading Churches, of both parties, cheerfully entered into the arrangement, and the course of fifteen Lectures was to be delivered in these five Churches in rotation, so that the whole could be completed within the three weeks of my Father's stay. But Bishop Henry Onderdonk remonstrated so energetically against the excitement likely to result, and so earnestly requested the abandonment of the intention, that my Father consented at once,

---

[1] It may be well to look back to the beginning of the painful education of the American Church on the subject of Episcopal Trials, to measure the advances since made in men's notions concerning it. Bishop McIlvaine writes, in the letter referred to (Feb. 7, 1844):—"I am the junior of the three offenders, *officially* and otherwise; and as you are the man of business of the three, skilled in the sort of questions which this matter creates, I lose no time in asking what you think should be done. I am not disposed to shrink from any responsibility which the Church demands. Is not this the very thing that was needed to bring the case to a head? Give me your views as to the question, Shall we *present?* If so, on *what charges?* It has occurred to me that if we do present, it might be well to increase the force of the presentation by getting others to unite in it. Meade, Johns, Lee, Elliott, Polk,—either, or all, I think, would. Then it is to be considered whether their position as judges might not be a little compromised, in the public view, by having part in the presentment." The notion of the respective positions of prosecutors and judges is not now quite so mixed as this anywhere. We have seen above, that Bishop Meade thought very differently from what Bishop McIlvaine supposed, on this subject; and he was probably equally mistaken in regard to the others whom he named.

though feeling somewhat hurt at this unusual interference with the rights of the parochial clergy in filling their own pulpits. The affair naturally led to the immediate publication of those *Lectures on the British Reformation.*

The agitation and excitement went on increasing during the whole season, one Diocesan Convention after another contributing its proportion of fuel to the flame. In October (1844) the General Convention met, which,—if universal expectation could be trusted,—was to witness the climax of heated discussion on the doctrinal points involved. And it is highly probable that if those questions had then concentrated the chief interest of the session, the decision would have been hostile to the further progress of the Church movement, by a large majority.

But a diversion of the doctrinal interest was effected, very happily, by the opponents of the General Theological Seminary, who succeeded in bringing about a formal Visitation of that Institution, by the Bishops in a body:—the first time they ever exercised their powers as Visitors. My Father had voted with the Low-Church minority on the Board of Trustees touching the confidence expressed in the Seminary; and he was one of the Committee of the House of Bishops to frame queries to be answered by the Professors. The result was, a large number of questions answered in a way to which no exception could well be made: and nobody was hurt. And this was not the only diversion which confused the simplicity of the attack. The unexpected opposition made to the consecration of the Rev. Dr. Hawks as Bishop of Mississippi proved to be a still more exciting and engrossing business: and a whole week's brilliant debate on that subject, with that closing speech by the eloquent Doctor himself which melted nearly every hearer to tears, threw the doctrinal discussion so far in the shade, that after worrying its slow length along till the thirteenth day of the session, it evaporated in a harmless resolution, adopted almost unanimously, which declared the present standards of the Church to be a sufficient statement of her doctrines, and that the General Convention was not the proper body to take cognizance of the errors of individuals.

But those who were opposed to the Church movement were about to deceive themselves in two very important particulars.

They are always stronger in personalities than in divinity; and would any day rather attack their opponents on moral grounds—if they can get a chance—than on theological. To the astonishment of the Church at large, Bishop Henry Onderdonk of Pennsylvania, by a letter under his own hand, resigned his Diocese, and asked for such discipline at the hands of his brethren as they might think deserved by the scandal which he had brought upon the Church by the too free use of stimulants, employed at first for reasons purely medicinal: and accordingly, his resignation was accepted, and on the seventeenth day of the session he was suspended from all public exercise of the ministry. My Father was one of the Committee to whom all the papers in this painful business were referred. Rumors began to be heard, too, that the still more obnoxious Bishop of New York was accessible in a similar way: and as the probability of such a warfare opened to the view, the charms of a dry and thorny theological debate rapidly paled in comparison.

Now the two points in which the opponents of the Church movement deceived themselves were these:—First, they thought that a personal triumph over these two High-Church Bishops on moral grounds alone, would be more than equivalent to the condemnation of their doctrines; and secondly, they took it for granted that all who might feel themselves compelled to act against these two men on moral grounds, would be, substantially, reliable acquisitions to the doctrinal strength of the Low-Church party. They evaded the perils of a doctrinal fight, but expected to win the spoils of a doctrinal victory. The two men went down, indeed, on charges that had nothing in the wide world to do with doctrine. So long as they were kept down, the Low-Church party flattered itself that it was doctrinally triumphant. Before it awoke to its mistake, the real victory had been won by the quiet growth of reading, and knowledge, and principle: and when the opponents of the Church movement at length became aware of their double error, it was too late to do anything but resign themselves to that gradual extinction which, as they now see and know, is all that the outlook into the future can reasonably promise them.

Chapter XIII.

THE ONDERDONK CASE.

THE subterranean activities that opened the way for the presentment of the Bishop of New York formed no slight part of the excitements which, below the surface, eddied and whirled around and through the latter portion of the General Convention of 1844. Illegitimate attempts to bring the rumors before the House of Bishops were foiled: but it was felt that the storm of reproach must be met in some mode; and three Bishops—in the exercise of a clear canonical right—undertook to act the part of Presenters.

After the rising of the General Convention they went to New York, and patiently examined all such charges as were brought before them. Some of the blackest stories against the Bishop evaporated under their more careful examination. Others looked less and less dark the more they were investigated. A little more care in one particular would have prevented the trial altogether. They found that the bulk of the charges brought against the Bishop were for acts which, if immoral *animus* could be proved, were of a very formidable character: but, if there were no such *animus*, and if reasonable allowance were made for such innocent exaggeration as would be natural on the part of young and imaginative persons when greatly startled or excited by mistaken ideas, the case would be so much altered that there would hardly be enough left to warrant so grave a proceeding as a trial for crime or immorality. Now it is due to the accused that it should be put on record, that, of all the specifications embraced in the presentment of Bishop Benjamin T. Onderdonk, there was one, and one only, which clearly established an immoral *animus:* and that was inserted upon the strength of the Rev. Clement M. Butler's affidavit of what his wife had told him; the subject being one of such delicacy that the Presenters (improperly but) naturally did not insist on direct testimony, on that point, from Mrs. Butler herself. But the *animus*, being thus established, spread its own contagion to all the other specifications, in a way that no subsequent correction could heal. When it came to the trial, however, and Mrs. Butler was put upon the stand, she totally denied the truth of that one damning story told by her husband, and on which really the whole Presentment rested; said that it never had happened, and that she had never told her husband that it had. Like an affectionate wife, she did indeed try to diminish the importance of her husband's error; and his explanation of the way in which he fell into the error showed it to have been so natural that no deliberate dishonesty can be charged to the account of either of them: but nevertheless, there is the strange historical fact, the result of all these blunders,—that had the Presenters been careful enough, at the right time, to examine Mrs. Butler herself touching the facts embodied in her husband's affidavit, there never would have been any Presentment at all.

On the 9th of November the Presentment[1] was formally made: and with it there came to my Father a grievous heaviness of heart, without which he could not remember the cloud that had already darkened the life of one of the two brothers Onderdonk, or contemplate that which now seemed about to settle down still more ominously upon the career of the other. At length the Court met, and the trial began.

It is hard for us now to realize fully the circumstances under which that Court acted. As if by a sort of fatality indicating a foregone conclusion, the course of the Accused was marked by error after error in judgment, each error tending to ensure the unhappy result. I have often heard my Father say, that the utter repugnance of the great majority of the Bishops to go into the trial was so great, and their anxiety to get out of the disagreeable necessity for proceeding was so eager, that if, before the lawyers had been introduced or the trial actually begun, the Accused had candidly acknowledged certain imprudencies of manner which had been misundertood, and which had given rise

[1] On taking down the bundle of Papers in this case, tied up together for many years unopened, I found that the "dauber wasps," so called, had long ago plastered the outer ends of the leaves all over with their clay nests: the only package of my Father's papers thus distinguished. The life and the venom were gone: only the dry dirt was left.

to scandal, and which therefore he had carefully guarded against for more than two years past, as was proved by the allegation of no grievance within that period; and if, in regard to the past thus complained of, he had thrown himself frankly upon the mercy of his brethren: they would at once have jumped at the chance, would have refused to go on with the trial at all, and would have dismissed the case forthwith, with merely a slight admonition.

But this wiser course was not followed. A total denial was preferred: and in engaging, as one of his counsel,[1] a lawyer who was not a Churchman, and whose chief professional reputation rested upon his skill in defending notorious criminals, another and still greater error of judgment helped to prepare men's minds for the result. Worst of all was the unhappy stress that was laid, by the Bishop's friends and counsel, upon the two witness rule: for when the general character and credibility of individual witnesses is left wholly unassailed, while the chief effort for the accused is expended in the attempt to prove the technical necessity of two witnesses to each several act, the result is, a *moral* conviction that the testimony of the witnesses, as given, is true as a matter of fact. And when women of irreproachable character testified positively to such facts as were sworn to on that trial, it was impossible to avoid the verdict. Moreover, the written paper read by the Bishop before sentence was passed, was understood as an acknowledgment of the facts as found by the Court, though denying the charge they were held to prove.

My Father believed that evidence with a firmness that nothing was ever able to shake for a moment, down to the day of Bishop Onderdonk's death.[2] He believed that the positive and

---

[1] Mr. Graham.

[2] It is a great mistake to suppose that the subsequent course of the majority of the Bishops, in refusing steadily to remit Bishop Onderdonk's sentence, was guided, or ought to have been guided, solely by the amount of evidence produced on the trial. Firmly convinced, as they were, that that evidence justified the verdict and sentence, they felt that they had a right to be guided by *moral* evidence as to the justice and expediency of his restoration; and that moral evidence reached them through innumerable channels, and in such a shape that the minds of ordinary men could not but find it irresistible. As a sample, I give the following letter from one of our Bishops, who, as a Presbyter and Deputy in General Convention, was not only known as a steady High-Churchman, but had openly impugned the legality of the Court, in the newspapers, over his own name, and was thus

clear proof of such things would be fatal for ever to the idea of that Bishop's returning to the exercise of his Episcopal functions, with edification to the Church. He believed that the tempest of public scandal and reproach called forth by the case, had branded and blighted the Bishop's official career for the rest of his life. And therefore he not only found him *guilty* of the Charges, but consistently voted for *Deposition* at each of the three scrutinies made before a majority of the Court agreed in the sentence of Suspension. There was no act of his life in which he was more clear in his own mind, more conscientious in his convictions, or more inflexible in his steady adherence to what he believed to be the cause of truth and righteousness. The duty of holding up a standard of high-toned personal purity in the members of the Episcopate, could not, by him, be made to yield to motives of kindness for an individual.

thoroughly committed to the public as one of Bishop Onderdonk's friends. Not very long after, writing to my Father in regard to that same newspaper article, he said:—"At the time the article you speak of was written, I urgently advised the resignation of Bishop Onderdonk, as a sacrifice rendered necessary by the perplexed condition of the Diocese, and the impossibility of his ever being enabled to do any good in the exercise of his ministry as a Bishop in New York. My advice was indignantly and rather insolently scouted by the person to whom I wrote, and who had previously told me more than was made to appear on the trial, of his delinquencies. In a conversation with Bishop De Lancey in 1847, he asked me what I thought of the restoration of Bishop Onderdonk. I replied, that from the observation I had been enabled to make in an intercourse with the Churchmen at Troy, Albany and elsewhere, I was decidedly of the opinion that, in the event of Bishop Onderdonk's restoration, he could never regain the confidence of his Diocese, and that his only course was, to resign his jurisdiction; and in this opinion I understood Bishop De Lancey to coincide with me. I desire what I have now said to be strictly confidential, for, though I have expressed the same opinion to several of the friends of Bishop Onderdonk, if it were known that I had expressed the same to you, it might involve me in what is my utter abhorrence,—a newspaper discussion." It was the abundance of appeals of this sort, renewed whenever there was a renewal of the agitation for his restoration, and coming from High-Churchmen, too, of character and standing, coupled with the fact that the Diocese of New York never by a plain square vote *asked* for unconditional restoration, that made the majority of the Bishops unshakably firm in the conviction that the verdict and sentence were no more than justice demanded, and that no true interest of the Diocese of New York itself, much less of the rest of the Church, would be served by the restoration of the suspended Bishop of New York. In corroboration of what is said in the above letter about Bishop De Lancey, it will be remembered that in 1859, at Richmond, after other motions, made by other Bishops in Bishop Onderdonk's favor, had failed, it was Bishop De Lancey who moved the remission of the sentence on his "placing in the hands of the Presiding Bishop a full resignation of his jurisdiction." But as Bishop Onderdonk telegraphed his refusal to accept this, the motion fell to the ground.—*Obsequies and Obituary Notices*, etc., pp. 146, 148.

Of all the written opinions of the majority of the Court, the Bishop of Vermont's was the strongest. The leading point to which he directed his attention was the claim, relied on by the Bishop's friends, that the two witness rule was of divine obligation upon the Church in regard to each fact charged: and this notion he so thoroughly demolished that it has never been heard of since in our ecclesiastical proceedings. The rule contended for by my Father,—that the principles of the Common Law are to be followed in ecclesiastical trials,—not only prevailed on that occasion, but has since been embodied in our written Canon Law.[1]

The fountains of bitterness overflowed for a long time after this trial was over; and the violence, personalities and injustice, the free imputation of motives, and often the scurrility of certain friends of Bishop Onderdonk, did much to fortify the minds of some of the Bishops against all possibility of change in his favor. They had no such influence upon my Father. The writers of anonymous articles against him in the papers, or the authors of anonymous letters sent him by mail, would have been sufficiently answered could they have seen the gentle indifference with which, after reading these effusions, he quietly twisted them up and used them to light his pipe.[2] But he often expressed his satisfaction at now knowing why the Providence of God had made him a lawyer, before calling him into the ministry. His familiarity with the principles and practice of law gave great weight to his opinions not only on this occasion, but on others of a similar character.

The violence with which all the issues connected with the Onderdonk controversy were fought, was so intense, that all other lines of division in the Church were for some time merged in these

---

[1] Title II., Canon 9, § vi. [4].

[2] During the greater part of his life, my Father did not use tobacco in any shape. After he was fifty years of age, on experiencing premonitory symptoms of bronchitis, he was recommended by his physician to smoke: and finding that Dr. Mott of New York had given the same recommendation publicly, for the same complaint, he became a smoker; often stopping the practice for weeks or months, to make sure that he was not a slave to the habit, and recommencing when he was sure of his liberty. He used to say, that if nobody would smoke until he was past fifty, and until it had been prescribed by two physicians of high standing, no great harm would follow from the use of "the weed."

only. The practical result was, apparently, for a while, to throw my Father wholly upon the Low-Church side of the House. The leading men of that party were fully aware of the importance of their acquisition, and no pains were spared on their part to secure him. The then editors of the newly started *Protestant Churchman* assured him that their paper was not Low-Church, but was determined to stand on the principles of Hooker, and the Bishop Hobart platform of "Evangelical Truth, Apostolical Order," merely avoiding the Tractarian "Novelties that disturb our peace": and for a while he believed them. Knowing his poverty, they offered him compensation for contributions from his pen. They flattered him, too, in a way peculiarly likely to influence him; and that was, by leaving to him the hardest parts of the work to be done in the one matter which had brought them together. As his Opinion bore the chief brunt of sustaining the verdict of the Court, so to his pen the chief defence of it was left, whenever it was again brought into question. They talked of him as if he were their standard-bearer and leader. Dr. Anthon wrote him:—"I have heard only congratulations on our arrangement by which we have secured the valuable aid of your pen. . . . I beg therefore that you will continue to stand in the forefront and cheer us onward." "Bishop McIlvaine," Dr. Anthon assured him, "makes the most favorable mention of your articles in *The Protestant Churchman.*'

So great was their confidence that circumstances and human nature must now render my Father wholly their own, and so violent was the tone of Bishop Onderdonk's friends towards him, that they did not hesitate in their letters to let him know plainly what they looked forward to. Dr. Anthon wrote (in February, 1845): "What shall we say of New Jersey and Maryland? Thorns and thistles will yet spring up in their path." Not very long after this, Bishop McIlvaine wrote to sound my Father as to "the need of some conference among us Bishops who think alike as to Tractarian errors,"—jumping at the strange conclusion that my Father now agreed entirely with him, and thus illustrating the queer mental impossibility of looking at any question except in a party light, which is so characteristic of some party men. He wished that they should come to "some common conclusion as to what we ought to do, in protection of the truth": and in feeling his way to this result, he had sent to a few of the Bishops the following question:—"In case a clergyman whom you know to hold the main distinguishing features of the Tractarian system, should present you a letter dimissory in due form, would you think it right to refuse to receive him into the Diocese? or what would you think the best course?" I have no copy of my Father's answer; but judging from his repeatedly published opinion that no cause of presentment could be found in the Carey ordination case, there can be no question that it was a dissuasive. The proposed meeting was not held.

In the Spring of 1846, when Dr. Seabury, in *The Churchman*, came out openly on the ground of Tract No. 90, my Father wrote a sharp pamphlet against him, which was published by the Harpers through Dr. Anthon's zealous agency, and with such rapidity that the whole of the proof was read by him within twenty-four hours after receiving the manuscript. The ground taken in the pamphlet was, the impossibility of so explaining away the Thirty-Nine Articles as to make them agree with the doctrinal decrees of Trent: and the indignant tone and sweeping denunciations of this pamphlet showed how far the events of the day had carried my Father beyond the ground he had originally taken himself in regard to Tract No. 90,—that "its ground-work may be admitted," and that it contained nothing "which had not been substantially asserted long before . . . by writers of unquestioned orthodoxy." The history of the English Reformation had not then been written up anew, as it has in our day. Dr. Seabury, therefore, in his reply, found it prudent to change his ground; and he maintained that what he meant was, not that the Articles could be explained away so as to agree with Trent, but that the Trentine decrees could be explained away so as to agree with the Articles. A second pamphlet, in answer to this new position, closed the controversy, leaving the victory clearly with my Father.

The congratulations of his Low-Church friends poured in

upon him afresh, and sometimes with forecastings of future possibilities which it was by no means my Father's design to encourage. Bishop McIlvaine wrote him, on the appearance of the first of these pamphlets:—"It is good, eminently. It hits the nail on the head. Go on, lead us all, dear Brother, in faithfulness and boldness. We want boldness and *unsparingness*, in these days." And then he goes on to say,—with a spirit which some of his own friends can fully appreciate in our days,—"Be sure we must get to discipline, now that the truth is being undermined on every side; and then, when the hand of discipline is put out, and some Puseyite, distinctly for Puseyism, is disciplined, the real fire of our furnace will begin.[1] But we must not fear. . . . I see with you the necessity of a Court of Appeal in certain cases." There is no doubt that if my Father had sanctioned this policy, the attempt would have been made, and probably with a success more embarrassing to the Church movement in this country, than was the year's suspension of Dr. Pusey from the University Pulpit to the movement in England. But he steadily opposed the idea, no matter how strongly he deemed it his duty to write, at the time, against what seemed to him a dangerous leaning towards Romanism: and without him, success was clearly impossible.

The value placed by his new friends upon his support was so great, that the sensitiveness they occasionally showed in their fear of losing him was amusing. In the summer of 1845, Dr. Seabury spent a Sunday in Burlington, and my Father—who did not know of his presence until the close of the morning service—asked him to preach for him in the afternoon, which Dr. Seabury did, very acceptably: and afterwards an invitation brought him out to our house to tea, and to spend the evening. No small portion of the

---

[1] For some years Bishop McIlvaine consulted my Father occasionally, as to points of discipline. On one occasion he inquired whether a distiller were so notorious an evil-liver that his suspension from the Holy Communion could be sustained. On another, he inquired whether it would be within the Canons to visit a parish by compelling its minister and candidates to meet him four miles off. His idea in doing such a thing was to punish the parish for "behaving so badly" towards him "personally and officially." His next letter shows what my Father's advice had been:— "Your view, and the reasons you give, are sufficient to prevent me from taking the course about which I inquired."

conversation, of course, turned upon the most important issues of the day; and each party expressed his own views with perfect courtesy and candor, though without much success in converting the other. The rumors about this simple intercourse of fraternal courtesy caused no small fluttering among his new friends of the other side in New York. And in the following summer, Dr. Anthon again writes in no slight uneasiness at "rumors" which confidently affirmed that, if the Convention of New York should request a remission of the sentence of Bishop Onderdonk, the Bishop of Vermont was pledged to vote for it: and what made the rumor more serious was, that the editor of *The Churchman* "had of a sudden become highly complimentary of the Bishop of Vermont,"—rather an unusual thing in those days. Dr. Anthon wished authority to contradict this mischievous rumor. "Your opinions," said he, "have deserved weight. Your name is a tower of strength. And if both (but in appearance) can be claimed and quoted, it will be done."

And yet, notwithstanding all their watchful and assiduous flattery, they found the Bishop of Vermont not a very manageable man, in the various turns and twists of their party warfare. They importuned him again and again to write editorials for *The Protestant Churchman*, or allow his communications to be used as such, whenever it might suit the editors. But he steadily adhered to his determination to publish only over his own name. A large part of his communications was simply the reprinting of his letters on Christian Education, which had originally appeared in *The Banner of the Church* in Boston.

But it was not long before my Father's peculiar jealousy over himself in regard to continuous action with any party in the Church, began to operate in his new sphere. When *The Protestant Churchman* committed itself to the idea that the suspension of Bishop Onderdonk *ipso facto* vacated the see, my Father wrote a strong and unanswerable argument against it, which he sent down to be inserted over his own name; and accompanied it with a card announcing that he withdrew from his position as a stated contributor to the paper.[1] A council of war was summoned

---

[1] It was not surprising that about this time the promised compensation for my Father's articles, long deferred, was found to be unattainable. Dr. Anthon wrote

at once to sit on the letter: the result of which was that they begged piteously that the withdrawal should not be published, and that the argument might be softened, or (still better) omitted altogether. As to the card of withdrawal, my Father yielded: but not so as to the other. Dr. Anthon still withheld it from publication, pleading hard that the hostility with which my Father was treated by the other side, should keep him from lending them a helping hand. "*The Churchman* of last Saturday," he wrote, "shows how eager its Editor is to seek occasion for an attack upon you. You are *the* grand stumbling-block in the way. Duer and Clark and Dr. Smith, and Dr. Taylor, Mr. Brown, Mr. Ketchum and myself, are of the same opinion as to the inexpediency of publication." But the Bishop of Vermont was obstinate about it, caring nothing for the opinions of men on either side: and Dr. Anthon, finding that his only option was, to print it in the columns of *The Protestant Churchman* or have it appear elsewhere, published it at last, but after more than a month had been lost in this epistolary negotiation. Among the letters of approval which my Father received on the appearance of this letter, was one from the clearheaded Bishop of New Hampshire, expressing his hearty concurrence in the views of that argument, and adding:—" I have always regretted that the voices for *Deposition* did not prevail, because that sentence, as respects Bishop Onderdonk, would not have involved greater severity than the sentence of indefinite suspension, while it would have left the Diocese in a situation infinitely better."

This had been my Father's chief reason for voting for "Deposition." He had said, in his Opinion:—" I do not think it necessary, by any means, to impute adulterous designs to the Respondent, nor to assume any secret motive beyond that which must, in ordinary construction, be connected with the acts themselves." And he had also said, in regard to the sentence for which he voted:—" Willingly would I have chosen the lighter

that he held himself personally responsible for the amount, and would pay it were he in funds: but added,—" with our present subscription list, we cannot do more than keep our heads above water." My Father was not quite poor enough to insist on a reluctant payment: and the increasing divergency of views between the editors and himself soon led to his ceasing his contributions to that paper.

sentence of indefinite suspension, if that would have relieved the afflicted Diocese of New York from a bond which can no longer be continued with any good result to its interests or welfare. But I do not see how the Court, in passing such a sentence, could avoid the risk of making many suffer for the sake of one, thus indirectly punishing the innocent along with the guilty."

When the Court, however, by a majority of one, had decided in favor of suspension, the Bishop of Vermont steadily set his face against all attempts to aggravate or add to the sentence thus passed. Therefore, when the effort was made in the Board of Trustees of the General Theological Seminary to displace Bishop Onderdonk from his Professorship, on the ground of his suspension for "immorality and impurity," nothing could induce my Father to advocate it. The Presiding Bishop—Bishop Philander Chase of Illinois—wrote earnestly urging the displacement of the suspended Bishop from his Professorship as a necessary measure "in withstanding the encroachments of the leprosy of vice and impurity, which evidently hath already begun its ravages among us"; and while saying, "for obvious reasons, I would wish my name not to be prominent," he added that he had written on the subject to Bishops Elliott, McIlvaine and Meade, but thought he should write in full to none others. Dr. Anthon and his circle of friends were equally urgent. But my Father held that it was clearly wrong to inflict an additional penalty beyond that pronounced by the Court; and with his usual boldness and candor, he did not content himself with absence from the Board or a silent vote when there, but advocated the right course, against all his new friends, openly in debate, to the best of his ability. Bishop Onderdonk retained that Professorship to the end of his life, though its duties were at no time after his suspension discharged in person.

Another subject of attack from Low-Church quarters was the sermon preached by my Father at the consecration of Bishop A. Potter of Pennsylvania, in September, 1845. In this sermon he not only took for granted the Apostolic Succession "in one unbroken line, by virtue of which our own ecclesiastical polity maintains its Apostolic title," asserting "the plain rule established for the administration of ordination and government, by those and those alone who stand in the rank of this Succession, so that it is impossible for us consistently to acknowledge Holy Orders, or the office of the Priesthood in the Church, except it be according to the Apostolic law which Christ appointed": but he went further, and asked:—"Is not the duty of government as distinctly apostolic as the duty of ordination? . . . . And if the episcopal right to ordain the ministry in the Church of Christ cannot be destroyed without incurring the awful sin of Korah, Dathan and Abiram, and laying a sacrilegious hand upon the Ark of God, how shall the equally episcopal right to govern be cast down and trampled under foot, without an equal amount of guilt and profanation?" He disclaimed entirely, however, the idea that a Bishop is to be " an arbitrary ruler," or " a supreme judge." He must govern only according to law: and this law consists not of the Canons of our national Church alone, but a Bishop is " obliged, if need be, to look beyond them to the law of our Mother Church of England, and beyond that to hold in due respect the Canons of the Ancient Church, especially those of the first four Œcumenical or General Councils, the decisions of which were always acknowledged to be of paramount authority." The ruling power would thus be, " not the will or caprice or fancy of the Bishop, but the law of the Church; of which he is only the constituted organ." Even as to Holy Scripture, " the Bishop must so expound and apply it, that he conflict not with the Canons of the Church." Moreover, he contended that the vows of canonical obedience " do not and cannot be held to bind the clergy, when the Bishop transcends his proper circle. For then he becomes a transgressor, and ceasing to pay respect to his own vows, he cannot lawfully demand that obedience which was only promised on the supposition that the Bishop himself should be obedient to the Church, according to the commands of her divine Lord and Master."

This sermon was courteously but most earnestly protested against by the *Episcopal Recorder*, as " an ecclesiastical enormity," worse than all " the tenets of Oxford" put together: and the phrase to which my Father's *Letters* had given currency, was boldly turned against himself:—" Of all the novelties which have recently been broached amongst us, this of Bishop Hopkins is the most truly novel; and it does appear to us that there is not one amongst them all which, in the end, will be so certain to 'disturb our peace.'" The instinct of the *Recorder* was right in finding that the Bishop of Vermont had expressed, in its quintessence, the principle which vitalized the whole Oxford movement: but its editor wasted his labor in denouncing him as a "misguided theorist" introducing a "novelty," so long as our Prayer-Book contains, in its Ordinal, the precious words:— "Brother, forasmuch as the Holy Scripture and the ancient Canons command."

It was about this time that an English Low-Church clergyman of some prominence wrote to sound my Father as to the practicability of getting a Bishop consecrated in this country for the Scottish schismatics who refused—while still calling themselves "Episcopalians" and using the Church of England Prayer-Book —to acknowledge the spiritual jurisdiction of their own Scottish Bishops. The ground upon which this appeal was made, will cause a theologian to smile:—" In arguing the case at a meeting of a few with whom I am intimate, I was thus appealed to:—'Is it not *heresy* to invoke the Holy Spirit to descend into the Bread and the Wine, and thereby make them *de facto* the Body and Blood of our Blessed Lord? And is it not persecution to excommunicate a man for not yielding to this?' This, I fear, is the plain state of the case, and I could urge nothing in reply, overcome by the perplexing difficulty." My Father, in his answer, dealt gently but very firmly with his correspondent. As to "heresy," he said:—" Nothing can be better established than the principle that we cannot lawfully hold communion with heretics. Now the Church of England and our American Church *do* hold communion with the Church in Scotland, and therefore we are directly involved in the charge." He then gave him some elementary instruction as to what "heresy" is, and what is "persecution," and also as to what is a "schism": so that after the exchange of two or three letters, his English correspondent was convinced that to consecrate a Bishop in America for the Scottish separatists "would be to create a schism," and that it was English business rather than American anyhow: and he dropped the subject with the following candid admission:—" Your elucidation of the Scottish Communion Office is the more important and valuable to me, who have hitherto been only guided by, and made myself the mere echo of, the sentiments of my brethren here, and who—such of them as I have conversed with on the subject—take a partial view, I fear, of the Scotch business, from prejudice in favor of those whom they regard as their ill-used brethren."

While on this subject of creating schisms, it may be *à propos* to quote from another Evangelical. About the time referred to, an exchange of publications with Bishop Daniel Wilson of Calcutta brought also a kind letter from that model Evangelical Bishop, who wrote:—" I take a deep interest in the American Episcopal Church, and I often wish her missionary Presbyters would plant themselves in my Diocese, instead of leaving the field to be occupied by the Missionaries of the Presbyterian Board, who, with all their personal excellencies, create schisms wherever they go."

In some of the most influential and thoughtful of the High-Church leaders, the results of the Trial of Bishop Onderdonk had wrought a deep dissatisfaction if not disgust. Something of that feeling which, we are told, maketh even wise men mad, led to the expression in certain quarters of a wish for the dissolution of our General Convention, and for the disintegrating of the American Church into a parcel of " independent Dioceses,"—so called. Of all those who had voted *Not Guilty* upon the Trial of Bishop Onderdonk, Bishop De Lancey of Western New York was regarded as the coolest, the most sagacious, and the wisest leader. When—shortly after that Trial—he introduced into the Board of Trustees of the General Theological Seminary a proposition for destroying the " general " character of that Institution, leaving it merely Diocesan, it was understood to be the feeler for the more important work contemplated. Of the three great bonds which consolidated the Church of America, it was felt that the Seminary was the weakest, the Board of Missions was far stronger, and the General Convention was the strongest of all. A wise and cautious general will attack the weakest defence of his enemy first: and if the attack on our Church organization failed in regard to the Seminary,—the weakest bond,—it would not be worth while to attempt anything at all elsewhere. Many true friends of the Seminary were greatly alarmed at such a threatening movement, from such a quarter. And when at length —after long-heralded expectations—Bishop De Lancey rose in the Board of Trustees, in 1847, and moved his scheme, commending it with all his ability as the best course to be pursued for the peace of the Church, his speech was followed by an ominous and dead silence. The friends of the Seminary, who were accustomed to look upon Bishop De Lancey as a leader and champion, were loth to break a lance with him. The Low-Church members of the Board, eager to defeat any measure proposed by Bishop Onderdonk's friends, were too few to accomplish anything, and feared to show their hand, lest their open advocacy should determine the question against them. The personal feelings growing out of the trial had put both parties in a false position, and each was disposed to vote against its normal convictions, in order to gratify the impulse of the moment. The silence was broken by my Father, who tore the plausible scheme to pieces so thoroughly, that all anxiety was at once relieved. When he had broken the ice, there were plenty of the old friends of the Seminary to follow him, their previous silence having been due to apprehension rather than consent. Bishop De Lancey's movement fell dead. It was never heard of after that debate.

While it is evident that the apparent affiliation of my Father with Low-Churchism, for some years, was by no means so close as was imagined by the great majority of either party, and that in fundamental Church principles there was in him no change at all: yet, on the one point that was then uppermost in the feelings of all party men, he acted with them, unswervingly, to the end. In the General Convention of 1847, the Memorial from the Bishop of New York was the first business laid before the House of Bishops; the resolutions from the Diocese of New York asking for relief from its anomalous position opened the session in the Lower House: and that question was the one engrossing question in both.

In the House of Deputies, the long debate culminated in Dr. Hawks's learned and eloquent speech to prove the vacancy of the see of New York, and Prof. Ogilby's spirited and conclusive reply. In the House of Bishops, a committee was appointed on the subject, by ballot, Bishop Brownell being chairman, but leaving the work of preparing the report to my Father, whose name stood second. That report gave as the first reason for rejecting the suspended Bishop's prayer for relief, that "the Memorialist, once convicted, on unimpeached and ample testimony, of the charge of immorality, can hardly hope to exercise again his high and holy office, to the honor of God and the edifying of the Church, in the face of the same community." It then went on to state that "The Office of a Bishop was conferred upon the Memorialist, not for his own sake, but for the benefit of the Church; and, therefore, it is not for his sake, but for the welfare of the Church, that the exercise of it should ever be committed to him again." The committee added that they "do not maintain the impossibility of his restoration, nor deny that he may hereafter satisfy the Church of the strength of his claims"; but that it would be inconsistent with the high and solemn responsibility of the Episcopal character to entertain the application of the Memorialist "until he can lay before them the most ample and satisfactory testimonials." And again, in the closing of the Report, they say that, while "the remission of that sentence is a possible event, in contemplation of law, they deem it but justice to the Memorialist, and to the Diocese of New York, to add, that they consider the probability of its occurrence so slender and remote, as scarcely to afford a reasonable basis for future action."[1]

That same General Convention, however, passed a Canon giving to the Bishops collectively the power to remit or modify any judicial sentence, and providing that for this purpose a

[1] In this Report, some points were replied to, as if they were contained in Bishop Onderdonk's *Memorial;* whereas in fact they do not occur there. They had been freely urged in *The Churchman*, however, which was so thoroughly identified with the Bishop's cause, that he was generally regarded as accountable for words over which he really exercised no control. I called my Father's attention to this fact after the adjournment; and in his reply he stated that, in preparing the Report, his object was, "to meet, in a short and simple way, every point which, in the public mind of the Church, seemed to require notice"; though he added, "I freely grant that if I had had the *Memorial* at hand when I wrote the Report, I should have modified the expression which has given my friends on the other side a handle. . . . I tried to have it corrected in the House, but the other Bishops, led on by Bishop Elliott, protested against altering anything, saying that it was just as it should be. It was near the close of our session, and, as time was pressing, I let it go."

special meeting of the Bishops "shall be convened by the Presiding Bishop on the application of any five Bishops, three months' notice in writing" being given to each Bishop, "of the time, place and object of the meeting." The request was made by five Bishops in October, 1849: but the Presiding Bishop (Philander Chase), taking it for granted that Bishop Onderdonk would have a better chance at a special meeting than when the attendance would be more full at General Convention, gave the Canon a twist which its framers certainly never intended. Instead of appointing a meeting in February, which would have given full "three months' notice" to all, he called the Bishops to meet on this subject on the 1st of October, 1850, the day before the assembling of General Convention: which was "three months' notice" and eight months more. My Father candidly wrote him that this was "rather stretching the law"; and on that principle of giving notice it is clear that the very object of the Canon providing that "a special meeting *shall* be called" might in every case be defeated. But the Presiding Bishop's feelings were very strong on this point. He wrote to my Father of the "horror" he felt at the idea of a meeting in February on this matter. "Not a moment's peace would I enjoy," wrote he, "were I to violate my conscience in termination of B. T. O.'s *suspension*, which was virtually *degradation*."

On assembling in Cincinnati in 1850, on the day before the General Convention, the very able document of the Standing Committee of New York was laid before them, and the discussion of the subject was very animated and protracted. The Canon of 1847 had not given the power of remitting or modifying to "The House of Bishops," but to "The Bishops of this Church who are entitled to seats in the House of Bishops": and it was clear therefore that what they did under this Canon was no part of their proceedings as a "House" of General Convention, and could have no proper place on its Journals. After full discussion,—my Father strongly advocating the change,— the practice was introduced by which the House of Bishops, whenever going into the consideration of any subject which does not require the coördinate action of the House of Deputies, resolves itself into a Council, or "goes into Council": a separate journal being kept of its proceedings in that capacity, which is not printed. This custom has ever since been continued, and it is one in which my Father took particular satisfaction. It was not until the 12th of October that the Bishops in Council made their reply, by adopting a Report, drawn by my Father (who again stood second on the Committee, and was again requested by Bishop Brownell, its chairman, to perform that duty). It called attention to the fact, that immediate restoration was not plainly asked for by any Memorial before them; nor was it implied that it was "the general wish of the Diocese that the suspended Bishop should again become its active head," while the New York document admitted that, if restored, the Bishop might find it expedient to delegate a portion or even the whole of his Episcopal visitations to others, or resign his jurisdiction altogether: and the Report therefore reiterated the conclusion announced in 1847, that "in the absence of any proof or even allegation of his innocence, of any profession of penitence, and of any sufficient evidence that the penalty, under which he was suffering, was inconsistent with law or equity, a remission ought not to be expected, and could not be allowed." The passage of the Canon permitting the election of a Provisional Bishop, at length secured Episcopal services for the Diocese of New York, and the question of the restoration of Bishop Onderdonk was not again agitated until 1859.

But in 1854 the case of Bishop Henry U. Onderdonk came up for discussion, the Hon. Horace Binney, in a pamphlet, attacking the majority of the Bishops with no slight energy for pronouncing a sentence which he declared to be unjust, uncanonical, illegal; and for harshness and oppression in refusing, in three successive General Conventions, to remit it. Bishop Meade replied; Mr. Binney rejoined; and my Father then, at Bishop Meade's earnest request, continued the discussion in a pamphlet, setting forth *The true Church principles of Restoration to the Episcopal Office*." He did not satisfy or convince Mr. Binney. But he set forth clearly and fully the principles on which he had himself acted all along in this painful business; and, considering the leading position accorded to him from the first whenever this subject came up for consideration by the Bishops, it is fair to conclude that these are the principles that guided the majority of that House to the end, in the cases of both the brothers.

In answer to the question, On what principles have the Bishops a *right* to restore Bishop Onderdonk? my Father replies,—"On the same principles which authorized his consecration. There are no others applicable. We know no others on which we can be justified before God and man." . . . He enumerates the election, the solemn testimonials from the Diocese, from the Clergy and Laity of other Dioceses, the consent of the majority of the Bishops, the good report of them that are without, and all the other required evidences that a Bishop-elect will exercise the office of a Bishop to the honor of God and to the edifying of the Church: and continues:— "Manifestly all this was necessary before the Bishops could have a right to consecrate him at all. . . . Now have we a right to restore him on any other principles? . . . I maintain that we, as *Trustees for God and the Church*, must have the same elements in the work of restoration, that we have in the work of consecration, since both acts produce precisely *the same practical result to the Church*, viz., the enabling an individual to execute the office of a Bishop who could not execute it before." And again he says:—"It is totally absurd to suppose that he can ever come before us with the testimony of the Church in his favor, and yet, without that testimony, the Bishops could not have consecrated him in the beginning. How, without an equal, or rather, I should say, *a much stronger testimony*, could we restore him now? For it is evident that it needs more evidence to countervail the past stain upon his character, than it needed at first to recommend him to confidence, when no *trust* had been violated, and no *solemn vows* had been broken." Towards the close of the pamphlet he quoted the saying of Bingham, "that the glory of the Ancient Church was her discipline," and vindicated Bishop Meade from the assaults made on him for being the leader in all the presentments against Bishops. "As for myself," said my Father, "I lay no claim to the Christian boldness and fearlessness which it required. But yet I should esteem it an honor far beyond any in my reach, if my epitaph could say:—

'Here lies the body of a Bishop, who was distinguished beyond all his brethren for his zealous, sincere and consistent support of pure Church discipline.'"

The hint thus more than once given by the Bishop of Vermont, that formal and solemn written testimonials must be laid before the Bishops before they would act in the case of a suspended Bishop, was at length taken. The application of Bishop Henry Onderdonk, which had been made and rejected in 1847, 1850, and 1853, was renewed in 1856, and would have suffered the same fate, but that a written testimonial, in language as strong as that required for a Bishop's consecration, received the signatures of a majority of the members of the House of Deputies, and of many others, including among "those that are without" even his old opponent in the controversy about *Episcopacy tested by Scripture*, the eminent Presbyterian divine, Dr. Albert Barnes. This was fairly meeting my Father on his own ground. The restoration was advocated by the Bishop of Pennsylvania. There was no entanglement of Diocesan jurisdiction in the way. And finally the remission of the suspension was carried in Council: my Father, however, being one of the last to consent, though his name stands, by right of seniority, as the first of the twenty Bishops signing the formal act of Restoration. That formal act, however, embodies in the clearest language the very principle for which the Bishop of Vermont had so long contended, for the Bishops therein say that they restore the suspended Bishop,— "being satisfied by the evidence laid before us, that he has led, during the twelve years which have elapsed since the said sentence was pronounced, a sober, godly and blameless life, and that the general mind of the Church, so far as it could be ascertained from the memorials addressed to us by a large number of the Clerical and Lay Deputies of the General Convention now in session, and others, earnestly desires that the said sentence should be remitted." On the evening of that day it was a keen pleasure to me to be allowed to accompany my Father in the brief call of fraternal congratulation which he made upon the restored Bishop.

It was a great mistake that the precedent thus set was not followed in 1859, on the occasion of the last attempt to secure the restoration of the Bishop of New York. The vote of the Diocese of New York was not for Restoration pure and simple, but for restoration conditioned upon restraints in regard to the exercise of jurisdiction, which in the minds of many were pregnant with evils. There was no formal testimonial as to character from the Convention of New York, or from members of the House of Deputies: but only from the Church of the Annunciation, New York. There was not on the part of Bishop H. Potter the slightest advocacy of the restoration; and the evils which he openly stated were sure to flow from the anomalous position in which it was proposed to leave the question of responsible jurisdiction, satisfied the minds of all that his icy neutrality was to be interpreted as a settled hostility. In this state of things, my Father remained true as steel to his old principles. I never in all my life strove one tenth part as hard to influence his course in any matter, as I did to change his voice and vote on this subject: but without the slightest success. The anxious, earnest, and often impassioned discussion in the Council of Bishops continued through eight days, sometimes until late at night. But all was in vain. As went the Bishop of Vermont so went the House. For unqualified restoration there were only *eight* votes. The greatest strength of Bishop Onderdonk was eleven or *twelve* as against *nineteen*, and that was only on the final vote to lay the whole subject on the table.[1]

The decided defeat of the most promising effort ever made on his behalf, slowly but surely broke the old man's heart: and in eighteen months he was at rest from all the trials of earth. He died with the declaration on his lips: "Of the crimes of which I have been accused, and for which I have been condemned, my conscience acquits me, in the sight of God."[2]

[1] *Obsequies and Obituary Notices*, etc., p. 148.
[2] This must not, however, be interpreted in such wise as to be inconsistent with the language of his last Memorial to the House of Bishops, in which he says:—" I presume not to say that I am entirely faultless, and have deserved no censure. I am not exempt from human infirmity, and . . . acknowledge that I cannot but believe parts of my conduct to have betrayed indiscretion, and that my demeanor must, in some instances, have been calculated to produce impressions injurious alike to the Church and myself, however such effect may have been unintended and unperceived on my part. I say that I cannot but believe this, because some of my fellow-Christians, and, among them, some of yourselves, brethren, felt bound to this extent to condemn me. I beg you, however, to believe me, when I most solemnly declare that, in this matter,

This painful subject was one on which I never after conversed with my Father. I knew that he had acted most conscientiously throughout. I knew that in nothing had the performance of his duty given him greater pain. There was no use in reviving painful associations when it was too late to be of any service either to the living or the dead. But so long as the Diocese of New York asked for restoration only under heavy conditions, and sent in no testimonials of character signed by the majority of Clergy and Laity, and Bishop Potter foreboded only evil: so long nothing in all human probability could ever have altered my Father's course, which was simply an unswerving adherence to the principles which had guided him from the first.

I was not the slave of deliberate impurity of intention. . . . But be my offences small or great, to whatever extent, brethren, I have brought reproach on the cause of our Master, or given just offence to any of my fellow-Christians, even without a purposed intention of wickedness, I am, without reference to your action on this request, heartily sorry, and desire to humble myself in penitence before God and man."—*Obsequies and Obituary Notices*, etc., p. 127.

Chapter XIV.

THE NEW JERSEY CASE.

IT is evident that some of the more bitter opponents of the Bishops Onderdonk were not satisfied with the success of the movements against them, but for years had contemplated proceeding against Bishop Doane of New Jersey, if not others of the High-Church party also.[1] At length, after the pecuniary failure of Bishop Doane (mainly due to his having alone carried S. Mary's Hall and Burlington College through the financial storms which had wrecked so many other noble enterprises of the same sort), the tongues which had made themselves busy with the Bishop's name for many years, resounded more and more loudly. They waited patiently for a year or two after the Bishop's failure, to ripen the harvest of scandal; but then, it was evidently time to act, if the case were ever to be acted upon at all. Accordingly, three Bishops made up their minds that it was their conscientious duty to rid the Church, if possible, of the grievous burden of Bishop Doane's misdoings, which were injuring the cause of Christ greatly in every place throughout the land, except New Jersey.

But the whole course of this attempt at Episcopal discipline was the reverse of that which had humbled the powerful Bishop of New York. At almost every turn where it was possible to make an error of judgment, the unhappy Bishop of New York made it; while his leading opponents, far from making errors of judgment, actually blundered into their chief advantages over him, without knowing it. But in the New Jersey case, all the errors of judgment were made by the Bishop's opponents, while the gallant defence made by him,—and he fought his own battle himself, without lawyers, from first to last,—was the most remarkable exhibition of boldness even to audacity, of adroitness, skill,

---

[1] See the Rev. James C. Richmond's *Conspiracy*, p. 13; also his *Reply*, p. 11 Also, Dr. Anthon's Letter, *ante*, p. 233, and Bishop McIlvaine's Letter, *ante*, p. 235.

endurance, eloquence, manly candor, and prudence, that has ever been seen, in that line, in the Church of America.

The three Bishops began with a blunder,—one of their worst. They sent to Bishop Doane, early in February, 1852, a joint letter, in which their object seems to have been to induce the Bishop to procure an investigation of the charges by New Jersey first. If—as they doubtless thought possible, believing the charges against the Bishop to be true—his own Diocese should present him for trial, the Three would be saved a very disagreeable and odious piece of business: and would not be disqualified from sitting on the trial. If the investigation should be refused, or made in an unsatisfactory manner, it would color the case more strongly against the Accused. They therefore feathered their first dart with the declaration "that action should first take place in the Diocesan Convention"; and added that "it was only when a Diocesan Convention refused to institute inquiry, or neglected to do it for too long a period, or performed the duty unfaithfully," that three Bishops could be expected to undertake the duty.

It was dangerous to make a mismove when Bishop Doane was playing the other side of the game: and when the Three went on to specify what they required as to the time of calling the Convention of New Jersey, and the sort of Committee that must be appointed, and so forth, they capped the climax of their blunders. Within three days Bishop Doane's "Protest, Appeal and Reply" was flying all over the country. He knew the Convention of New Jersey, and they knew him. He knew he had their hearts, and they knew he deserved to have them. In 1849 when the charges were first brought before them without being backed by a responsible name, not a single voice—not even that of the mover of the resolution—voted for a Committee of inquiry; while the unanimous *No* went up like a shout. The idea of such a Convention being dictated to by the Bishops of Virginia, Ohio and Maine, and under a threat too, welded the whole Diocese like one man, in a white heat of outraged feeling.

The four names signed to the complaints received by the three Bishops were, as nearly as possible, of no account whatsoever in the Diocese of New Jersey: and when the Special Convention met, it declared its full confidence in its beloved Bishop, and uttered its indignation at the course of the Three with the utmost cordiality. Whereupon, the Three went on to make their formal Presentment, and the Presiding Bishop (Philander Chase of Illinois) lost no time in the performance of his canonical duty, fixing the 24th of June for the day of Trial, in Camden.

When Bishop Doane stated these facts to his Convention at their annual session in May, that body remembered its pledge made in 1849 to investigate any charges made against their Bishop on responsible authority: and, considering the Presentment to be the first thing worthy of that name coming before them, they appointed a committee to investigate everything contained in the Presentment. Thus their investigation would precede the trial, and the original blunder of the Presenters would be turned against themselves.

But in this curious conjuncture two other blunders were made. The enemies of Bishop Doane felt so sure of their trial before the Bishops, that they laughed at the idea of appearing before "the whitewashing Committee of the Convention," as they called it; and, though often invited, not one of them would come and tell his story to Jerseymen: which enabled the Bishop's friends to say, that his accusers had made default, and did not dare to substantiate the charges.

The other blunder was made by the Presiding Bishop, certainly not through partiality for Bishop Doane. But it was the year of the Jubilee celebration of the venerable Society for the Propagation of the Gospel in England, and, in response to a very hearty invitation, certain of our American Bishops were ready to go over as representatives of our Church at the festival. But their attendance at the time appointed would be impossible, should the Trial open on the 24th of June. Now Bishop Chase had received more kindness and more money in England than all the other American Bishops put together; and he was therefore anxious that this first formal invitation from the Mother Church should not remain unimproved. It might, indeed, turn out to be the beginning of something which should become vastly more important than a joint celebration; and therefore Bishop Chase was easily persuaded to change the day for the meeting of the Court, from June 24th to October 7th. This he had no Canonical power to do, but thought he had guarded sufficiently against evil consequences by asking and receiving a pledge from Bishop Doane (who also had many friends in England) that he would take no advantage of the postponement. The Presenters, however, were very uneasy if not indignant at the change, which had been made without their consent. Bishop McIlvaine wrote strongly concerning the "singular blunder of our venerable Primus," declaring the postponement to be "illegal, without authority, and void": and adding that their counsel [1] and other legal friends were of opinion that they ought to meet on the 24th of June and adjourn formally to the 7th of October. But as there was a chance for a blunder as brilliant as that of the venerable Primus, the Presenters concluded to make it: and so, without withdrawing their Presentment, they formally made a new one, the last signature to which was not written until the 11th of August, whereas New Jersey's investigation was completed on the 14th of July, and was enthusiastically accepted by the Convention as abundantly sufficient, before the new Presentment was even made! The new Presentment—with the exception of a few specifications put in to make a difference—was the same as the old. Those few additional points, there was no doubt, would be cleared up by the Convention as satisfactorily as the others, so soon as they had the opportunity: but, since the new Presentment was served exactly the Canonical 30 days before the Trial was to begin, and the Constitution of New Jersey required four weeks' notice for the meeting of a Special Convention, this little remnant of their loving labor in defence of their Bishop must needs be postponed till after the meeting of the Court. A Committee had been appointed, however, to appear before the Court, and claim it as the Canonical right of the Diocese, that its investigation should render all further proceedings under the presentment needless.

My Father had had enough of Episcopal trials. He believed

---

[1] The Canon said:—" The accused party may have the privilege of appearing by counsel ; and in case of the exercise of such privilege, but not otherwise, those presenting shall have the like privilege." The Presenters, it seems, employed counsel from the start.

that it was the duty of every Bishop, when summoned, to appear and take his seat, unless he had a valid excuse for shirking the unpleasant obligation. Such a mountain had been made of the kindly expression of a difference in opinion on one point, as making him a " doctrinal and personal opponent " of Bishop Onderdonk, that he now hoped to be fairly excused from sitting on the Trial of Bishop Doane, because of the sharp though almost forgotten controversy with him just before leaving Boston for Vermont. He stated to his own Convention his determination to ask to be excused, and the reason of it; and on the assembly of the Court he made his request in writing, with his reasons :—

> Some twenty years ago, when our accused brother and myself were Presbyters in the Diocese of Massachusetts, there was a serious difficulty between us. I have no intention to enter into the details of the matter, nor do I ask you to say whether he or I were in the wrong, because I do not stand here to enter the slightest complaint against him on account of the transaction, nor am I conscious of any bias whatever as regards the present case, unless it be that of sympathy on his behalf, and a desire that his course may be vindicated to the satisfaction of the whole Church, after due investigation. But yet, when I learned that a Presentment had been made, and I reflected upon the duty which I, as one of the judges, might be called on to perform, this old and almost forgotten difficulty rose to my memory, and I could not feel satisfied that I should be acting with due delicacy and consideration for him, if I did not decline to act as one of his judges, so far as my own individual opinion was concerned ; and thus give him the benefit of the right of challenge, by challenging myself. On this ground, therefore, I request to be excused from attending the Court as one of its members. I have put my application into writing, in order that it may appear on the Record, with the decision thereupon ; and I tender it in person, as a point of respect towards the Court, and as a proof that I consider it the solemn duty of every Bishop to answer to his name on the canonical summons of the Church, unless hindered by the act of Providence ; and to submit the validity of his excuse for withdrawing, to the judgment of his Brethren.

He was not excused: and Bishop Doane very handsomely expressed his full assent and wish that my Father should be a member of the Court.

Its opening services were marked by one of those startling coincidences which so often, in times of high excitement, flash forth from the services of the day. The first act of the Bishops on assembling at Camden was to unite in the Morning Prayer of the Church; and my Father, as senior Bishop present, officiated. It was the 7th day of the month, and the moment the first words of the first Psalm for the day were uttered, every man's heart was in his mouth. There is no other such Psalm in the whole Psalter, to speak for a man unjustly arraigned by his enemies:—

Plead thou my cause, O LORD, with them that strive with me : and fight thou against them that fight against me.

Thenceforward we watched the verses. The Presenters themselves had to respond:—

Let them be confounded, and put to shame, that seek after my soul : let them be turned back, and brought to confusion, that imagine mischief for me.

And again, they had to say :—

Let their way be dark and slippery: and let the angel of the LORD persecute them.

And again :—

Let a sudden destruction come upon him unawares ; and his net that he hath laid privily catch himself : that he may fall into his own mischief.

There was hope in the words:—

All my bones shall say, LORD, who is like unto thee, who deliverest the poor from him that is too strong for him : yea, the poor, and him that is in misery, from him that spoileth him?

As to the charges, the language was clear:—

False witnesses did rise up : they laid to my charge things that I knew not.

As to the ingratitude shown for kindnesses done to those connected with one of the Presenters, the words,

I behaved myself as though it had been my friend or my brother : I went heavily, as one that mourneth for his mother,

recalled to the minds of many the great kindness and constant attention shown by Bishop Doane to the mother of Bishop McIlvaine, who died a resident of Burlington, New Jersey. The seizing upon the Bishop's failure as the chance to attempt his ruin, echoed from the words:—

But in mine adversity they rejoiced, and gathered themselves together:

yea, the very abjects came together against me unawares, making mouths at me, and ceased not.

And when one remembers the use that was made by the Bishop's enemies (not the Presenters, of course) of the *Police Gazette* and the vilest newspapers as channels of unmeasured defamation, " the very abjects " described them precisely. The element of personal feeling, which was so irrepressible on both sides, spoke out with vehemence :—

O let not them that are mine enemies triumph over me ungodly: neither let them wink with their eyes that hate me without a cause. . . .

Let them not say in their hearts, There! there! so would we have it: neither let them say, We have devoured him.

Their claim of having full evidence in their hands was thus replied to :—

They gaped upon me with their mouths, and said, Fie on thee! fie on thee! we saw it with our eyes.

This thou hast seen, O Lord : hold not thy tongue then ; go not far from me, O Lord. . .

Judge me, O LORD my God, according to thy righteousness : and let them not triumph over me.

Even the Bishop's friends were not forgotten by the Psalmist :—

Let them be glad and rejoice, that favor my righteous dealing : yea, let them say alway, Blessed be the LORD, who hath pleasure in the prosperity of his servant.

And the Psalm ends with this burst of pious confidence and gratitude :—

As for my tongue, it shall be talking of thy righteousness : and of thy praise, all the day long.

There were many of us present at that service, who had about as much of neutrality in our hearts as is to be found in that Psalm : and we were from that moment convinced that God was fighting for the good Bishop, and would bring him safe through all his troubles ; and that there was no danger of his sharing the fate of the poor Bishops Onderdonk. But, as in many other cases, the path by which Providence brought about this happy result, was one of great intricacy and complexity, and many things were accomplished that were not intended.

Three of the Bishops, including the Presiding Bishop,[1] had gone to their rest between the summoning and the meeting of the Court. Of the thirteen who sat, my Father, the senior, was elected President of the Court by ballot. The Presenters had their lawyers in attendance, ready for use: but the Canon gave them no right to appear by Counsel unless the accused first claimed the like privilege. Confident in his own abilities, Bishop Doane determined to be his own lawyer, and was easily more than a match for the three Presenters, who were thus compelled, within the Court-room, to do all their own work.

The first *Order*, on the organizing of the Court, was to adjourn its sessions from Camden to Burlington. Camden was the place in New Jersey nearest to Philadelphia, which, as the headquarters of Low-Churchism, had always been most hostile to Bishop Doane. Burlington was his own home, where nearly all his alleged offences had been committed, and where all his witnesses were. The next thing done was the reading of the communication from the New Jersey Committee, asking that the Diocese should be heard before proceeding further. This was denied, by the close vote of 7 to 6, on the ground that the point could better be considered later in the case: and a further *Order* then at once fixed the time for hearing New Jersey to be immediately after the reading of the Presentment. This was carried by the same vote of 7 to 6; but there was only one Bishop who was in the majority both times. Bishop Doane—far from courting concealment—moved that the doors of the Court-room be opened to the public: but it was not done.

New Jersey was heard,—the Committee being admitted in a body, and their Chairman reading their long argument and appeal with all the force that a warm heart and fervid elocution could give. The Presenters took two days to prepare a written reply, which cut up many parts of the fervid appeal with equal severity and justice: but it was cold-blooded work, and the hardness of tone with which they closed, helped them with nobody.

The Bishop was permitted to reply on behalf of his Diocese: and he threw himself into the work with the whole force of his

---

[1] The other two were Bishops Gadsden of South Carolina and Henshaw of Rhode Island.

character. He openly declared, from the first, his comparative carelessness of his own personal issues: but announced his conviction of the great evils already brought on the Church of America by the previous Trial of a Bishop, and his fixed determination to do what lay in him to "make the Trial of a Bishop hard." And he kept his word. In the discussion, continued by him and the Presenters for some days, he had the advantage of them increasingly, in ability, in fertile resource, in turning all their errors to the best account, and in winning the sympathy of all who had hearts to feel: while the Presenters won sympathy from none but those whom they brought with them. Burlington had an uncongenial atmosphere for such: and the sympathy for the Accused grew stronger and stronger every day of the session.

On the last day but one, the members of the Court delivered their opinions in full; and on adjourning that day the result was still undecided, the Bishop of Mississippi having yet to make known his judgment, which would either tie the Court or carry it for New Jersey. He had given no intimation as to the leaning of his own mind.

On the morning of the last day, as Bishop Doane was walking, alone, from his house to the Court-room, with bundles of papers under his arm, a snake wriggled out across his path on the sidewalk. Instantly the Bishop's heel was on the reptile's head, and after grinding it into the gravel until the work was complete, he kicked the now harmless carcass off the sidewalk, and quietly went on his way. When the Bishop of Mississippi began reading his opinion, it opened with a declaration that he was "one of those who are disposed to hold the Clergy to a strict account"; that in his opinion, a Bishop who had "once been convicted of wilful impurity or dishonesty, should be *lastingly* deprived of his high and holy office"; and that "under these solemn convictions" he had "come nearly two thousand five hundred miles to be present on this occasion." The opponents of Bishop Doane thought the case was theirs, when they heard these words. But the rights of the "independent Diocese" inclined the scale the other way, before the document was ended. And it was the Bishop of Mississippi's vote which decided that the Court was not called upon to proceed further, because "previous to the making of the Presentment now before the Court, the Convention of New Jersey had investigated most of the matters contained therein, and had determined that there was no ground for Presentment": and it was added, that the Convention's pledge of further investigation as to the few new specifications might safely be relied on. Thus the blunders of the original concession in the "private letter" and the making of the new Presentment, were fatal.

The Presenters then had the face to produce the old Presentment, and offer to go to trial on that: but this was a little too much. The Court promptly declined to receive it: and the "first Trial of Bishop Doane" was ended,—being no Trial at all.

But there were six Bishops who dissented on the main question, —the Court just escaping a tie vote: and the first of the six was the President of the Court, not a single High-Churchman being among the other five. To understand my Father's position in this matter, we must remember the original condition of the American Canons, by which a Bishop could be *tried* only by his own Convention,—an utter abomination to any one with Catholic principles; and must remember also the Bishop of Vermont's long and patient efforts to secure our recognition of the true principle, that Bishops are amenable, not to their own Clergy and Laity in Convention, but only to their own Order. The Constitution had been changed, and the Canons had recognized the right principle, notwithstanding the imperfections that yet marked its practical workings. To the Diocesan Convention (under severe restrictions) was left the power to present its Bishop, but not to try him: and to render still clearer the amenability to their own Order, any three Bishops might also present. There being nothing in the Canon to indicate that either of these two coördinate presenting powers should have precedence over the other, of course the first that should *make* a presentment would exclude the other.

It has already been said, that the hardships flowing from the Onderdonk case had irritated many High-Churchmen into an abnormal admiration of the idea of Diocesan independence. In the stress of the battle to make the trial of a Bishop hard, this same feeling proved to be the most available and the most effective weapon for the defence: and the blunders of the Presenters enabled Bishop Doane to grasp it by the handle instead of by the blade. But, being the author of the change himself, my Father knew that the intent of it was thus entirely misunderstood and misrepresented. To him, the idea that because one presenting power was resolved not to act, therefore the other (expressly provided to meet such a contingency) should be considered incapable of acting, was absurd. And to see a Court of fourteen Bishops, canonically brought together to try a Presentment canonically made, and then and there resolving to go home without action, because *seven laymen* of the Diocese of the Accused had already tried the case, looked like going back to the original slough of unprincipled American novelties, and losing all that had been gained by his long years of labor for something better. He sympathized fully with the Accused, so far as personal feeling went: and no one could behold unmoved the enthusiastic devotion of the clergy and laity of the Diocese to their Bishop. But Catholic principle and Canon law and common sense compelled him to dissent from an *Order*, at which he was nevertheless personally rejoiced, as well as greatly relieved. In his *Opinion*, he says, after discussing the claimed right of the independent Diocese of New Jersey :—

> If these be the rights of Dioceses, I should be glad to know when they were conferred, or by what branch of the Church of Christ they were ever claimed or exercised, before they were assumed by the Diocese of New Jersey. With respect to the other phrase, "an independent Diocese," a definition is equally desirable. According to my judgment, it is a phrase without any meaning, unless it be a very bad one. A Diocese cannot be independent in its legislation, because its laws must always be subordinate to the General Convention of the whole Church, of which it is but one member. If its Bishop be infirm, and it be required to give him an Assistant, it cannot be independent, because it must have the consent of the whole Church for the consecration of the elected person. If its Bishop be dead, it cannot be independent, because, without the same consent, it cannot have a successor. And if its Bishop be the subject of evil report, it cannot be independent, because the other Bishops are the only tribunal in the Church who are authorized to try, and either acquit or condemn him. The truth is, that this phrase can never be reconciled with genuine Catholicity. It belongs of right to the Puritan school, and its influence all tends in a schismatic direction.

Among the letters which my Father received, showing that the principles for which he contended in that *Opinion* were not wholly lost sight of in the strong and general sympathy for Bishop Doane as a man, there was one from Bishop Williams, of Connecticut, in which he says:—"I do not believe an abler Opinion was ever penned: nor am I alone in my views." And in point of principle, the result vindicated the correctness of this approval.

The Presenters, with a courage and perseverance certainly remarkable, felt it their bounden duty, in conscience, not to let the matter end with a mere *ex parte* Diocesan investigation by laymen, without any real hearing of the only parties who professed to have anything against the Bishop of New Jersey. Bishop Meade's feeling of indignant disappointment and disgust was, indeed, plainly manifested in the Court-room. After the *Order* of the Court was adopted, he did not wait for a formal adjournment; but gathering his long cloak about him, taking his black satchel in his hand, and deliberately putting his hat on in the presence of them all, he turned his back on the Court, and slowly and grimly stalked out of the room. Nor did he even so much as enter a house in Burlington; but walked straight down street to the steamboat dock, and there sat on a wooden bench in the open air until the arrival of the boat which took him Southward once more. It was not long before a list of 130 names was procured in New Jersey—so it was claimed—requesting the Presenters to make their Presentment for the third time: which they did accordingly, and this time without any entanglement. The importance of all the principles involved was at length thoroughly understood; and they succeeded in getting together the most numerous Court of Bishops that ever sat in this country.

Twenty-one members of the Court took their seats, on Thursday, September 1st, 1853. The Presenters had hired a Hall in Camden for the use of the Court, and this fact decided the Presiding Bishop, Dr. Brownell, to fix the meeting of the Court there. Bishop Doane again moved to open the doors to the public, and the Presenters were also willing: but the Court refused by a strong majority.

The Presenters, however, had not yet lost the art of making blunders. As before, Bishop Doane managed his own case alone, thus compelling the Presenters, according to the Canon, to do without counsel in the Court-room. But the Hall which they had hired was provided with a convenient little chamber, opening into the Court-room by a door: and in that room the Presenters had accommodated their Counsel and other friends. When Bishop Doane called the attention of the Court to this as unfair, since *he* had not employed counsel, and *his* friends were excluded, Bishop Meade pleaded in vain for his friends. The Presenters were directed by the Court to request their friends to withdraw.

This was not the only blunder. Bishop Meade having mentioned the Memorial from 130 Jerseymen requesting this third Presentment to be made, Bishop Doane asked if the 130 were Communicants of the Church. Bishop Meade "did not know." Bishop Doane then demanded, as a right, to see this Memorial, with its list of names: and Bishop Meade promised that it should be forthcoming. But on subsequent conference with the other two Presenters, the promise was forfeited.

Still a third blunder was added. In reply to one of Bishop Doane's arguments, the Presenters read a written opinion, drawn as they said by a "distinguished jurist." Upon pressure from Bishop Doane, the Presenters had to give the name of this "distinguished jurist"; and it turned out to be the name of one of their own counsel:—which was hardly the correct thing for them to do, when the Canon shut them out from the open aid of counsel. Every error of theirs, however, only strengthened Bishop Doane.

The chief point of debate was the one on which the previous decision had turned: namely, whether the Diocese of New Jersey should be heard, and interpose her investigation by seven laymen as sufficient to supersede the necessity of going on under the Presentment made by three Bishops. In other words, the chief points made by the Bishop of Vermont in his *Opinion* came up for decision afresh. The first was, whether the Diocese should be admitted by its Committee; which was decided in the negative, thus overruling the decision of the first Court. A motion by Bishop Johns that "the Court entirely *recognize the right*" of Bishop Doane to lay before them the result of the New Jersey investigation, was lost by a tie vote: but it was with no wish to deprive the Bishop of the benefit of it in the minds of the Judges; for Bishop Elliott's motion " that at this or any subsequent stage of the proceedings the Court will *cheerfully hear* from *the Respondent* the result " of the New Jersey investigation, was adopted unanimously. Bishop Doane was quite correct in considering this as " altogether the rejection of his Diocese " in its claimed "*right*" to intervene. They also, four to one, decided that they would hear the Respondent read any paper prepared by the New Jersey Committee, and receive the testimony and acts of the Convention: and an attempt by the Presenters to have this order rescinded was defeated. The Court, however, more than four to one, explained that it refused to rescind, because willing that the Respondent should have all the advantage he could derive from those Diocesan proceedings; "at the same time distinctly declaring that, by this action, the Court does not recognize any *right* in the Convention of New Jersey to appear as a party before this Court." The Diocesan Documents were then read: but they were not placed on the Journal.

Three whole days were spent, after the settlement of these points, in arguing Bishop Doane's motion that the Presentment be dismissed: on the ground that it had been dismissed by the previous Court, for good and sufficient reasons, which still existed in full force. Ten days of the session had now elapsed: and the eleventh day was spent in secret session, closing with the appointment of the seven Bishops who were not members of the previous Court, as a Committee to confer with the Presenters and the Respondent, and see if any common ground could be agreed on, without going into the trial. Bishop Elliott of Georgia was the leading spirit on this Committee (but strongly aided by Bishops Brownell, Otey, and Polk). He was ranked at that time on the Evangelical side, and was a warm admirer and personal friend of Bishop Meade: but he had lost all his own property in an attempt, like Bishop Doane's, to build up two noble Church Schools in his Diocese, and he knew how to sympathize with pecuniary embarrassments arising from such a cause.

In his conference with this Committee, Bishop Doane showed that his candor, his prudence, and manly wisdom, were equal to the other great qualities which he had displayed throughout the whole of this most painful struggle. His frank and voluntary acknowledgment of " such error as his conscience accused him of " was given at once, and to the satisfaction of all, except the Presenters. And the Presenters made their last blunder, by refusing to be satisfied with " any such acknowledgment of error as the Respondent would be willing to make ": and they placed upon the Record their persistent cry that the trial should go on, whether or no.

The Committee, taking all the circumstances into consideration, and expressly specifying each, unanimously reported in favor of dismissing the Presentment, and discharging the Respondent without delay. But they also reported two other resolutions, the first of which, once more, solemnly reiterated the principle for which the Bishop of Vermont had contended from the start: " That no order or decree of the Court in October, 1852, or of this Court, shall be taken to admit *the right* of any Diocese to come between a Court of Bishops and the Respondent Bishop, after canonical Presentment first made by three Bishops." The other declared the belief of the Court that the Presenters had " acted in good faith," and " in a desire and determination to carry out the law of the Church in such case made and provided, in the painful duty which they felt themselves called upon to perform ": which was judiciously worded, and unquestionably true. And having thus prepared the way, the whole twenty-one Bishops unanimously adopted the order to dismiss the Presentment. Bishop Doane, thrice presented, and twice brought before a court of his peers, went forth uncensured to the amount of the slightest admonition, and without ever having been called on even to plead guilty or not guilty.

My Father was one of the last to give his consent to a course which was so incompatible with all his old legal principles. " The case," he said, speaking of it afterwards,[1] " was peculiar and much embarrassed by previous irregularity. But although it would be impossible, in my mind, to reduce the action of the Court to any strict legal principle, yet the final disposition of the

---

[1] Vermont Con. Journal for 1854, p. 15.

presentment was probably as near substantial justice as the position of the matter allowed. And therefore, notwithstanding its incongruity with judicial form and order, I assented to it, for the sake of unanimity; believing, as I still believe, that under all the circumstances, I ought not to stand alone in resisting a sort of compromise, which put a final close to an agitating controversy." He added: "The result, however, will doubtless be the improvement of our ecclesiastical system in the important point of discipline, so as to regulate and define its future exercise with more clearness and accuracy."

This prognostication of changes in the working system of Episcopal Trials, as proved, by experience, to be needed, was fully verified by the various plans for modifying the Canon of 1844, which were laid before the General Convention of 1853. My Father contributed one draft to the number, though neither his nor any of the others continued the presenting power in the hands of any three Bishops. These various schemes finally ripened into the Canon of 1856, every portion of which was most thoroughly discussed previous to its adoption. Dr. Hawks was the engineer of the present Canon in the Lower House, and feelingly exclaimed "*Laus Deo!*" when it was declared by the President of the Lower House to be adopted. The power of making a Presentment is now given neither to the Diocesan Convention nor to three Bishops. But, except in doctrinal cases, an intermediate body,—a Board of Inquiry, of eminent Clergymen and laymen,—will sift all charges brought against a Bishop by his accusers; and unless this Board of Inquiry think fit to make Presentment, nothing can be done to touch a Bishop in the way of discipline. The trial of a Bishop is thus made so "hard" that it is never likely to be attempted again, except in cases which shall be too clear and strong to admit of a reasonable doubt.

We can now look back upon the whole series of events connected with our Episcopal Trials, and see the Constitutional gain which was wrought out for us in the furnace and the heat of some of the most exciting struggles through which we have passed. My Father was the first—so far as I know—to make a steady and pertinacious effort to abolish that uncatholic Americanism by which each of our Bishops (except in Vermont) could be tried by his own Clergy and Laity. Without this power, the notion of Diocesan independence—so dear to some American minds—is a transparent absurdity. The first step was, the proposed giving the Presenting power to any three Bishops. The next was, the alteration of the Constitution, so that Bishops should be tried only by their own Order. The finishing touch of the change is, the further protection of that Order, so that not even a Presentment shall be made, until after such careful previous examination, that there will be no future trials of Bishops except in extreme cases.

The whole Apostolic Order is thus, with us, advanced to a position much more nearly approximating its ancient and original standing in the Church, than could have been deemed possible during the first generation after the Revolutionary War. And the circumstances of the contest have been such as to make the change perfectly homogeneous and unquestionably secure, because it has *not* been merely the triumph of one party over the other party. Naturally, the principles of the High-Church party would have led them to work steadily for the change, and those of the Low-Church party would have led them to work as steadily against it, since Diocesan independency (involving the equivalent of the political doctrine which asserted the right of secession) was the only theory by which the strength of our ecclesiastical system could be weakened at any future time. But since it was only High-Church Bishops that were subjected to Presentment and Trial, High-Church partisanship cannot be charged with the whole of the result: while the Low-Church party, as a whole, was so intensely interested in hunting down those whom it regarded as wicked High-Churchmen, that it committed itself, without exception or reservation, to that great change which has elevated the Apostolic Order to something like its old position of Apostolic solidarity and power. When the Presenters themselves, including such eminently representative men as Bishops Meade and McIlvaine, denounced the action of the "independent Diocese" of New Jersey as "a gross invasion of the prerogatives of the Court of Bishops"; when they said that the Court of Bishops was "created by the highest authority known to the American

Church"; that it was "not in any particular subordinate or amenable to the Convention of the Diocese of New Jersey"; that it "drew its authority from a source paramount to the laws and Canons of the Diocese of New Jersey, and which that Convention is bound to obey"; and that unless the Canons of the General Convention *gave* to New Jersey the authority she claimed, it "*did not exist,* but was an *illegal usurpation*" : when all this was said by those Low-Church leaders, they clinched the nail that had already been driven home by minds more Catholic than their own. With the passing away of the personal issues, all High-Church dissatisfaction has long since disappeared: and Low-Church dissatisfaction with the "paramount" authority of General Convention will never be able to unsettle the system now, by so much as the turning of a hair.

No one had labored more earnestly in the cause of this great improvement than the Bishop of Vermont.[1] None was more rejoiced than he at the outpouring of good feeling which accompanied the unanimous decision in the closing of the New Jersey case, and which proved that that work was now substantially *done.* He wrote to my Mother an account of it in which he said:—"The cordial union and good feeling which have thus been produced were exceedingly affecting and delightful, and I have never seen the Bishops so admirably harmonized with each other on any other occasion. We have great reason to thank God, whose work it is." Even as to the Presenters, he says— after mentioning the frank acknowledgment of Bishop Doane— "The Presenting Bishops themselves allowed that if he had admitted as much at first, they would not have presented him at all": and my Father adds that "they did not oppose the course proposed, of dismissing the Presentment," although they did not feel that they could sanction it. As this places them in a much more amiable light than they have made for themselves on the record, we are glad to mention it here, to their credit.

---

[1] During the protracted investigation into the Canon Law of the whole Church which he prosecuted during these years of effort, he copied nearly the whole of the *Reformatio Legum* with his own hand. The work was so rare that he could not buy it, and it was only with difficulty that he could borrow the volume long enough to answer his purpose. In later years he more than once expressed his regret that the work had not been better worth the trouble he took about it.

Chapter XV.

BOOKS AND PAMPHLETS.

IN giving a connected view of the important subject of Episcopal Trials, the unity of subject has been preserved, rather than that of time. We must therefore retrace our steps in order to complete the narrative of my Father's activities in other departments during the period referred to.

In his parish at Burlington, he was subject to the drawback of his numerous and protracted absences on higher duties; at one time, indeed, in 1845, he made two official visits to Philadelphia and two to New York, involving an absence of one fourth of the year. Still there was growth. In 1846 a floating debt of some hundreds of dollars was extinguished. In 1848 he was elected Rector of the parish in S. Alban's, to the no little indignation of the Church people in Burlington, who manifested so warmly their reluctance to part with their Bishop, that the invitation was at once declined. In 1850 a convenient house near the Church was secured, for the use of a Rector or Assistant Minister, when one could be supported giving his whole time to the parish; and there began to be some talk of enlarging the Church.

This enlargement was carried into effect in 1851, the improvements costing about $7000. My Father was, as before, both architect and superintendent, having unusually vigorous coöperation on the part of one of the laity. In the Chancel, a large portion of the adornment was the work of his own hands. He painted six tablets, on canvas, for the three compartments on each side of the Chancel wall. The selection of texts embodied a brief summary of God's dealings with man, from the Creation to the Day of Judgment. He painted every letter himself, and each letter was shaded with three different colors. He then painted six Angels over the six tablets, the expression of the countenance of each being in correspondence with the general subject of the texts over which he spread his wings. Last of all, he modelled with his own hands the crocketed canopies that projected over each above, and the foliaged brackets that supported each below. His lively practical interest in Church architecture and adornment had brought him several invitations to become a Patron of the New York Ecclesiological Society. This, however, he thought it wiser to decline, though expressing "the most friendly feeling towards its objects and its labors,"[1] and the first embroidered altar-cloth ever made under the supervision of that Society, was completed for the Altar of S. Paul's Church, Burlington, where it still remains. The reöpening of the enlarged and beautified Church was on Christmas Day, 1851: and was a joyous festival to the parish.

The publications that appeared during these years were too numerous to be all specified here.[2] The fanatical error of Millerism was very rife in Vermont, as in some other parts of the country. At the request of many of the Clergy and Laity, the Bishop of Vermont preached and published, in 1843, two sermons exposing its fallacies unsparingly. They passed through four editions, and were read to the people in more than one parish Church.

It was about the year 1844 that my Father completed his eighteen years' work, in reading through the whole body of the Old Fathers and Councils of the Church. After S. Bernard, "the last of the Fathers," he took up also the *Summa* of S. Thomas Aquinas, with which he was so greatly delighted, that he began a translation of it, with such slight adaptations as might make it useful for the training of our own Clergy. This work was left entirely incomplete: but I have often heard him say that he

[1] As early as 1844, he thus gave to his Convention his judgment as to choral services and similar "advanced" practices:—"To the extent of the Cathedral Service of our Mother Church of England, I consider it *lawful* for any rector to proceed so long as there is no Canon of our own Church which forbids him: while the *expediency* and *wisdom* of going beyond the usual custom of our own oldest and best established Dioceses, is another question, which I shall leave to every parish minister to decide for himself." So long as doctrine was safe, he was "perfectly willing that every parish in the land should imitate the model of a Cathedral, if the Rector and his people prefer to have it so." He did not introduce these changes, however, into his own parish.

[2] A complete list of my Father's publications (or nearly complete) will be found in the *Appendix*, arranged chronologically. See pp. 449-452.

never consulted Aquinas on any point without replacing the volume on its shelf with a greater respect for the Angelic Doctor than when he took it down.

During the years 1846 and 1847, poverty pressed him so heavily that he made great efforts to earn something in the drudgery of preparing elementary books for instruction in drawing: and the *Vermont Drawing Book of Flowers*[1] and the *Vermont Drawing Book of Figures* were the result. It was thought advisable that my name should stand upon the title-page rather than my Father's: and it is true that a considerable part of the work was mine. But much the larger part of the work, and the whole of the design, were my Father's. Those of his sons who were then at home and able to help, spent many weary months during those two years in coloring the prints of the flowers. But no money was made out of it after all: and it was many years before the losses incurred in the effort were all made up by other means. He was totally destitute of the commercial faculty: and none of his sons at that time were able to supply the deficiency. In the autumn of 1847, however, through the kindness of a friend, a sum was advanced sufficient to pay the original purchase money of the Rock Point farm ($3500), with the more pressing of my Father's pecuniary obligations: the increased value of the property being by that time an abundant security for the money.

The decided change in my Father's tone towards Oxfordism, after 1842, owing to the defections to Rome, and the long deferred perversion of Dr. Newman himself,[2] who was received into the Church of Rome in October, 1845, led to some trouble of the same kind in his own Diocese. One of his clergy, who had spent part of his preparatory course under my Father's roof, and had for years been one of the most earnest, faithful and laborious of his parish clergy, had sympathized with Dr. Newman throughout; and his personal relations with my Father had been friendly and generous to an extent equalled by no other clergyman in the Diocese. But in July, 1846, he was received into the

---

[1] Begun some years before.

[2] This long delay was entirely misunderstood then: and was not fully cleared from the suspicion of treachery, until the publication of his exquisite *Apologia pro Vita Sua*.

Communion of the Church of Rome, with his wife and children, a published correspondence between him and his Bishop having, some months previous, satisfied all that his continuance with us would probably not be of long duration. This clergyman had married into a Burlington family, one of the old pillars of my Father's parish: and a portion of this family sympathized so strongly with their relatives, that in the latter part of the following year they followed the example. The number influenced, by these important and deeply regretted defections, was very small: but the pain of this experience was one which my Father never ceased to feel.

The stress of his opposition to the more advanced writers of the Church movement in England at that crisis, led him into positions on several points, which further and cooler investigation in after years compelled him to change. In one of his letters to me, for instance, when I had consulted him about some views of the Rev. Mr. Maskell before his abandonment of the Church of England, he replied:—

Maskell's doctrine that all which the Church of England did not *expressly repeal* at the time of the Reformation is still binding, proves too much. For, by that rule, we should oblige her to use Holy Water, the Vestments,[1] lighted candles by day upon the Altar, Chrism, the Episcopal ring and Pastoral Staff, the sign of the Cross with Chrism on all consecrated vessels, and (without Chrism) on the person, the giving persons of both sexes liberty to assume the vows of conventual or monastic life before the Bishop, and keep them so long, at least, as they thought proper, with many other matters of which the Liturgy, the Articles and the Canons of the Church say nothing directly. But this is nonsense, because the meaning of the Church must be gathered, not from the *bare letter of her written law* but from *that and her practice together*. If she had intended that these things should have continued as before, *they would have been continued*. And if they were dropped, and there was no attempt made to enforce them for three centuries together, how preposterous is it to pretend that the Church of England could have made the change *if* she had specified it in writing, but that *if the writing were omitted*, or were *thought unnecessary*, her public and unanimous action should go for nothing! By that rule the Church of Rome herself would be obliged to go back to

---

[1] In my Father's Sermon before General Convention, in 1847, he declares that these among other things were "abolished" at the time of the English Reformation, except the surplice and gown.

the old penitential Canons, which have never been directly or expressly repealed; and the legal doctrine would be totally destroyed which holds that laws become obsolete by *non-user*, through the lapse of time and change of circumstances.

This extract is given in full, as one of the evidences of the great—though to some degree unconscious—change which my Father's mind achieved in subsequent years. When he gave more thorough investigation to the subject, he soon saw that to admit *practice* as having the power to abrogate all previous *law*, was tantamount to making the lowest period of the Church—the practice of the dead eighteenth century—the standard for all future time, and the condemning of *all* improvement over the practice of that age as *illegal*. He found that the "legal doctrine" as to "*non-user*" was exactly the opposite of what he hastily supposed it at first. He not only, however, lived to publish the most categorical refutation of the above letter, both in principle and detail, in the latest book printed by him during his lifetime;[1] but even so speedily as in the year 1850 he had discovered that this principle which he at first thought to be correct in the Church of England, was a transparent absurdity when practised by the Jesuits in the Church of Rome: and he called pointed attention to the "admirable coolness" with which these same Jesuits "lay down the comprehensive rule THAT THE LAWS OF THE CHURCH LOSE THEIR FORCE WHEN MEN NO LONGER OBSERVE THEM!"[2]

But even in the highest climax of this feeling of opposition to those who seemed to him to be dangerously extreme, he never became narrow in his personal relations with brethren in the Church from whom he differed. Not long after the time when his pamphlet against Dr. Seabury appeared, an eminent Low-Church clergyman in New York was scandalized to learn that one of the Vermont candidates for Holy Orders, then at the General Theological Seminary, was attending on the ministra-

---

[1] See *The Law of Ritualism*, pp. 70-72. It is surely no discredit to my Father, that, on the first practical suggestion of the subject, he should have jumped at the same conclusion which, after all the additional light of the quarter of a century's active discussion, was in the year of Grace 1871, announced by the Judicial Committee of the Privy Council in England. My Father grew wiser as he grew older. Of the Judicial Committee, I fear, there is not so much ground to hope for permanent improvement.

[2] *History of the Confessional*, p. 238.

tions of Dr. Seabury, and informed my Father of the fact, taking for granted that it was without his knowledge and consent, and that he would put a stop to it. My Father replied, that he had never given any special permission to his candidate to attend the Church of the Annunciation, because he had never considered such permission necessary: "but," he added, "I have said, that I had no objection to his attending any of our Churches which he preferred, on his own responsibility." And he continued:—

> My own opinions, so far as they differ from those of Dr. Seabury, are published and known. Apart from these, I have no fault to find with him. And if I had, so long as a minister is in full communion with the Church, and no ecclesiastical proceeding is commenced against him, I have always set my face against any *indirect* mode of proscribing him or his official ministrations. So far have I carried this principle of fraternal communion with my ministerial brethren whose sentiments on many subjects I disapprove, that I have always made it a point to preach for them when invited, and to invite them to preach for me, *without distinction*, however fiercely the storm of party might be raging at the time. Nor can I, after twenty-five years' consideration, make anything less than this out of the duty of Ecclesiastical Communion. If they cannot understand or appreciate the principle on which I have acted, and blame instead of approving, I may regret, but I cannot help it. I am not looking for the praise of men, but simply trying to follow what seems to me the path of duty.

The application of this rule of straightforward good sense and right feeling, would have saved many searchings of spirit and floods of irritating eloquence, which have been a chronic complaint in the Board of Trustees of the General Theological Seminary, and elsewhere. As for himself, he thoroughly understood what it cost to keep thus aloof from practical identification with either party,—the being "between hawk and buzzard" as he used pleasantly to call it: and in answer to some notion of mine concerning him about those times, he wrote:—" My brethren do not like me well enough on either side of the house to advocate any increase of my influence. I paid that price for my independence many a long year ago; and I should be reckoning entirely without my host if I were to calculate upon rescinding my bargain." His influence, however, in moderating the excesses of party feeling, cannot easily be overrated.

In 1848, he began a work which he had contemplated for many years, fondly hoping that it might absorb the ripest energies of his remaining life. This was a commentary on the whole Bible :—a gigantic labor, which he entered upon with a full consciousness of its greatness. He wrote me his general plan of operations :—

> I have a book such as they have for the Town records, the page being about twice the superficial size of letter-paper. This I place in the middle of a high desk which I have planted just under the picture of the Holy Family, and I stand at this desk from morning till night, or rather, to be more precise, from half-past eight A.M. till eleven o'clock P.M.,—taking out dinner, tea, and our evening prayer time ;—say about thirteen hours a day, for four days in the week on an average. On the one side of this desk I have D'Oyly and Mant's Commentary,[1] and on the other Poole's *Synopsis Criticorum*, and on the table near the window, Bagster's great Polyglott and Arrius Montanus's version of the Old and New Testament. From these I write what pleases me, expressing my own views freely, and endeavoring to produce a useful and thorough Commentary, for all practical purposes. And to this I devote the right-hand page, leaving the left entirely blank. On this plan my intention is to go through the Bible first, and thus securing a *good general Commentary*, which will take from four to five years, I design next to take up the Fathers and Councils, on the blank page, under the head of "Extracts from the Fathers and Councils," giving them a distinct place to themselves, and availing myself of all my large body of MS. Notes on the Fathers, as also of the Indexes to the passages of Scripture which are found in the Appendix to each volume. I design to give another distinct place to critical remarks on our English Version, with a special view to the differences between ours and the Roman, or the Latin Vulgate, showing their chief departures from the Hebrew Text. I shall moreover take all possible notice of the army of commentators who have appeared since Poole, by reading what they have said and using as much of it as seems to be good and useful. And I shall state their names with all due credit to them in my *Introduction :* but I shall rarely quote from them individually. That preëminence I shall reserve mainly for the Fathers and Councils.

At first, he found these long hours of standing very wearisome ; but after a fortnight's steady labor, it became much less so, and he was actually growing stronger under it. The work was begun on the 27th of September, and with such energy did

---

[1] The one then in most common use among American Churchmen, and for which my Father had very little respect. He would consult it mainly to show what was wanting, but not to obtain material to supply the want.

he prosecute his task that by the 23d of February next succeeding he had gone through the Pentateuch with the first branch of his labor, and had reached the 4th Chapter of the Book of Joshua, with the 9th verse of which the manuscript stops. Nearly four hundred of those great double folio pages in less than five months, was certainly no mean amount of labor, even if he had done nothing else during the interval, though of course his parochial and other duties were discharged as usual. No part of this Commentary was ever enriched by the subsequent additions, from other sources, which he contemplated. No part of it ever received his last correction for the press. Nothing was ever added to it from that day onward. Yet, in many places where I have examined both, for the very purpose of testing them, it compares not unfavorably with the valuable and learned Commentary of Bishop Wordsworth, of Lincoln: in many points being, of course, excelled; but in others being decidedly preferable.

This great work was interrupted by the unusual prominence given among us, just at that time, to the Romish practice of enforced Auricular Confession, which it was supposed that Bishop Ives of North Carolina was attempting to introduce,[1] filling the columns of all our Church periodicals with controversy. Many appeals were made to my Father to take up the subject, and he at length determined to interrupt the Commentary for this, which appeared to be, for the time, the more pressing duty. The result was his *History of the Confessional*, published by the Harpers in the summer of 1850, in the compilation of which he once more went through no less than forty of the volumes of Patristic divinity, which had been his favorite study for so many years. This work was fairly noticed in *The Churchman*, and was received with very general acquiescence, although there is a large amount of sound Church teaching in it which the Low-

---

[1] Bishop McIlvaine was ready once more for the ultimate resource, and in a letter to my Father expressed the conviction that Bishop Ives ought to be presented for trial. Years afterwards, in 1865, in a letter to the Rev. Dr. Clover, he "solemnly believed" that the same remedy of "presentment" should be tried upon Bishop Whitehouse, for some delay in issuing a Letter Dimissory; thus showing that time had only confirmed his original conviction in regard to the usefulness and varied applicability of the Canon for the Trial of a Bishop. The Tate case has since been equally expressive, as to the inferior clergy.

Church party would not have received with so little objection from any one else.

The testimony of this volume to the deliberate and intended permission, in the Church of England, of private and auricular Confession to a priest, is the more weighty, since the whole tone of the book was decidedly hostile to the general use of that liberty. While showing clearly, and making the most of, those points in which " the allowance of voluntary auricular confession, as retained by the Church of England," varied from " the enforced and compulsory exactions of the Church of Rome," he nevertheless quoted fully the well-known passages from the English Communion Office and that for the Visitation of the Sick, and said:—" In these two places, therefore, the Church of England authorizes her priests to receive private confession, and to administer the sentence of absolution in language borrowed from the Church of Rome." He also quoted fully the English Canon 113, which straitly charges and admonishes all English priests that they " do not at any time reveal or make known to any person whatsoever, any crime or offence committed to their trust and secrecy " by any man who should " confess his secret and hidden sins" to them : " under pain of irregularity." [1]

In accounting for the existence of this part of the English Prayer Book, my Father gave two reasons as probable. The Reformers, he thought, " may have been influenced by a benevolent disposition to favor the feelings and habits of a large proportion of the nation, in whose judgment the principles of the Reformation had not yet become fully established, and who, therefore, whenever their minds became alarmed and dejected, might naturally long after their accustomed course, and derive a certain comfort from hearing the old and familiar words of positive personal absolution. . . . The Reformers had been long accustomed to this mode of administering absolution. They doubtless anticipated the result, that, by making its use to depend entirely on the voluntary request of the laity, it would soon die away. And meanwhile, in order to facilitate the conversion of Romanists, and prevent their thinking that they would lose any

[1] Pp. 42, 46.

real privilege in coming to a pure Church, they determined to tolerate it in this optional shape, which still continues."[1] This reason was an admission of the fact, that the voluntary Confession and Absolution still continued in the Church of England is substantially and practically the same that was customary before the Reformation: but the idea that this continuance was meant to be temporary, does not agree with the fact that those two passages have been left unaltered at every subsequent review of the English Book; and the latest review, in 1662, was just after the deluge of Puritanism, when there was surely no occasion to conciliate Romanists.

The other probable reason given by my Father he thinks may be "more satisfactory," namely: "that the use of private confession and absolution, in certain cases, was allowed, not to accommodate the habits of Romanists, but in order to agree as far as possible with the system of the German Reformers, Luther and Melancthon; for they had retained a far closer resemblance to the Roman discipline in this matter. They called absolution a sacrament, and required auricular confession and priestly absolution of every one, as a regular preparative for the Eucharist; although they abolished the rule which authorized the priest to act as an inquisitor, and severely denounced the whole Romish doctrine concerning works of penance or satisfaction": and he then goes on to prove what is the Lutheran doctrine. If, however, the Church of England arranged her formularies on this subject to harmonize with Lutheran practice, it is not easy to prove to Protestants that she meant this arrangement to be merely temporary. The changes made in these two places in our American Prayer Book were strongly urged by my Father as against any general revival of auricular confession and private absolution among us: a revival which he then considered to be, practically, quite out of the question.

He sent a copy of his book, as soon as published, to Bishop Ives; and, not long after, was very much gratified at receiving from him an acknowledgment of the receipt of the volume, in which he said (Nov. 14, 1850):—

[1] Pp. 242, 3.

Accept my warm thanks for this token of kindness, and for the pleasure and profit I have had in its perusal. I have not sufficient knowledge to enable me to speak confidently of its numerous details. But of its results and reasonings, I can say in all sincerity that they have long since been my own. I may not agree with you on every point of expediency. But in reference to what Rome holds and our Church holds on this subject of Confession, I agree with you entirely. And I feel bound to add, that I do regard, and have ever regarded, the *Romish Confessional* as fraught with the most serious evils; while at the same time I am free to confess my continued conviction of the great desirableness of restoring to our people that kind of Confession contemplated in our Prayer Book.

That there was, about this time, however, a decided reäction in the Bishop of North Carolina's mind, consequent upon a re-examination of the whole question, together with kindred points, is clear, partly from his course in his own Convention, and partly from another letter, which is here placed on record as a proof of the singular vacillations which preceded the abandonment of his See by Bishop Ives. His final submission to the See of Rome took place but about sixteen months after the following was written to my Father:—

RALEIGH, August 7th, 1851.

MY DEAR BISHOP:

Upon my return from a long visitation I hasten to acknowledge your kind letter of last month. It was most grateful to my heart. Next to the approbation of my own conscience in the sight of GOD, is that of my brethren in the Episcopate. And yours, my dear brother, under the circumstances, I feel to be peculiarly valuable, - We have not always thought and acted together; and hence your judgment of my recent course could hardly have been the expression of party bias or too favorable regard. I am allowed to look upon it, therefore, as the dictate of simple truth and justice prompted by fraternal sympathy and affection. You have my warmest thanks for it, and my prayers to GOD that, under His blessing, it may result in that mutual confidence and coöperation so desirable, I may say so *essential*, in our holy brotherhood.

I have been placed in a most trying position, partly by my own fault, partly by the disingenuousness of others, and wholly by the wise and merciful providence of GOD. But, by His Grace, I have been enabled to see my own error, to extricate myself from the snares of designing associates, and to submit with, I think, a humble heart to the divine discipline.

My determination to retrace my steps, and do what I might to undo the evils—unintentional, but no less real—of my error, was formed more than a year ago; and I only waited till my diocesan difficulties should assume a shape to leave me master of my own movements, to carry out my intention. The moment, therefore, that I found myself relieved of all *personal* questions, and surrounded by a large majority in my Convention of warm supporters, I took the course I did; and that, too, without even the *knowledge, on the part of any one, of my real purpose.* I mention this, that you may be put into possession of the means to dissipate any doubts which ignorance or prejudice may impute to my motives.

In what I have said or done in the way of *retraction*, I know you will understand me as only having renounced those views and practices which are distinctly *Romanizing* in their tendency; and not such as are usually embraced under the denomination of *High-Church*, and were taught by Hobart and Ravenscroft. I feel that I cannot renounce what I have hitherto held and taught of the *Sacramental System*, without renouncing the plain teachings of the *Prayer Book*. But *Confession*, founded on *judicial, priestly absolution; the necessity of such absolution to the forgiveness of post-baptismal sin; that high sense of the Real Presence of Christ in the Eucharist* which *cannot well be distinguished from Transubstantiation;* and all the *practices* which are the legitimate offspring of these views, *do not belong to this System as set forth in the Prayer Book*, and *I renounce them*.

Begging your prayers and counsels, and hoping to hear from you often, I remain, dear brother, most sincerely and affectionately,

Yours in the Lord,

L. S. IVES.[1]

Towards the close of his life, my Father gradually ripened into the conviction, which he often expressed to me, that the first Book of Edward VI., in 1549, was the purest and truest expression of the real mind of the English Reformation, before it had been marred by Continental Protestantism from abroad or by Puritanism at home: and he frequently quoted the closing words of the *Exhortation* in that Book (omitted in 1552 and thereafter), as the highest wisdom, the happy golden mean, on this subject: —" requiring such as shall be satisfied with a general Confession, not to be offended with them that doth use, to their further satisfying, the auricular and secret Confession to the Priest; nor those also which think needful or convenient for the quietness of their own consciences particularly to open their sins to the Priest, to be offended with them which are satisfied with their humble con-

---

[1] The italics in the above represent exactly the underscoring in the original.

fession to God, and the general confession to the Church; but in all these things to follow and keep the rule of charity; and every man to be satisfied with his own conscience, not judging other men's minds or acts, whereas he hath no warrant of God's Word for the same."

As the Commentary had been interrupted for *The History of the Confessional*, so the completion of the latter had in turn been suspended for the preparation of a pamphlet on the Gorham question, which was then agitating the Church of England. At the time of writing this pamphlet, my Father had not seen the full report of the examination of Mr. Gorham, on which the Bishop of Exeter's action was grounded; and he missed, therefore, the peculiarities which distinguished that clergyman's views. My Father supposed that he only held the ordinary Low-Church notions on the subject, and that the result of a decision in the Bishop of Exeter's favor would result in driving the whole Low-Church party out of the Church of England. Under this impression he wrote the pamphlet, declaring that his own convictions as to the true doctrine of the Bible and the Church were—so far as he knew—the same as those of the Bishop of Exeter: but contending for the historic standing of the Low-Church party as being rightfully within the intended comprehensiveness of the Church of England. The pamphlet brought him warm letters of thanks from Bishop Meade and other prominent Low-Churchmen; but otherwise fell from the press almost unnoticed.

In correspondence with my Father on this subject at the time, I in vain tried to convey to him the peculiarity of Mr. Gorham's errors: but his replies contained some expressions which it may be well to record. In one letter, he said:—"The question was *not* whether infants and adults alike receive the remission of sins in Baptism. This Mr. Gorham was nowhere charged with denying. . . . Neither is there anything involved about the sacrament being a *naked sign*, which Mr. Gorham nowhere asserted. Of course, *that* would be heresy." And in another letter, he says:—"The adult must receive previous grace to repent and believe, beyond dispute. But yet this does not hinder our maintaining that his sins are not yet actually remitted until he becomes a subject of his Saviour in the appointed sacrament of Baptism.

If, then, the previous grace which *prepares* the adult for the beneficial effects of Baptism, in no respect interferes with the blessed privilege conferred in the Sacrament, why should an act of previous grace interfere with it in the case of the infant?" But it is no sin to have failed to appreciate quite correctly the idiosyncrasies of such a crotchetty errorist as Mr. Gorham.[1]

In the year 1850, my Father added the delivering of popular lectures to his insufficient means of support; and for many years thereafter filled occasional appointments of that sort in various parts of the country, from Maine to Louisiana. One of his earliest lectures, delivered at Buffalo and Lockport, was on the vexed subject of Slavery; and in it he took the ground which he so ably defended many years after, that there is no Scriptural condemnation of the relation of master and slave in itself, and therefore that it is not a sin: but that, nevertheless, the abolition of the institution in this country was highly expedient, desirable, and probably inevitable; and he therefore urged that it might be done, by general agreement, in some constitutional and fraternal manner. The Lecture was printed at the request of the three rectors of our Church parishes then established in Buffalo, with others; and brought him very warm letters of cordial approval both from Daniel Webster and Henry Clay. These two distinguished statesmen both doubted, however, the practicability of the mode suggested by my Father for removing the evil,—a question of which none but practical politicians could be competent judges. My Father had originally thought of laying his views on this subject before the public in a letter addressed to Senator Phelps, of Vermont. I opposed, as energetically as I dared, this entrance on the political arena, and that letter to Senator Phelps was not printed: but my Father wrote me:—

My present impression is that I shall make a much larger and more thorough thing of the subject, with proofs from the Councils, Commenta-

---

[1] Mr. Gorham distinctly attributed to the "prevenient grace," and *not* to the Baptism itself, each and every benefit ascribed to Baptism in Holy Scripture and in the Standards of the Church. It was by "the prevenient grace" that sins were remitted, membership in Christ was given, etc. If this did not leave Baptism "a naked sign," while all the substance was attributed to the "prevenient grace," it would be impossible to say that his language had any meaning at all. But this is not the common Low-Church view.

tors, etc., worth looking to as a standard. I do not at all agree with you in thinking that I am out of the line of Episcopal duty in the matter. The Abolition spirit will soon attack ourselves ecclesiastically. We must vindicate our position as the Church of Christ on *the religious question;* and yet, along with this, show ourselves the friends of abolition on the *ground of expediency.* . . . And here, as in other cases, I am indebted to your variance of opinion, since it leads me to do a better work than I contemplated in the beginning. . . . You must be convinced, if you read the doings of Congress thoughtfully, that the agitation has not at all subsided. Nor can it subside, until the South either adopt some scheme of abolition, or the Union is dissolved.

The Compromise measures, in which Henry Clay and Daniel Webster did their utmost to prevent an open collision, postponed the stress of the pressure for some years. My Father dropped his plan of a book on the subject, partly on the playful ground of the " Spring fever " (it was April), but adding :—" It is a plausible argument for doing nothing more in it, that *one person* (viz., my dear son Henry) will be pleased, whereas the book, if it were written and published, would most probably please no one." The design thus temporarily dropped was long afterwards fulfilled, in much more eventful days, as we shall see hereafter.

It had been part of my Father's design at one time, in carrying on the controversy with Rome, to prepare a specific answer to Milner's *End of Controversy*,—the book which Bishop Kenrick had invited all our Bishops to read, and thereby be converted to Rome. On finding that the learned Dr. Jarvis had already assumed this enterprise, my Father dropped the idea. But the publishers of Dr. Jarvis's work, having found by the experience of some years that his volume, though slender and cheap, had not the element of a popular style, so that its usefulness was restricted, requested my Father to resume his original idea, and prepare a work which could be looked to as the standby, whenever Milner was found to be doing mischief among Church people. The preparation of this—my Father's most elaborate work in that department—involved a still further postponement of the Commentary. It appeared in the year 1854, and has passed through three editions. Perhaps its most valuable part to the scholar, though not the most interesting to the ordinary reader, is the condensed historical summary of the evidence, especially from Councils, that a Reformation of the Church in the head (the Pope) and the members had been called for uninterruptedly for hundreds of years before it broke out. Many other parts, such as his vindication of the venerable customs of bowing at the mention of the Sacred Name and Prayer for the Faithful Departed, are permanent testimonies to the lawfulness of things too generally neglected among us, notwithstanding our boasts of Primitive Catholicity. The general style is so clear, pointed and vigorous, that though it occupies two volumes, it is by no means heavy reading. The author of it was gratified by many letters of thanks from persons whom Milner had strongly inclined towards Romanism, but who had been rescued from that danger, and confirmed in their attachment to the Church of America, by the perusal of "*The End of Controversy*" *Controverted*.

In the Spring of the same year, a pamphlet was printed by him on the subject of the Jerusalem Bishopric, occasioned by some misunderstanding of editorial remarks in *The Church Journal*,—a paper which had then been rather more than a year in existence. It brought him letters of thanks from a number of leading Low-Churchmen, and Bishop Meade bought ten dollars' worth of the pamphlet for circulation in Virginia; but otherwise it attracted little attention. It embodied, in very strong shape, a favorite idea of my Father's, which he adhered to with great pertinacity, because it was verbally Patristic. He proved, from the Fathers, that they freely used the term "heresy" in regard to certain errors, without waiting until those errors had been formally condemned as such by a General Council: and he contended that, as every Bishop is *ex officio* a judge of heresy, the Bishop of Vermont had now the same right to condemn any error as a "heresy," which was exercised by individual Bishops in primitive days. But as this was never a living question in any of the issues of the day, his idiosyncrasy on the subject attracted little notice, and did no harm. The voice of a single Bishop who really represented the faith of an undivided Christendom, was one thing. The judgment of a Bishop who does not, in the matter of which he treats, represent the voice even of the whole of his own Communion, and when the whole of his own Communion forms but a minority of a divided Christendom, is rather a different affair.[1]

But the most noticeable circumstance in this pamphlet was his determination not to be swayed in any theological opinion by the fact that the supporter of the error was his own son. Only a few weeks previous, he had written to me:—" While I have no idea in the world that, at your time of life, you should vary from what you hold to be the truth, merely because your father thinks you mistaken, so, on the other hand, I cannot, at my age and in my office, suffer any one to suppose that I am ready to give up what I hold to be the truth, in consideration for the notions of my son. If ever you should be led to what I consider a false position (which God forbid!) I should consider myself bound to disclaim and oppose it, the more distinctly, for the very reason that you are my son : because I could not in conscience be satisfied, as I would not have you or any Christian teacher be satisfied, that the earthly bond of family affection should be suffered to overcome the spiritual allegiance which I owe to the Redeemer and Judge of us all. *He that loveth father or mother more than Me, is not worthy of Me, and cannot be My disciple.*" The pamphlet proved that this was no empty form of speech : and he was ready to act on the same principle as unhesitatingly, to the end of his life.

It was about this time that *The Episcopal Recorder* changed hands, and came under the control of Mr. Francis Wharton, who made repeated attempts to secure editorial contributions from my Father. "Our great object," he wrote, " is, to make the *Recorder* the organ of *Broad Church* (in a true sense) as well as literary views." He went on, very candidly, to add concerning his own friends, the Evangelicals :—" Intolerance of dissent, breaking out often into harshness of language, narrowness of literary and social

---

[1] My Father probably did not remember, at the time, that in his Charge of 1842, having shown that by law in the Church of England nothing can be adjudged to be heresy " but that which *heretofore hath been so adjudged* by the authority of the Canonical Scriptures, or by the first four General Councils " (in his latter years he would have said *six* instead of *four*), he adds :—" Now such being the established law of heresy in our Mother Church, *it is also the law in ours*, because it was so at the time of our separation, and remains so still, of necessity ; at least until we set up, by the authority of our General Convention, some other standard ; which I, for one, should question our right to do."

views, desire to construct a purely doctrinal platform, have heretofore marred their newspaper organs. . . . As it is, we are much behind the Tractarian papers in literary ability." But his request, though repeatedly urged, and backed by offers of compensation to the amount of ten dollars a column, were steadily declined by my Father, who contributed only three articles in review of Bishop Ives's *Trials of a Mind*,—the weak little book written by him after hanging up his pectoral cross in S. Peter's at Rome.

CHAPTER XVI.

DIOCESAN AND GENERAL.

THERE was nothing very eventful, during these years, in the history of the Diocese. Occasionally some incident a little out of the usual quiet routine would give a flush of fresh life and interest; but the double depression, partly from the failure of the attempt to secure a Diocesan School and a local supply of clergy, and partly from the continued emigration of native Vermonters to the West, weighed down the hearts and hopes of all. For some years, the good fruits of that enterprise were still felt: but after two or three years [1] the falling off in the numbers of clergy and of persons confirmed was very painful. In speaking of these losses in 1844, he said:—" Few of our ministers have left Vermont during the thirteen years of my Episcopate for any other reason than the want of means to live in decent comfort." In 1846, the number of clergy had fallen from twenty-eight to *nineteen*, and there was not a single candidate for Orders.

In that year, he recommended that Vermont should at length conform to the practice of all the other Dioceses, in repeating the General Confession. When the House of Bishops in 1835 recommended that the people should say each petition "*with*" the Minister, instead of "after" him as the Rubric directs, the Bishop of Vermont considered it to be in reality an illegitimate mode of altering a rubric without following the rules prescribed in the Constitution: and accordingly Vermont kept up the old practice. But in 1846 he took the ground that eleven years' compliance with the recommendation, and in all the Dioceses except Vermont, was morally a full equivalent for the approval of two successive General Conventions: and since 1846, therefore, Vermont has fallen in with the innovation.

[1] In 1842, owing to a change of time in holding the annual Convention, a double visitation was reported, showing 230 persons confirmed (the whole number for the three years previous was 249). In 1843, there were 190 confirmed, the largest number thus far in any single visitation.

In 1847, the Bishop's Address again alluded to the evils felt from the constant changes in the ministry. Of the sixteen parishes strong enough to have a clergyman at the time of his Consecration, nine had had five different rectors apiece, two had had six, one had had three, and three had had two; while Rutland and Burlington alone had been without change. His request that the Diocese should avail itself of the new Canon, authorizing the Bishop, with the consent of the Standing Committee, to ordain deacons without full literary and theological qualifications, was acted on: but with little benefit.

The year 1848 was that of the lowest depression of the Diocese during my Father's long Episcopate. There were only 66 persons confirmed in all; and in no less than twelve of the parishes *none*. In that year, in accordance with the Bishop's repeated recommendation, the Standing Committee of the Diocese was constituted of an equal number of Clergy and Laity, having before been all Clergy. From that year there began a very slow but steady improvement. In 1850, some of the stronger parishes were induced to give up the appropriation they had all been receiving from the Land Fund; which could thus be better concentrated on those parts of the Diocese that were most in need. In 1851, the Bishop could say: " At no former period during the nineteen anniversaries of my Episcopate has the record which it is my duty to lay before you been prepared with so strong a sentiment of gratitude to the favoring Providence of God."

In one case he mentions that most of the persons confirmed " were younger than I have usually seen prepared for the reception of the Apostolic ordinance, but not too young to perform this duty according to the system of the Scriptures. And hence it is so expressly declared by the Church, that *all* who have been rightly instructed should be ready to take their baptismal covenant upon themselves, as soon as they have arrived at years of sufficient discretion to do so with suitable intelligence and sincerity of heart." He speaks of the fear entertained by most persons that those confirmed so young may not be found able to remain firm against the assaults of temptation; " But," replies he, " experience and observation abundantly justify the system of the

Church, by showing that those who are not brought in early life to adopt the service of Christ, are but too apt to postpone it until their best powers have been wasted in the cares and follies of the world; and, in multitudes of cases, decline the duty altogether, and die without any religious hope or consolation."

A Convocation of the Clergy had been formed that year (1851), and had held two meetings, with his cordial approval.

In 1853, the improvement had been so decided, that the Bishop was encouraged to look back and give a retrospective summary of the twenty years of his Episcopate. The eleven[1] clergymen whom he found in the Diocese on his arrival were increased to twenty-five; the sixteen Church buildings had become twenty-eight, besides two entirely rebuilt, one much enlarged, and many others greatly improved; the one parsonage had become seven, with others in contemplation; the confirmations had been 2595 in all; and the property of the Church was generally free from debt and embarrassment. Compared with the population,—which had been nearly stationary,—Vermont had no reason to be ashamed of her Church strength, notwithstanding all her drawbacks. In the proportion of Clergy to population, Vermont was indeed excelled by Connecticut, New York, Rhode Island, Maryland, New Jersey; but in her turn outranked Massachusetts, Pennsylvania, Virginia, and pretty much all the rest. The Bishop then alluded to the divisions among the Clergy when he came:—"I found my little Diocese about equally divided by High and Low Church differences, and there was a large amount of irregularity, and a plentiful supply of the elements of strife." Afterwards came all the excitements of the Oxford Tracts, and Episcopal Trials, and perversions to Rome:—"Suffice it to say, that the period of my Episcopate has embraced the most perilous times which the Church in this country has ever encountered, and that our internal peace and unity were never exposed to such imminent danger."

But now, what is the result within our own borders? I state it with humble gratitude to the Giver of all good, as a special ground of devout

---

[1] Two of those who voted at his election in 1832 left the Diocese almost immediately after.

thanksgiving. There is not, from one end of the Diocese to the other, a single root of bitterness or dissension. Our Clergy meet together, without one exception, as a band of brothers. The lines of party spirit are all merged in the unity of the Church. And I doubt whether it is possible to enjoy, in this poor imperfect world, an ecclesiastical condition of greater harmony, peace and affection, than the blessing of the Redeemer has worked out for us, to the praise of His gracious and holy Name!

That year, the whole work of Diocesan Missions was placed in the hands of the Convocation, which was duly constituted the Diocesan Organization for that purpose, as it still continues to be: no Missionary to be appointed or removed without the consent of the Bishop. My Father had at first supposed that one object of the Clergy in their attending Convocation was, to be able to confer freely with one another, unembarrassed by the presence of their Bishop. But in this year, the repeated and earnest representations of the Clergy themselves, not only public and formal but also private and confidential, satisfied him of his mistake: and thenceforward he was never absent unless in obedience to some call of superior duty.

There are a few points of more general interest which it may be well to mention here.

In the summer of 1849, when Dr. Upfold had been elected Bishop of Indiana, the then Presiding Bishop, Chase of Illinois, refused to consent to his consecration, on the pretext that, four years previous, in talking about the Onderdonk trial, he had slandered the Court of Bishops; and he went so far as to send a circular to the other Bishops, stating his reason for refusal. This led to not a little correspondence. My Father exerted all his influence with Bishop Chase to remove his objection (which was really groundless); and of course consented promptly to the Consecration himself. The opposition failed, although receiving some countenance from a quarter whence such a course should not have been expected.

While on this subject, it may be well to put on record some facts in regard to the attempts made by Bishops to stop, for various reasons, the consecration of a Bishop-elect.

Bishop Ravenscroft refused to consent to the Consecration of Bishop Meade, without some proof that he was more sound in the Catholic faith than he supposed him to be: but he failed to obtain the doctrinal statement, and failed to stop the Consecration.[1]

Bishop Ives tried to get Dr. Burgess to explain his views on the subject of Baptismal Regeneration, before acting on his Consecration: but Dr. Burgess steadily refused to submit to any such pressure, on the ground that it " might compromise the rights of Dioceses and of Bishops-elect "; and he was consecrated accordingly.

When the Rev. Dr. Young was elected Bishop of Florida, an attempt was made, in which Bishop Coxe of Western New York had a hand, to obtain from him some disclaimer of my Father's book on *The Law of Ritualism*, he having been one of the clergymen who united in the request to the Bishop of Vermont to give his views on the subject. Dr. Young resisted, steadily refusing to give any such disclaimer: and was consecrated accordingly.

The Rev. Dr. Wm. C. Doane was another of the signers of that request to the Bishop of Vermont: and when he was elected Bishop of Albany, Bishop Coxe, with perfect consistency, attempted a pressure in the same direction once more: and with the same success. Dr. Doane refused to make any disclaimer, and was consecrated accordingly.

The result of all these cases (perhaps there are more of a similar sort) would seem to be, that it is regarded as an impertinence, and is properly resented accordingly, when any personal requisition is made upon a Bishop-elect, beyond the Canonical Testimonials. Any Bishop is of course free to withhold his consent to a consecration, for any reason satisfactory to himself, and with responsibility only to God for the mode in which he exercises his discretion in such a matter. But to put private pressure upon any Bishop-elect, to obtain from him a declaration on points which are left open in the standards of the Church, and under the implied threat of withholding consent to his consecration unless his response is satisfactory: is a course which has

---

[1] Bishop Johns's Memoirs of Bishop Meade, p. 192. See also, *Appendix*, pp. 456-458.

never yet—so far as I know—been submitted to in a single instance, and has never in a single instance been successful in stopping the consecration of any man upon whom it has been tried.

In the General Convention of 1844, besides the Canon for the Trial of a Bishop, on my Father's motion a Joint Committee was appointed "to take into consideration the Canon Law of the Church,[1] with a view to the preparation of a complete Code, which may suffice to all the demands of Order and Discipline." The difficulty of getting the Committee together,—my Father was not the Chairman,—or of inducing them to give any real attention to the matter, was great, as usual. Shortly before the General Convention in 1847 to which they should have reported, one of the clerical members of the Committee wrote my Father:— "I shall feel myself justified in devolving my portion of the herculean labor assigned us, upon your broad shoulders. You can bear it. And you must do it, if it is done at all, and especially if it is well done." This was more complimentary than comforting to one who wished to get other people to help in doing hard work. The report in 1847 amounted to nothing; but the Committee was continued, to equal purpose; and in 1850 the subject was "indefinitely postponed."

The General Convention in 1850 met in Cincinnati—the only meeting which has thus far been held west of the Allegheny mountains. My Father's Sermon before the Board of Missions was a continuation of the theme on which he had preached at the opening of the General Convention in 1847. Then he had shown that the true idea of the Church did not exclude, but plainly from the first included, parties of men who on some subjects differed from each other in convictions, in sympathy, in practice. In 1850, he showed that all the needful differences and diversities of party, need not and ought not to weaken the deeper fraternal unity, which in essentials bound every member of the One Body together in the holiest of fellowship.[2] This

---

[1] Journal, p. 123.
[2] In this sermon, while acknowledging his early opposition to our present Mission system, he reminded his hearers of the apparent fusion of parties at the time of its adoption, and declared that the aspect of the matter was "entirely changed," in his judgment, by the controlling necessity which he saw for unity. "The Church,"

sermon was received with a sort of extravagant satisfaction, which I do not remember to have seen on any other occasion. It was ordered to be printed immediately, for the use of the Convention, besides the usual and more leisurely publication afterwards in New York. It was repeatedly alluded to in the debates, and many ascribed to it, in a considerable degree, the good feeling which characterized the proceedings of the whole session.

In the leading debate, on the Provisional Bishop Canon, for New York, the Bishop of Vermont was the Chairman of the Committee of Conference which harmonized the conflicting views of the two Houses. And on the next chief subject which drew out the strength of both Houses, he was once more heartily with his old High-Church friends, and was one of the Joint-Committee which put their principles in the form which was finally adopted. The ill-advised Low-Churchmen of Maryland, who asked the General Convention to decide that the Bishop should not administer the Holy Eucharist in any parish of his Diocese without the consent of the Rector, were beaten, two to one, in both Houses. At this General Convention,—seeing that the Committee (of which he had no control, not being Chairman) on a general Code had come to nothing, the Bishop of Vermont introduced and read a plan for a Court of Appeals, which was referred to the next session. The third section of this scheme contains, in fact, the germ of the Provincial System, in accordance with which the whole American Church would have been divided into Provinces, each containing not less than three or more than seven Dioceses. Immediately after it was read and referred, Bishop De Lancey offered for the first time his proposal for dividing the American Church into four Provinces, General

said he, "for fifteen years has sustained the plan amidst heavy difficulties: and I would deprecate, under existing circumstances, any movement in favor of change. This is no time to make sacrifices to party spirit, or to weaken a single fibre of the bonds which hold us together. This is no time even to seem to falter, as if the institutions of the Church were failing through internal strife. In union, under God, is our strength. . . . Once solemnly committed to the work of Missions, as a duty of the whole united Church, it would be an open sign of discord if it were now abandoned to party organizations. And therefore I, for one, cheerfully sacrifice my individual preference to the paramount interests of that fraternal union, which ought to be regarded, in due obedience to Christian truth, as at once our highest privilege and our holiest obligation."

Convention to meet thenceforward only once in twenty years: which was referred also.

On his return homewards, he made a visit to his old flock at Pittsburgh, and wrote to my Mother his grateful surprise at the warmth of his reception:—

> It would have melted you down outright, if you had been here, to witness the crowding up around the Chancel, and the knots waiting in the alleys and at the doors, many of whom I scarcely remembered, all full of delight apparently, dashed with sorrow, countenances changed by age and trial, youths and maidens whose parents reminded me that I baptized them, young fathers and mothers who told me that I had married them, and from the whole the kindest inquiries about you and our children, and the warmest assurances of their pleasure at seeing me again, with regrets that I had ever left.

In 1853, the happy dismissal of the Presentment against Bishop Doane, and the presence of a Bishop and other eminent clergymen as representing the English and Colonial Churches, in return for the American deputation that took part in the Jubilee of the S. P. G. the year before in London, tended to a remarkably united and pleasant session: but its symmetry was marred by the deposition of Bishop Ives, who had abandoned his Diocese and resigned his jurisdiction. The Canon under which this was solemnly done, was drawn by the Bishop of Vermont. As Chairman, moreover, he had at last gotten his joint Committee to work, at a rate that made up for lost time; for nearly fifty pages of fine print in the *Appendix* of the Journal are filled with the projects of Canons, partly reported by the Committee, and partly proceeding from a minority of their number. Such a mass of matter needed to be digested still further by another Committee, of which also my Father was Chairman; and at the following Session the present Canon for the Trial of a Bishop was the result. Time was not yet ripe for the rest. At this session, besides being for the first time appointed Chairman of the Committee on Canons of the Upper House,[1] my Father was also elected by ballot one of the Committee of three on the Pastoral Letter.

---

[1] This position he retained until called in 1862 to preside, owing to the absence of Bishop Brownell.

During all these years, and indeed until the close of his life, the frequent intercourse with the Canadian Church was kept up, kind invitations taking my Father every year or two to Montreal or Quebec or both, to preach on set occasions, or to make speeches at meetings of the Church Society, or in some other way to be the most frequent visible exponent of the full and fraternal intercommunion of the Churches. One of the pleasantest of these occasions was on the first arrival of Bishop Fulford in this country, when the Bishop of Vermont, by special invitation, met him as he passed through Burlington from New York, and accompanied him to Canada, Bishop Mountain awaiting them at S. John's, and both remaining with him until he had received his hearty welcome to his See of Montreal. The assistance my Father gave to the Canadian Bishops, at their request, in the difficult task of organizing the synodical system of the Canadian Church, especially in helping them to secure the right of a vote as a separate Order, each in his own Diocesan Synod, was warmly acknowledged by the Bishops of Quebec, Montreal and Toronto, and very kindly remembered by them ever after.

Chapter XVII.

THE VERMONT EPISCOPAL INSTITUTE.

IN the Spring of 1854, an invitation to deliver the Price Lectures took my Father to Boston, and kept him there for several weeks. It was during this visit that one of his old creditors, whose original claim of $8500 had been punctually paid to the amount of $7500, used the coercive power given him by the law of Massachusetts at that time,[1] and arrested his debtor for the remaining $1000 and interest. Two kind friends, George and Thomas A. Dexter, went bail for him, and saved the Bishop of Vermont from actual imprisonment. But the total destitution of ability to discharge so large a sum from his own means, and the knowledge that two kind friends were now bound for it besides himself, brought him home with a heavy weight upon his heart.

During his absence, his younger children had been industriously improving the flower-beds near the approach to the house, looking forward to his smiling approval,—his quick eye being prompt to notice such marks of diligence and good taste. And when he came, and passed through their handiwork without once looking at it;—and when, for many weeks, there hung a veil of silent sadness and abstraction on his usually open and cheerful countenance, all felt that something very grievous and unusual had happened;[2] but he shut up the sorrow in his own heart, and never mentioned it to any living soul, by letter or by word of mouth, until he had reached, in his own mind, a plan of relief from the strait in which he was placed. It has always been regarded as a proof of rare courage and ability, when a man is able to make

---

[1] Imprisonment for debt could then be employed against the citizens of another State. The final abolition of imprisonment for debt became law in Massachusetts on the 4th day of July, 1855.

[2] For a slight expression of his feelings at this time, see the lines given in the *Appendix*, pp. 459, 460.

his darkest misfortunes the foundation on which to build up his greatest successes: and my Father's reflections on his apparently hopeless situation, resulted in the formation of a plan for the revival of that scheme for Church Education in his Diocese, which had so disastrously ruined him fourteen years before. It was combined with new features, however, which touched the commoner sympathies of humanity somewhat, and therefore gave additional chances of success.

It may be best to state this plan in the words used by my Father in laying it before his Convention in September of that year. After recalling fully the history of his former failure, and the pledge of the Convention, then, to renew the effort at some more favorable time, and proving the need of some such effort from the fact that the number of the Clergy had *diminished* from 26 in 1840 to only 20 effectives in 1854, he thus proceeded to unfold his plan, with some personal details which formed its basis :—

The year 1841, which followed the loss of all I had, while $13,000 of debt remained without any means of payment, saw me and my family occupying an old and dilapidated house in the village, as my parish had no parsonage for my accommodation. Under these gloomy and uncomfortable circumstances, my eldest son suggested the idea that I might induce some of my friends to unite in purchasing a tract of 100 acres, lying on the lake shore and forming the extremity of the bay, within a moderate walk of two miles, with which we were well acquainted, and give him a lease of ten years,[1] with liberty to cut down the timber for building and improvements, and with a covenant besides to convey to him the title in fee, at any time within that period, if he should have it in his power to tender the original purchase money and the interest. In this mode, he thought that he could have the satisfaction of providing for us a more retired and suitable home. The property would increase in value. My younger sons would have a constant supply of wholesome exercise and occupation in the intervals of study. And should it please Providence to prosper his own industry, he might be able to earn enough to pay for it, within the interval prescribed.

On this suggestion, I consulted several friends, and the result was, that with the aid of one gentleman in St. Alban's and another in Keeseville, who, between them, provided for three eighths of the sum, the

---

[1] This was the intention from the outset. The lease, however, was made out to my Father first, and, after the eldest son came of age, it was duly assigned over to him.

arrangement was made, according to my son's proposal. The timber was sold as it stood, for a dollar a cord, which sufficed very nearly to put up a substantial dwelling. My son went soon afterwards to Georgia as a teacher, which enabled him, in a couple of years, to remit $1250 more. The personal labor of myself and my family was added. And thus the wild tract of 100 acres, which previously was only valued as a timber lot and hunting ground, was transformed into a valuable farm, remarkable for its extraordinary beauty of location, as many of yourselves can testify.

Before the original lease expired, a wealthy friend in New Jersey, since deceased, gave my son a loan of $5000 for ten years, secured by mortgage on the property, which enabled him to purchase the title. And such is now the position of the matter. Of this sum, however, $1500 were applied to pay my own arrears of the previous rent and other debts, nor is this the only occasion on which I have been indebted to his filial devotion.

But since he entered the ministry, and his thoughts became concentrated on the interests of the Church, he has resolved to dedicate this beautiful property to the service of religion. He authorizes me, therefore, to offer it to the Convention at such price as your Committee shall approve, to be the residence of your present and future Bishops, and the site of your Theological Seminary and your Schools, with the express agreement on his part that the whole purchase money beyond the mortgage shall be appropriated to my old creditors. It gives me pleasure to say that those creditors are very few in number, that they have acted for the most part with perfect kindliness to the present hour,[1] and deserve this proof that their claims have not been forgotten, either by him or by me.

He then enumerated the benefits that would result from the execution of the plan. Their Bishop would be relieved from those old debts which he had now no other means to pay, and which were not creditable to the Diocese. The Church would possess a beautiful estate, of steadily growing value. A small outlay would enlarge the building sufficiently to accommodate the Diocesan library and the theological students, with lecture-room and chapel; and the grounds would furnish room for a Diocesan school for boys and another for girls, whenever the time for that work should come. The Bishop, as chief Professor, would need no additional salary; and the support of one other Professor and of the students themselves (who would spend a few hours each day in labor on the farm) would not be a heavy burden to the Diocese. He himself was "ready to undertake any

---

[1] The Boston creditor was the *only* exception.

degree of personal labor which the execution of the plan may require ": and he thus closed this portion of his Address :—

> I confess that I feel the deepest interest in the result. I wish to be instrumental in establishing a permanent institution for the Diocese, to be a memorial of my labors after I shall have passed away. I wish that the personal toils and hardships of the last fourteen years may contribute to the religious and temporal advantage of future generations,—that the candidates for your future Ministry and the scholars of your future Seminaries may enjoy the shade of the trees which I had trained, and gather fruit from the orchards and gardens which I had planted, and use the library which I had collected, and occupy the walls which I had built, and think, while they do so, that the first Bishop of Vermont, notwithstanding his failures and errors of judgment, had not quite lived in vain. And along with all this, I wish my friends and brethren to know, that the rights of creditors have never been forgotten ; that I have a son who sympathizes so fully with his father, and who is ready to sacrifice all that he possesses of worldly property, if an arrangement can be made, by which the welfare of the Church, the claims of justice, and the reasonable dictates of natural affection, may be brought to harmonize together.

The basis of this plan had been secured about the beginning of August, and then, for the first time, his long and sad silence was broken. "The clouds began to break away," as he expressed it, "and he saw the sunshine once more." The first mention of the idea in Burlington was so favorably received, that from the greatest despondency my Father was suddenly lifted to a height of faith and hopeful confidence which never afterwards failed him. He at once prepared in advance, and read to one and another, the portion of his Conventional Address devoted to the subject. One wealthy gentleman of Burlington, specially attracted by the idea of furnishing the Bishop with a home which should be secured to him for life, subscribed five thousand dollars,—a sum to that time unheard of in donations to Church objects in Vermont. With such a beginning, twelve others followed the example, with smaller ability but equal good-will, so that when the Bishop laid his plan before the Convention in September, he could show nearly $8000 of the amount needed subscribed already in Burlington, on condition of the approval of the Convention being given to the plan. The Convention very promptly and unanimously came to the resolution to approve of the plan proposed by the Bishop, " inasmuch as the people of Burlington had subscribed so large a portion of the sum necessary for that purpose"; and a Committee of five laymen was appointed, with the chief subscriber at the head of them, to obtain a proper Charter of Incorporation from the State Legislature. "The Bishop" was also "requested to solicit funds for the ends in view."

After this happy beginning, the Charter was obtained without difficulty, the Governor affixing his signature on the 14th of November. A fortnight later, an arrangement was made with the Boston creditor, by which he agreed to accept $1500 of the first receipts collected, and stop all suits, and give a full release of all liability: the money to be paid, or security given, before the 1st of August following. On the 2d of December the Trustees held their first meeting (the Bishop, Mr. A. L. Catlin and Mr. Thomas H. Canfield being present), organized, accepted their Charter, and signed the agreement made with the Boston creditor. Before the expiration of the same month, the land was deeded to the Trustees, "for the purposes therein set forth and specified, and for no other purposes," my Father himself drawing the deed, and beautifully engrossing it on parchment with his own hand. All the other creditors, being Churchmen and old personal friends, showed their sympathy for the enterprise by cheerfully accepting fifty per cent. of their original claims, or less, and giving releases in full. The price of the farm—estimated by disinterested parties as worth from $15,000 to $20,000—was fixed at $12,000, of which, provided it could be raised, $5000 would go to the extinguishment of the mortgage, and $7000 would wipe out all the old debts.

The work of getting "*The End of Controversy*" *Controverted* through the press, and the arrangement of these preliminaries with the creditors, had absorbed nearly all the leisure that could be taken from parish duties, and further effort was postponed until after Easter: but the bright prospect of success was a wellspring of joyous hope watering with gladness all the services of the Lenten season of 1855.

Meanwhile, however, very different thoughts were going through the heads and entrenching themselves in the hearts of some of the good Church people of Burlington. They remembered his former zeal in the great cause of Church Education, which had so far outrun his pecuniary ability as to bring about his financial ruin, with a long and dark train of embarrassments and sorrows. They thought they saw in him such a rekindling of the old fires as would surely lead him on to a similar catastrophe once more in his old age. Their comprehension of the Church's wants was not clear enough, nor their love for her sufficiently strong, to lift them up to the level of loving conviction in which he worked. Doubtless, some fear of possible complications neither very comfortable nor very creditable for themselves, contributed to the result of their meditations, which was, that the kindest act they could do for their Bishop would be, to render impossible the execution of this new scheme, which seemed to them to involve for him such an enormous amount of toil, trouble, distress, and eventual failure.

This new view of the case was extensively talked over during the latter part of the winter, and while he was so happily engaged during Lent, in the preparation of a large Confirmation Class, and a number of Catechumens. No one told him a word, or gave him a hint, of what was going on. His earnestness and confidence were so great that no one of them, singly, liked to face the avowal of what they thought. A paper was therefore prepared, and was passed round privately until it had received the signatures of twenty-eight members of the parish. It embodied various reasons for a request with which they concluded: as, for instance,—That sufficient reflection had not been given at the outset; That the subscribers had not entertained the thought that it would be seriously undertaken; That the times were so hard that they were unable to aid any new object; That the enterprise could not obtain means enough anyhow to secure the object aimed at, and they doubted the expediency of such an institution even if the money could be had; That the parish yet owed $3200 for the last improvements of the Church three years previous, and they could not pay that and aid the Institute plan at the same time; and so forth. They therefore closed with the cool request "that the Trustees surrender the subscription thus far made, to those who have subscribed it, and that they abandon all future efforts in the prosecution of the object."

My Father had for some weeks been trying to get the Trustees together for their second meeting, but some obstacle which he did not understand had prevented it. At length on the evening of Thursday, March 29th, that second meeting was held in the house of Mr. Thomas H. Canfield: and my Father, in the height of his happy confidence, was called on to give audience to two gentlemen of the parish, as a Committee, to present that Memorial and Request, which they meant as a real kindness to him personally. It was the sort of kindness, however, which he was the last man in the world to be able to look upon in that light. The darling project of his life, essential to the growth of his poor Diocese, which had been revived in his old age, and started so favorably by the Burlington subscriptions, on the faith of which the Convention had unanimously approved the plan, and the Legislature had given the Charter, and the creditors had all consented, and the property had been deeded, and they were all committed publicly to the effort before the Church and the World: all this was now about to be digged down by the hands of the very Burlingtonians of his own parish who had laid the foundation! He was kindled to a white heat, and in a long and excited interview told them plainly that the persistence in that course would compel him to resign both the Parish and the Diocese. He would say nothing about it until Easter Day: but then he would speak out.

The "Committee" left, in no happy frame of mind. The Trustees adjourned without action on the subject. He went on with his Lenten Services, once more with a heart heavy in its silence, the grief being harder to bear than the burden of the summer before: but it only gave increased depth and earnestness to his ministrations among the younger members of the flock, who little dreamed of the intensity of his sufferings. Twelve adults were baptized and twenty-one persons confirmed (thirteen others were added during the year) on Good Friday. The morning service of Easter Day was devoted to the commemoration of the Great Feast. But on the afternoon of that day, in an extemporaneous sermon on the words of Malachi, "*Will a man rob God?*" he broke ground on the length and breadth of the whole subject, with all his energy. Not a few heads hung down, one after another, in the congregation, during the delivery of that sermon: and it closed with a notice that his written resignation of the rectorship would be read at the parish meeting the next day, at which a full attendance of the people was requested.

That night four of the leading laymen—only one of whom had subscribed the Memorial—called upon their Rector, requesting that the written resignation might be read to them in advance. It was a long document, going fully and unsparingly over the whole ground, and its tone was pitched upon the highest key:—

> I set aside the personal wrong to myself. The disappointment of my creditors, the necessary result of the disgrace attached to my name when I am seen to have made pledges which cannot be redeemed, and represented the *written engagements* of my own parishioners as *realities*, instead of being only *promises made to be broken*. I pass over all this now, because there is a higher and more solemn question involved, namely, my own *official rights and duties*, which no man or men shall ever set at naught, with my consent or allowance. The Convention of the Diocese, which is the constituted organ of the whole Church in Vermont, has approved this measure, and committed its execution to the Bishop, and the Bishop is bound to *carry it through*, instead of *abandoning it*. That duty I must perform, or *cease to be the Bishop*. As Rector, too, I cannot admit the propriety or consistency of my parishioners proceeding to set themselves against the Convention, and putting their names to a conclusion which virtually negatives the whole authority of the Church, while they neither consulted me, nor sought the advice and counsel which it was my place to give them. Of course I cannot regard this extraordinary act as anything else than a total rupture of the relation which I have so long sustained to them, as Bishop and Rector.

Their reasons for their course he dissected with unsparing keenness, saying in regard to the plea of pecuniary *inability* to meet the debt of $3200 and their subscriptions to the Institute: —" When these gentlemen declare, as they have done, their *inability* to pay both these claims, they would be still more sorry than I should be, if any man believed it." But the categorical resignation contained in this paper was thought to be more than the case called for as yet : and the four laymen continued their friendly importunity until, late at night, the promise was made that that document should not be read the next day.

On the morning of Easter Monday there was of course a full parish meeting. The Rector made them a long speech, going fully over the whole ground of fact and argument contained in his paper, and telling them plainly what their course would involve if persisted in. "In such a case," said he, "as the only power we can exercise is in the conscience of our people, and there is no human tribunal to enforce obedience, nothing is left to a Bishop who knows his duty, but to resign and abandon, publishing his reasons, and leaving the parties to the judgment of the Great Day." The speech was listened to with deep attention. At its close, the Rector withdrew, and left them to themselves. They adjourned until the evening, and then followed a long and excited debate, lasting until midnight. The result was a compromise. A resolution "approving" the Bishop's plan of the Institute and pledging their "cordial coöperation," was unanimously rejected; and the Memorial of the twenty-eight was unanimously "approved." But with equal unanimity, on the other hand, they "disclaimed any intention to dictate" to the Bishop "the manner in which he was to perform his duties, or to interfere with his prerogatives as Bishop or Rector"; and testified their "sincere desire that he continue his relation to the Diocese as Bishop, and to the Parish as Rector," and that he be "requested not to offer his Resignation."

Their Bishop and Rector was grievously disheartened by such a *unanimous* rejection of his plan by his own parish. To make it worse, the chief subscriber, whose generous opening with $5000 had given such a brilliant start to the whole scheme, took this occasion to withdraw his subscription, and declare that he considered it no longer binding upon him in any way. This looked like a total and ignominious collapse. It had been made the Bishop's duty, by the Convention, to solicit funds for the execution of the Plan; and he meant to do it: but with this example set by Burlington itself, he was hopeless of any success in the rest of the Diocese. "It is evident," said he, "that if here, where the proposed Institution is to be located, and where, if successful, all its advantages would be directly profitable to the character and business as well as to the religious privileges of the place,—if here it is discountenanced and condemned, it is perfectly vain to expect much available support from any other quarter." It was therefore with something like settled despair, that, on the Saturday after that parish meeting, he left home to visit the rest of his Diocese, officiating no more in Burlington until the attitude of the other parishes should be determined : but thoroughly resolved, in case of equal failure there, to resign both the parish and the Diocese. My Aunt, writing to me, at the time, concerning the feeling of my Mother and the rest of the family at this prospect, simply said : " We are all ready to go with him to the ends of the earth. God's will be done."

In the midst of this sudden and desolating storm of opposition in Burlington, little did any of the excited actors in it dream that, just one week before the presentation of that Memorial, in the poor and quiet little town of East Berkshire, a consolation was provided in advance, to double the amount of the loss in wealthy Burlington. Dr. Ambrose Willoughby, a very aged and childless Churchman, on the 22nd of that same March, added a codicil to his will, in which he " gave to the Vermont Episcopal Institute, to be located at Burlington, Vermont, as a fund for the support of a Professorship, the income of ten thousand dollars, so long as that Institute shall remain in operation."

With this indication of what a kind Providence was preparing, no faithful reader will be surprised to learn that the Bishop did *not* find the parishes so ready to follow the example of Burlington as he had supposed. Parish after parish rose to the nobler and more hopeful and generous course. The priest of one poor flock mentioned one day, to one of the faithful women of his congregation, some of the difficulties that were making the Bishop think of resigning his Diocese. Tears started in her eyes, and she said :—" I have only an hundred dollars of my own, but I will give *them* for the Seminary." The Bishop was not able to visit every parish, nor was he able to canvass any one of them thoroughly : but the result of this his first attempt was a subscription of nearly $7500, without counting Burlington at all. No less than fifteen of the clergy were themselves subscribers, poor as their salaries were; and with unwearied and cheerful zeal they accompanied their Bishop from house to house. Many of the laity said that they would double their subscriptions, if necessary. "Indeed," said the Bishop in his address to the ensuing Convention at Windsor in September, "I did not anticipate—I could not have anticipated—so universal and generous a display of kindness and good-will as the occasion called forth; for they answered my application in a manner which converted what is usually a repulsive task, into the purest pleasure. I cannot deny that it affected me deeply and gratefully, nor can I otherwise regard it than as the richest reward for my poor services which I could have hoped to receive, on earth, from the goodness of God." Even Burlington did better than could have been expected from her unfortunate beginning. The large subscription was the only one withdrawn. Though there were six of the other subscribers among the twenty-eight, not one of them withdrew his signature, and several fresh names were added: besides which, the parish debt of $3200 which was such an insuperable obstacle in March, was reported "entirely extinguished" in September.

There were now no fears remaining as to the final success: but opposition was not yet over. The *Fundamental Statutes* of the Institute, adopted at the third meeting of the Board of Trustees, on the Monday before Convention, were in one point objected to by one clergyman; while another opposed strongly a proviso in the codicil of Dr. Willoughby (with which my Father had nothing to do, being ignorant of the bequest until some months after it was made), requiring that the Professor supported by that bequest should "promise true conformity to the published works of the first Bishop of the Diocese."[1] But the vigorous support of the laity more than counterbalanced the hesitation of the clergy, and the strength of opposition was at length exhausted. The time of the meeting of future Conventions was this year changed, from September to the first week in June.

Full of confidence and hope once more, my Father, about the middle of October, set out to see what could be done in other

[1] In the case of each election to this Chair, the promise of this conformity was made in writing, the form being drawn up by my Father, and in his handwriting; and the Professor-elect declaring, "I do hereby make the promise and profession required by the Will of the Founder, as the same is understood between the Bishop and myself, namely, that the conformity required extends not to matters of *opinion*, but only includes matters of *faith or doctrine*."

parts of the Church. He had accepted invitations to deliver a series of lectures both in St. Louis and New Orleans. In the former city he was very cordially received by the Bishop and Clergy, and at the request of the Bishop of Missouri he had the pleasure of ordaining to the priesthood his son Theodore Austin, then Rector of S. George's Church, St. Louis, and the second of his sons who had entered Holy Orders. He reached New Orleans about the end of November, and was the guest of Bishop Polk during his stay. His lectures there attracted larger audiences—so he was told—than any lectures ever delivered in that city before: and the number of hearers steadily increased until the end of the course.

After spending the Christmas time at Home, he resumed his work early in January in Philadelphia, whence he soon wrote:— "The clergy are most kind, and go with me in person,—a thing which they never do in ordinary cases. And the laity applied to have in no case declined, but subscribe with the greatest readiness: while the satisfaction expressed in my success on all sides is of the most cordial and gratifying character." In Baltimore the clergy formed a committee themselves to aid in raising the money. In Pittsburgh his old friends were all warm and active, and many new ones besides. But the work was wearisome and monotonous at the best. From Pittsburgh, in reply to inquiries about his health, he wrote home: "I am quite well, thank God! and would be very homesick, if I dare." New York was reached early in March, and on the 17th of that month his Boston creditor received his last remittance, and recorded his "satisfaction" in due form. Finding how seriously the work was interfering with his parochial duties, and seeing the probability that it would continue to do so for a long while to come, he resigned the rectorship at Easter, but consented to retain it temporarily for some time longer, his absence being somewhat made up for by the services of William Cyprian, the third of his sons who had entered the Ministry of the Church. The effort in New York was continued until some time in May: when, like the wandering bee, he returned with the rich rewards of his industry. He had obtained over $8600, outside the Diocese; while the sum subscribed in the Diocese outside of Burlington had increased a little to $7727, the Burlington subscriptions remaining at nearly $3000. Five Vermont parishes were yet to be visited. So that they were sure of about $20,000, besides the legacy of $10,000; nor had he yet been to Boston, or Brooklyn, or over so much as one-third of the ground in New York.

The preparation of his volume, *The American Citizen*, which was undertaken at the request of a New York Publisher, was the literary work of the year. And after the General Convention in Philadelphia, 1856 (at which he wrote, and read, the Pastoral Letter, and gave the parting Benediction), he resumed his labors for the Institute, correcting the proofs of *The American Citizen* between times, collecting the subscriptions in the cities, paying all the other old creditors, and satisfying the mortgage, which was duly cancelled, the executors of the mortgagee kindly releasing the interest then due to the amount of $450 : so that the property now belonged to the Church without incumbrance. On the 26th of March, 1857, the Trustees accepted the Bishop's report, together with the plan prepared by himself for the Seminary building. On the 25th of June the year before, my Father had visited the aged and infirm Dr. Willoughby for the last time, and given him his farewell blessing : soon after which he had entered into his rest. The legacy therefore was now available, and was formally accepted, with grateful thanks, by the Trustees.

The Bishop then entered upon a second visitation of his Diocese during this Conventional year, at both of which, as he gave them notice, subscriptions were not to be made, but paid. And he states as the result :—" It gives me much pleasure to say that our friends came up to their engagements with a prompt zeal and heartiness which were not only most creditable to themselves, but gave the best warrant for the genuine interest which they had taken in the enterprise. Certain it is that, in the whole course of my life, I never saw money paid in with more apparent cheerfulness and satisfaction. And I felt it most sensibly, as another proof of the Divine blessing " His notice of the falling in of the Willoughby legacy, not only occasioned a just and beautiful tribute to that faithful servant and steward of the Lord, but the Bishop also enlarged with great emphasis on the duty of every Christian in making his last will and testament :—

There is no way of escaping the conclusion, in any thoughtful and religious mind. Every Christian who has property enough to make it worth while to dictate his last Will and Testament, is solemnly bound, before God and the Church, to consecrate a fair proportion of it—never less than a tenth part—to the maintenance of religion. If he have no offspring to provide for, that proportion should be increased, as in the case of our departed friend, by adopting the Church instead of children. But never, in that solemn act, should the cause of Christ be omitted or forgotten. Never should he fail to place, on this last earthly record, a testimonial of his faith; nor distribute his possessions without a suitable memorial of his pious gratitude to that GOD who had so kindly prospered him.

There is a circumstance connected with that legacy which ought to be placed on record here. Though childless, Dr. Willoughby left an aged widow, for whose wants it seemed, at first, that sufficient provision had not been made; and she therefore applied to the Trustees for a temporary diversion of a portion of the income from the legacy, for her more congenial and comfortable support; which was at once granted, as she expressed it, "in a very feeling and sympathetic manner." But she was of a like spirit with her departed husband; and finding, soon after, that she did not need it, she wrote:—"I have finally (as I am happy to inform you) withdrawn said application, and confirmed the original appropriations, by approbating and acquiescing fully in the same, and the estate will now proceed at once to a final settlement accordingly."

Shortly after the Convention closed, the ground was marked out for the new building, the foundation was dug, and the walls began to rise, the whole building being erected of rough stone, of a light tint, quarried on the place.[1] The mild weather that autumn continued late enough to permit the completion of the walls to the top of the basement, when the work was covered in for the winter. Meanwhile, the financial convulsion of the autumn of 1857 had swept over the country, making such vast changes as to tie up, if not render for ever unavailable, a large portion of the subscriptions for the Institute: $4700 being now

---

[1] It is a silicious limestone, which will bear a very good polish, but is much too hard to be worked to advantage as marble.

past due, and the $1500 yet unexpended in the treasury would not justify the proceeding with so large a work as the building.

In the Spring of 1858—Burlington having been at length supplied, some months previous, with a very acceptable rector—a new duty was laid upon my Father. Bishop Alonzo Potter's health had so far broken down under the labors of his large Diocese, that he had been compelled to go to Europe; and during his absence, his Standing Committee requested a visitation of part of the Diocese from the Bishop of Vermont. He did not accept, until assured that the request to him was with the knowledge and approval of their absent Diocesan. On the feast of the Annunciation he left home for this duty, which he found much more onerous than he had expected. Within fifty-seven days of incessant labor, he visited 63 churches, delivered 114 sermons and addresses, confirmed 1331 persons, ordained 2 deacons and 4 priests, having travelled in this service over 3000 miles. The Convention of Pennsylvania thanked him in terms of unusual warmth for what he had thus done; and, besides the action of the Diocesan authorities, some of the Churchwomen of Philadelphia had a new set of Episcopal robes made for him, which in some respects differed from the pattern commonly worn by his brethren, each deviation, however, being expressly sanctioned by himself.[1] Though the excessively hard work and pressure of excitement was almost too much for him, yet he was glad to render this service to a Diocese with which the earlier years of his ministry were so wholly identified.

It was evident, however, that unless the default in the paying

---

[1] The material and the color were the same as usual. He would gladly have taken purple instead of black for the chimere, but thought "it would not do," as yet. The chimere was cut, however, exactly as a cope should be, a semicircle (with a very slight accommodation for the neck). The armholes were exactly on the quarter lines of the semicircle, so that the weight before and behind the arms was the same. The whole of the diameter of the semicircle was embroidered (in black) with the vine and grapes, enclosing the sacred monogram where the hood of the cope should be. The rochet was made with long close sleeves, like an albe, embroidered in white round the neck and the wrists. The lawn sleeves were like short surplice sleeves extending rather more than halfway from the elbow to the wrist, and embroidered with white trefoils all along the lower edge. These robes were not only much simpler in appearance, but were far lighter and more convenient than the absurd and inexplicable ugliness of the heavy, stuffy, baggy "magpie costume" in which the Anglican Episcopate swelters, groans, and endures, without having the moral courage to return to something better.

up of the subscriptions (and Burlington was more largely behindhand than any other place in the Diocese or out of it) were made up from fresh sources, the Institute building could not be finished. The Convention in June met at Burlington; and in this year, 1858, for the first time, was marked by an unusual feature, which continued to be repeated, with increasing interest, for eight years afterwards. On the afternoon of the first day, Wednesday, the whole Convention went out to Rock Point, in carriages and omnibuses provided for the occasion, where they spent the afternoon inspecting the unfinished building, and roaming over the beautiful grounds of the Church property, while the Trustees of the Institute were in session: and towards sunset, a collation, provided and prepared by the Churchwomen of Burlington, was served by their own fair hands to the Convention as their guests; after which, all returned to Burlington, as twilight approached, in time to attend the Missionary sermon in the evening. It was hoped, in this way, to increase the personal interest of all the members of the Convention in the great work to which they were all contributing: while, in itself, this feature of the annual Conventions rendered them more enjoyable than any similar gatherings in our part of the country.

The union of effort in this good work had indeed borne fruit already in more than one direction. It was about this time that one of his elder clergy wrote him:—"For the year past I have seen nothing, and have heard nothing, but the kindest expressions and most cordial approval from every quarter. We have seemed to me in a delightful state; all our clergy unite in love to one another, and in the bonds of affection to their Bishop. I believe there was never a sweeter concord than has existed among us for many months past, or than still exists."

For five months during this year, he had managed to give each alternate Sunday to the parish at Brandon, which was feeble and almost extinct. At the close of that period, several were baptized, 17 were confirmed, a lot was purchased, and a church plan drawn by the Bishop was adopted; nor was it long before a beautiful stone building was erected according to that plan: since which time the parish has gone on growing steadily until it is one of the strongest in the Diocese.

The next winter found him once more in New York and the other large cities, raising money for the Institute; but he often wrote that he made "very slow progress." There had been financial troubles; and in Philadelphia especially he found "four times as many refusals as before." The claims upon Church people for the West were also just then peculiarly pressing. But notwithstanding, he obtained $5400 from New York and $2300 in Philadelphia and Baltimore, so that the great building which was partly under roof late in 1858, went on during the summer of 1859, without serious interruption, the founder making advances from his own narrow funds when the Seminary exchequer was empty.

The General Convention of this year was of unusual interest, meeting as it did for the first time further south than Baltimore. On the second day of the session, on my Father's motion, a committee was appointed on the subject of the relations of the Churches of England and America, in reference to the transfer and discipline of clergymen:[1] as the result of which, the Presiding Bishop, Brownell, corresponded with the Archbishops and Bishops of England, and was answered "kindly and hopefully." It was a slight step towards something of more importance. At the Consecration of the Bishop of Texas in the Monumental Church, the Bishop of Vermont presided, preached, celebrated, and was the consecrator of Bishop Gregg, aided by several other Bishops; three other consecrations of Bishops taking place on the same day in other Churches, for no one building in Richmond was large enough to hold all who desired to attend a service never before seen in that whole region of country. But one of the leading features of the session was the adoption of our *Digest* of the Canons, arranging our Church law in a systematic form, instead of its being incoherently scattered through all the Journals of General Convention. This was substantially what my Father had suggested long before, and striven for through session after session against the indifference of nearly all others. On this occasion he wrote home :—

---

[1] Provided for partially in the Lambeth Conference. See p, 39 of Proceedings of the Adjourned Meeting in December.

The idea was started by myself, many years ago, but nothing effectual could then be done. The Hon. Murray Hoffman of New York took it up, however, some six years since, and he and Dr. Hugh Davey Evans of Baltimore, with the Rev. Dr. Hawks and others, have carried it through. It is not the only case, by many, in which I have suggested what other hands have performed. "One soweth, and another reapeth." And so that the good be done, what does it signify who has the credit? It is a privilege to be chosen as the Lord's instrument, in any degree, for the benefit of His Church, although our agency may be forgotten.

The task of raising more money for the Institute was again resumed, immediately after the close of the General Convention, in order to make up for the unpaid subscriptions in Vermont. But no encouragement was held out at Troy; and New York friends were by no means sanguine of the success of a third application there, while the Bishop of Vermont felt a special repugnance to stating that the want of punctuality on the part of Vermont subscribers was the real cause of the difficulty. While pondering what had best be done under the circumstances, he received a very unusual offer, which enabled him to obtain money in a way he never dreamed of.

The Bishops of Louisiana and Georgia had been the leaders in that noble and beautiful scheme for The University of the South at Sewanee, Tennessee, where the Churchmen of ten Southern Dioceses, with united strength, were beginning to found an Institution on the most magnificent and far-reaching plans. They had secured land in one parcel, to the amount of nearly ten thousand acres, situated on a sort of level mountain top, with lovely inland views on every side, and well supplied by nature with timber, stone, water, and coal. Here they proposed to retain the property of the soil, and draw a moderate ground-rent from every building erected by others; while striving to make it a growing centre, of summer residence at least, for many of the most refined and cultivated families of the South. In the general laying out of this vast property, they were anxious to secure the services of my Father's taste in matters of art; and they offered him therefore $1500 for six months to be spent there in this work.

An absence from the Diocese was requisite whether or no, in order to raise the money: and my Father was rejoiced to think that he could earn it by his own labor, rather than beg it from other people, to say nothing of the uncertainty of success in the latter just then, anyhow. Without even going home to say "good-by," he wrote to my Mother his determination, closing with the cheery encouragement, "Keep up your spirits, my good, brave wife!"˙and at once turned his face southward nearly a thousand miles, arriving at University Place on the 5th of December. He had promised to comfort her for his long and unexpected absence by being a much better correspondent than usual; and the scenes were indeed fresh and picturesque. Everything of course was yet in the rough:—

<blockquote>
I occupy the best of a set of log houses, in which is the office of Col. Barney.[1] It is a good large room, with a fine open fire. The logs are hewed smooth, outside and in, and my bed and table are both very comfortable. It reminds me strongly of Bassenheim, and the cabins where I listened to "*O Richard! O mon roi!*" sung to the harp by a charming young lady some forty-five years ago. If she were only here to talk to, what a romantic couple we should be!—both, indeed, much older and wiser than we were in those days, and yet young enough in feeling and affection to be far more happy than any married pair of our acquaintance.
</blockquote>

He had not been there a week before he found an extraordinary benefit to his health. For several years he had been troubled more or less all winter with a persevering cough, and it seemed disposed to attack him a little earlier each successive autumn. It was about at its worst when he left New York: but he had not been more than a week at Sewanee when he found himself perfectly free from cough and cold, in that admirable climate where in December the thermometer is hardly at the freezing point at night, and the air always pure and delightful. Nothing was needed but the open fire, and there was not the slightest occasion for stoves or furnaces, from both of which he always suffered grievously: while the water—and there are sixty natural springs upon the property—flowing through sandstone rock, was the softest and purest he had ever tasted, except upon the Allegheny Mountains in Pennsylvania. He was in raptures, too, with the place in other respects. All along the outskirts of the elevated

---

[1] The skilful engineer and general manager of the University Estate.

plateau he found beautiful views of valley and distant mountains: while the interior was filled with noble old trees, the oak, hickory, walnut, chestnut, tulip tree, etc., and would constitute, when properly improved, the finest park one could desire. "If Lake Champlain could be thrown in," he said, "it would be absolute perfection." Nor was it only that the weather was so delightful in winter: the Spring opened in February: and the extreme healthfulness of the situation, where fevers, rheumatism, and consumption were never known, combined with all its other advantages, marked it out beyond any spot within his knowledge, as the very place for a preëminent Church University.

Soon after his arrival, he established regular family prayer, morning and evening, at the cabin where he stopped, reading in the morning a Psalm, and in the evening a portion of the Gospel with a brief familiar lecture; and on Sundays the full regular service besides. The people around, amounting to nearly twenty, young and old, seemed to be much interested from the first. One Sunday, about a fortnight after his arrival, he went to preach at Winchester, about ten miles distant, where there was a Church parish; and was agreeably surprised by the arrival of Bishops Polk and Elliott, who accompanied him back to the Mountain. On Christmas Day (which fell on Sunday that year) the three Bishops held service at their little log boarding-house, the congregation consisting of about twenty, all told. Nor was my Father the only one of the three whose thoughts were somewhat, on that festival, at Home. He wrote:—"I thought of you, however, and our dear ones with you, worshipping in the Church at Burlington, with all its solemn and appropriate beauty, and receiving the Sacrament of our Saviour's love: and it was a delightful feeling to be *sure* that you were thinking of your wandering but faithful husband, and that our prayers, though from places so far apart, ascended to Heaven together."

The few days spent in the congenial society of those two remarkable men, were highly enjoyed by my Father: and I have often heard him recur to them in a way which proved the loving warmth with which they had impressed his memory. After full conference and exchange of views concerning the great work, they left the Mountain two days after Christmas, and he continued his pleasing though laborious task alone. He never saw either of them again, on earth.

About three months were spent in the work of the University, drafting maps of roads and sites, and plans for buildings, and making water-color drawings of striking views.[1] He was happy in being able to enjoy his artistic tastes with a triple pleasure, not only serving the Church University of the South, and his own Vermont Institute at the same time (to which he gave the whole amount he received for this service), but adding also, in regard to the personal hardness of part of the work :—" We ought to be thankful for an opportunity to set an example of some self-denial, and I never felt more happy than in this instance of labor, in the best of causes, beyond the degree which any one had a right to expect of me. How small a sacrifice is it, at last, for Him who has given us all things!" His wife was like-minded with him, in the readiness for self-denial and rigid economy in order to give the more to the good cause. He had sent her several cheques for household expenses; but she had kept her secret, and at last told him that she had been able to get along without touching any of his remittances. This called from him an enthusiastic letter of thanks, for " the unexpected and very welcome intelligence that you have had money enough for your expenses, my darling Manager and Prime Minister, without using my cheques! So much the better, as we shall need it all."

Having persuaded his Southern friends that in this three months of activity he had done them pretty much all the service that was in his power, they cheerfully released him; and sure, now, of the $750 which would finish the Chapel of the Institute, he sent from Sewanee the appointments for his next visitation, and rapidly closed his work. At his last Sunday service, on the 25th of February, there were four adults baptized—to three of whom he had for some time been teaching the catechism—and three infants : no small proportion of fruit to gather from so small a flock, though the Sunday congregations had increased to forty or fifty, and would have been larger but for the wretchedness of

---

[1] Nearly all of these were destroyed by the United States troops during the War, when the corner-stone (laid in the ensuing October) was taken up and broken in pieces, and other needless acts of what was then supposed to be " loyalty " were performed.

the roads throughout that region of country. On the 27th he left for Home, where he spent only one day, and then started on his Visitation : " Hard work, my dear son," as he wrote me, " but rest will come by and bye."

He did himself no harm in his Diocese by showing that he was even more ready to work for the Institute with his own hands, than to beg for it. And when the visitation was over, he pressed forward the work of finishing the building. The entire dimensions of this edifice are, in length 125 ft. ; in breadth 44, one wing being 57 ft. deep, and the other, with a Tower 60 ft. high, being 66 feet deep : and the accommodations are sufficient, at present, for seventy or eighty boys. The Diocesan library has a fine room appropriated to it; and it was originally intended that the Willoughby Professor and the theological students should occupy one end of the building ; but it was afterwards found more convenient that the theological part of the work should be done elsewhere. The highest richness and ornament were of course bestowed on the Chapel, to which chiefly the money earned in Sewanee was devoted. It combined, and far surpassed, the attractions of both the Oratories spoken of before. There was now a real open-timber hammer-beam roof with traceried spandrils, and recessed chancel, and stained glass windows ; and marble font, and Altar, and choice Altar plate parcel gilt, enamelled and engraved. An organ was provided ; and over the organ a picture of King David in his royal robes playing upon his harp, painted by my Father's own hand : and over the door the Madonna and Holy Child, also painted by him, after a part of the Sistine Madonna of Rafaelle.

All being thus complete, the Chapel was consecrated at the opening service of the Diocesan Convention that same year, 1860. The venerable Bishop of Quebec was present, with two of his clergy, and three of my Father's sons in Holy Orders, besides the clergy of Vermont, and representatives from other Dioceses, and a great crowd of friends from all sides : the ladies of Burlington performing their part of the hospitalities with cheerful profusion. At the meeting of the Trustees that day, a Professor was elected on the Willoughby Foundation,—the Rev. Dr. Hicks, a graduate of the General Theological Seminary, and the senior Presbyter of the Diocese: and the Academic Department was put under the charge of the Rev. Theodore Austin Hopkins, the first of my Father's sons to enter Priest's Orders. It was found that, under their Bishop's personal superintendence, the whole work had been completed for about $5000 less than it could have been contracted for, as certified in writing by the leading builders and carpenters in Burlington. And had all the subscriptions been paid in, there would have been no debt, and several hundred dollars in the treasury. But in fact, even the Sewanee contribution did not fill the gap, and some future effort would be needed to complete the work so nearly done. Thus far, perfect unity and harmony, in the Executive Committee and the Board of Trustees, had marked their whole proceedings: and there had been such kindly interest among all the workmen, that the task of the architect and superintendent was regarded by him as a pleasure and a privilege. Special gifts had graced the crowning of the work : and my Father found it not only one of the happiest days of his life, but remembered it " as one of those special manifestations of loving-kindness from our Father in Heaven, which are sometimes vouchsafed, in the progress of the Church, to cheer the hearts of his faithful people."

In September he was called to the Rectorship of Trinity Church, Rutland, where they expected him to spend, on an average, about three days in the week; and for which he was to receive a salary of $1000. He accepted it in the hope of stirring them up to the building of a new Church,[1] and also in order to earn another thousand dollars for the Institute; and a somewhat similar arrangement at another time and for a briefer period at Brandon was applied in the same way. During the years since the work began, moreover, my Father had advanced from his own earnings,—whether from his salary, his lectures in various places, or his books,—other amounts, the whole of which, to the figure of $4000 (besides the Sewanee contribution), he made a gift to the Institute in the following year, 1861.

[1] During his rectorship of a year, he raised a subscription of $8000 for the new Church: but the War prevented the progress of the work for awhile. The energies of the parish rallied, however, before the War was over; and, with a plan from my Father, they put up a beautiful stone Church, which was consecrated in the summer of 1865.

But he still regarded the scheme as incomplete until, on the Foundation thus laid, he had provided for the girls of the Church, as well as for the boys and the candidates for Orders. In the Winter of 1861, therefore, he set out on a new campaign in the great cities for that object: and since the family at Home had been gradually diminishing, as one child after another grew up and was fledged from the paternal nest, my Mother, for the first time in her life, felt free to join him as his travelling companion. My Aunt spent part of the time with one of her nephews, and part with another: and the Homestead that had been the scene of such busy life, was shut up, and pretty much left to the cats. At the time of their marriage, wedding tours had not yet come into vogue: and so my parents called this tour their "wedding trip." In Philadelphia, and most specially in Baltimore and Pittsburgh, they met their friends of former years, and brought back the mellow memories of the olden time; and sometimes the two sang together, for their friends, the same songs that had given so much pleasure nearly half a century before.

The expedition was much more successful than could well have been expected during the then troubled state of the country. No less than $5170 was subscribed, of which $1550 was paid down. But the War interrupted this good work, among many others, rendering collection of the subscriptions so difficult, and the obtaining of others so entirely out of the question, that at length my Father obtained the consent of the subscribers to transfer their amounts to the "general fund" of the Institute treasury. In the autumn of 1863 an eligible and beautiful lot was purchased for the girls' school; but three years later it was taken by the City of Burlington, at an advance of price, for their new public "Lake-view Cemetery." When the War was over, the effort was made to push this good work once more: but the claims of the South, in her destitution and misery, were so pressing, that the attempt was postponed. During the last year of my Father's life, he set the quarrymen to work, and quarried out a large quantity of stone near a site on the Church Farm where he had finally determined to place the girls' school: but he never saw even the corner-stone laid; and the quarried heaps have slept undisturbed since his departure. That one earnest longing of his heart was unsatisfied. If it had pleased God to spare his life and health two or three years longer, that rounding out of the completeness of his plan for his Diocese would doubtless have rejoiced his heart with its fulness, ere he went hence, to be no more seen.

Chapter XVIII.

THE CIVIL WAR.

ON the 15th of December, 1860,[1] when Secession was rapidly ripening into Civil War, the Bishop of Vermont received a written request from a number of personal friends in New York, that he would give them a brief statement of his views concerning the recognition of Slavery in the Bible, and the constitutional position of the two threatening parties in the country. My Father's views had been long and well known on this vexed subject of the Scriptural sanction of slavery. He had published them in full in the *American Citizen,* and in several of his *Lectures* which he had delivered in various parts of the country, North and South, without offence to any. His friends thought that the wide circulation of a cheap tract containing the substance of the Bible teaching, might do much to cool down the fiery zeal for the abolition of Slavery as the one great Sin of the times, which was a leading element in the mixed cup of the country's dangers.

The pamphlet was completed on the 20th of January, 1861; was rapidly rushed through the press in cheap form; and was somewhat widely circulated: but it was too late in the day for anything of that sort to exercise an appreciable influence on the whirl of events which soon issued in open War. The greater part of the pamphlet was devoted purely to the Bible question, and only a small part, at the close, to the constitutional point, of the right of the Southern States to secede. In regard to this, he said :—" In my humble judgment, they have a right to secede; although I grant that the point, being entirely new, is not without considerable difficulty." Every one who has studied the history of the adoption of our Constitution knows the large amount of evidence that may be brought together on this side of the question, includ-

[1] The formal printed letter is dated the 20th: but the original, informal request was received on the 15th.

ing the fact that the great State of New York claimed that right openly in the very act by which she acceded to the Constitution in the first place: but as the best mode of settling this long-vexed question, he said:—" Let the dispute about the right to secede, and the question of treason, be submitted to the Supreme Court, whose office it is to construe the Constitution." And, as this is precisely the course which was, for some time later, advocated by a person of such unquestionable " loyalty " as Gen. B. F. Butler, there was surely in this no evidence of a want of attachment to the Constitution and the Union. Even in this pamphlet, as in his book some years before, he expressed his conviction that, for many reasons, the abolition of slavery would be the better plan; and that it was, in the course of things, inevitable. " But," said he, " it belongs to the Slave States themselves to take the lead in such a movement. And meanwhile, their legal rights and their natural feelings must be respected, if we would hope for unity and peace." And this was simply what our wisest statesmen had held from the beginning.

There were many who, to the last, clung to the hope that a return to the original principle of fraternal union might restore the original feeling; and an " American Society for Promoting National Unity " was formed for the issuing of publications likely to promote that end. On the 3d of April (the attack on Fort Sumter had not yet been made) the Secretary of that new Society wrote my Father that their first issue, their " leader," was to be 20,000 copies of his *Bible View of Slavery*, omitting the prefatory matter and the brief portion referring to Secession.[1] He was urged, also, to allow his name to be used as one of the Vice-Presidents of the Society, among whom the Bishops of Ohio and Kentucky, he was informed, had already consented to be enrolled: but this last he declined, as being too distinctly a political position. The fall of Fort Sumter, a few days after, flashed the torches of civil war into a blaze from one end of the country to the other: and the well-meant work of that Society, like so many other amiable things, was lost in the storm. But the pamphlet will be heard of again before long.

[1] This pamphlet, in the following year (1862), was translated and published in the Netherlands.

Only a few days after the appearance of the original edition of it, my Father wrote, on the 15th of February, to Bishop Polk, immediately on seeing in the daily papers the statement that the Diocese of Louisiana was to follow the example of Secession set by the " Sovereign State " of Louisiana. In this letter he pleaded most earnestly against any such action, showing the difference between the crisis then breaking upon us and the rupture with England at the time of the Revolution, and contending that even though the country should unhappily be divided by civil strife, there was no reason why the Church should not continue to act as one body. But the answer to this letter, though kindly, showed that the time had not yet come for considerations of Ecclesiastical Union to prevail. Bishop Polk wrote him from New Orleans, April 30th:—"This great city is one military camp, and so is all my Diocese, and the whole South. May God have mercy on us all, for, I fear, vain is the help of man."

In answer to a similar letter from my Father, urging the same great arguments, the venerable Bishop Meade, who, down to the appearance of the President's Proclamation calling for 75,000 men, had been earnest in his devotion to the Union,[1] replied on the 10th of May in a strain which left no room for hope, though the old affection breathed through it still:—

> Had our friends at the North only approached to the just views on the subject in dispute set forth in your late letter, the South would never have commenced the work of secession. . . . But the die is cast, and our ecclesiastical and civil Union is sundered; and, I fear, never to be restored. The whole South is now united, as one man, in a war which is honestly believed to be a defensive one, and which will be waged as such with the utmost vigor, and with the most assured belief of success in resisting the attempt at enforcing reünion. . . . One thing I feel: that I shall be under any circumstances a friend and brother to all whom I have loved and still love throughout the Lord's Church. I see a notice for a meeting of delegates from the Southern Conventions in July. I think it is hasty, but suppose I ought to go to it. . . . Most truly yours in the Gospel of Peace,
>
> W. MEADE.

Unsuccessful in his efforts at the South, my Father was only the more earnest in laboring to prevent the needless increase of

---

[1] See Bishop Johns's *Memoir of Bishop Meade*, pp. 490-500.

alienation by acts of injudicious loyalty at the North. In his Convention Address of 1861, while strongly insisting on "allegiance and support to the Constitution, the laws, and the authorities under which the Providence of the Almighty has placed us," as a religious duty, and the further duty of prayer, "for all that are in authority," he also said:—

> Political preaching and political preachers have always been firebrands in the community, and it is the glory of our Church that she has thus far continued, as I trust she will always continue, free from these too popular abuses of the House of God. Of course we are all, as individual men, citizens of the Republic, and, as such, we have all the same right to hold and express our personal opinions. But when we come together as Christians, in the Sanctuary of the Most High, we approach the mercy-seat of the Prince of Peace, and have no right to discuss any subject which is not fairly connected with the advancement of His everlasting Gospel.

There was no political resolution passed, or even offered, in his Convention during the War. If any political sermons were preached by his Clergy, I never heard of it. But with his full approbation several of his Clergy went into the Union Army as Chaplains, and did good service there, one of them being his son William. One of his sons-in-law, from another Diocese, devoted himself to the same noble work: while two grandsons and three cousins were in the ranks, and three of the five fought their way through the whole war from beginning to end, with no promotion in any case except what they won by merit.

A few days after the Convention in June, a letter was received, which had been drawn up by the late Bishop Burgess of Maine; was signed by him and by the late Bishop Chase of New Hampshire; and was sent to my Father, with the request to forward it to Bishop Williams of Connecticut. The letter was a "Protest," addressed to the Domestic Committee, against paying any longer the stipends of Missionaries of the Board in Alabama, that "Diocese" having "seceded." My Father refused to sign the paper, and in his letter to Bishop Williams urged a variety of reasons why no such severity should be shown towards the few poor Missionaries in Alabama:—

> Brotherly kindness, patience, and an affectionate spirit of conciliation seem to me imperatively demanded of us all, in these perilous and alarming times. I have no faith in the healing power of coërcion. Nor am I an advocate for coërcion in any form which absolute necessity does not require. That necessity is the plea which seems to justify the defensive war of our Government; and I fully admit, as a citizen, the force of the political argument. But I do not perceive the same necessity for the coërcive preservation of union in the Church, because the organization of the Church depends not on the mutable shape of earthly constitutions, but on the abiding laws of spiritual truth and order.

Undeterred by his failure with the Bishops of Louisiana and Virginia, my Father could not bear the idea that the Southern Bishops should hold their meeting at Montgomery in July, without at least one earnest and affectionate voice from the North, pleading against their needless haste (as it seemed to him) in snapping the bonds of our Ecclesiastical Union. His *Letter to the Bishops and Delegates now assembled at Montgomery* was printed at New York, reïterating and enlarging upon the arguments already presented in vain to some of his Southern brethren; and the package of pamphlets was sent to the Rev. Dr. Craik of Louisville, by whose kind agency it was forwarded so as to reach Montgomery just before the work of their Convention began. But the course of events was too strong: and the well-meant pamphlet exercised no perceptible influence upon the deliberations of the body.

Following the example of most of the Bishops, my Father put forth special forms of prayer to be used during the War, though he did not think them absolutely necessary. He was careful not only to avoid any phrase which could be construed into a political test, but he also expressly permitted his Clergy, if they so preferred, to confine themselves to the form provided in the Prayer Book for use *In time of War and Tumults*, or to select any other prayers set forth by any other of our Bishops in any Diocese. Independent himself, in all matters where he was free by the law of the Church, no man had a more delicate and conscientious respect for the independence of other people: and nothing would have been more abhorrent to his whole character than to use his canonical power for the purpose of forcing his Clergy to use prayers which expressed his private or political opinions, not theirs.

At the annual Convention of 1862 he was able to say that the number of clergy in the Diocese was greater than it had ever been before, while there were no less than *six* candidates for Orders,—a very unusual number for so small a Diocese. As it was just thirty years since his Episcopate began, he was tempted to a comparative retrospect of results: and—notwithstanding all the peculiar disadvantages with which he had contended—he found that, in the number of Clergy, the Church had within that time gained two hundred and fifty *per cent.* on the growth of the population: and that her attained ratio of communicants to population placed the little Diocese of Vermont actually ahead of the great Dioceses of Pennsylvania, Virginia, and Ohio, and nineteen other Dioceses besides. He found also, that while there were then twenty-seven States out of thirty-three superior to Vermont in population, there were only sixteen which exceeded it in the number of Communicants, and only seventeen outranked it in the number of the clergy.[1]

At the General Convention in New York, that year (1862), the chief subject of discussion was, the state of the country, and the duty of the Church in regard to it. The Bishop of Michigan, in the opening sermon, struck the true keynote of duty, when he declared that the introduction of politics into our Church Councils would be "high treason against GOD." In the Lower House, the first symptom of the dreaded intrusion was tabled by a vote of more than two to one of both Orders.

But this—the true and instinctive utterance of the Church—was at length somewhat overborne by the stress of the times. The New York State election was impending, and to be decided only a few days after the adjournment of Convention. The Hon. Horatio Seymour was a lay deputy in the Lower House, and was also the Democratic candidate for Governor of the State at the approaching election. That party went into that election

---

[1] The average total population to each Communicant in the Dioceses referred to was then as follows:—Massachusetts, 148.9; Vermont, 149; Pennsylvania, 179.8; Virginia, 199.7; Ohio, 385.5, etc. The population is taken from the Census of 1860, the Church statistics from the Journals of 1861.

on the War platform, in professing which they were loudly accused, by their opponents, of being insincere. In order to have a favorable effect on that very important election, the Democratic members of the House were more willing to "do something" than they would have been at any other time. The Republicans, of course, were earnest for any action that would tend to strengthen the hands of the Government, and in their eyes politics and patriotism were conscientiously identified. There was a day set apart for "Solemn Humiliation, Prayer and Fasting," with a special service in Trinity Church: and the two letters from Cabinet Ministers expressing gratification with that special service (one read openly in the House of Bishops, and the other shown privately) created the impression that some of the Rt. Rev. Fathers were more solicitous to please the powers at Washington than the Powers of Heaven. The courage for resisting the intrusion of the secular issue became more and more quiet during the session. In the Lower House, Dr. Mead, Dr. Hawks, the Hon. Robt. C. Winthrop, the Hon. Washington Hunt, Dr. Mahan, Judge Chambers, and many others, fought the battle with the utmost bravery and pertinacity; until, after more than a week's continuous debate, the whole subject was very nearly laid on the table again. The long resolutions of the Committee of Nine, which meant as nearly as possible just nothing at all, and whose mild apparent censure was carefully put in the potential mood and in the paulo-post-future tense, passed by a very small majority;—even the slightest stiffening of its censures being voted down. The one determination from which there was no flinching, was, that nothing should be said or done which could be used as a serious obstacle to the spontaneous reünion of the Church after the War should be over. It was a great gratification to my Father, that, without one word from him to influence them, the Vermont delegation, clerical and lay, voted right on every division, without exception.*

But towards the end of the long debate, it leaked out that the current in the Upper House was beginning to set the other way. The confidential relations apparently existing between the Government and the Bishop of Ohio—who had been sent abroad on a semi-diplomatic mission, along with Archbishop Hughes, and had breakfasted with the Queen, and who came to the Convention from Washington where he had been the guest of a leading member of the Cabinet—gave him an extraordinary degree of prestige, which was not diminished by his reception of letters from the same quarter during the session. My Father presided, as the oldest Bishop present, the aged Bishop Brownell of Connecticut being too infirm to attend. The subject of the Pastoral Letter was referred to the five Senior Bishops,—being those of Vermont, Kentucky, Ohio, Wisconsin and Michigan. At their first meeting, no other member of the Committee having prepared anything, my Father read a draft which he had written, and in which the Scriptural principles of allegiance to the "powers that be" were plainly and fully set forth; but nothing properly political was introduced. Several modifications were suggested,—not a word being said on the political issue,—and notes were made of the suggestions, and at a subsequent meeting it was voted, on the motion of the Bishop of Ohio, that the draft thus amended should be laid before the House.

Before this was done, however,[1] the Bishop of Ohio requested, in writing, that the Committee might be called together again, but without specifying any reason. My Father of course complied with the request; and on assembling, the Bishop of Ohio expressed his conviction that something more was needed at the present crisis: and he accordingly produced a draft of a Pastoral Letter which he had prepared, and in which the Clergy and Laity of the Church were not only instructed as to what was the true interpretation of the Constitution of the United States in regard to the vexed subject of State Sovereignty, but the ground was taken that the Bishops taught this "as official expositors of the Word of God," and that "they could not teach less, without unfaithfulness to the Scriptures." My Father suggested that, if they could not all agree on one draft, the better plan would be to prepare a majority and minority report; but this not being satisfactory to the Bishop of Ohio, my Father's personal delicacy about seeming to contend for a document written by himself, induced him to rise, and quit the Committee, leaving the remaining

[1] The Pastoral Letter is not generally acted upon until towards the end of the Session.

members of it to arrange the matter as they pleased. The Bishop of Ohio was wiser, and remained; and the Bishop of Kentucky was in favor of his draft: the other two Bishops preferring the one already voted on. The four being thus left equally divided, nothing could be attempted except to lay both drafts before the House. And when both were read there, on motion of the Bishop of Maryland the draft of the Bishop of Ohio was adopted as the Pastoral Letter of the House of Bishops. The importance of the issue was thoroughly well understood. The number of those saying *Aye*, was small. The number saying *Nay* was still smaller. The larger number of the Bishops sat silent. One of them shortly after, passing behind my Father's chair, said in his ear:—" You are the only really courageous man among us."

The point of personal delicacy being now out of the way, the Bishop of Vermont was determined to make his opposition to the principle involved, as effective as possible. On the day after that vote, he was absent from his place, but hard at work; and on his resuming his chair on the following morning, he read his " Solemn *Protest* against the political aspect of the Pastoral Letter "[1] which they had adopted. It stated strongly and clearly the true principles upon the subject, such as have been held and practised upon unanimously in all parts of our American Church, except during that brief stress of storm: but notwithstanding the intense excitement of the occasion, its solid strength is not weakened by a single word of harshness.

He declined to bury his *Protest* in oblivion, by suffering it to go " on file " among the papers of the House of Bishops; but gave it all the publicity in his power through the weekly and daily papers. Nor was this all. Every attempt was made to add religious prestige to the political Pastoral. For the only time since the organization of our American Church, the General Convention was closed with a morning session, at which the Bishops all attended in their robes, the Pastoral Letter was read in place of a Sermon, and finally the Holy Eucharist was offered. This—which ought, one would think, to be done always—was done then, and then only: and if it be supposed that the object of this exceptional course was simply to give the greater weight to that

---

[1] This Protest will be found in the *Appendix*, pp. 461-465.

political Pastoral, I know of nothing to urge in proof that the supposition is incorrect. But it also gave the greater emphasis to the *Protest* against that Pastoral: for the chair of the Bishop Presiding, in the crown of the apse of S. John's Chapel, remained vacant until the reading of the political Pastoral was ended. Immediately after its close, the Bishop of Vermont came out robed from the sacristy, and took part with his brethren in the Eucharistic service, as usual.

The storm of opposition and dissatisfaction, roused by that political Pastoral, raged through the papers for weeks afterwards. In many Churches it was not read at all. In others, the day when it would be read was announced beforehand, so that all who did not wish to hear it could stop away. The discussions drew out a number of facts, every one of which strengthened the political complexion of what had been done. The fiftieth part of the large edition of the Pastoral, ordered and paid for by the General Convention, was sent to two members of the Cabinet at Washington. The Pastoral was addressed to the Clergy and Laity of the Church: but a letter was published in all the papers from the Secretary of State, addressed to the writer of that Pastoral, informing him that it had been "submitted to the President" of the United States, who was not a baptized man, and had never been even a habitual attendant on the services of the Church. "He authorizes me," said the Secretary of State, "to assure you that he received with the most grateful satisfaction the evidences which that calm, candid and earnest paper gives of the loyalty of the very extended religious communion over which you preside." He was "further instructed to say, that the exposition which the highest ecclesiastical authority of that communion has given in the Pastoral Letter, of the intimate connection which exists between fervent patriotism and true Christianity,' seems to the President equally seasonable and unanswerable." It leaked out, moreover, that a large number of the Bishops had signed a Memorial to the President, requesting the appointment of a day of General Fasting and Prayer, in terms which were very carefully guarded, but

---

[1] It appears that at this very time, as for years previous, and until the end of his life, Mr. Lincoln was what is commonly known as an infidel. See Ward H. Lamon's Life of Abraham Lincoln.

would have been popularly understood, in those excited times, as a demonstration in sympathy with the War;—the Memorial, however, not having been sent, partly because one or two Bishops who had signed it felt that it would be likely to increase their embarrassments in their own Dioceses; and partly because it was believed the President would not grant the request. All these straws were moving the same way, and the publicity given to them helped to counteract the mischief done by the political tone of the Pastoral. For some weeks, of course, the Bishop of Vermont was one of the best abused men in the country, in certain quarters: but it strengthened the foundation for his future influence; and in some churches, his rejected draft of a Pastoral was openly and acceptably read instead of the official document.

It was on the 16th of the following February (1863)[1] that a well-known layman of the Church in Philadelphia wrote to my Father, requesting permission to reissue that part of the pamphlet of 1861 which referred to slavery. On the 15th of April the request was more formally made by six gentlemen of Philadelphia, three of whom were known to him as communicants in the Church, of high standing and character, and none of whom were known to him, at the time, as active politicians. He took the invitation to be substantially of the same kind as that which had been made to him by some gentlemen of New York in December, 1860; and he saw no reason why he should not make the same response. Since they mentioned the pamphlet of 1860 as meeting their views on that subject, he placed at their disposal the part of it referred to, in its original form. They reprinted it, and a large Philadelphia edition was soon disposed of. In June it was again reprinted by "The Society for the Diffusion of Political Knowledge," in New York, and very large numbers were struck off. It was not until July that it was proposed to make use of the Democratic Clubs throughout the country as the most convenient means of further distribution, not in Pennsylvania alone, but in other parts of the country also. Having given his consent to the reissue of the pamphlet, my Father conceived that he had no right to interfere with any mode of distribution which the gentle-

---

[1] This could hardly be said to be "on the eve of the election" which did not take place until eight months after.

men who printed it might think best to adopt. He knew it would be more widely circulated with the aid of the Democratic Clubs than without them. His only object was, to enable the truth to reach the minds of men: and he would have been doubly well pleased if the Republican Clubs had taken hold of the same work, only with more zeal.

For the general views of that pamphlet—which only discussed the teachings of Scripture on the subject of Slavery—were precisely the same that nearly all steady-going, conservative, religious people had held time out of mind; the same that he had himself delivered in lectures in various parts of the North and South for thirteen years, with the warm approval of such thorough Union men as Clay and Webster; and nearly all Commentators, of all ages and all varieties of religious belief, were agreed in the leading points of his interpretation of the Word of God, down to our own day. He could not, for the life of him, understand how the mere change of circumstances should make any difference in regard to holding or proclaiming the Word of God: nay, the more unpopular that Word was likely to be, the higher was the duty in him to proclaim it afresh. He did not realize that the War-fever—which is a sort of madness while it lasts[1]—tests everything by the one standard of its own heat; and that all blood which will not rise as high and beat as fast, is at once set down as being in sympathy with the enemy: or, if he did realize it, he supposed that it was true only of the world at large, and not to any great extent true of the Bishops and Clergy of the Church.

But active and practical politicians look at these things in a light which is totally removed from the illusions of the abstract. A Churchman was the Democratic candidate for Governor of Pennsylvania in the October election, and the Churchmen among his prominent supporters were flooding the State with Bishop Hopkins's *Bible View of Slavery*. If—as was evident—*they* thought this to be a good electioneering document for their party, —though never so intended by its author—it is no wonder that the Republicans looked at it in the same light exactly: and nothing could be thought of more likely to outweigh the prestige

---

[1] As Mr. William Welsh said, in the General Convention of 1865: "We have all been crazy; and some of us are not over it yet."

of a Bishop, than to enlist the services of another Bishop on the opposite side. By the end of September—which was "upon the eve of the election" in October—it was evident that something must be done. The Bishop of Pennsylvania—the able and influential Alonzo Potter—was well known to sympathize strongly with the Government, and was conscientiously convinced that his was the true standpoint for every truly national man. "Being assured that the pamphlet was used widely and industriously to mislead people both as to the subject and as to our Church," Bishop Potter himself, in response to pressure both from Clergymen and laymen, drew up a form of *Protest* against it, in language somewhat stronger than that which was finally used: but he prudently made his signing it contingent upon its being signed indiscriminately among a good proportion of the Clergy in the city of Philadelphia and its immediate vicinity, because, as he said, "the *moral* value of such testimony depends largely upon its embracing a respectable number of those of different Ecclesiastical sympathies." Having thus started the movement, he left town almost immediately after, and was with a sick member of his family in the State of New York for more than a fortnight.

Meanwhile, a meeting of City Clergy was held, the language of the *Protest* somewhat modified from the original draft, and a committee of three appointed to circulate the document throughout the Diocese for signatures. In the form finally adopted, they censured my Father's pamphlet as, "in their judgment, unworthy of any servant of Jesus Christ," and added that it "challenged their indignant reprobation." There were only two or three weeks before the election, and there was no time to lose. Printed copies were forwarded to every Clergyman, with a request "to sign the enclosed paper and return it IMMEDIATELY." More than 160 signatures were thus obtained, the most conspicuous publicity being given to the whole affair, and in many cases the sharpest pressure being brought to bear on clergymen to compel them to sign, or find their refusal made the means of running them out of their parishes. It must be remembered, also, that about the time the circulation of that pamphlet actively began, Pennsylvania was invaded by Gen. Lee's army, the battle of Gettysburg being won by the Union forces on the first days in

July, 1863. The whole State was, in September and October, yet quivering with the intense excitement, to a degree felt in no other part of the North during the whole War: and the bulk of the Republican party looked upon the active canvass of the Democrats as a self-evident collusion with the enemy.

Under these circumstances, it is not to be wondered at that a much more vigorous use was made of the *Protest* than the Bishop of Pennsylvania contemplated. On his return about the middle of October, he found to his surprise that the *Protest* had been signed by the Clergy in the interior, and was evidently being circulated throughout the Diocese. He "foresaw, at once, that in some smaller and more isolated congregations it might be the occasion of unnecessary trouble, and that the younger Clergy were liable to be embroiled in unseemly discussions, unless much circumspection and self-restraint were used." More than a fortnight after the "Public *Protest*" had been sent out for immediate signature, therefore, the Bishop, on the 15th of October, sent out another " Circular " to his Clergy, marked "*Private*," in which he alluded to "the vortex of our election contest," saying to his Clergy:—" It is especially our parts and duties to shun whatever may tend to needless recrimination or uncharitableness. Many things occur in our party canvasses which all regret in their cooler moments; and there is nothing which I more ardently desire, nor is there anything which appears to me more congenial with the spirit and precepts of the Gospel, than that our Clergy should be known as lovers of the truth, in the meekness of fear, and as pursuing assiduously the things that make for peace, and that they may edify one another." This Circular was marked "*private*," as the Bishop afterwards explained, "not because I courted concealment, but because I thought much of its good effect would be lost if it reached the Laity prematurely, or if it gained publicity through the newspapers."[1] The good Bishop's solicitude is considerately expressed, and reads well in his *Memoirs :* but it was as accurately timed as the *Protest* in regard to the work it was to do. It was perfectly safe for him on the *fifteenth* of October that year to " pursue assiduously the things

[1] See Dr. Howe's *Memoirs of the Life and Services of the Rt. Rev. Alonzo Potter*, D.D., LL.D., p. 240.

that make for peace," for on the *thirteenth*, just two days before, the election battle in the State of Pennsylvania had been fought and won.

In all this the Bishop of Pennsylvania as earnestly—and doubtless as conscientiously—as the Bishop of Vermont, repudiated all idea of political partisanship. "That the *Public Protest*," said he, "was meddling with politics (as that word is commonly understood) is a great mistake. It was an earnest remonstrance against debasing such momentous questions as the fate of an entire race, by mixing them with vulgar party canvasses." But the practical working of the thing, when the prominent and more violent Republicans seized upon it and pushed it as their most available electioneering document, was very different, and the bitter waters flowed freely on every side. Letters began to pour in upon my Father in a flood, especially from poor country clergymen, who found the Public Protest headed by their Bishop's name thrust at them with imperative demands that they should sign, while they had his "Private" circular in their pockets, virtually exhorting them to do no such thing. As men took time to reflect, moreover, the extraordinary character of the circumstances began to impress itself more and more. Here was a whole Diocese vehemently drummed for signatures to a Protest in which the strong censures already quoted were pronounced by clergymen, and even by young deacons, against a Bishop, and he next to the Presiding Bishop in the order of Seniority. The Pamphlet, as circulated, moreover, contained not a word of politics, being solely devoted to an examination as to the teachings of the Bible: whereas the Protest was avowedly against the "Rebellion." So great was the pressure, that many signed who had never read the pamphlet condemned; some signatures were attached to the Protest without authority; and some signers had the manliness to withdraw their signatures, when, on reading the Pamphlet, they found how greatly its substance had been misrepresented.

My Father was wounded very deeply by an assault so injurious in its terms, circulated in so strange a way for the signatures of even the youngest of the Clergy, and which had been mailed to all the clergy in Vermont as if with the purpose of making it a firebrand there also. But the deepest grief of all was, to see a Bishop of the Church, and so many of her Clergy, thus denouncing a pamphlet which merely contained the substance of the teaching of Holy Scripture as understood in all ages of the Church. He replied to the Protest in a letter addressed to the Bishop of Pennsylvania, in which he showed that neither pungency nor power had yet begun to fail his pen. The fact that a Bishop and more than an hundred of the Clergy of the Church had thus come out in denunciation of the teachings of Holy Scripture, determined him to carry into execution at once the resolution which he had formed years previous, and had then abandoned, partly at my solicitation. Accordingly, in his reply to the Protest he said:—

> I do not believe in the modern discovery of those Eastern Philanthropists who deny the Divinity of our Redeemer, and attach no importance to the Bible except as it may suit themselves. I do not believe that the venerated founders of our American Church were ignorant of the Scriptures, and blind to the principles of Gospel morality. I do not believe that Washington and his compatriots, who framed our Constitution with such express provisions for the rights of slaveholders, were tyrants and despots—sinners against the Law of God and the feelings of humanity. But I do believe in the teaching of the inspired Apostles, and in the Holy Catholic (or universal) Church, which you and your Clergy also profess to believe. I *know* that the doctrine of that Church was clear and unanimous on the *lawfulness* of slavery for eighteen centuries together; and on that point I regard your "protest" and "indignant reprobation" as the idle wind that passes by.
>
> I wish you, therefore, to be advertised that I shall publish, within a few months, if a gracious Providence should spare my life and faculties, a full demonstration of the truth "wherein I stand." And I shall prove in that book, by the most unquestionable authorities, that slaves and slaveholders were in the Church from the beginning; that slavery was held to be consistent with Christian principle by the Fathers and Councils, and by all Protestant divines and commentators, up to the very close of the last century, and that this fact was universal among all Churches and sects throughout the Christian world. I shall contend that our Church, which maintains the primitive rule of Catholic consent and abjures all novelties, is bound, by her constitution, to hold fast that only safe and enduring rule, or abandon her Apostolic claims, and descend to the level of those who are "driven about by every wind of doctrine."

The Bishop of Pennsylvania did not reply. He left that task

to one of his clergy, who thought it not unworthy of him to hunt up the original issue of the pamphlet in January, 1861, and reproduce the few words touching Secession, none of which had appeared in any of the numerous subsequent editions. My Father responded with undiminished freedom, candor, and force: and forthwith went to work at his proposed book, with all his might.

Once more, I did my utmost to dissuade him. Every reason which had seemed to me strong before, was now of tenfold strength. The certainty that "the institution" was doomed; the hopelessness of getting men to reason, in the midst of the passions of a protracted Civil War; the increasing of bitterness and divisions among our own Church people,—heretofore so free from the curse of agitations about slavery; the impossibility of persuading the ordinary mind that his argument was not *ipso-facto* an advocacy of "the Rebellion"; the possibility of drawing upon himself the pressing attentions of the Government; and last and chiefest, the prospect of injuring if not totally destroying his influence for good in his own Diocese,—Vermont being so intensely Republican, that it is the only State in the Union which has never at any time voted the Democratic ticket: all these pleas were urged; but to all he had one invariable answer. He allowed the truth and force of everything that was pleaded, confessed the hopelessness of results so far as passing events in the political world were concerned, and admitted the truth of apprehensions as to his usefulness in his own Diocese; but none of these was his first care. The real attack, he said, was upon the Word of GOD: and *that*, it was the first duty of every Bishop to defend, cost what it might. He was ready to face every consequence without flinching, even if it involved the being driven from his Diocese and thrown penniless upon the world when past the age of threescore years and ten. He had made up his mind that he was doing his highest duty: and all remonstrance was utterly idle. And yet the thought of separation from his Diocese must have been peculiarly painful to him: for at the Convention that year he had expressed his humble gratitude to God for the general aspect of prosperity which had rendered his last visitation on the whole the most gratifying that he had made during the thirty years of his Episcopate.

Day and night his work was pushed,—Holy Scripture, Commentators ancient and modern, Fathers and Councils, besides a wide range of other authors, being all put under requisition,—and by the middle of January (1864) the book which was begun in October was so nearly ready for the press that he went to New York to find a publisher. The correcting the proofs, and the finishing of the work itself, delayed the appearance of the volume until about the middle of March. This intense application had been continued in spite of the fact that his health had begun to suffer from it. In answer to affectionate apprehensions on this account, he wrote Home:—

> As to my cough, my darling wife must not give herself any anxiety. Until this book is off my hands, I cannot feel nor appear as usual, because I have still to work on the latter part of it, and it absorbs my thoughts so that neither appetite nor sleep are as good as they should be. But the cough itself is no worse than I have often had at home, at this season of the year. And my strength is such that I walk to the printer's every day in the week (Sundays excepted) three miles and a half, and then walk back again, making seven miles a day.

More than once, too, as I remember well, that whole distance was accomplished on foot in the midst of furious storms of snow or sleet. As a consequence of this " heroic treatment," he could write, about a week before the book was out, " My cough is about gone, and my health and strength are excellent. . . . As to my nerves, my labors have not disturbed them in the slightest degree. The goodness of the LORD fits His servants for their work ; and instead of feeling any the worse for mine, I have not felt in better health for the last two years than I am just now."

The work produced under these exciting circumstances, ran through four editions in a few weeks, and the seventh was put to press before the demand was satisfied. Some attempts were made to answer subordinate parts of the argument: but the main substance of the book is unanswerable, being history, not argument.

The consequences, to my Father, were by no means as formidable as he had prepared himself to expect. He was attacked and ridiculed in all the Republican papers as a matter of course, and was lauded and defended in the Democratic papers with equal unanimity. One of the Burlington papers was specially pertinacious in its attacks, which were kept up for weeks together. All invitations to attend meetings of Democrats as such, were promptly and politely declined. But there was not a ripple of trouble in his own Diocese. Perhaps there were some half dozen of the laity in all, who let it be known that they would not attend Divine Service when the Bishop came on his visitation: and that was all. Not a word or a lisp of personal disrespect, or of organized opposition, could be heard in any of the parishes: and the congregations, wherever he went, seemed as large, as attentive, and the people as affectionate, as ever.

In April, 1864, just after the publication of his book, the state of things in the Church of England seemed to call for some expression of brotherly sympathy on our part. The Judicial Committee of the Privy Council had given judgment in the *Essays and Reviews* cases, in a way which seemed to weaken the testimony of the Church from the beginning in regard to the Inspiration of Holy Scripture and the eternity of the Second Death. A Declaration had been drawn up on these two points, by Dr. Pusey, which was pushed by the hearty coöperation of his friends on the one side, and the leaders of the Low-Church party on the other: and it received the signatures of between eleven and twelve thousand of the Clergy of the Church of England, besides being largely signed in the Colonies. At the suggestion of my Father, —Bishop Brownell, the then Presiding Bishop, being first consulted and giving his consent and signature,—the same Declaration, word for word as to doctrine, was sent round among our American Bishops for signatures. Of course, there could be no direct communication with the Southern Bishops, during the continuance of the War. Some of the Northern Bishops, moreover, had strong and well founded objections, on general principles, to the getting up of Declarations on any doctrinal point, without the solemnity and wise safeguards of actual meeting and free discussion. Subsequent experience has proved that, even with these helps, doctrinal declarations had better be let alone, unless there is such a compliance with constitutional requirements as will give them some authority. But, with all these drawbacks, the disposition to give a cordial support to our English brethren, in their hard battle to protect the Faith against the underminings of a lay Court of Appeal, prevailed to such a degree that, of the twenty-seven Bishops then accessible, all but four gave either their actual signatures or their substantial approval of the doctrinal truths embodied in that Declaration.

Meanwhile, the bitter local controversies created by the *Protest* in Pennsylvania had been burning their way corrosively in many a parish; and high party feeling produced unusual excitements at not a few Easter elections, the issue being whether the parson should be allowed to remain in such peace as he could find, or should be asked to resign because he was not sufficiently "loyal" to sign the *Protest*. Bishop Stevens, then the Assistant Bishop of the Diocese,—who was ordained at the South, where he had spent many years of an acceptable priesthood, and had married a Southern wife,—refused from the first to sign the *Protest*, and for a long time after was the butt of unmeasured "loyal" obloquy. In the Western part of the State, the Rev. Dr. Van Deusen, then rector of St. Peter's, Pittsburgh, was the leading representative of similar sufferings, and fought his battle bravely and triumphantly. His parish stood by him at the Easter meeting, by a handsome majority.

In May, the annual Convention, for the first time in the history of the Diocese, met West of the mountains, and the opening service was held in S. Peter's.[1] All the debates, however, took place in Trinity Church,—my Father's old parish,—and in the edifice which, with slight alterations made after a partial fire, still stood as built from his designs. The chief discussion—and one attended with great excitement—was on political issues, the resolutions offered being very strong and bitter in their language. The business of the *Protest* was, of course, too recent and too hot to escape notice. The Rev. Dr. Washburn (then rector of S. Mark's, Philadelphia), one of the earliest signers, startled the House on Thursday morning with the bold declaration that he would sooner have lost his right hand than sign the *Protest*, had he known that it was to be forced upon other men as a test of

---

[1] It was supposed, the year before, that Trinity Church would, at the time the Convention met, be torn down for rebuilding: but this not being the case, the subsequent sessions of the Convention were adjourned to the old mother church, Trinity.

loyalty. Others, of equally assured loyalty, made similar declarations. On the other side, one who claimed to have been in personal communication with the President of the United States, declared, that the President desired " most of all, to know that he was supported by the religious sympathy of the country, and was upheld by the Episcopal Church as well as by other religious bodies": and the proceedings of the Old-School Presbyterian General Assembly were read to show Pennsylvania Churchmen the sort of thing which it was their duty to pass. One layman even went so far as to move a censure on the Bishop of Vermont's book, and the approval of the course of the Bishop of Pennsylvania on that subject, but was not seconded:—a proposal which brought out a breeze of hisses. Bishop Potter promptly sent a private message to the mover, begging him to let that matter drop; and it was dropped accordingly. One of the striking features of the debate was the speech of Judge Shaler,—an old parishioner and personal friend of my Father's, past his threescore years and ten, and totally blind,—who described in touching terms the former freedom of the Church from these political issues, which were now relentlessly forced upon them: and he then took up the political gauntlet, and excoriated the Administration with all the energy of an old-fashioned, life-long Democrat. The friends of politics were evidently getting the worst of it, when at length Dr. Van Deusen moved a substitute, couched in words taken from a letter written by Bishop Stevens in aid of the Sanitary Fair, and which were familiar to everybody in the House, as they had been sent by circular to every parish in the Diocese. Bishop Potter said, from the chair, that this substitute would be sufficient, and it was finally carried: a portion of the original preamble, softened by omissions, being all that was saved from the wreck.

Less than two years elapsed, and a very different scene was witnessed in that same Trinity Church, Pittsburgh, so dear to my Father's recollections. It was the Feast of the Conversion of S. Paul, in the year 1866. Bishop A. Potter had departed to his rest. Bishop Stevens was lying near by, too ill to take part in the service. A great company of Bishops, Clergy and laity crowded the venerable building in every part, to witness the Consecration of the first Bishop of Pittsburgh. The Bishop of Vermont, as Presiding Bishop, occupied the Chair filled on the former occasion by Bishop Potter. The service of the day was not only the long-delayed and now fully ripened fruit of my Father's early labors in that parish and the region round about; but—far nearer to all hearts there—the War was over; the Church had been reünited; and—in no small measure owing to the position of the Presiding Bishop—the policy of love had triumphed everywhere, within the Church, over the policy of hatred and bitter denunciation. The long procession entered at the west door, and moved up to the Chancel. The solemn service began. One of the signers of the Protest was appointed to read the First Lesson for the day,[1] and with the opening words of it some people began to prick up their ears, while, as verse after verse was heard, the strange coincidence grew stronger and yet more striking:—

Then shall the righteous man stand in great boldness before the face of such as have afflicted him, and made no account of his labors.

When they see it, they shall be troubled with terrible fear, and shall be amazed at the strangeness of his salvation, so far beyond all that they looked for.

And they repenting and groaning for anguish of spirit shall say within themselves, This was he, whom we had sometimes in derision, and a proverb of reproach.

We fools accounted his life madness, and his end to be without honor:

How is he numbered among the children of God, and his lot is among the saints?

Therefore have we erred from the way of truth, and the light of righteousness hath not shined unto us, and the sun of righteousness rose not upon us.

We wearied ourselves in the way of wickedness and destruction: yea, we have gone through deserts, where there lay no way: but as for the way of the Lord, we have not known it.

What hath pride profited us? or what good hath riches with our vaunting brought us?

All those things are passed away like a shadow, and as a post that hasted by. . . .

But the righteous live for evermore; their reward also is with the Lord, and the care of them is with the most High.

[1] Wisdom v.

Upon the hearty welcome among his old friends and their descendants, and the other joyous circumstances of this occasion, I need not dwell. It was my Father's farewell visit to the scene of his earliest labors for the Church: and none more appropriate, more significant, or more beautiful could easily be imagined.

But this is anticipating the true order of events.

Chapter XIX.

THE REÜNION OF THE CHURCH.

THE departure of good Bishop Brownell, in a ripe old age, on the 13th of January, 1865, left my Father the Presiding Bishop of the Church of America. He had for many years been primitive enough to lose all admiration for our present American rule, which makes the Senior Bishop by consecration the Presiding member of our national Episcopate: nor was his opinion changed when the operation of the rule brought the honor to himself. It rather sharpened the sense of its unwisdom. "What could be more absurd or unprimitive," he would often say to me, "than to make the Bishop of such an out-of-the-way, little, insignificant Diocese as Vermont, the Presiding Bishop of so vast a National Church as ours?" The office, he thought, according to the almost universal practice and law of the Primitive Church, should belong as a matter of course to the Bishop of New York or Philadelphia: and he anticipated that the growing inconveniences of the present plan would before many years give way to a wiser conformity to the ancient and far better way.

But his coming to this position just as the Civil War was drawing towards a close, gave to the whole Church the full fruit of his courageous adherence to truth and principle while the tempest was at its height. This result had not been anticipated by him: for single-hearted as was his devotion to the old Union, he had from the first despaired of its preservation by means of War. He and I had had many a long discussion on the subject, but neither could convince the other. "The world had never seen," he urged, "twelve millions of people, inhabiting a country so vast, reduced to submission by the sword." And the considerations urged on the other side from the condition of the population, the physical peculiarities of the country, and the wonderful differences produced by steam on land and water, were not enough to persuade him that we were making History in this land on a different scale from that which had been the general rule in the past.

But none rejoiced more intensely or more deeply at the prospect of peace [1]: and his first and dearest care was turned towards the reünion of the Church. His voice had been the last to be heard, pleading for continued ecclesiastical union, even after the dogs of war had been howling throughout the land for months: and now his voice was to be the first official utterance looking towards reünion after the War was ended. But the difficulties in the way were very great. Some of us had foreseen the actual state of things. We had, with unwavering confidence, anticipated the triumph of the United States, and the eventual restoration of the old Government, after a longer or shorter period of suffering and trouble. This confidence was our support under all the reproach, showered on us during the continuance of the War fever because we insisted on keeping the political agitations out of the Church. Armies and artillery might bring back the Southern States: but the Church had no armies or artillery to operate in bringing back the Southern Dioceses to our General Convention. If they came back at all, it must be of their own free will, as brothers returning to their old place, to be welcomed once more by brethren.

The prospect of this at first, from one point of view, seemed but small. The essence of the Low-Church party is, to sympathize with any popular movement among the Protestant denominations, far more readily and strongly than with anything distinctive connected with their own Church. Before the War, slavery issues were easily avoided among us, because the Low-Church party, which alone was likely to try to introduce them, was in a minority and could not afford to divide its forces: and Massachusetts and South Carolina, Virginia and Ohio, were all in that minority together. But the War fever swept everything before it among the denominations, the Methodists going so far as to insert the oath of allegiance in their Ordination Office. Our Low-Churchmen, therefore, as a body, went the same way: and during the War, Church interests, and even their Evangelical party interests, were nowhere, in comparison with " saving the life of

---

[1] See *Appendix*, p. 459.

the Nation." When the War ended, they had not yet gotten over this predominance of secular interest: and to such a degree was it rampant, that on the 6th of May, 1865, three weeks after Gen. Lee's surrender, a leading editorial in the *Episcopal Recorder* of Philadelphia, then the chief Low-Church organ, demanded of the Government that some of our leading Bishops and Clergy at the South should be hanged, on the ground that they had been leaders in the original movement for Secession. As the General Convention was to meet that same year, in October, in that same city of Philadelphia, one can easily see how difficult it must have been to persuade Southern Churchmen that they would be welcomed to its sessions as brethren.

In contrast with this, the Bishop of Vermont's course had been such as to bring applications from the South for his Episcopal services, even before the War was ended. On the first day of the year 1865 a request from eight of our clergy in New Orleans was sent to him, asking him to go down to that City, and visit the parishes within the Federal lines. The Diocese of Louisiana was then without a Bishop, no Convention having met since the one which, owing to the "secession" of the State of Louisiana, declared the Diocese to be no longer a portion of the Church in the United States. The acceptance of a military command in the Southern Army by Bishop Polk, and the early occupation of New Orleans by the Union forces, prevented the calling of any other Diocesan Convention: so that Louisiana was never united formally with "the Church in the Confederate States." The members of the Standing Committee were so reduced and scattered by the casualties of war, that the meeting of a quorum was impossible. The Clergy of New Orleans were unanimous in their request: and, among others, the venerable Bishop Kemper wrote, warmly urging the fulfilment of it. But my Father knew that the feelings of the Laity, in such times, were harder to control than those of the Clergy: and in his reply, while expressing his willingness to go, he made it a condition that the request should be united in also by the Vestries of all the parishes within the Federal lines, in their official capacity; as well as by such members of the old Standing Committee as could be reached. The Vestries were found unwilling to act as such, though, as individuals, their members expressed every desire for the visit. The military authorities were sounded, and were heartily willing not to interfere.[1] The refusal of the Vestries satisfied my Father that the movement was premature: and he did not go. A similar request was received from the Memphis clergy in February, and was repeated from the Standing Committee of Tennessee in April: that Diocese being then vacant by the lamented death of Bishop Otey, and the Diocesan Convention being unable to meet. But here also it was finally concluded not to act. Some at the South might have misinterpreted an unwise haste in bringing a Northern Bishop to perform Episcopal acts in Southern Dioceses, without the Canonical invitation. It was better to be too cautious in trenching on the rights of others; and that caution was more likely to conciliate the confidence of Southern Churchmen generally.

Immediately upon the cessation of hostilities, the minds of Northern Churchmen thought first of all of the reünion of the Church; and the Presiding Bishop naturally felt that the chief responsibility for action lay upon his shoulders. It was a most favorable circumstance, that the Presiding Bishop of " the Church in the Confederate States," at the close of the War, was Bishop Elliott, whose warm personal attachment to my Father had never been interrupted. He had, indeed, been one of the most ardent in the Southern cause, and the failure of it at the last destroyed utterly one of the favorite dreams of his life, and doubtless paved the way for his sudden departure before two years more had passed. But, as he told his people, " We appealed to the God of battles, and He has given His decision against us. We accept the result, as the work, not of man, but of God." From his point of view, the chief difficulties in the way of reünion were to be expected from the South. Defeated, humiliated, impoverished utterly, with their whole system of labor temporarily if not permanently demoralized, and compelled to accept a political union which they detested: nothing was more natural than that they

---

[1] In a letter to me at the time, my Father said:—" The military Governors have been applied to, and express their hearty assent, but decline to put it on paper, because it is a matter with which they do not think they have any right to interfere. A very correct opinion!"

should cling to their Southern ecclesiastical organization, as a sphere in which they could indulge their passion for separation, with no danger of interference from governments or armies. This feeling was for some time dominant there: and with such editorials as that of the *Episcopal Recorder*, and the reprinting in similar organs, for weeks, of every paragraph that could keep up Northern prejudice against Southern Churchmen, the prospect of immediate success was not cheering.

The attempt therefore was delayed for awhile. But on the 22d of June, my Father prepared the draft of a Circular Letter to the Southern Bishops, expressing to each of them the hope that he and the Deputies from his Diocese would be seen in their places at the General Convention in October: and this draft was sent to all the Northern Bishops for their signatures. But, on the 3d of July, he wrote me that he had "received only three answers, all declining to sign, though all friendly to the kind treatment of the parties concerned." One of the three had already written to the South of himself; the other two thought it best to abstain from any concerted action. As to the rest, it afterwards appeared that all—or nearly all—were willing that the Southern Bishops and Dioceses should return; some even heartily desired that result: and no one would have offered any decided objection thereto. But they were not willing to make the first movement. They thought that as the Southern Dioceses had gone off of their own accord, they should come back of their own motion; and that the first word spoken of reünion should come from them. Some even were so far from being willing to ask them, that they would have exacted certain terms to be complied with before those who were willing to return should be admitted to their old seats.

Under these circumstances, my Father saw clearly that the only thing to do was to write in his own name, as Presiding Bishop, addressing a copy of the circular letter to every Southern Bishop, including, of course, the Bishop of Alabama, who had been consecrated during the war without full compliance with all the canonical prerequisites. In this letter, he said:—

> I consider it a duty especially incumbent on me, as the Senior Bishop, to testify my affectionate attachment to those amongst my colleagues from whom I have been separated during those years of suffering and calamity;

and to assure you personally of the cordial welcome which awaits you at our approaching General Convention. In this assurance, however, I pray you to believe that I do not stand alone. I have corresponded on the subject with the Bishops, and think myself authorized to state that they sympathize with me generally in the desire to see the fullest representation of the Churches from the South, and to greet their brethren in the Episcopate with the kindliest feeling.

The letters were promptly forwarded through the Secretary of the House of Bishops, the Rev. Dr. Balch, who had been ready and anxious, ever since the day of Gen. Lee's surrender, to perform this service. Private correspondence in various quarters between North and South, and public discussion in other journals than the *Episcopal Recorder*, helped—together with the lapse of time—to prepare men's hearts and minds. The action of several of the Southern Diocesan Conventions, in the meanwhile, showed that the way was preparing, with quite as much of rapidity as was consistent with united action there.

On the morning of the first Wednesday in October that year, as I was going up the southern flight of stone steps to the porch of S. Luke's Church, Philadelphia, to attend the opening of the General Convention, I saw, leaning against the iron railing at the halfway landing, the beloved Bishop Atkinson, of North Carolina, and round him a group of clergy and laity, welcoming him most cordially. He was the first Southern Bishop I had seen since the War began: and while joining my congratulations to those of the others, my Father came up the steps, and I had the delight of witnessing the greeting between the two, when both their hearts seemed too full to permit of easy utterance. All united—none more strongly than my Father—in urging the Bishop of North Carolina to return at once to his own place, and enter, robed, in the procession with his brethren. But he steadily refused: giving, as his reason, his delicate regard for his Southern brethren who had not come on. He was unwilling, even in appearance, to separate himself from them, or act in so important a matter without them; and he therefore took his seat in the body of the Church, with the congregation. But when, in the midst of the service, the call was again made upon him, openly and by name, he could refuse no longer, but rose, advanced, and was welcomed at the Altar with joyful thanksgiving.

This joy was still further enhanced when the Bishop of North Carolina, along with Bishop Lay (now of Easton, Md.), who arrived shortly after, on waiting below, and sending up to the House of Bishops to ask what would be required of them in order to their admission to their old seats: received for answer, sent by the House through the Bishop of New York, that all that was required of them was, to "trust to the love and honor of their brethren." Whereupon they entered, and, after a warm fraternal greeting all round, the *Gloria in Excelsis* was sung. Three Southern Dioceses, too, were represented in the Lower House, in both orders of Clergy and Laity,—Texas, North Carolina and Tennessee. The consecration of Bishop Quintard for the vacant Southern Diocese of Tennessee crowned the work of reünion, so far as it could be consummated at that session; and the wise and loving moderation with which all the delicate points involved were handled, ensured the voluntary surrender of the Southern organization within a few months: since which time not even a ripple has remained to tell that there ever was any such separation at all.

The presence and happy influence of the late Metropolitan of Montreal, Bishop Fulford, with several of the Canadian Clergy, indicating the gradual drawing together of the two Churches of the United States and Canada, and pointing forward not uncertainly towards a possible meeting at Lambeth; the Addresses received from the Provincial Synod of Canada and the Synod of Nova Scotia; the presence also of the Bishop of Honolulu; the public thanksgiving for the return of Peace and Unity; the refusal of the Bishops, 15 to 7, to infuse the slightest political tint into the services of that Thanksgiving Day; the election of three new Missionary Bishops; the resolution strongly supporting the noble Bishop of Capetown: all these were additional glories of that General Convention of 1865,—the first of our Reünion after the War, and the only one in which my Father ever presided over the Upper House in his own right.

But there was one drawback at the close, in regard to the Pastoral Letter. Those who had appeared to carry everything their own way in 1862, found themselves in a very small minority in both Houses in 1865. They failed, on the opening day, to defeat the reëlection of the Rev. Dr. Craik as President of the Lower House; and the rule of seniority by consecration made the Bishop of Vermont—the most obnoxious man on the bench, to them—President of the Upper House. That he should have the honor of writing the Pastoral Letter besides, would have been very hard for them to bear. Moreover, the Bishop of Vermont remembered the painful experience of 1862; and when the subject was first brought up in the House, he rose and stated, that, as he did not wish to be exposed to the same difficulty again, he would not take any part in the matter, unless the action of the House committed it to him. The Bishop of Ohio, however, was fully prepared, having brought with him a draft of a letter, which was read in the first meeting of the Committee. On being read by him in the House, however, it was promptly met by the Bishop of Maryland, who moved "That the House do not adopt the letter read by Bishop McIlvaine as the Pastoral Letter"; and the matter was referred back to the Committee of the five senior Bishops. From conversation with the other Bishops it was clear that there was no chance for that Letter. The eulogium on President Lincoln and the disquisition on slavery were, in tone, at least three years removed from the tone of the Church in 1865; and the long examination of the errors of Colenso was unsuited to the general character of a Pastoral Letter. The probability was, that no Pastoral would be issued. On the evening of the last Sunday during the session, therefore, my Father prepared a draft at one sitting: and it closed with a brief but feeling tribute to the late Bishop of Pennsylvania, whom he had never met since the issuing of the Pennsylvania Protest in 1863, but who had breathed his last about three months previous, and for whose lamented departure the Church in which the General Convention sat was still draped in mourning. This draft was read in Committee next morning, and ordered to be reported to the House.

But meanwhile, the other Bishops had not been idle on the subject. Having received the impression, from my Father's opening remarks, that he would not have any thing to do with the Pastoral Letter, and being satisfied that the Bishop of Ohio's paper could not be made to answer the purpose, a large number of them had consulted and agreed that it was "inexpedient, under present circumstances, to address a Pastoral Letter to the Church"; but that the Bishop of Ohio should " be requested to issue so much of the able paper read by him as relates to the subject of Rationalism, in the form of an Address to the Clergy and to Theological Students": and the Bishop of New York was to move the resolutions accordingly, whenever the matter came before the House again.

On Tuesday, the last day of the session, therefore, when the business of the Pastoral was called up, the Bishop of New York immediately rose and moved the resolutions agreed on: but, on learning that my Father had prepared a draft of a Pastoral, which he desired to read, the Bishop of New York waived his motion, and the draft was read accordingly. The closing part—relating to the late Bishop of Pennsylvania—was uttered with evident emotion: and after such a graceful tribute to his departed brother, it was peculiarly hard for the Bishop of New York to proceed. There was dead silence for a moment. Bishop Kemper moved that the draft just read be the Pastoral: but, the other Bishops being committed in advance, no one seconded the motion. The Bishop of New York's resolutions were then put and carried. My Father was firmly convinced that the concerted action on the part of the other Bishops was arranged by those who knew that he had prepared a draft of a Pastoral: but I have never heard from him or from others any evidence that his impression was correct. Yet there was irritation at the North, which required to be considered by wise men, as well as the irritation at the South: and to concede the negative triumph of no Pastoral Letter was but a small counterpoise to all the positive victories of the session, every one of which was won by the friends of Peace and Reünion in Brotherly Love.

This was the last General Convention my Father ever attended: but his experience in various points induced him to put on record a few hints under the title of—

SUGGESTIONS FOR THE GENERAL CONVENTION OF 1868.

The Presiding Bishop to open the House of Bishops with a written Address, giving an account of his acts since the last General Convention,[1] and making suggestions for this session, viz.:—

---

[1] This was done in 1868 and 1871.

1. That a Master of Ceremonies be appointed.

2. That the Pastoral Letter hereafter be in the style of the old *Synodical*, giving information of the Acts of the Convention to the Church at large, with such explanations as may be deemed expedient. That the Presiding officer draw up this statement after the Report on the State of the Church is handed in, and legislation is ended. And that two of the younger Bishops be a Committee to furnish him with a sufficient abstract for the purpose.

3. That the close of the Convention shall be with full Morning Service, the reading of the Pastoral Letter, and the Holy Communion, that all things at the last, as well as at the first, may be done " decently and in order."

4. That *Rules of Order* be established for the House of Bishops.[1]

5. That the Canon on Bishops resigning their Dioceses be repealed, so far as it renders them ineligible for the future.

6. That there should be liberty for the Clergy to choose their own Hymns, without restriction.[2]

It is an additional proof of the degree to which my Father was in advance of his day, that two General Conventions have been held since his departure, and only two of the above suggestions have yet been carried into effect.

The Presiding Bishop soon began to find that his office was one of labor and expense, not of honor alone : and that the labor was the greater, the more he was personally beloved. With only one exception, all the Bishops consecrated during his term of office requested, as a special favor, to be consecrated by his own hands, they cheerfully bearing all his travelling expenses, without which a compliance would have been simply impossible. Within about three weeks after the rising of the General Convention he was at Chicago, at the consecration of Bishop Clarkson, and where—for the first time in this country—the *Veni, Creator Spiritus* was sung at the consecration of a Bishop. With one accidental exception, this was repeated on every subsequent occasion of the kind at which he presided; and the custom thus introduced by him has been followed in divers other cases since.[3] In the

---

[1] Carried into effect in 1868.

[2] My Father was aware that the Clergy have this liberty already (see page 435); but so few seem to understand it, that he thought it ought to be made generally known by some act of the General Convention. In 1871, for the first time, a joint-resolution declared the contrary : but a joint-resolution is not law.

[3] The simple melody used on all these occasions will be found in the Rev. Dr.

alternate lines, sung by him alone, the sweet tone of his truthful voice, with just enough of the marks of age in it to give it a more touching tenderness, never failed to move many to tears. On Holy Innocents' day in the same year he presided at the consecration of Bishop Randall in his old parish of Trinity Church, Boston. And on S. Paul's day ensuing, as we have already mentioned, he consecrated the first Bishop of Pittsburgh, in the old Church designed and built by himself at the opening of his ministry.

But towards the close of the year 1866, the acceptance of the pressing invitations to him to preside in New Orleans and Louisville at the Consecrations of Bishop J. P. B. Wilmer for the Diocese of Louisiana and Bishop Cummins as the Assistant of Kentucky, showed him, more vividly than he had ever known before, the depth and strength of the hold which he had gained over the affections of Southern Churchmen. The reünion of the Church was complete. There was no longer anything to prevent the full manifestation of their love and admiration for him under whose Presidency it had taken place so easily and happily, when, with some others at the helm, it might have been, to say the least, more complicated and protracted. It was my good fortune to be his companion on that journey, which was made both ways by land. The manifestations of kindness at Jackson, Mississippi, at New Orleans, at Memphis, at Louisville, were more than I could enumerate. In some cases, formal deputations waited upon him, with addresses of fervent feeling: in others, persons rushed into the railway car for the pleasure of taking him by the hand even for a moment. Nothing could exceed his own humble surprise at the manifestation of a feeling the like of which he had never known in his life, and which was as remote as possible from either his expectations or desires.

The fatiguing journey of four thousand miles by land, proved to be not too heavy a strain upon my Father's strength: and indeed he was rather benefited by it. His usual winter's cough was already severe before he left (its tendency was to come

Tucker's *Parish Hymnal;* also, in his issue of *The Hymnal, with Tunes New and Old* [F. J. Huntington & Co., New York]; or it may be obtained, printed on card, of E. P. Dutton & Co., 713 Broadway, New York. It is in several of the other new *Hymnals* also.

earlier and remain longer each successive year), and at one time he thought it would compel him to abandon the idea: yet he found himself not only entirely cured, owing to the change to a milder air, but the cough thus broken did not return during all the rest of that winter. On our way home again, however, we were thrown from the track on the New York Central Road, a few miles beyond Syracuse, at about 2 o'clock in the morning. We were in the sleeping-car, which was left on the side of the embankment at an angle of nearly 45 degrees. We were all instantly shaken out of our berths in the darkness, and were tumbled into the most promiscuous confusion, the concussion putting the lamps out: and the dust that filled the car made my Father—who was a passionate devotee to fresh air—feel as if he should certainly die of suffocation. But the opening of a window soon gave him relief; and a tedious groping search in the dark finally recovered everything for him, except a meerschaum. A long, dark and disagreeable walk, with an unpleasant waiting at a wayside tavern, was the only other unfavorable result of an accident which might so easily have proved horribly fatal.[1]

There was only one disappointment in that Southern journey, and that was, the failure to meet the beloved Bishop Elliott of Georgia. He was to have preached the sermon at the Consecration of the Bishop of Louisiana: but was unexpectedly prevented, at the last moment, from leaving home; so that my Father was called on to preach, extemporaneously, in his place. This disappointment was followed within a few weeks by the tidings of his sudden, nay instantaneous, death on S. Thomas's day,—a loss which weighed heavily on my Father's heart, and he wrote to me concerning it:—"There is no one of my Episcopal colleagues whose loss to the Church would affect me equally." Neither of the two was a good correspondent. They seldom wrote to one another, except when Church business called

---

[1] Not many days after his return, his old friend, the Bishop of New Hampshire—not a man predisposed to enthusiasm, by any means—wrote him: "I desire to express my admiration at your endurance of bodily exposure and official toil. Without a watchful Providence and sustaining grace continually present, your labors are enough to crush out the spirit from the most perfect of vital energies. It is truly wonderful that at the age of seventy-four you are so fresh, and can endure so much. The LORD be praised for His mercies! I am two years younger, and truly there seems little of me left." Yet he survived my Father more than two years.

for it. But their mutual confidence and affection was great: and perhaps I can place it before the reader in no way so well as by giving, in full, the only letter without ostensible business which my Father ever received from Bishop Elliott, and which was written in the summer of the year in which he died: it forms, moreover, an appropriate close for that portion of our work which refers to the War and the Reünion of the Church. The family and personal allusions will be pardoned, as they are not easily separable from the rest:—

SAVANNAH, July 13, 1866.

MY VERY DEAR BISHOP:

I have been intending, for a long time, to write you a letter of pure affection, which should have nothing official about it; and I know no better time than now, when you have just been celebrating two such events as your Golden Wedding and the finished Reünion of our beloved Church.

Most heartily do I congratulate you upon having enjoyed the rare privilege of receiving under your roof, after fifty years of wedded life, with your long-loved wife by your side, so many descendants, children and grandchildren, and among them several ministers of the glorious Gospel of Grace: fully realizing the promise of God, that He will show mercy unto thousands in them that love Him and keep His commandments. And among them stood my adopted son, John Henry, of whom I feel so proud, whose wise and judicious counsels have done more than almost any human means besides, to bring about the reünion of the children of God at the North and South. I wish, my dear Bishop, that you could have welcomed all your children at your blessed festival. But, alas! some were absent; and some "were not." May your present circle continue unbroken for so long as God shall see it good for you; and may your own valuable life be spared to the Church for many, many years. Will you present my compliments to Mrs. Hopkins, and to any of your children who may yet be with you, with my best wishes for their welfare, and the assurance that any descendant of yours will always find a friend in me.

In the Journal of my Diocesan Council, which I send you by mail, I have turned up certain pages for your special notice. The first of these contains my reasons for the course which I pursued in relation to the reünion of the Church, and which differed somewhat from your opinion and that of your excellent son. I offer them to you as the excuse for my presumption in venturing to differ from you. I should not have done so, had I not believed that I knew the state of feeling among the Clergy and Laity of the South better than it was possible for you to know it; and that time was needed, to calm the feelings, and to give Church allegiance

—which was much stronger than any political allegiance—opportunity to work its effects. As it is, there has been great difficulty in bringing South Carolina and Virginia back at all, and I sincerely believe that any other course than that pursued, would have prevented it for a much longer time, if not altogether. Most sincerely do I rejoice with you in the happy result, which is very much due, under God, to your conservative counsels, and the Christian firmness of your administration as Presiding Bishop of the Church. The South can never forget your manly consistency and dignified self-reliance during all the madness of the people ; and future times will do full justice to your wisdom, and your Christian sympathy with a persecuted, oppressed, and now ruined people.

The other passage to which I have directed your attention in my Address, stands connected with Emancipation. I felt it to be due to the Southern Church that those words should be spoken and published to the Church,—spoken by me, as the one who sanctioned the whole course of the South, and who presided over the Church as long as it was separate ; and published for the future guidance of the Church in her dealings with the emancipated race. The mischief, I fear, is done : and we must abide the consequences.

We were hoping, my dear Bishop, to have seen you here during the last winter. I hope we shall not be disappointed the coming season. You will receive a warm welcome from every one in Church and State. No man in the whole country would find more cordial greetings awaiting him than yourself. I have not written to you upon this subject before, because I did not wish, so long as reünion was doubtful, to embarrass you and ourselves : but now that everything is settled, and Old Virginia has worked off her bitterness, and "is humble enough to shake hands with a dog," I feel that you can mingle freely with a people who will delight to do you honor.

I have a daughter at the North this summer, born while your son was in my house, whom I desire above all things to meet and know you. (She is travelling with Mrs. L—— of this place, and who has resided for many years in Florence.) Your son has already found her out, although she has been in New York but four days. Pray if you should hear, in any of your travels, of such a young person as Miss Hesse Elliott, of Savannah, introduce yourself to her, and give her your blessing.

I am, my very dear Bishop,
Most affectionately yours,
STEPHEN ELLIOTT.

To the Rt. Rev.
John Henry Hopkins, D.D.

Timid people have sometimes been afraid of a schism of some sort or other in our American Church. The only approximation to such a thing was from the year 1861 to 1866. And when the head of the one portion can write to the head of the other such a letter as the above, in the first year after the termination of such a vast and bitter Civil War as ours: the fears of timid friends and the hopes of malicious foes in regard to the possibility of a schism, may safely be laughed to scorn.

CHAPTER XX.

THE GOLDEN WEDDING—POETRY—CANONICAL POINTS.

THE Golden Wedding Festival, to which Bishop Elliott alludes, was held in 1866, a few weeks later than the actual anniversary, in order to reach a pleasanter part of the season, and make it coincide with the week of the Diocesan Convention. The testimonials of affection and respect were not only such as might naturally be looked for upon an occasion not common in ordinary life, and still more rare among our Bishops: but there were some features worthy of special note.

Just before the opening of Divine Service, on Wednesday morning, the first day of the Convention, all being robed in the sacristy, the Clergy of his Diocese presented him with a Pastoral Staff, of oak, carved and adorned with color, silver, gilt, and enamel. In the crook was the figure of the Good Shepherd, standing with a lamb in his arms and a sheep on either side, all of silver. Eight enamelled medallions on the knop gave the condensed Apostolic Succession from S. Paul through S. Augustine of Canterbury, Matthew Parker and Bishop White. A few brief and well-chosen words of cordial feeling accompanied the gift, which was declared to be for him and his successors in office: and it was then borne into the Chancel by one of the Clergy, and placed beside the Bishop's chair. This is the first Pastoral Staff made in this country and presented to one of our Bishops by his own Clergy. In accordance with the expressed desire of the donors, my Father bequeathed this Pastoral Staff to his successor: and it was accordingly delivered to the present Bishop of Vermont on the day of his consecration.[1]

There was plenty of rain in the afternoon: but the weather

---

[1] Many years previous, however, my Father's old friend, Bishop Doane of New Jersey, had received as a personal gift from his friend Mr. Beresford Hope,—the munificent restorer of S. Augustine's, Canterbury,—a simple pastoral staff carved of the oak that still remained sound, of the woodwork of that ancient monastic foundation. It is now the property of his son, the Bishop of Albany.

cleared off with a beautiful rainbow near sunset. In the evening the Bishop's House was open to the Convention and all his friends, and was thronged for several hours. The approaches to the porch—the night being rather cloudy and dark—were illuminated by railway headlights, making every tree sparkle with its raindrops. The most striking point of the evening's entertainment was to see the venerable couple led to the Piano, where he sat down and played the accompaniment, while she stood beside him, and they sang a duett of his own composition, both words and music,—one which had been familiar to them both for many years, and which called up so many associations that it was not easy to keep their voices quite firm to the end. It is not often that such music is made by those who are in the seventy-fifth and seventy-second years of their age.

The next day, in the afternoon, after the adjournment of the Convention, the family dinner was spread, in the large room in the centre of the house. Even that was not large enough to accommodate all the guests, for there were thirty-seven descendants present, including those who had married into the family; and fourteen were yet absent in various parts of the world, besides those who were in Paradise. Two additions were therefore made to the long table, one on each side, giving it the form of a Cross: and after the grace, when all were seated, the aged couple walked slowly round the whole table, counting over their living treasures, their faces beaming with love, and with gratitude to God. At the close of the dinner, a copy of a brief *Autobiography in Verse* was presented by my Father to each descendant, only a few impressions being privately though quite handsomely printed for this festival, at the Riverside press.

The showers were not yet over, and one fell during the dinner-hour: but the clearing up, just afterwards, was the most remarkable sight of the kind I have ever seen or heard of. My Father had taken his seat on the front porch, looking towards the city of Burlington, and had lit for the first time a remarkably beautiful gold-mounted meerschaum sent in honor of the occasion by an absent son in California, when cries of delighted surprise soon drew us all out there by his side: and we saw, bent over the city of Burlington, no less than *five* complete and perfect rainbows.

The three inner arches were decidedly the brightest in tint, and were not all concentric, two of them overlapping at the right end, and making that double the intensity of the rest. The two outer arches were fainter, as the secondary rainbows generally are. But the whole five were unbroken, and of almost equal brilliance throughout, each of its own kind. This whole extraordinary series of rainbows spanned the entire city, the right foot of the arches resting on the reflecting waters of the Lake, the other reaching far over beyond the hill: while all the atmosphere inside the inner arch seemed composed of rainbow luminousness not yet organized into circles, but poured forth so as to bathe the whole city in showers of glory. Our voices were subdued with something like awe as we gazed at this wonderful sight until it began to break and fade away, the double intensity of the overlapping portion being the last to disappear. But it is not to be wondered at that we children saw in it a beautiful coincidence with the occasion which had brought us together. The repeated storms with their rainbows were like the stormy trials of the long day of life then drawing towards its sunset, each followed by the beauty of a victory gained in the cause of truth and peace. The three bright inner arches were the three dear aged ones around whom we were gathered; two of whom had been for half a century joined together in one, thereby making that unity of double brilliance: and the two outer arches were the generation after generation of descendants: each spreading out more widely, and yet with feebler light, than those inner circles without which their own existence had been impossible. And it seems, moreover, as we look back upon it, to have pointed forward to a sunset of life which should be more glorious than any portion of the previous day.

Early next morning, Friday, the closing day of the festival, there was another reünion, at the Altar in the Chapel of the Institute. My Father was the Celebrant, assisted by three of his own sons, two priests and one deacon; and by two sons-in-law, also priests, while still another priest—husband of a granddaughter—was among the gathered company of the faithful. All the *Amens* and *responses* were chorally rendered, another son presiding at the organ; and still another—three thousand miles away—had composed and sent on the music for the *Gloria in Excelsis* which was sung on the occasion, all the rest of the music used being either by my Father himself, or some of his descendants. The Gospel was, by appointment of the Bishop, the narrative of the Marriage in Cana of Galilee: and in reading it, a new shade of meaning glanced upon the words, "but Thou hast kept the good wine until now."

There was only one drawback to the enjoyment of this three days' festival. It was the ever-present consciousness of a sunset now so near, that the beautiful rainbows could not much longer remain unbroken:[1] and that probably there would never be so many of us assembled in one place again, until it were to look into an open grave. It so happened that, on the Sunday after my Father's burial, three of us who had been brought together by that event stood once more around that little Altar in the Chapel of the Institute. It was the Second Sunday after the Epiphany: and the Marriage in Cana of Galilee is the Gospel for that day. As the blessed words were read, the associations of the past were almost more than could be borne: and when we thought of Him—no longer among us on earth but with the saints in Paradise—the words, "Thou hast kept the good wine until now," struck chords of feeling well-nigh deep enough to choke the utterance altogether.

During the previous Winter and Spring he had resumed his efforts to raise the means for adding a girls' school to the Vermont Episcopal Institute: but found the claims from the destitute South still so pressing that he could use little urgency, and contented himself with very slight success; being resigned to await more promising times. During this absence he held confirmations in several Churches of the Diocese of Maryland, at the request of their Bishop, whose health was greatly impaired: and a similar invitation was extended to him by Bishop Johns of Virginia, to confirm a large class in his old parish of Emmanuel Church, Baltimore. My Father was there, and had the pleasure of meeting Bishop Johns once more,—the first time since the outbreak of the War. Speaking of this meeting afterwards in his

[1] The same thought must have been strong in my Father's mind also: for his Last Will and Testament was executed within a week thereafter.

own Convention, my Father said: "It would not be easy to describe the emotion of gratitude to God with which I looked upon his face and grasped his hand once more, in the confidence of our reünion." It was another pleasant incident of the winter's trip, that the Rev. Dr. Howe (now the Bishop of Central Pennsylvania), who had been prominent among his opponents in the Pennsylvania *Protest* business in 1863, wrote him a friendly letter requesting him to be his guest on his way through Philadelphia, to confer with him in regard to the acceptance of the Missionary Episcopate of Nevada, which Dr. Howe then had under consideration. This was a gratifying evidence that the alienations caused by the other affair were passing away: and, prompt to respond to any such feeling, the invitation was accepted, and a day and a night were spent with his host very pleasantly.

Nothing proves more conclusively the singular activity of my Father's mind, than the fact that he had learned to utilize, for some years past, the time which was spent in long journeys by rail. He could not do much in the way of prose composition, indeed; the form of it giving so little aid to the memory. But he had found that he could put together several lines of verse, and retain them so as to be able to jot them down in pencil while stopping at the stations on the road: and this habit became so settled during several of the later years of his life, that the quantity thus produced was something unusual. He used to say, indeed, that it was "only rhymes tagged together, and not worthy of the name of poetry": but there was always sound sense clearly expressed, and often forcible argument couched in strong and manly form. In this way he finished a long poem begun in his youth, and left incomplete for many years.[1] He then prepared a volume of "The Gospels Versified" according to the order of the Ecclesiastical Year: which was finished in the brief space of seven weeks. *The History of the Church in Verse* was another fruit of his activity in this line, intended, like the other, "for use in Sunday-Schools and families." And about the beginning of June, 1867, only a few months before his departure, he began a long poem, entitled, *Satan*, which, to the length of nearly two thousand lines, was left unfinished in the midst of the Sixth Canto, and with

[1] See page 58.

no portion of it revised for publication. Besides these, there were many briefer pieces, of course; but none of the larger works was ever printed, except the *History of the Church in Verse*, which appeared in a neat volume within the last year of his life. The spirit of the whole of these metrical labors of his is very clearly embodied in the last three stanzas of the *Introduction* to this last-named work :—

> 'Tis true, my simple verse may often seem
> Too weak its noble subject to sustain ;
> But to do justice to so high a theme
> An Angel's talents might aspire in vain.
>
> I ask indulgence for an old man's zeal,
> Whose life is hastening to the closing hour,
> Claiming no merit, though his heart may feel
> The wish to do the little in his power.
>
> That little at the Saviour's feet I lay ;
> And may His grace the humble gift approve
> When He shall come, at the appointed day,
> To rule His Church in heavenly light and love !

At Easter, 1866, a vacancy occurred in the rectorship of S. Paul's Church, Burlington, on the resignation of the faithful and devoted priest who for nine years had served the parish, being its only rector since the Bishop had resigned it in order to prosecute with more energy his work for the Institute. As sometimes happens, the circumstances attending the change were such as to leave the parish too much divided in feeling to be able to agree at once upon a new rector : and after five or six weeks of consideration, they unanimously requested their Bishop to take charge of them, which he consented to do, until they should be able to agree in calling some younger man. This position he continued to hold almost to the end of his life.

And it was a great pleasure to him to resume his old relations to his old parish. He visited assiduously from house to house, and devoted a degree of time and attention to his parochial work which proves how dear it was to his heart, even when there were so many other and weightier responsibilities that might have excused him for being easier with himself. The expressions of satisfaction with which many of the elder parishioners welcomed his reappearance among them, were a great gratification to him: for, with conscientious delicacy, though continuing to reside in Burlington, he had during those nine years seen as little of them as possible, and was rarely present in the Chancel of S. Paul's Church except on official occasions as Bishop;—his design being to leave the charge of the flock to their Rector without the slightest chance of interference from those feelings of affection which his twenty-seven years of pastoral service would naturally produce. But his entire abstinence—perhaps somewhat overdone on his part—was carried out at the cost of no little hearthunger for that old pastoral intercourse, which had previously been uninterrupted during his whole ministerial life. Nor was the warmth of his feeling without its due effect among the people: for, in the only parochial report which he lived to present, it appeared that the number of persons confirmed during the first year of his renewed care more than doubled that of any one of the six years previous, and had not been equalled since his resignation of the rectorship in 1855.

The change in the parish was further signalized by a great enlargement of the church building, due entirely to the energy and indefatigable perseverance of Mr. Thomas H. Canfield, who, as one of the staunchest friends of the rector who had lately resigned, and as the son-in-law of the Bishop, rightly conceived that an exertion calling for the combined strength of the whole parish would be more likely than anything else to produce harmony of feeling once more. And this was resolved on, and the Bishop was applied to once more for plans of the enlargement, before he was called to the acting-rectorship. While this was in progress, the same leadership secured the purchase of additional grounds at the corner: so that the property of the parish now includes a solid half block, on which stand the enlarged Church, the parsonage and the Sexton's house, together with ample open space for shade-trees.

The design of the enlargement—the last work of his life in the department of architecture—was not what my Father would have preferred: but he was tied down to the preservation of the old original nave, with its faults of outline, proportion, and low roof. All that he could well do, therefore, was to remove the Chancel which he had added in 1851 (preserving and using again a large part of its ornamental work), and to replace it with transepts (not the full width of the nave), having a new Chancel beyond,—the whole ground plan being cruciform. The panelled roof was continued in the new part, further enriched with color: and the apsidal arrangement of the interior of the Chancel enabled him to preserve something of the Basilican plan, which was his favorite as the most ancient, and artistically the most beautiful. The Altar stands out on the chord of the apse, the Bishop's throne is at the crown, and the *corona presbyterorum* extends on either side of it round the semicircle, with seats for twelve of "the second throne." The tablets painted by him in 1851 still adorn the sides of the apse. No one was more conscious than its architect of the points in which the building is open to professional criticism: but it is remarkable that so pleasing an effect, on the whole, has been produced under such heavy disadvantages. The work was not entirely completed at the time of his departure: and the first day on which it was opened for public service, was the day of his funeral.

There were two canonical points which came up for action during the last two years of my Father's life, on which I think it worth while that his decision should be recorded.

One of the great objects for which he had labored for many years, with nothing but disappointment for his reward, was the establishment of a canonical Court of Appeal, by which a ready and safe remedy would be provided for any oppressive use of Episcopal or Diocesan authority. This he regarded as necessary, in order not only to complete the primitive arrangement which we profess to reproduce, but also to render safe, and even possible, that enlargement of the administrative powers of the Bishops which is so sadly needed among us for the efficiency of our working system. This enlargement is coming practically, though slowly, by the mere multiplication of sees: for, as a general rule, a Bishop is a much more important man among fifteen or twenty priests than he is among two or three hundred. But it will not come, to the degree needed, so long as there is absolutely no remedy for ignorance, prejudice, indolence, carelessness, partisan injustice, want of judgment, or personal tyranny, on the part of any Bishop, except at the cost of attempting the difficult if not impossible work of having him tried by a Court of his peers: and even if tried and condemned, our present system provides no means whatever for the correction of that injustice to clergy or people for which the condemnation may have been awarded. It is a high testimony to the moderation of our Bishops and the love of order which animates our clergy and people, that it should have been possible for us to get along so comfortably for nearly a century under so defective a judicial system.

Anxious as he was to establish a Court of Appeal canonically, my Father was ever ready to act in the spirit of it, both as to his own doings and those of his Brethren. No one was more independent than he, in the formation and utterance of his own judgment and the exercise of his own rights. And no one had a more delicate regard for the rights of others, or a greater abhorrence of anything that even looked like an improper use of prerogative or superior authority in order to crowd down one whose personal standing gave him no chance for an equal contest.

Now it so happened that in a thoroughly High-Church Diocese, whose Bishop and Standing Committee were generally in the closest accord with one another, a difficulty arose in regard to an applicant for Holy Orders. His papers were regular; his first interview with the Bishop had been very cordial and satisfactory; his testimonials were signed by the Standing Committee; and he was told by his Bishop that he might consider himself duly entered on the list of Candidates in that Diocese. About two months afterwards, he received a very cold and formal note from the Bishop, surprising him with the information that his name had *not* been actually entered on the canonical list, and advising him to withdraw his application, but stating no reason for this sudden and entire change of determination. It was evident that the Bishop had heard something to the man's prejudice, which in his mind was sufficient ground to bar the ordination of the applicant: and it is very probable that the cause was sufficient, and that the Bishop's judgment in regard to it was correct. But he refused steadily, from first to last, and in response to every effort made personally or through friends, to give the slightest hint as to *what* had changed his mind, or as to the person or persons on whose information he was acting. The Standing Committee appointed an investigation into any and every rumor against the applicant which they could get wind of: and as the result of it all, stood unanimously by their written testimonials in his favor.

In this state of the case, the applicant laid his case before the Bishop of Vermont, with full papers, proofs, correspondence, and letters from members of the Standing Committee referred to. Nothing seemed to him more clear, whether on principles of law, of equity, or of Christian charity, than that no man ought to be condemned thus secretly, all knowledge being denied him both of the charge made and of the accuser by whom it was brought. No matter how guilty or unworthy a man might be, that mode of trying and condemning him was far worse: and the Bishop of Vermont was ready to act at once.

The Canon[1] requires that no such person " shall be admitted as a Candidate in any other Diocese, until he shall have produced from the Bishop, or, if there be no Bishop, from the Standing Committee of the former Diocese, a certificate, declaring the cause for which he was refused admission, or for which he ceased to be a candidate." This provision had already prevented action in another Diocese, where application was made before sending the case to Vermont: the Bishop of that Diocese considering that, if the first Bishop refused to give such a certificate, every other Bishop was prevented from acting. My Father took a different view of the case. His Standing Committee unanimously signed the testimonials of the applicant: and thereupon the Canonical request was forwarded at once to the first Bishop,[2] " to know whether any just cause exists why the Candidate should not be ordained ": and in the course of correspondence he took the ground that " The Canon, requiring a certificate in such cases, ' declaring the cause for which the applicant was refused admission, or for which he ceased to be a candidate,' makes it the duty of the Bishop to give such certificate, according to my humble judgment, by necessary implication." The first

---

[1] See § ii. of Canon 2 of Title I. of the *Digest*.
[2] According to Canon 4 of Title I. of the *Digest*.

Bishop maintained his original position (which he had consistently maintained also in answering the other Bishop to whom application had been made), refusing to mention anything definite, or any accuser, but speaking in the strongest terms of his own entire conviction that the cause was sufficient and insuperable.

The candidate was at once admitted in the Diocese of Vermont (after consulting and obtaining an elaborate opinion from the Hon. Murray Hoffman on one or two points involved); and the beginning of his Candidateship was dated back to the day of his application to the Bishop of Vermont. The first Bishop "solemnly protested" against the ordination: but—owing to the dating back of the admission to Candidateship—the protest was not received until a few days after the ordination had taken place.

In justice to the first Bishop, it must be said that he retained his strong convictions to the last. "If I had acted from caprice, or with imperfect knowledge of the facts," he wrote, "it is conceivable that I might have changed my course. . . . But I hope there is no Bishop in the Church who would resist an application as I have resisted Mr. ——'s, without reasons, which would make it utterly impossible for him ever to grant what he had repeatedly refused." And he added, in his final letter on the subject: "If Mr. —— or his friends (many of whom have acted sincerely, on imperfect information) desire to bring this whole case before the public, I shall be most heartily content, and there will be some chance of a public recognition of the truth." Nothing could more clearly prove that the writer was convinced in his own mind that he was acting justly towards the applicant, and with friendly delicacy protecting him, by this mysteriously impenetrable silence, from serious injury to himself: and the conscientious adherence to his course, in spite of the very strong pressure from various quarters to change it, proved the highest devotion to a conviction of duty. But my Father had not forgotten the fundamental principles of law: and no amount of delicate conscientiousness in the motive in the present case could reconcile him to the idea that it could ever be right for a public officer to hear only one side of a story, refuse to hear the other or even say what he had heard, and then be so sure that his "knowledge" of the case was not "imperfect," as to act officially to another man's prejudice without giving him a chance to say a word for himself.

The other canonical point alluded to was in regard to the election of an Assistant Bishop in Virginia, while there was no evidence that the Bishop of that Diocese was "unable, by reason of old age, or other permanent cause of infirmity, to discharge his Episcopal duties": and when, indeed, the Bishop's Address, at the very Convention which made the election, showed a larger amount of Episcopal work done than in any one year before; with only a few days' interruption from a transient indisposition during the whole year. The final steps taken by my Father in this matter were postponed until his return from England, and he departed this life before the result was ascertained: but he left his convictions so clearly and strongly expressed in many ways, that it is due to him to put them on record. It was peculiarly difficult for him to take the position he did, because of his kind personal relations to the amiable and warm-hearted Bishop of Virginia, of whose cordiality and that of his Diocese the Presiding Bishop had received so many proofs. Nor was the slightest shade of personal dissatisfaction expressed with regard to the person chosen, and who has given such general satisfaction throughout the Diocese since his consecration. The difficulty in question was purely canonical, and therefore the opinions on either side may be clearly and strongly expressed without offence to the other. Our Virginia brethren were doubtless convinced in their own minds that their action was quite as canonical as at the time of the election of Bishop Johns himself, to assist the late Bishop Meade: and there has been no age of the Church in which, on some canonical points, there have not been two opinions, if not more.

At first the Presiding Bishop thought of sending a Circular to the Standing Committees, calling their attention to the chief points involved:—

The principle established from the beginning of Diocesan Episcopacy is well understood, namely, that there should be one Bishop, and only one, in each Diocese. The allowance of an Assistant Bishop, therefore, is carefully guarded by our Canon, so that it must appear to be a measure of necessity: "When a Bishop of a Diocese is *unable*," etc. On this ground alone does the Church place the exception to the general rule. And hence the plain result, that every Convention which desires to claim the benefit of the exception should record the fact of the Bishop's inability to perform his Episcopal duties before they proceed to elect an Assistant Bishop, because this fact is the very basis of such action, and if there be no evidence of it on the face of the record, it cannot appear that they have any authority to elect at all.

He next went on to show that, in Episcopal elections during the recess of the General Convention, the Diocese electing is required to communicate its " desire to the Standing Committees of the Several Dioceses, together with copies of the *necessary testimonials*"; and the consents of a majority of the Standing Committees "together with other testimonials" are to be forwarded to the Presiding Bishop. He then continues:—

Here it is quite manifest that the consent of the other Dioceses rests upon the testimonials transmitted by the Diocese concerned. But as those "*necessary*" testimonials include, by express direction, a precise statement of the election and the qualifications of the individual for the office of a Bishop, how can they be considered complete if they omit the all-important fact of the present Bishop's incapacity, which is the indispensable foundation of the whole? When, therefore, these documents furnish no evidence of that fact, they must be held insufficient: and the defect must at least be supplied by some other satisfactory proof, before the Standing Committees are authorized to consent, or the Presiding Bishop can be justly expected to call on his colleagues for their approval of the elected person's consecration.

But, while preparing this document, my Father came to the conclusion that it would appear to be going beyond his duty as Presiding Bishop; and he therefore left it unfinished, and turned his attention towards private efforts to procure either from the Standing Committee or the Bishop of Virginia something which would answer as an approximation, at least, toward a proof of the existence of the canonical inability plainly required. In this he did not succeed. The case was left without one particle of additional strength beyond the facts as on record in the action of the Diocesan Council which elected Dr. Whittle.

Meanwhile, the discussions in the Church papers were giving rise to more of obstruction in the Standing Committees than was at first deemed probable by any one. One Standing Committee after another declined to act on the testimonials of the Assistant-Bishop elect, on the ground that the election itself was clearly uncanonical. Things were beginning to look serious: and at length, to satisfy the scruples of the Standing Committee of Massachusetts, a certificate was issued from Virginia declaring it to be "a fact within the knowledge of the Standing Committee of Virginia, that the Bishop of the Diocese, by reason of old age, and other permanent cause of infirmity, is unable to discharge his Episcopal duties." But unfortunately, when viewed in the light of the incontestable facts, that the Bishop—though past seventy years of age—had performed more Episcopal work in his own Diocese during the previous year than it had ever known before, besides confirming some hundreds of persons for his really disabled brother the Bishop of Maryland; and that, during all this discussion about his health, he was going on with his visitations during the heat of the dogdays as regularly as if he was in his prime; and that his own Diocesan organ, while trying to demonstrate his "inability" in one column, admitted accounts of those visitations in another column, which—in spite of his fatigues—declared the venerable Bishop to be "in excellent health": in the light of these facts, the certificate of the Standing Committee of Virginia did not seem, to some, to be using language exactly in its ordinary sense.

The Standing Committee of Pittsburgh, therefore, wrote to the Bishop of Virginia himself, nearly two months later, respectfully asking him the plain question, whether he was actually "unable, from old age or other permanent cause, to discharge his Episcopal duties." And the Bishop honestly replied:—"I cannot but commend your caution, though it may deprive me of your consent to the consecration of the Bishop-elect of Virginia. Neither age nor infirmity from other causes have thus far prevented me from rendering to this Diocese the amount of Episcopal service required by the Canon."[1] If this letter had been published

[1] It must not be supposed for an instant that Bishop Johns was indifferent or opposed to the Consecration of Dr. Whittle, who was, I believe, his own favored candidate: and in his letters, to the Presiding Bishop and others, he did his utmost to show that the action of Virginia was correct, and that the "strict construction" of the Canon was not imperatively called for. But he was too truthful to do otherwise than give a plain answer to a plain question, even to the prejudice of what he most desired.

earlier, it would probably have defeated the Consecration of Dr. Whittle: but a very small majority of the Standing Committees had acted favorably before it was written; and it was not published until more than three months later.

When the evidence of the consent of the majority of the Standing Committees was at length sent to the Presiding Bishop, his determination was already formed. His first idea was, that he should 'feel obliged to govern his official course according to his own conclusions, so long as it might please Divine Providence to continue him as the Presiding Bishop": in which case he would have declined to communicate the requisite testimonials to the other Bishops asking their consent to the consecration, but would have published his reasons for declining, instead. If he had done this, there would certainly have been no Canonical mode of consecrating the Assistant Bishop of Virginia. But here, once more, he abstained from taking a course that might seem like an attempt to force his own views of canonicity upon others, who had just as full knowledge of the facts, and just as much right to form their own opinions, as himself. "It is not the duty of the Presiding Bishop, *as such*," he wrote, " to influence, or *try to influence*, the other Bishops, in such a matter. I have a judicial judgment for my own course as the Bishop of Vermont: but as the Presiding Bishop, I am only an executive officer, under the Canon, to carry into effect the decision of the majority." He wrote to the Bishop of Virginia, that as an individual Bishop he could not give his consent to the Consecration, and placed his refusal on record among the other papers of the case: but he sent out the notices to the other Bishops as usual. He had no idea that the Consecration could be defeated, however: for he wrote me at the time:—

> I have no doubt that the usual indifference to strict law, and the general disposition to be accommodating which governs on such occasions, will insure a pretty unanimous consent. . . . Dr. Whittle, therefore, will undoubtedly be consecrated. I shall take no part in the matter, beyond the official necessity of directing others to discharge the duty which the majority have the canonical power to authorize. I shall appoint Bishop Johns to be the Consecrator, and of course shall stay away.

Providence placed the final arrangements in the hands of another, who, of his own accord, made the same appointment which had been contemplated by my Father: but his opinion in regard to the uncanonical character of the election was much more strongly supported than he thought possible. The votes were so close, that the case was not decided until the Bishops met for the election of a Missionary Bishop of Oregon: and then, on correcting the lists, it was found that twenty had consented, and twenty-one had not: whereupon, one of the latter changed his vote, thus barely saving Virginia from defeat. Morally, it *was* a defeat: and has rendered it certain that the elasticity of that Canon will not be stretched so severely in future, at least for a long while to come.

At the same time, there is not a little to be said in behalf of the noble old Diocese of Virginia. Their beloved Bishop Meade—for twelve years an Assistant Bishop himself—had obtained an Assistant under circumstances not a whit more strictly canonical than those under which Bishop Johns followed his example. The mode in which the State of Virginia had been divided into two States during the War, made the very idea of dividing the Diocese at that time passionately repugnant to the feelings of the most devoted Virginia Churchmen. Moreover, with the trifling exceptions of less than a year at one time and about six years at another, Virginia had had *two* Bishops ever since August, 1829; and had come to feel as if that were decidedly the regular rule for that Diocese, though it is the exception in all the rest of Christendom. Nor can it be wondered at, that a Diocese which has been always predisposed to give a hypothetical interpretation to some very plain words in the Prayer Book, should not feel bound to give a very strict construction to the words of a Canon which is of far less solemn obligation than the Prayer Book. It is a comfort, too, to know that the votes given on the occasion did not coincide with either the sectional or the theological lines that usually find expression in the decision of disputed questions: and thus there was the less ground for personal irritation either in the points raised or in the decision reached. Nor was it the least consideration, in the minds of most of those who consented, that the Diocese of Virginia was the last and the most reluctant to return to her old union with the General Convention,—a return which then was yet young and tender: and, in view of the natural and most commendable desire to do nothing which would cause her needless pain or embarrassment, the only wonder is, not that the opposition to Dr. Whittle's consecration did not prevail, but that it was made at all.

Chapter XXI.

THEOLOGICAL OPINIONS—RITUALISM.

DURING all his life my Father continued to be a rapid and constant reader. His remoteness from the large cities and the shortness of his purse compelled him to be limited in his buying of new books; but he bought where he could, and borrowed where he could not buy. His common phrase used to be, —that he "expected to know something in ten years": and the growth in certain parts of his theological views was gradual, though decided.

In the Spring of 1866 he was in New York City for some time, and we had many long conversations on subjects of Church interest,—as had been the custom, indeed, for more than thirty years whenever we were together, so that there was no other person living who was so fully acquainted with his views on all subjects as I was. In one of these conversations, I happened to allude to the common Protestant proverb that "Justification by Faith only is the test article of a standing or a falling Church": when he broke in, with the use of a contemptuous slang word very rare with him: "That is all *bosh!* On the subject of Justification there is no fault to be found with the Council of Trent." I have looked through all the volumes of his works devoted to our controversy with Rome, and I find that Justification is made a leading issue in none of them; nor is there more than a slight allusion to the subject in any even of his earlier books. He never made it a prominent subject in his preaching, or conversation: but I was myself surprised at the energy and contemptuous terseness with which he swept the foundation of all Protestant dogmatism into limbo.

It was during that same visit that, in my room, he read my copy of Dr. Pusey's *Eirenicon*. He devoured it at one sitting, being absorbed in the perusal to a degree unusual even with him: and as he rose, and stretched himself for physical relief after the many hours of continuance in one position, I asked him: "Well, Father, do you find any disloyalty to the Church of England in that book?" "Disloyalty to the Church of England!" exclaimed he, with a look of surprise. "Not a speck, not a particle! Why, who says such a thing as that?" It will be remembered that *Tract* No. 90 was the point on which he had, in 1843, turned sharply round from his previously favorable view of the *Tracts for the Times:* and he had very steadily maintained his hostile tone towards that particular Tract ever since, though without re-reading it. I called his attention, after his strong approval of the *Eirenicon*, to the fact that its principles were precisely those of *Tract* No. 90; and asked if he had seen the new edition of that Tract, with Dr. Pusey's *Historical Preface* and Keble's reprinted *Letter*. He expressed a great desire to see them, and the next day sate down to their perusal as eagerly as he had done to that of the *Eirenicon*. When he had finished, he looked very grave,— a touch of tender sadness with the gravity: but said nothing. And I asked him no questions; but ever after, when alluding to *Tract* No. 90, there was a gentleness in his language such as I had never known before. In one point, however, he always expressed himself as unable to agree with the *Eirenicon:* and that was, the *practicability* of a reünion with Rome by means of explanations to be given of the present apparently contradictory standards of doctrine accepted on either side. His idea was, that Rome was irreformable, and would never condescend to explain anything whatsoever for the purpose of rendering it easier of acceptance to those not now in communion with her. Even in this point, however, his supposed difference was rather overstrained: for Dr. Pusey does not go so far as to say that he thinks any such course is actually practicable; but only that the formal documents on either side were at that time in such a shape that mutual explanations, removing apparent contradictions, were theologically possible, provided there were a willingness on both sides to come to a common understanding. As to what was likely to happen, he rather sadly forebodes[1] "a collapse of faith, through the amount of that, taught as 'of faith,' which was no part of GOD's revelation to the Church;" and that this "collapse of faith," due

---

[1] See *Eirenicon*, p. 334.

to the Church of Rome, may "issue . . . in the coming of Anti-Christ": which is quite as severe as anything ever held by my Father.

In one of our walks together, I sounded him on another point. He had always been decided in maintaining that Anthems in the words of Holy Scripture were not only allowable in our American Church, as declared by the House of Bishops in 1814, but that when used, they ought to be used in the place provided by Rubric in the English Book,—the American Book having provided no other: and that is, after the third Collect, and before the Prayer for the President of the United States. I knew how very strenuous he was in opposition to any thing like Mariolatry. After drawing from him a reïteration of his views about the lawfulness of Anthems, I asked whether there was any objection to the repetition of any one particular Anthem. He said, "Certainly not: they may sing the same one every day in the year if they like." I then asked: What objection could be made, if the words of the Anthem were those of the Angelic Salutation, "Hail, Mary, thou that art highly favored," etc., and if they were used at every service throughout the year? He looked very grave; walked on silently for some minutes; and then replied deliberately, though rather reluctantly, that "no fault could be found with it, provided the words used were simply those of Holy Scripture, without the unscriptural addition of 'Pray for us sinners now and at the hour of our death.'"

It was during that same visit that he was one day expressing rather strongly the views which I had often heard from him before, and which he had first formed while yet a presbyter in Pennsylvania;[1]—that a number of things had been dropped practically since the Reformation, which at that time it was intended should be retained, and which would have been of great practical advantage to the Church of England had they been continued in use from that time to this. I remarked, that these very subjects were then undergoing the liveliest discussion; and that if one whose anti-Romish position was so well known as his, should publish the views which he had just expressed, it might have a good effect in allaying the unreasonable panic of some excitable people who

[1] See page 115.

did not know the difference between such things and "popery": adding, that I thought those who were, in the midst of heated opposition, trying to reduce his principles on the subject to practice, had a moral right to the support of his name and published opinions on the same side. He said that his opinion on the subject had not been asked for; and that I knew his conviction that it would be his *duty* to respond, should his opinion upon any Church subject be requested by any respectable number of clergymen or laymen. He was assured, in reply, that the request would not be long in forthcoming. In a few days he received it, in due form, signed by seven priests and eight lay communicants of the Church, and he promised to comply with it as soon as his official engagements would allow.

The result of this was his little volume on *The Law of Ritualism*,[1] which made its appearance towards the end of September, 1866, with a smoking censer on the cover. A great many good people were at that time as "daft" on the subject of "Ritualism" as they (or others like them) had been about "Tractarianism" twenty-five years before. The sensation caused by the little book in blue and gold was therefore more marked than that caused by any previous publication on the subject. It had hardly been out a week, when, on the 3d of October, the Bishops met, to consider Dr. Howe's refusal to accept the Missionary Episcopate of Nevada, and—as it turned out—to elect the Rev. D. S. Tuttle as Missionary Bishop of Utah. At the close of the second day's session,[2] my Father was informed privately that some of the Bishops were anxious to bring up the subject of Ritualism for a ventilation, and for action if possible: and that his book would probably be alluded to. On the following morning, therefore, he absented himself from the House, sending a note to the Bishop of Connecticut, by me, asking him to tell his Brethren the reason of his absence, and that he thought some of them might express their minds about his book more freely if he were away. But he was evidently deeply hurt by the readiness of the Bishops to condemn a work which had been out only a few days, and which the most of them had not even read. It was something unprece-

---

[1] Published by Hurd & Houghton, New York City.
[2] This was his last day's service in the House of Bishops.

dented, too; for never before had any book written by an American Bishop been the subject of such discussion by the House: and it seemed strange that he who had been so singularly Protested against by even priests and deacons in 1863, should now, when Presiding Bishop, be subjected to the indignity of such a discussion as was contemplated on that day.

The note was duly delivered at the opening of the session. In the evening, when I called upon him again, I found him sitting in the same place where I had left him in the morning, and with that look of peculiar and settled gravity mingled with grief, which was seldom seen upon his cheerful face. "What is the matter, dear Father?" said I. "What makes you look so sober?" "My son," he replied, "I have been thinking the whole matter over again as carefully as I know how; and I am satisfied that I have never done the Church a greater service than by that little book on *The Law of Ritualism*. We have the old Catholic Creed; we have the Apostolic Succession; we have valid Sacraments; we have an admirable Liturgy; we have all the grand substantial features of a true Branch of the one Catholic and Apostolic Church. And yet the practical working of our system seems to have an almost inevitable tendency to run down into semi-stagnation,—a half-dead-and-alive sort of condition,—and the most constant exertion is needed merely to keep ourselves above that level of deadness. Now what is the reason of this?— except that we have unwisely thrown overboard so many of those beautiful and impressive usages, which are thoroughly authorized in Holy Scripture; which have always been freely used in the Catholic Church; which God Himself made to be agreeable and interesting to human nature; and which were consecrated of old to His service by His express command. If, therefore, in addition to all we have already, we could only regain a rich and gorgeous ceremonial, we should no longer have the old stagnation to contend with, but the Church would feel new life and vigor throughout her whole body, and to the very ends of her fingers and toes!" This conviction only strengthened, as long as he lived.

Meanwhile, the House of Bishops had a protracted and animated discussion that day, Friday, October 7th, on the subject.

The fears of many were expressed in terms of absurd exaggeration, as might have been expected: but the resistance on the part of the wiser and more learned Bishops was outspoken and—to a certain extent—successful. The Bishop of New York, in particular, ridiculed the alarm on the subject of Ritualism as "a Mrs. Partington sort of business," and told his brethren that they might as well try to keep down the rising tide of the Atlantic Ocean with a broom, as to stop the movement for increasing the " glory and the beauty " of the public worship of the Church. As a House, the subject was dismissed without action. But it was understood that three Bishops,—of whom Bishop Coxe of Western New York was the Secretary and the leading spirit,—should prepare a *Declaration* concerning Ritualism, to be signed as individuals, by such of the Bishops as should approve of it.

It was agreed that no direct reference should be made in that *Declaration* to the Bishop of Vermont's book. But, as Bishop Coxe explained in a letter dated October, 1866,—the very time when, as Secretary of the Committee, he was circulating that *Declaration* for signatures—there were only two things that called for action at all: some ritualistic doings in New York City, and the Bishop of Vermont's book. The former he regarded as "simply absurd": "but the appearance of the Bishop of Vermont's little book," he added, " is a serious thing, as it opens the door for experiments which are not unlikely to be made in respectable Churches, if not in some of the most important seats of the Church's dignity and strength." It is therefore impossible to understand the *Declaration* in any other light than as meant for a demonstration against the Bishop of Vermont's "little book": but this was not comprehended equally well by all the signers of it, especially the more remote. For five months it was on its travels in search of signatures, and at length appeared, with the names of twenty-eight Bishops appended to it.

But the signers were careful enough not to pledge themselves in advance as to what they would do with it, " leaving to each Diocesan his own course as to its publication, or reception, in his own Diocese "; and besides this, in the document itself, every signer expressly " reserved each for himself his rights as Ordinary of his own Diocese, and also his rights as a member of the House of Bishops sitting in General Convention": which was very prudent in the signers, but added no force to the *Declaration*. The Bishops of sixteen Dioceses,—Vermont, Maine, New York, New Jersey, Pennsylvania, Maryland, North Carolina, Georgia, Florida, Mississippi, Louisiana, Arkansas, Tennessee, Missouri, Illinois, and Oregon,—did not sign: and of those who did sign, not half a dozen ever raised a finger towards " its publication or reception in his own Diocese": while pamphlets and newspapers dissected its ignorance and clumsiness, its bulls and blunders, with merciless ridicule. It succeeded, indeed, in advertising the Ritualistic movement in this country, in many quarters where it was before entirely unknown, thus doing more good than harm to the cause which it professed to oppose. So thoroughly was it killed by this discussion, that when in 1868 it was moved in the House of Bishops that the *Declaration* be adopted as an act of the House, the motion was laid upon the table, although a decided majority of the House then present were among the signers.

And the advance since then has been very rapid. Every attempt to legislate against ritualistic details failed in the General Convention of 1868. And in 1871 the failure was only still more illustrious. The Report of the Five Bishops condemning a catalogue of details was thrown overboard without any serious consideration of it in either House. Dr. Mead's amendment to the proposed Canon on Ritual began by embodying ten of the prohibitions reported by the Five Bishops; but even he felt compelled to throw aside seven other paragraphs of their proposed legislation before he could stagger under the remainder. And one of the most amusing incidents of that six days' Ritualistic discussion was to hear the venerable Doctor lighten his load every time he read his amendment, until he had thrown overboard no less than *six* of the proposed ten prohibitions, and among the six thus parted with were the prohibitions of Incense, Altar-lights, Crucifix, and Mixed Chalice, while at no time did he undertake to prohibit Vestments. Moreover, when his proposal—even after it was razeed to its briefest proportions—was supported by only ten or eleven Dioceses out of forty, the totality of his failure in the Lower House (he had previously, for many sessions, been the leader of that House), may be appreciated.[1] In the Upper House, on the last day of the session, when the Bishops were preparing their Canon against Eucharistical Adoration, one of them moved as an amendment to add to it a prohibition of incense and Altar-lights: and it was one of the three Bishops that got up the *Declaration* of 1867, who begged him not to press that amendment, because such a prohibition would be sure to kill the Canon; and thereupon the amendment was voted down by an overwhelming majority. The Canon against Eucharistical Adoration failed in the Lower House all the same, however.

The result of these two General Conventions has thus been, to prove conclusively that the leading principles of the Bishop of Vermont's "little book" on *The Law of Ritualism* were quite correct. By attempting to legislate against the things which he declared to be lawful, his opponents confessed that there was no law against them at the time he wrote his book. And by their repeated failure to effect any prohibitory legislation since, they reluctantly confess that there is no law against them now.

Meanwhile, the public did not wait for the five months' incubation of the *Declaration* of the Twenty-eight, but formed its own opinion by reading the "little book" itself. Four editions were rapidly exhausted, besides which it was reprinted in London in a cheap shilling edition, upon the advice of two of the most influential laymen in England in such matters. It was noticed more extensively in England than any of his previous works. Thanks for it poured in from the most unexpected quarters, at home and abroad. An aged American priest, well known for his deep learning and incisive style as an author, but no Ritualist, wrote him on reading the book:—"I am glad that some parts have fallen into the hands of one who has been a lawyer. Your argument about the continuance of the Canon Law of England until repealed by us, pleases me much. If we have not something like this to fall back upon, we are utterly afloat." And he added, "I wrote to Bishop —— *before* I read your book, that he had better *head* Ritualism, so as to control and guide it; adding,

---

[1] At the beginning of the Session, Dr. Mead was heard to say, that he "would never leave Baltimore until he had secured a Canon against those Ritualists!" so sure did he feel of success. He left, however, after the adjournment.

that if he meant to fight it, he would have a long battle." Another aged American priest, never suspected of Ritualism himself, wrote: "Most heartily do I thank the Supreme Head of the Church that there is *one living* Bishop who is not afraid to say, to preach, and to print, what he thinks, what he knows, and what he believes." Neither of these two had ever been under my Father's jurisdiction. Even the Bishop of Western New York, writing to the Bishop of Vermont within three months after the appearance of the *Declaration*, said, touching Ritualism: "I think you will allow, that if, on that point, I have differed from you (less in theory, than as to what is expedient, for our Church), it has been with entire respect and deference." In thus making the question to be one of expediency, not of theory or of law, the *Declaration* is virtually explained away by the very prelate who was chiefly instrumental in getting it up.

From abroad the expressions of satisfaction were even more emphatic and gratifying. A prominent English layman wrote:— "It is gratifying to find that the Father of the American Bishops views without alarm—or rather that he approves and justifies— the great movement of which we in England now see the beginning. The book, coming from such a source, has a value which it could not have possessed had it been written by any other living man." The writer enclosed a letter of strong approval from "one of the ablest and most learned ecclesiastical lawyers in England." The Council of the English Church Union voted to send a copy of the Bishop of Vermont's book to every English Bishop. But the crown of all came when the author was no longer on earth to enjoy it. Sir Robert Phillimore, the highest ecclesiastical Judge in England, in his famous Judgment in the Mackonochie case, cited *The Law of Ritualism* among his authorities, as one of "the writings of the late most distinguished American prelate, the Bishop of Vermont." To be cited as an authority by such a Judge in such a case is a higher compliment than has ever been paid to any other American Bishop, so far as my knowledge extends; and more than atoned for some opinions of a different sort entertained and expressed nearer Home.

In that little book, nothing had been said on the subject of Eucharistic Adoration. It treated of "the *Law* of Ritualism," not of the doctrine of the Holy Eucharist. But foreseeing that the controversy about Ritual was sure to gravitate steadily towards the doctrine which was, or was supposed to be, the real heart of the whole movement, and being anxious to obtain from my Father his deliberate judgment on that subject also, after full examination: I sent him Dr. Pusey's two works,—*The Doctrine of the Real Presence, as contained in the Fathers*, and *The Real Presence of the Body and Blood of Our Lord Jesus Christ the Doctrine of the English Church*,—together with Keble's " Golden Tractate " on *Eucharistical Adoration* : asking him not only to read them very carefully, but to mark the margin of the page in every case where he thought they had gone too far. He read them, as he afterwards assured me, with the greatest care, and specially expressed his delight at the perfect fairness with which Dr. Pusey had quoted all the passages that seemed to make against him, as well as those that were more favorable. But he did not make any marks on the margin, and thus I had not the measure of his difference of opinion quite as sharply defined as I wished.

But our prolonged conversation on the subject then, and often subsequently, gave that opinion to me with sufficient distinctness for all practical purposes. He acknowledged always, without hesitation or qualification, that the doctrine taught by Dr. Pusey and Keble was clearly within the intended comprehensiveness of the Church of England; and therefore, that the idea of disciplining any one for holding and teaching that doctrine was preposterous. He also acknowledged, that, the doctrine being thus legally allowable, the ritualism which expressed it was, by logical implication, equally allowable. But as he had already proved the lawfulness of Ritualism, it seemed to him the height of absurdity to attempt to put down a Ritualism which was clearly legal, on the ground that it taught symbolically a doctrine which was also clearly legal. Touching his own opinions, however, he seemed anxious to make out that there was some shade of difference betwixt himself and those distinguished theologians. As to " the Real Presence," he always stoutly maintained it,—name and thing. He acknowledged that it is objective,—that is to say, that it is a Presence other than that which abides in the heart of each true believer; a Presence which is in the Sanctuary before the communicant comes to receive It; a Presence dependent upon valid Consecration by a true Priest of the Apostolic Succession. To adore that Presence could not be forbidden. But he did not like to consider that Presence as so rigidly and locally¹ identified with the consecrated Elements, that the act of adoration should be specially and visibly directed towards them. He did not like to say that the Body and Blood of Christ were "given" by the Priest. He preferred to think of Christ as Himself so present that, at the instant when the Priest gave the consecrated element, Christ gave Himself to the faithful receiver, passing by those whom He knew—and none but He could know—to be unfaithful or unworthy. This last point my Father defended solely by the words of the 29th Article: but in all our conversations I never heard him quote as proving it either Holy Scripture or the Ancient Fathers. He considered that the words " in no wise are they partakers of Christ " excluded the idea of the wicked receiving Him in that Holy Sacrament to their condemnation. In no other point could I ever perceive any appreciable difference between his opinion and that of the learned theologians already mentioned. In celebrating the Holy Eucharist, he made no change in later years from the reverent mode which had been his custom during his whole ministerial life: but he always preferred the ancient Basilican position of the celebrant, when it was in his power.

When writing the "little book," he did not anticipate the practical rapidity of the movement, or the probability that he would, at his advanced age, make any visible change in the habits of his previous life. But he soon began to find that things were practicable now, which he had supposed would only become so after the lapse of years: and having published the convictions which he had arrived at so many years before, he found that the putting them into practice was not so difficult as he had supposed. S. Paul's Church, Burlington, needed two new surplices and stoles, which were ordered shortly after his return from the meeting of the House of Bishops that discussed his "little book":

¹ My Father's difference of opinion here, seems, to me, to be exactly what Dr. Pusey means when he declares that Presence to be "*supra-local.*"

and he ordered the stoles to be made of purple,—the first appearance of a colored vestment of any sort in the Diocese of Vermont. Moreover, the chancel of that Church was very dark, and his eyesight was steadily failing, so that he really needed more light. Christmas Day saw both the innovations for the first time; and on the next day he wrote me:—" The surplice has arrived, and I wore it yesterday at Church, with the new stole, and with the two lights on the Altar. Quite an advance towards Ritualism! But S. Paul's is so dark that I really could not see to read with the wall lamps lighted by gas as usual. Thus I have had a very good *practical* argument for the remedy, which I intend shall be a permanent improvement in the right direction." In accordance with this determination, the young priest who was called to the parish as his assistant, and began his services at the time of my Father's sailing for England in August, 1867, was expressly directed by him to continue the use of the Altar lights during his absence.

Nor was his practical advance confined to the parish in Burlington. It was seen, also, in the services of which, as Presiding Bishop, he had the direction: though here he was very much more tender in consideration for those brethren whose consciences are so weak when anything is proposed to increase the glory and the beauty of God's service, and so strong and noisy whenever anything is done which they themselves do not happen to fancy. At the Consecrations of new Bishops, subsequent to the General Convention of 1865, the service was generally more or less choral. At the Consecrations of Bishops Neely and Tuttle, early in 1867, there was full choral service, with large surpliced choirs of men and boys, and processional and recessional hymns. And on the last occasion of the sort at which he presided,—the Consecration of Bishop Young of Florida on S. James's Day, in Trinity Church, that same year,—besides the above, his Pastoral Staff was borne before him by a deacon. There were some fifty surpliced choristers, more than an hundred clergy and six Bishops in the procession, which moved all the way down the North Aisle, then round and up the middle alley, chaunting psalms all the way. The service was fully choral. The *Nunc dimittis* was sung during the consumption of the remainder of the Consecrated Elements at the close of the service; and the procession retired as it entered, singing "Seven-fold Spirit, Lord of Life," from the People's Hymnal,—a collection which has never been "allowed" or "licensed" by any Bishop or Convention. It was, as a whole, the grandest and most impressive service of the kind ever seen, as yet, in the Church of America; and a noble and appropriate culmination of his public services as its Presiding Bishop.

Immediately after finishing *The Law of Ritualism*, in the summer of 1866, my Father prepared a treatise on a very different subject, which had occupied more or less of his thoughts for years. It was on the Personal Reign of Christ and the future Supremacy of Israel when converted to the Faith. The leading idea of it is, that the Bride, the Lamb's Wife, is the converted Church of Israel, the chosen people, to whom and to whom alone —the Virgin, the Daughter of Zion—the Lord declared Himself, by the mouth of his prophets, to be an Husband; and that the Gentile churches all over the world are but "the virgins that bear her company," and are brought with her unto the King. Not having been successful in finding a publisher for this work, and being unable to print it at my own risk, it still remains in manuscript.

After its completion, on reviewing *The End of Controversy, Controverted*, for a proposed new edition, he found that there was one point of some importance on which he had entirely changed his mind. He wrote me, on the 4th of February, 1867:—

I also find, what I had entirely forgotten, viz., that I adopted and defended largely the current Protestant view of the Pope being the great Antichrist. The lapse of twelve years has changed my mind on that point. The new edition must therefore omit all that, and I shall prepare for the *Church Review* (to be also in pamphlet form) the reasons for my "Retractation."

The work grew upon his hands, however, until it made enough for a small volume, of about the size of *The Law of Ritualism*: and it was finished and forwarded to me. After reading it, I placed it in the hands of my dear friend, the Rev. Dr. Mahan, now also in Paradise: and I give his estimate of the work and its author the more freely, because he was generally reticent in such matters, possessing that dignified sensitiveness of conscientiousness which made him sparing of words even when his feelings of admiration or love were deepest and strongest :—

I consider your Father's Antichrist Retractation a sublime thing for one at his time of life. It looks like a special crown of grace, a fit reward of an honest life, that he should be inspired to bear such a testimony in his declining years. So subtile a brain is seldom found at the end of such a strong backbone. He is our American Exeter,—and a little more than Exeter.

It was indeed, to the natural man, a hard thing to do. The pride of consistency in opinion was as strong with my Father, naturally, as with any man I have ever known : and the more so, because he never committed himself in print on any subject without having examined it so thoroughly as to be convinced, in his own mind, that he had worked through both sides of it. His convictions as against the peculiar claims of Rome had been the result of the studies and labors of a half century; and on the general issue he was as immovable as a rock. His certainty that Rome would ever resist such changes as could alone render possible the Reünion of Christendom, shaped all his convictions as to the personal coming and reign of Christ. Yet he never closed his mind against further reading and further thought : and he was thus constantly gaining in breadth, depth, and clearness of conviction ; while on some points, differences that had seemed to him of great importance in earlier years, fell to their true proportions as mere misunderstandings or things of comparatively trifling importance. And this change was so quiet and so constant that, for the most part, he was not aware of it himself, until brought face to face with his former opinions in some of his printed works.

His *Candid Examination of the Question Whether the Pope of Rome is the Great Antichrist of Scripture* was completed too late to permit of its publication before sailing for England. And after his return, it was his intention to retain it, until he could read and examine all that had been said on the same subject both by Archdeacon Wordsworth (now Bishop of Lincoln) and Dr. Döllinger. But this he was unable to do during the few weeks after his return from England : and therefore the treatise was published after his decease, without his final corrections. At the close of the manuscript were found memoranda of a fresh and sharp reading of the *Homilies*, which—though not connected with the treatise—were printed at the end of it, as indicating the freedom of criticism which he applied to those old sermons without hesitation. The treatise itself, with yearnings after a Reünion which he could not see to be practicable, gives utterance to the kindliest and most charitable feeling towards Rome on the one side, and towards the Protestant Sects on the other, with a final reïteration of the great burden of his life-work :—

There is no scheme of unity worthy of the slightest confidence, but that which shall honestly go back to the principles of the Primitive Church, when she was united, three hundred years before Popery began its perilous innovations; since that is the true source from which we can alone derive the great and leading rules of the Gospel dispensation. For what other standard can those modern denominations regard with equal reverence? If the Church in that early day was united,—which no one can dispute,— and if it is now split up into more than a hundred divisions, how is it possible that it can be united again except by returning to its original condition, before the work of division began?

And, after comparing the controversies among Christians to quarrels among brethren by blood, whose relationship as brethren remains notwithstanding, and cannot be denied without absurdity: he thus concludes the treatise, with words which were a beautiful closing of the work of authorship which had occupied so much of the best strength of his life :—

How much more shall Christians acknowledge that, since a true and living faith in the Divine Redeemer, sealed in our Baptism, makes us the adopted sons and daughters of the Almighty Creator, we must be brethren by virtue of that spiritual relation! And therefore, although we may not expect, in these last degenerate and evil days, that outward union will be restored before the end of this dispensation, yet we may and ought to remember that the same Saviour died for us all; that the same God, for His sake, regards us as His children; and that even in our strongest denunciations of error, the spirit which animates our hearts should be in harmony with the wondrous pity and love of our Lord, when He uttered on the Cross that gracious supplication: " Father, forgive them ; they know not what they do."

But his incessant literary activity was not carried on with entire impunity. Several times he felt symptoms of oppression about the head, which were not a little alarming. One year—

the summer of 1863—I persuaded him, with great difficulty, to let me take him on a brief trip of a few days among the Adirondacks. He had been living in sight of them for more than thirty years; yet had never gone a foot further towards them than was necessary in performing occasional priestly or Episcopal functions in the parishes on the western shore of Lake Champlain. We landed at Port Henry, and, with a horse and buggy, drove over the mountains on the direct road towards Elizabethtown, but turning to the left at a little schoolhouse, and descending the hill to New Russia, getting the glorious view of the Dome and the immense mountain wall that flanks it on either side, in the purplish shadows of evening. From Elizabethtown to Keene, thence to Scott's in North Elba, and around through the marvellous Wilmington Pass, across the hill from Wilmington to Lower Jay, looking back almost every moment to enjoy the magnificent view of Whiteface Mountain; and thence by way of Ausable Forks and Keeseville to Port Kent, where we took boat for Burlington: such was the brief and only trip my Father ever took in the Adirondacks. A similar brief trip followed, shortly after, from Rutland up through the Green Mountains by way of Mendon and down the remarkable gorge of Sherburne, as far as Bridgewater: and returning next day by way of Plymouth Notch, and under Killington and Shrewsbury Peaks, to Rutland. On both these trips, his sketch-book was his constant companion; and whenever a particularly fine view struck his fancy, we stopped until he had secured its characteristic features on paper: and several of the sketches taken on these trips were afterwards enlarged by him on canvas.

But the most serious physical trial of his later years—far more so than the winter's cough which was usually his companion for some months of the colder season—was the failure of his eyesight. This began, years before his departure, with a cloudy spot in the vision of his right eye, which gradually enlarged and darkened, until it ended in entire loss of the sight of that eye. On examination by one of the ablest oculists in New York, it was pronounced to be cataract: and the left eye was beginning, very perceptibly, to sympathize. His handwriting began to show gradually increasing traces of the evil, being larger, heavier, and looser than the firm clear character of his earlier years: and in some of his latest manuscripts, in attempting to erase a word, the erasing lines at times pass entirely over the word without touching it. Yet he would not lighten the burden laid upon the one failing eye that was left. It only made him feel that his time was short, and that he must work the harder while that one eye was left. He used a "Student's Lamp," which gives a very bright light: and sometimes after working by it in his study all evening, with the flame turned up so high that it almost filled the room with its smoke, he would at length come down-stairs complaining that "the oil was so poor in these days, that the light was miserable": not conscious, for the moment, that the growing dimness was from within. Yet he was, in reality, fully conscious of the dark prospect before him, and was ready to try any remedy but idleness. He expected,—should his remaining eye fail him,—to submit to an operation on the right eye: but was well aware that a favorable result cannot be depended on with certainty. He said little about his failing sight, indeed; for he was most tender in his anxiety to spare the feelings of those who were nearest and dearest to him. But they knew it, nevertheless: indeed it could not be concealed, in the nature of things. And, as early as October 11, 1866, my Mother wrote me of him:—"He told me a day or two ago that his other eye is beginning to fail, and looks forward to total blindness with the resignation of an angel."

Chapter XXII.

PREPARATORY TO LAMBETH.

ON the 28th of March, 1851, the then Archbishop of Canterbury, Dr. Sumner, invited the Bishop of Vermont, as he did all the American Bishops, to take part in celebrating the third Jubilee of the venerable Society for the Propagation of the Gospel in Foreign Parts. In his answer to that invitation, my Father suggested—and so far as I know was the first to suggest[1]—such a meeting of Bishops of the Anglican Communion as was held in 1867 at Lambeth. His letter was printed in full in the English papers at the time, and was the subject of comment, besides being well remembered at least by some of the more thoughtful minds on that side the water. About a year after, the Bishop of Maryland—then in England—repeated the suggestion in a public speech which gave rise to some discussion in both countries. At the Consecration of the present Bishop of New

---

[1] The Bishop of Moray and Ross, the *Primus* of the Scottish Church, addressing his Diocesan Synod on the 2d of October, only a few days after the Conference was over, gives to that letter of the Bishop of Vermont the credit of the first suggestion of the idea:—" In looking to the origin of this great Conference, it is worthy of remark that, although it met at Lambeth, it was not suggested or initiated by the Home Bishops of the Church of England. The first suggestion of such a Conference with which I am acquainted appears in a letter many years ago from the American Bishop of Vermont to the late Archbishop of Canterbury, from which I make the following extract:—
' I fervently hope that the time may come when we shall meet in the good old fashion of Synodical action. How natural and how reasonable would it seem to be if ' in a time of controversy and division ' there should be a Council of all the Bishops in communion with your Grace ; and would not such an assemblage exhibit the most solemn and, under God, the most influential aspect of strength and unity in maintaining the true Gospel? It is my own firm belief that such a measure would be productive of immense advantage, and would exercise a moral influence far beyond that of any secular legislation.' God's time was not then come for such a meeting. Eighteen years have passed since that suggestion was offered ; and now the time was come, a time of even greater controversy and division than when those words were penned, and I had the pleasure and privilege of sitting by the side of that good Bishop of Vermont, now the Presiding Bishop of the Church in the United States of America, in a Council of all the Bishops in communion with his Grace of Canterbury, when his fervent hope was fully realized." *

* See Church Journal, Nov. 13, 1867.

York, Bishop Fulford, first Metropolitan of Montreal, and the first Anglican Bishop who united in an American Consecration since we received the Episcopate from the Mother Church, preached the sermon: and renewed the suggestion of such a meeting, with a special view to the repudiation of the New Dogma then about to be proclaimed as *de fide* by the Bishop of Rome. It was extensively discussed in the papers: being specially and repeatedly advocated in the *Church Journal*, which, on the 7th of December, 1854, said that such a Council "would form not only a more auspicious, but also a more important, era in the history of Christianity, than any Council held anywhere in the Catholic Church for more than a thousand years." And the same paper, in reply to inquiries from England as to what might be meant by all this, replied, on the 15th of February, 1855:—

> Unless the initiative be taken in England, it is not likely that the suggestion will go beyond newspaper discussion or private conversation and friendly correspondence. Willing and desirous as many of our American Bishops undoubtedly are for such an event, and freely as they may individually speak of it, or even write to friends abroad upon the subject, it cannot be expected that they should so far forget propriety as *themselves* formally to invite the Archbishop of Canterbury to give them an invitation. An informal suggestion is all that can—or probably will —be done in this country, until something be done in England. But if any such invitation were given by the Archbishop of Canterbury . . . it would certainly be cheerfully and joyfully accepted by a large majority of our Bishops. . . . We speak solely from our own conviction. Yet we hesitate not to say, that if the opportunity be given, the action of our American Bishops will be precisely what we have indicated above. We know perfectly well what we are talking about, and future events will prove our present words to be weighty with the authority of Truth.

It took much longer for the idea to mature elsewhere. It was more than ten years before the Metropolitan of Montreal succeeded in procuring from the Canadian Bishops an Address to the Convocation of Canterbury, expressing the desire for some such meeting: but even then it was limited to the inviting of the Indian and Colonial Episcopate to meet with the Archbishop and the Home Bishops of Great Britain. Both Houses of the Convocation of Canterbury afterwards united in requesting the Archbishop to issue the invitations; but they extended them to their true limits, so as to include all Bishops who are avowedly in Communion with the Church of England. There was subsequently a numerous though informal gathering of English, Irish and Colonial Archbishops and Bishops, at Lambeth,—the Bishop of Illinois being also present, to speak for the American Bishops —and the same request was unanimously made to the Archbishop by them.

Accordingly, on the 22d of February, 1867, the Archbishop sent his invitation to all the Bishops in the world professing to be in communion with the Church of England, except Dr. Colenso, then by the Letters-Patent of the Queen (but not by the Grace of God) Bishop of Natal. In the letter of invitation the Archbishop stated that the meeting was to be under his Presidency, at Lambeth, on the 24th of September and the three following days, and that, besides "uniting together in the highest acts of the Church's worship," there would be "brotherly consultations," in which, said he, " we may consider together many practical questions, the settlement of which would tend to the advancement of the Kingdom of our Lord and Master Jesus Christ, and to the maintenance of greater union in our Missionary work, and to increased intercommunion among ourselves. Such a meeting would not be competent to make declarations, or lay down definitions on points of doctrine. But united worship and common counsels would greatly tend to maintain practically the Unity of the Faith, whilst they would bind us in straiter bonds of peace and brotherly charity." The Archbishop added, —showing how entirely open the field was left at the time of the invitation,—" I shall gladly receive from you a list of any subjects you may wish to suggest to me for consideration and discussion. Should you be unable to attend, and desire to commission any Brother Bishop to speak for you, I shall welcome him as your representative in our united deliberations." As the invitation was an autograph circular addressed in the same terms to each Bishop, no one could possibly guess, from the language quoted above, that any private understanding with a few Bishops at home in England was to narrow the range of topics thus freely offered to the Bishops abroad, and on the faith of which they undertook their long and expensive journeys from the ends of the world to Lambeth.

The original circular was received by the Bishop of Vermont on the 3d of April, and was at once accepted—provided his Diocese should supply the means: and on the 16th of May he received the Archbishop's personal invitation to be his guest at Addington Park during the session. On meeting his Convention in June, at St. Alban's, he could say, as to his Diocesan work, "No former period has been marked by a larger amount of Episcopal labor, nor by results which, on the whole, were more satisfactory." More than double the usual number had been confirmed: the large addition to the Church in Burlington was in progress; the Institute was flourishing, and had over $4000 in the treasury. He also mentioned his increasing duties as Presiding Bishop:—

In addition to my parochial duties in S. Paul's Church, Burlington, and the visitation of my own Diocese, I have been called four times to New York, in the service of the Church, as the Presiding Bishop, and also to New Orleans and Louisville: five Bishops having been consecrated by me since our last Convention, one year ago. The growth of the Church, keeping pace with the vast increase of our territory and our population, has made the duties of Presiding Bishop vastly more laborious than they have been at any previous period. It is, moreover, purely an honorary office, entirely without pecuniary support, and involving some expense, as well as time and toil. But I am devoutly thankful to the gracious Providence of God that, notwithstanding I have long since passed my threescore years and ten, my health and physical vigor have been thus far abundantly sufficient for the work, and have sustained no injury, as yet, from fatigue or travel.

He laid before them the subject of the invitation to Lambeth:—

That such an imposing Council of reformed Bishops will attract the most universal interest, cannot be doubted. Nothing like it has ever been known, since the great Reformation. And although, so far as I am individually concerned, my attendance may be a matter of small importance, yet the position in which I am placed, by the Providence of God, as the Presiding Bishop of our Church, invests my name with a certain value in the judgment of others, and for this reason my absence would be a matter of much greater regret.

The question of defraying the cost was thus frankly laid before them :—

> My income, as your Bishop, is $1200 a year, and it is no larger now than it was before the war, although the expense of living has been doubled. The salary has been paid out of the Land Fund, and the parishes have never been taxed one dollar for their Bishop. Of the small amount of this salary I have not complained, nor do I complain now. But I mention it in order to show how impossible it is that I could pay the cost of a voyage to England. Whether the Diocese will feel disposed to supply the expense under these circumstances, my brethren, it is for you to decide. Thus far, if your Bishop has not served you well, he has at least served you cheaply. It is possible, I am aware, that you may not think my attendance at this great Council worth the cost. It is possible that my remaining at home because my Diocese does not feel able or willing to provide for my travelling expenses, may not seem, in your judgment, to involve any reproach to the liberality of Vermont. And in that case, I shall only have to send my apology, and honestly state the reason. That part of the question rests with you, and I wish you to settle it solely with regard to the interests of the Church, and the character and credit of the Diocese.

While asking no increase of salary for himself, however, he went on to plead earnestly for something of the sort for his clergy, declaring " an insufficient support " to be the sole reason for removal with nearly all the clergy who had left the Diocese for other fields of labor. And then, as if with some presentiment that this was the last time he should ever meet with his Convention, he thus concluded :—

> The time is approaching, and will arrive ere long, when you will be obliged to provide for your next Bishop on a very different scale,[1] or you will fail to obtain his services. But for the remainder of my course, I prefer to continue, as I have been, one of the poorest Bishops in the land. The good Providence of God has brought me nearly through my humble work on earth. When I entered the ministry, forty-three years ago, it was at a large pecuniary sacrifice. When I came as your Bishop from Boston to Vermont, my income of $2500 was exchanged for $1200 ; and my whole career, for almost thirty-five years, has been one of small remuneration to myself, so far as money is concerned. Yet the sources of supply have never dried up. The basket and the store have always been replenished.

---

[1] On the election of Bishop Bissell, his successor, it was voted that his salary " be fixed at $3000 *per annum*, until he takes the use or possession of the farm and residence of the late Bishop, at Rock Point."—*Journal*, 1868, p. 27.

And through many of my latter years, the favor of my divine Master has enabled me to live perfectly free from debt or difficulty.

I may be permitted, I trust, to state these facts without the reproach of offensive egotism, because I do it for the encouragement of my brethren of the Clergy, and in accordance with the example of S. Paul, who gloried in his poverty, and desired no other riches but those which the love of Christ lays up for His faithful followers in a brighter world. With me, it is regarded as no hardship, but rather a privilege, to be the poorest of the Bishops. And I should be sorry to change my condition, at this day, with the proudest monarch that ever occupied an earthly throne. The little sacrifices which I have been called to make in earthly profit, have been repaid more than an hundredfold in far more important ways, to me and mine. And however humble my personal claims, and however small my services, the result may at least prove the certainty of the Divine promises to all the servants of the Sanctuary, who can cast their worldly cares on Him Who careth for them, and whose chief aim is to worship and obey their glorious Redeemer in spirit and in truth."

He used habitually to say, that the promise, "Dwell in the land, and be doing good: and verily thou shalt be fed," was enough for him. And his closing words on the subject are recorded here as some slight protest against the periodic eruption of communications and editorials in our Church papers, complaining that the poor support of the Clergy is the reason why their ranks are not more numerously recruited; while others, with an equally contemptible whine, think that no more ought to be ordained until a comfortable support is first given to all who are in Orders already. Worse than all is the triumph of Mammon in requiring preliminary endowment, as a *conditio sine qua non*, for the erection of a new see: a condition now choked down upon the neck of all further growth in this direction, by its embodiment in the Constitution of the American Church. Such words and deeds are worthy only of men who shall first renounce all spiritual relationship with those noble old gentlemen who went about in sheepskins and goatskins, and lived in dens and caves of the earth; who were destitute, afflicted, tormented; of whom the world was not worthy. Perhaps, if there had been a comfortable salary for each of the prophets of the Lord in the time of Ahab, instead of only bread and water in a cave (and even that an unusually good living for them under the circumstances), there might have been more than an hundred of them in all Israel. Perhaps even some of the four hundred and fifty prophets of Baal might have 'verted: which would have been so great a gain for the worship of the true God, the jealous God of Israel! And who knows but that the worthy Demas might have stuck to the ministry of the Word, and not have forsaken S. Paul, if the Apostle could only have made him sure of " a good living " ?

But to return to our subject :—A Committee of three laymen, appointed on the subject of the invitation to Lambeth, reported resolutions declaring that invitation to be " the most hopeful sign and the most important step taken since the era of the Reformation "; that, " as our Bishop is at present the Presiding Bishop of the Church in the United States, we recognize the greater honor to ourselves and the greater importance to the Church, of his presence upon that extraordinary occasion "; that the constant prayers of the Diocese would ascend not only for his safe return, " but that the blessing of the Holy Ghost—that God who maketh men to be of one mind in an house—may rest upon the thoughts, words and deeds of all the Bishops who may there assemble in the name of the Prince of Peace ": and naming a further Committee of five laymen to raise funds at once to defray the Bishop's expenses. Nearly $1300 was the result,—a sum, it is believed, actually larger than was provided for the purpose by any other American Diocese: and especially gratifying to my Father from the promptness and cheerfulness with which it was given.

At the close of the month, he preached and presided at the Commencement of the General Theological Seminary; his sermon reaffirming the great truth that "outside of the Apostolic Succession of Bishops, there can be no true ordination to the Priesthood. The law of God had thus settled it, and no uninspired man had the right or the power to change it." The Reformation—however much it might have been needed in some things—" left the old essential foundations of the Church unchanged." It was no inappropriate farewell to an Institution in which two of his own sons had been trained for the Ministry, and in which he had always felt a deep interest.

On the 14th of August, at about 3 o'clock in the afternoon, we sailed from New York for England, in the steamer *Chicago*,

Bishop Odenheimer and two of his family being our fellow passengers, and adding greatly to the enjoyment of the trip. Neither my Father nor I were ever troubled with sea-sickness; and there was pleasant weather for the earlier part of the voyage. After three days of such cloud and rain that it was impossible to take the sun at noon, we found ourselves, at night on S. Bartholomew's day, in the midst of a gale, with driving rain dead ahead, and looking over the phosphorescent waves for Fastnet light on the wrong side of the bow: for we were inside Mizen Head instead of outside, and had rather a narrow escape from running on the rocks. But our careful Captain found out the error in good season, and the ship was put about instantly. Fastnet light was in sight before one o'clock the next morning. The day dawned beautifully bright and clear after the storm, giving the loveliest views of the Irish coast all day long, from the Old Head of Kinsale to the Tuscar light. There was both Morning and Evening Service, my Father preaching at the latter, and making a very touching allusion to our deliverance from danger on the night previous. We saw Holyhead light before retiring; and early on Monday morning, August 26th, after watching the beautiful alternations of sunshine and mist on city and river, we landed in Liverpool. The first door we entered was that of the office of the Steamship company, where we paid for our tickets, and selected our berths, on the *Minnesota*, the return steamer of October 15th. At Evening Prayer that day, in Chester Cathedral, we returned thanks for our safe arrival. On Tuesday, the 27th, we left Liverpool; and after glimpses of Morecambe Bay and Barnard and Brancepeth Castles by the way, we arrived towards sunset at Durham,—the unrivalled view of Cathedral and Castle and City from the Railway station being at its very best, glowing with the Western sunset light. The next morning we were at the Cathedral betimes; and after the service, and examining the venerable pile, we wandered under the trees at the West end, and across the Prebend's Bridge. The exquisite view from the further end of this bridge was a temptation which the aged artist could not resist. Blind as he was in one eye, and with the curtain of dimness daily descending lower over the other, he took out his sketch-book, and made a rough, hasty outline of the towers of the Cathedral emerging from the hill of green foliage, and with the rippling Wear flowing at the foot. It was his last sketch from nature. This was on Wednesday.

The same evening we arrived at York; and on the following day, after a brief hour in the Minster, he retired to a seat under one of the green trees towards the north of the Nave, and there —while his younger companion was examining every part of the building—he sate for hours, and smoked his quiet pipe, while continuing his labors on some verses which he had begun at Durham, and which were added to as he went from place to place, being finally completed in London.[1] These lines express very forcibly his feelings on witnessing the cold and perfunctory style in which the Choral Service of the Cathedrals was rendered, and especially the chill that was made most painfully prominent at the celebration of the Holy Communion.[2] On Friday night we reached Lincoln: and I had said so much to him about the first view I had had, both at Durham and York, in the mingled mystery of starlight and gaslight, before any inspection by day, that he determined to share it with me at Lincoln. Shortly after climbing the long hill, therefore, we sallied from the White Hart tavern, passed under the old arched gate-way of the Cathedral close, and slowly went all round the great and splendid pile, beginning at the West with its broad wings and towers, and following the Southern path round both transepts and the east end, and beyond the quaint Chapter House with its low flying buttresses. We spent the Saturday and Sunday at Lincoln, and very kind attention was shown him by the Canon in residence at the time. On Monday we reached Peterborough in time to catch the greater part of Matins; and at Ely, the same day, we heard the Vespers exquisitely sung. The splendid new work in Ely Cathedral gave my Father the keenest enjoyment. Tuesday afternoon found us at Norwich, and on Wednesday afternoon, Sept. 4th,

---

[1] These lines, entitled *Reflections on the State of the Church of England*, will be found in the *Appendix*, pp. 466-471.

[2] The custom seemed to be, that the *Ter Sanctus* should be sung as an Anthem just after the Sermon; and then that the whole choir should leave the Church, only an handful of people remaining behind, while all the rest of the Communion Service was without a single note of music!

we reached London, and took rooms at the Westminster Palace Hotel, at a convenient distance from Lambeth Palace.

He remained quietly in London until after the Conference was over, accepting few invitations and refusing many, his chief object being to husband his strength for the one service which had brought him there. After no little solicitation, he preached extemporaneously one of the remarkable series of sermons that gave such prominence, at that time, to the city Church of S. Lawrence, Gresham Street; but this was the only sermon he preached in London. He commonly attended divine service, unofficially, in the Abbey: and the hospitable kindness of his near neighbor, Archdeacon Wordsworth (now the Bishop of Lincoln), was one of the chief pleasures of his sojourn in London. Part of his hours passed in reading such publications as gave a clearer idea of the practical working of the great Church movement. One of these, I remember, was the account of some years of city mission experience in the East of London, by one of the faithful priests[1] who has so long devoted himself to that work. Coming in, one day, when he was about half through this pamphlet, I asked him what he thought of it. "My son," said he, "I believe that I was converted to Christ a great many years ago: I am beginning to think that I shall need to be converted to the Church yet, before I die." When he had finished it, he said that "it made him feel as if he had lived to the age of more than threescore years and ten, and had not yet *begun* to work for the Master." Speaking of the systematic use of private confession and absolution, as one of the leading features of that work in the East of London, he again, and still more strongly, reïterated the views I had heard from him in later years, that there was no difference worth mentioning on that subject between the Anglican and Roman Communions, except that Rome exacted it of all, by compulsion, while our Church leaves it free to each individual, to use it, or not, as he may find best for his own spiritual health.

One of the few institutions which he visited was the Sisterhood House of All Saints' Church, Margaret Street. The living-rooms

---

[1] The Rev. C. F. Lowder.

were as plain and common looking as those of the working classes, though as neat and clean as possible. The Chapel, however, was adorned with the utmost richness and beauty: and those who were there silently kneeling at their private devotions did *not* turn round to see whether we were watching them. We found that that company of devoted women were carrying on no less than *five* distinct and separate charities; and that for only one of the five—a Convalescent Hospital—there was at that time going up, in the outskirts of London, a new building which would cost about $350,000. I never knew my Father to be more deeply touched than he was by this his first and only direct contact with a Sisterhood in the Church of England. There was a tone of sadness mingled with tender humility in the little that he said about them. He understood now, he assured me, why they were called " the Religious,"—a term to which he had often in previous years expressed strong dislike when distinctively applied to members of the Orders. " He thought he had been living a life of devotion to Christ: but as compared with the lives of these women, and the work they had wrought, it seemed as if his whole life had only been secular after all, and that he had accomplished next to nothing." In not one point did he have one word of fault to find with the revival of the Religious Orders so hopefully begun within our own Communion.

Three days, from Friday, September 13th, to the following Monday, were delightfully spent at Addington Park, as the guest of the Archbishop of Canterbury, whose unaffected cordiality, and simple, unpretending dignity, gave peculiar grace to his hospitality. While there, the Archbishop showed him the immense petition sent in to his Grace, asking that proceedings be instituted against the Bishop of Salisbury for the bold assertion, in his famous *Charge*, of the Real, Objective, Spiritual Presence of Christ in the Holy Eucharist, and the proper adoration of Him thus present: and the Archbishop asked my Father's advice as to what could, or should, be done in the matter. He carefully read the *Charge*, in the Archbishop's copy: and then gave it as his deliberate judgment that there was no cause for any action whatsoever, as the Bishop of Salisbury had not gone beyond the clearly intended comprehensiveness of the Church of England, as understood from the time of the Reformation down to our own day. While at Addington, the Metropolitan of New Zealand (now the Bishop of Lichfield) also arrived as the Archbishop's guest. It was the first time my Father had ever met him, and the meeting was a great pleasure. Bishop Selwyn, as a man of real power of the highest order, impressed him more deeply, on the whole, than any other person whom he met abroad.

Meanwhile, the arrival of American and Colonial Bishops in London, one after another, betokened the approach of the day appointed for the opening of the Conference: and in connection with this, there was not a little said as to the preaching of the sermon on the first day. Some time before leaving home, the Presiding Bishop had been notified by the Archbishop of Canterbury that it was his " anxious wish " that the opening sermon should be preached by one of the American Bishops, but leaving it to their " Episcopal House " to make the selection. With the distances of American sees from each other, it was simply impossible for the American Bishops to assemble before sailing, to settle a point like that. The Presiding Bishop therefore wrote to the Bishop of New York,—the prominence of whose see naturally entitled him to the first place of importance,—and to the Bishop of Illinois, whose connection with the call of the Conference gave him also a peculiar claim, telling them both precisely how the matter stood, and asking each of them to prepare himself for the honorable service, in case he should be called to perform it: he wrote also to the Archbishop, mentioning what he had done. The Bishop of New York at once replied declining the office peremptorily, and wrote to the Archbishop also, expressing the same determination to him. The Bishop of Illinois promised to prepare a sermon, though too greatly pressed for time to be able to do justice either to the occasion or to himself: but kindly added that the Presiding Bishop was, of all others, the one who ought to preach that sermon, begging my Father to write one accordingly, and pledging himself that he would secure the unanimous request of the other American Bishops on their arrival in London, that their Presiding Bishop should be their preacher. He was so very earnest about it, that my Father had accordingly prepared a sermon for the occasion before leaving home: and as it was the last sermon he ever wrote, some things in it may well be worthy of note, though it never was delivered. Once more he reiterated the ancient Catholic doctrine, that the Bishops are the Successors of the Apostles; that the testimony of the Fathers is unanimous upon this point; and that "through the long course of fifteen centuries he that would find a Church without a Bishop would seek in vain." Once more he pointed out the tyranny and usurpation of Rome, mainly based upon the false decretals, and adding one corruption after another to the ancient faith, until the Reformation was a necessity. Once more he showed that "the Protestant sects," in setting up a ministry of their own, outside of the Bishops to whom alone was given the power of ordination, were in "rebellion" against the divine Constitution of "the Kingdom of Heaven," and that this rebellion is "a greater crime" than "rebellion against the government of a nation":—

> The latter is human. The former is divine. The one involves the interests of time. The other extends to the interests of eternity. Shall Christians be commanded, as they are, to be subject to the ordinances of man, and shall they not much more be required to obey the ordinances of the Almighty? The familiar example of Korah, Dathan and Abiram stands on record to prove the judgment of God on all who wilfully set themselves against the government which He ordains for the religious direction of His people. Those rebels did not mean to assail the authority of the Lord. They only attacked the right of Moses to confine the priesthood to Aaron and his sons. But this, in itself, was virtually an act of treason. And the Almighty visited their crime with a severity which was doubtless designed to be a solemn warning to the end of time, although there are few minds, in our distracted age, willing to make the application.

In glancing at the condition of Christendom, he mourned over "the distracted and divided state of our Protestant brethren, split up into more than a hundred sects—the Lutheran and Calvinistic branches overrun with heresy, while infidelity, false philosophy and spiritualism are all around us." The question of the Swedish and the Moravian Episcopate he alluded to, as still "unsettled." The Papal Church was "shorn of her former power, reduced to half her ancient strength, and less than half of her potential influence," flourishing only where she is "deeply indebted to the principle of religious toleration," though she "has never taken one step in that direction where the rights of others are concerned." The Pope has not, indeed, renounced any one of the extravagant assumptions of his predecessors; but "thousands of his own priests are clamoring for Reformation. Thousands of Romanists, who once regarded the Church of England as heretical, are now studying her system with a favorable feeling, and longing to be united with her on the pure and Apostolic platform." And this "desire for unity" now "possessed the minds of men who are worthy of the highest esteem in both communions." As to the Anglican Church, he claims that she is "free from all corrupt innovations save one small addition to the Creed," where he is "free to confess that the Greek Church has the best of the argument,"[1] though he does not consider the Oriental Church without fault in some other particulars. As to reünion in the Truth, though not himself personally sanguine as to its success before the end of this dispensation, he says "it is very certain that we may lawfully labor and pray for it, as a most desirable consummation. In so far as our Unity Societies, on both sides of the Atlantic, work for such an end, we may surely sympathize with them most cordially." As to our own Communion, his tone was naturally more cheerful:—

Has she not spread abroad throughout the world, and planted Bishops and priests on every continent? And is she not, at this day, more flourishing and prosperous than ever? Our own unity, therefore, my beloved brethren, seems, in my humble judgment, to be the great object which should occupy our minds on this deeply interesting occasion. The assembling of so many Bishops from distant lands, and living under such widely different forms of society, is, in itself, a striking demonstration of this unity: and if the results of our meeting should amount to nothing more, it will at least prove that the Church of England possesses a spiritual bond of union, independent of all the changes of human policy, and derived from those principles of her organization which are indeed divine. Possessing, as she does, all the proper characteristics of a Patriarchate, as it existed in the Catholic era of the fourth century, I have sometimes wished that she might adopt that venerable title, as more expressive of her real dignity, for assuredly there is no Patriarchate in the world of so

---

[1] He adds, "although, in our interpretation of the clause, there is no real difference of doctrine." The Roman interpretation, however, does not give the same doctrine as the Greek.

much importance, nor one so well adapted to sustain the interests of Christian truth, unalloyed with error.

But with all our grateful acknowledgment of the special favor of God to our highly privileged Communion, I am far from claiming that the condition of our Church is perfect, and cannot be improved. On the contrary, we are all aware that there are evils to be remedied, lost ground to be recovered, Catholic usages to be restored, and better means to be adopted for reaching the masses of the population. It would be a happy work, if it could be accomplished, to bring all our Liturgies into the same form, by a judicious collating of the First Book of Edward VI., the Scotch and the American Books with the present Order of the Church of England, so that, allowing of course a special prayer for the officers of each government, there might be a closer bond of union in the general system, and a still better conformity to the Primitive type. How far it may be practicable to effect any of these objects, it is not for me to say. But I suppose it will be universally admitted that it is the duty of the Church, as well as of the individual Christian, trusting in the grace of God, to go on unto perfection.

After glancing at the probable subjects of their action, among which he anticipated resolutions affirming the great principles of the Church, or rebuking heresy and schism, the discourse closed with exhortations to brótherly love, " with due respect to the primitive allowance of liberty in lesser things, and with a generous indulgence towards the various dispositions of men, so long as the sacred doctrines of the Creed and the established order of the Church are safe from invasion." It was a noble close to his life-long battle for Primitive Truth and Primitive Order, that he should thus have advocated a Liturgical Revision which should be even *more* completely Primitive than the First Book of Edward VI., a further restoration of " Catholic usages," and the formal recognition of the Archbishop of Canterbury as a Patriarch of the Catholic Church. It is not often that an old man of nearly seventy-six years of age is found so far in the advance of any onward movement: and as he was the first to suggest such a gathering of Bishops as the Lambeth Conference, perhaps some future meeting will show that these other suggestions have also within them the germs of life.

Nor have they the weight of his name and approval alone. The sermon was read and warmly commended by a number of the American Bishops as they arrived, and by none more cordially than by the Bishop of Illinois, who, on his reaching London, exerted himself to the utmost to redeem his promise, and to secure for the Presiding Bishop the honor of preaching that sermon at the opening of the Conference. But my Father himself, peremptorily and repeatedly, refused to allow his name to be used in that connection. The Archbishop of Canterbury, having received from the Presiding Bishop of the American Church the names of only two Bishops, one of whom had at once declined, naturally took it for granted that the other would be the preacher: and we found, on arriving in England, that the published arrangements for the Conference had already announced the Bishop of Illinois as the preacher. To make a change, after such publication, my Father was satisfied would not be properly understood by the public, and would be interpreted by many to the prejudice of the Bishop of Illinois: and therefore the friendly importunity of the latter, reïnforced at his instance by others of his brethren, was entirely without avail. My Father was highly gratified, however, with the cordial approval of his sermon, given by all of his Episcopal brethren who read it.

On Tuesday, September 17, a preliminary meeting of the Bishops was held, at the House of the venerable Society for the Propagation of the Gospel, and some very important questions were settled. It is exceedingly instructive to see precisely the same practical points emerging into prominence, which have been for so many ages mooted in regard to General Councils: and it is well for our wise men to look ahead a little, and take care that worse than Roman precedents are not set, and are not hardening into yokes upon their necks, before they think of it. Every step becomes of the greatest moment, when viewed as a precedent likely to be appealed to at future meetings. And the vast and far-reaching importance of that meeting is my justification for giving it a much greater proportion of attention than a mere biography would require.

First of all, the Archbishop of Canterbury did right in merely "inviting" a meeting which he had no authority to "summon."

Next, it would seem that one who invites, may, in the invitation, fix the limit of the visit which he requests. This is quite correct socially: but when viewed ecclesiastically, it gives the

Archbishop the power to limit absolutely the length of the session in advance. The essential difference between one who "invites" and one who "summons" is, that the former claims no official power, while the latter does. But in thus limiting the session in advance, the Archbishop really exercised a greater stretch of power than was ever ventured upon by any Emperor or Pope that ever summoned a General Council. It was not meant, indeed, as a stretch of power: but a precedent which is set from one motive, may afterwards be appealed to and enforced from a very different motive. From another point of view, nothing is more clear than that to invite Bishops to come from the ends of the earth at their own expense, to sit at Lambeth for only *four days*, was neither more nor less than a cowardly insult. Yet it was not meant so: and, thank God, it was not taken so. It was merely the uncontrollable timidity which, in the chief Prelate of an Establishment, naturally marred an act that in itself transcended in boldness anything done by any of his predecessors. And the peculiar difficulties surrounding that first tentative experiment in a direction so full of imaginary dangers and terrors to the Episcopate of an Established Church, were too keenly appreciated by all concerned to render possible such a calamity, as the construing of that limitation into an insult. But either that, or a more than Papal stretch of power, is what it will mean hereafter, if it be deliberately repeated: and the attempt to repeat it should therefore be enough to defeat any future meeting under any such invitation. When my Father first saw that limitation, he could not believe that it was really intended. Even when he found that the Church Congress at Wolverhampton was fixed for the week following the Conference, he felt assured that the Bishops would adjourn over to the week next ensuing after the Congress. And his conviction as to the necessity of such adjournment for the completion of important business, was proved correct by the adjourned meeting of the Conference, held on the 10th of December. It is a very unsatisfactory way of transacting such business, however, that there should be a large attendance at the beginning of it, and very few present at the completion of it in the final and authentic form. Hence the thin adjourned meeting in December merely received and published the reports of the Committees on important subjects, without considering or acting on them in detail: and its action, therefore,—no matter how wise and important those reports may have been,—has amounted to very nearly nothing at all. The whole weight of that extraordinary assembly was concentrated in its short September session.

Another point settled was the right to preside. When the Emperors called the "undisputed General Councils," the Emperors appointed the Presidents. When the Pope began to summon Councils in his own right, he also claimed and exercised the power to appoint the Presidents. The Archbishop, in sending his invitation, settled this question in advance, by asking his brethren to meet "under his Presidency." It may have been wise. It was not generous. Under the circumstances, there was no one else who could have been thought of for a moment: and it would have been equally safe, and perhaps better as a precedent, to have left that point of the programme to the acclamations of the Bishops when assembled. But it may be considered as settled that the Archbishop presides in person, if present. It is not settled that he can appoint deputies to preside in his absence, or that no meeting can be held should the See of Canterbury chance to be vacant on the day of assembling.

The previous arrangement of an order of business is a great convenience in facilitating the action of any number of men. It becomes almost a necessity, if the number of members be large, and the session be short. Any thing done in this line must, from the nature of things, be done by the Archbishop and his English brethren, and cannot be done by the other Bishops while scattered throughout the world. The advantage of central circumstances is so great, that the Pope has gradually converted it into claiming and exercising the absolute right of the initiative: and his commissions of divines sit for months in advance, and prepare everything that is to come before a Council. No new matter may be brought in by any member, except through the Pope's Commission. At Lambeth, there were some signs that looked like a tendency to imitate the Papal example. When the Archbishop, in his original invitation, said to each Bishop, "I shall gladly receive from you a list of any subjects you may wish to suggest to me for consideration and discussion, he apparently recognized a power of initiative in each one of them; but a slight emphasis on the little words "*to me*," would indicate that *he* was to be the sole judge whether or no the subject thus "suggested" should be actually discussed. Moreover, the private pledge given by his Grace to the Bishop of S. David's and to Dean Stanley that the Colenso question should not be discussed or acted on, shows that both he and they were persuaded that the finger and thumb of his Grace controlled an absolute throttle upon the action of the Conference, like that of the Pope on the Council of the Vatican. But the result, at Lambeth, was such, eventually, as to provide both for convenience and for liberty. The Archbishop's printed programme of business for each of the four days was very convenient. But at the preliminary meeting on the 17th of September, it was settled, in behalf of liberty, that any amendment might be moved, by any member; and also, that new matter, not on the programme at all, might be introduced, on motion. And as to the Archbishop's private pledge, though, out of courtesy to his Grace, and a reluctance on the part of his guests to punish him too severely for his really discourteous blunder, the subject was not pushed to formal action at once in the Conference: yet it was introduced, was very largely discussed, and was partially acted on in September, to the loudly expressed disgust of some to whom the pledges were made; while the action of the Bishops outside the Conference was decisive: and the adjourned meeting in December accepted and sent forth a Report of a Committee which asserted substantially all that had been voluntarily withdrawn in September. Liberty of debate and freedom of action are therefore secured: though the contest for these was the sharpest of the whole session.

Another point ruled at the preliminary meeting was, that a stenographer should be present, who should make a verbatim report of the proceedings of the Conference, for publication. This was right: but it was afterwards reversed touching the publication, as we shall see further on.

Another point ruled, was, that none but Bishops should be present at the Conference, which was *wrong*, because utterly opposed to every ancient precedent, from the Council of the Apostles in Jerusalem down to our own days. It is worse than wrong; it is stupid: and the policy will have to be abandoned sooner or later.

The question of introducing the Colenso business was discussed at that preliminary meeting more fully than any other. The Metropolitan of Capetown, in a long and very able speech, urged that the Conference should act on the subject: and he was supported by the Bishops of Vermont, New York, Illinois, and other Americans, as also by the Metropolitans of Montreal and New Zealand. There was perfect unanimity among those present as to the spiritual validity of Colenso's excommunication: but many saw difficulties in the way of dealing directly with the question in the Conference. Nothing was decided at the preliminary meeting, in regard to that special question.

On the evenings of the ensuing Thursday, Friday and Monday, a number of the Colonial Bishops met at the house of Archdeacon Wordsworth in the Cloisters of Westminster Abbey, to arrange for united action in bringing the Colenso matter squarely before the Conference. My Father was requested to meet with them: but he declined, deeming it hardly delicate in an American Bishop to take part in meetings which might be regarded as a "caucus" for opposing the Archbishop's programme. He told those who invited him, however, that he was clear that the subject ought to come before the Conference; that it was a Colonial question, and therefore the Colonial Bishops should arrange for action in such shape as would suit them; and that they might rely upon his support, in whatever shape they should bring it up. They did not know, however, how much, or how little, this might mean. Though they had among them two such admirable men, for ability, courage and practical wisdom, as the Metropolitans of Capetown and New Zealand, yet the prestige of the Lords Bishops at Home over the poor and comparatively unimportant Colonial Bishops was so overwhelming, that at each successive meeting their numbers were smaller, and their courage lower, than before: so that at the last, they concluded upon a perfectly colorless resolution, which did not commit the Conference by a single syllable that was more in favor of the Bishop of Capetown than of the Bishop of Natal. The entanglement of the complicated relations of Church and State at Home were the chief obstacles to be contended with, no doctrinal sympathy with Colenso being expressed by anybody: but the failing to deal with the question in some way, was sure to be misunderstood as implying a doctrinal sympathy, or at least an indifference, so far as popular effect was concerned.

Meanwhile, the programme prepared by the Archbishop had been seen by many influential persons, not members of the Conference, and had failed to give universal satisfaction. Dr. Pusey in particular, wrote a most earnest letter to my Father, desiring that three alterations of importance should be made. First, those words should be struck out, that seemed to set up the Anglican Reformation as the model for all Christendom. Secondly, some words should be inserted, acknowledging that we had some faults and shortcomings as well as other Branches of the Catholic Church.[1] And thirdly, and most important, there should be express recognition of *six* General Councils, and not of *four* only: for the idea that the Anglican communion was about to throw overboard two whole General Councils accepted by all the orthodox heretofore, and expressly recognized in the Homilies, would be disastrous in the extreme. A personal interview of several hours with Dr. Pusey at Oxford enabled me to lay his views before my Father more fully than could well be done by letter: and this distinguished theologian doubtless made known his criticisms to other and more influential prelates than the Bishop of Vermont. But when the acts of the Conference came to be published, it was found that all the three blots were removed, and each of his requests was punctually complied with.

[1] This point was fully embodied in my Father's *Sermon*, see p. 406.

Chapter XXIII.

THE LAMBETH CONFERENCE.

ON Tuesday, September 24th, the Conference of seventy-eight Bishops met at Lambeth, more quietly than any seventy-eight Bishops had ever met before. They held their service in the Chapel where Provoost and White and Madison had been consecrated. The sermon was preached by the Bishop of Illinois, and the Holy Eucharistic Sacrifice was offered: but no one was permitted to be present except the Bishops,[1] and there was no note of music from beginning to end.

On proceeding to business,[2] it was found that the introductory Resolution on the programme gave rise to discussions which consumed the whole day, and the debate was adjourned to the morrow. That introduction included two of the points objected to by Dr. Pusey,—the setting up Anglicanism as a model, and the recognizing of only four General Councils. On this last subject my Father moved that the four be changed to "*six*," and sup-

---

[1] On walking over Lambeth Bridge with my Father that morning, I found at the Palace gate a little crowd of Americans and others, all indignant at the order for secret sessions, and that those who had travelled thousands of miles to be present, should have the doors of the Conference room shut in their faces. Each morning of the session I walked over from our Hotel to the inner gate of the Palace with my Father, and came back for him in the afternoon, pacing before that gate an hour or so, or waiting in the Hall up-stairs, until he made his appearance wearied out with the excitement of the day's discussions. The Archbishop had kindly invited us to be his guests at Addington during the session: but when my Father found that he should be compelled to oppose the published programme, he felt it more delicate to excuse himself, on the ground that the ten miles to and fro from Addington to Lambeth and back again every day would be a serious addition to the fatigues of the session, which at his advanced age would not be advisable: and therefore we continued to enjoy the hospitality of our Hotel,—the parlor of the Presiding Bishop being naturally a sort of headquarters for the American Bishops in attendance.

[2] It may be interesting to some to know the order of arrangement in which the Bishops sat. The Archbishop was in the centre, in the President's chair. On his right hand sat the Archbishop of Armagh, then the Presiding Bishop of the Church in the United States, then the Primus of the Scottish Church, then the Metropolitan of Sydney. On the President's left hand sat first the Archbishop of Dublin, then the Metropolitans of Montreal, New Zealand, and Capetown. The other Bishops sat in a body before them, without any special designation of order or place.

ported his amendment in an earnest speech, in which he showed the immense importance, in the controversies of the present day, of the action of the Fifth and Sixth General Councils: for the Fifth had condemned a number of errors, some of which were identical with some of those set forth by Colenso; while the Sixth was famous for having condemned Pope Honorius as a heretic. The omission of these two General Councils, therefore, would be, as he urged, a triumph both to Colensoists and Romanists, the two chief parties with whom the Church was at present compelled to fight the good fight of Faith. His amendment was not carried in that precise form: but to the effect of his speech it was mainly due that the phrase was finally settled as "the undisputed General Councils," which is the same thing: the mover of this amendment being the (late) Bishop of Winchester.

On Thursday the Colenso matter came up. When the Colonial part of the programme was reached, the Metropolitan of New Zealand rose and moved the amendment finally agreed on by the Colonial Bishops in their meeting at Archdeacon Wordsworth's. It declared

> That, in the judgment of the Bishops now assembled, the whole Anglican Communion is deeply injured by the present condition of the Church in Natal; and that a Committee be now appointed at this general meeting [to consider the case and inquire into all the proceedings which have been taken therein, and] to report on the best mode by which the Church may be delivered from the continuance of this scandal, and the true faith maintained. That such report be forwarded to his Grace the Lord Archbishop of Canterbury, with the request that he will be pleased to transmit the same to all the Bishops of the Anglican Communion, and to ask for their judgment thereupon.

But in the speech which he made on moving this, the courageous Bishop of New Zealand went beyond the text of his amendment, and declared that the whole question, "Do we believe that the judgment of the Bishop of Capetown is valid or not?" ought to be met and settled by the Conference. He was seconded by the Bishop of Montreal.

The Bishop of Vermont then rose and declared it impossible for him, on such a question, to content himself with voting for a resolution which did not utter a syllable of sympathy for the

Bishop of Capetown any more than for the Bishop of Natal: and which, by proposing a Committee to inquire afresh into the whole case, put it in the power of the friends of Colenso to claim that it was the acts of the Bishop of Capetown which were to be inquired into and reported on, rather than anything said or done by the Bishop of Natal. He could not consent to leave it thus doubtful which party was really on trial. He therefore moved the following substitute for the resolution offered by the Bishop of New Zealand:—

Whereas the Bishops of the Holy Catholic Church in communion with the Church of England hold it to be their sacred and imperative duty to maintain the unerring truth of the Holy Scriptures, as the Divinely inspired rule of Christian faith and practice, and to condemn as false and heretical all doctrine which is opposed to the same;

And whereas Doctor John William Colenso, sometime Bishop of Natal, has taught and published many great and grievous errors, against the authority of the Holy Scriptures, and utterly subversive of the Catholic Faith, which errors have been condemned by the Convocations of Canterbury and York, by the Synod of the Episcopal Church in Scotland, by the General Convention of the Protestant Episcopal Church in the United States, and by every Provincial Synod of the Colonial Churches;[1]

And whereas the said Doctor John William Colenso, after due and repeated admonitions, has been deposed and excommunicated by the Metropolitan of the Province of South Africa, with the unanimous consent of the Synod, for the said grievous and notorious errors, involving the most destructive heresy, and nevertheless refuses obstinately to submit himself to the united voice of the whole Anglican Communion, and now contumaciously acts in defiance of the same, scattering and oppressing the flock of Christ which he was appointed to gather and to feed with the saving truth of the everlasting Gospel:

Therefore, *Resolved*, That the Bishops of the Holy Catholic Church assembled from every quarter of the Anglican Communion in this present Conference, do hereby declare their entire approval of the deposition and excommunication of the said Doctor John William Colenso, as valid, righteous and just. And while they abstain from pronouncing any opinion concerning the judgment of the secular courts, they will hold themselves bound to regard the said Doctor John William Colenso as a heretic, cut off from the communion of the Church, until, by the grace of God, he shall renounce his grievous errors, and be openly reconciled by lawful authority, for which we devoutly pray.

---

[1] This last statement is a little too strong, but the inaccuracy was unintentional.

This substitute he supported in a speech of great earnestness and vigor, handling the subject with a boldness and pungency which made a decided impression upon the Conference. He was supported bravely by the Bishop of Salisbury, whose manly and outspoken defence of the right on this occasion my Father often afterwards spoke of with grateful admiration: but, if I am correctly informed, no other English Bishop stood with him in this.[1] The battle was left to the Colonial and American Bishops.

All the opposition, however, came from the English Bishops. The Bishop of S. David's—their chief spokesman on this occasion—rose and objected to the discussion of the subject in any way whatever.[2] He protested against entering into the question, on the ground that to do so would be a breach of faith towards himself and perhaps others; and he threw himself upon the President's "honor and good faith." The President was in so delicate and disagreeable a predicament, that he did not at once speak out. A long discussion ensued as to whether the whole case should be gone into or not, during which several Bishops, especially those of New Zealand and Grahamstown, declared that they were not bound by the Archbishop's programme, of which they knew nothing until they reached England; whereas they had come from the ends of the earth expressly for the discussion of this question. The Bishop of New Zealand added that it would be most unfair if Bishops, who had been accused of uncanonical proceedings, and claimed inquiry, were not heard; and dwelt

---

[1] I am not quite sure as to the time at which the Bishop of Salisbury spoke: but of the fact, and the impression produced thereby on my Father, there is no doubt.

[2] The account of this debate—with some additions mainly concerning my Father's action—is taken almost word for word from the letter written by the Bishop of Capetown on the 24th of February, 1868, after consulting the *verbatim* Report at Lambeth to refresh his memory. His letter was published in the *Guardian*, and was thence copied into the *Church Journal* of April 1, 1868. It closed a discussion which began with the original account of that debate given in the New York *Church Journal*, and which was thence copied into the English papers, drawing out two letters to the *Guardian* from the Bishop of St. David's. These letters were ingenious attempts on the part of his Lordship to prove that the *Church Journal* account was "grossly inaccurate," in which he signally failed. The Bishop of Capetown wrote two letters in reply. He says, however, "I have not professed to give a report of this most interesting but most painful discussion,—I should not have felt justified in doing so,—but I have stated very briefly what is deeply imprinted on my mind; and which I find to be verified by the authorized report of our proceedings." Imperfect as it is, however, it is the fullest that has as yet seen the light.

strongly upon the Bishop of S. David's assertions upon the subject in his late *Charge*. During that discussion the Bishop of S. David's appealed *four times* to the President, and called upon him to close the debate, as its continuance would be a breach of a solemn engagement.[1] At length the Archbishop, thus compelled to speak, ruled that neither the Bishop of Vermont's substitute nor the Bishop of S. Andrew's amendment (which had been moved during the debate, and with which the Bishop of Capetown had expressed himself satisfied) could be submitted to the

---

[1] In his letter to the *Guardian*, dated February 15, 1868, the Bishop of S. David's while doing his utmost to persuade his readers that the view given above was "an entirely erroneous impression," acknowledges that the introduction of the Colenso question was "a breach of the *tacit compact* under which I and perhaps others had attended the meeting—viz.: that the discussions were to be confined to the subjects of which notice had been given in the original announcement." A "tacit compact upon which I and perhaps others had attended the meeting" is a queer description of a "proposed" programme which was published to all the world alike. Dean Stanley, in a hot debate on the subject soon afterwards in the Convocation of Canterbury, used stronger language:—"There was a programme set forth by his Grace the Archbishop, but when the Bishops met, that programme was entirely set aside, and that too against his Grace's own wishes; and thus *the pledges given to persons inside and outside of this Convocation* were entirely broken through, and questions were brought forward and discussed which it was his Grace's intention should not be included in the programme." And again, he said, "We do know that his Grace *gave a pledge* that the question should not be discussed; and we also know that it *was* discussed, and that a resolution was arrived at respecting it." Dean Stanley thus understood even the neutral-tinted resolution moved by the Bishop of New Zealand to be a violation of the "compact" or "pledge," as well as the substitute offered by the Bishop of Vermont. By the passage of that resolution he declares that the Archbishop's "pledges" were "entirely broken through." But the Dean's dissatisfaction really dates still further back. In his letter to the Archbishop declining the use of the Abbey for the closing service, and written on the 21st of September—*three days before the Conference opened*—it is evident that he did not wait for the moving and carrying of the Bishop of New Zealand's substitute, to make up his mind: and in his introductory words he says "the allusions in his letter to the intentions of the Primate refer to *expressions used by his Grace* in *previous communications assuring him* that *all party questions would be avoided*." Then again, in the letter written to the Bishop of Vermont some days after the close of the Conference, Dean Stanley speaks of a pledge as made *to himself*:—"the pledge which *I* had received, that no question exciting party differences should be introduced into the meeting." In excluding the Conference from the Abbey because it was ready to defend the Catholic faith against Colenso, the Dean showed the rigidity of his conscientiousness in his guardianship of the Abbey, against all "party questions" or "polemical considerations." In subsequently communicating, by invitation, Mr. Vance Smith, the Unitarian minister who could not join in the Nicene Creed, the Dean showed the elasticity of his conscientiousness to be equally remarkable. Of course, in *that* act, there was no regard paid by him to "party or polemical considerations." But nevertheless, to us outsiders, at a distance, it seems that whether the Dean's rigidity or his elasticity is to be employed in any given case, depends solely upon whether the Catholic faith is to be defended, or betrayed.

Conference: but that it was no breach of the previous understanding to discuss, amend or adopt the Bishop of New Zealand's motion. The Bishop of Vermont, on this decision, rose and withdrew his substitute, making a closing speech, however, in which he alluded to the pressing and imperative importance of the question; spoke of his own advanced years, and of the short time within which he must stand before the Judge,—the great Head of the Church,—to render his account; and said that his sense of responsibility to the Master would not have permitted him, for any earthly consideration, to say one word less than he had said that day. But the responsibility, he added, was now in other hands, and there he left it.

The Bishop of Capetown then rose and stated that he had had no intimation, when invited to attend the Conference, that there would be any restriction put upon it as to the subjects to be discussed thereat; that had he been informed that this case would not be gone into, he would not have come; that he had hoped to enjoy the opportunity of vindicating himself from the aspersions which had been cast upon him and upon his proceedings; and that there should have been some expression on the part of the members of the Conference, either that they did, or that they did not, accept the validity of the spiritual sentence upon Colenso. He then read a resolution which he had himself intended to submit to the Conference, and sat down, saying that he submitted to the ruling of the President.

The Bishop of New Zealand's resolution was then adopted, omitting, at the suggestion of the President himself, the words enclosed above in brackets.[1] The Bishop of Oxford (now of Winchester) a few moments after, privately asked my Father to permit the use of his substitute as a *Declaration* to be signed by as many of the Bishops as might desire so to do: but he declined, on the ground of delicacy; saying that if any paper of that sort were to be signed, it ought not to be left to an American Bishop to originate it. He therefore brought his substitute home with him, and on reaching his room in the Hotel endorsed on the back of it these words:—" Resolution offered at the Council of

[1] See page 414.

"Resolutions of
Synod at the
Convent of Lambeth, but not acted on, because of the understanding between the Archbishop & the Bishop of St. Davids' that the subject of Dr. Colenso should not be introduced
London, Sept 26, 1867.

Lambeth, but not acted on, because of the understanding between the Archbishop and the Bishop of S. David's that the subject of Dr. Colenso should not be introduced. London, September 26, 1867."[1]

But the discussion had gone too deep into the hearts and consciences of the Bishops to lie still under the Archbishop's private understanding with some few individuals. On the last day of the session, Friday, the Bishop of S. Andrew's earnestly appealed to the Bishop of S. David's to waive his "understanding" with the Archbishop, in order to introduce for action a *Declaration* drawn up by the Bishop of Oxford touching the fact of the present *status* of Dr. Colenso. But the Bishop of S. David's refused to waive a pledge which had been given to others besides himself. The *Declaration* referred to was then produced, notwithstanding, as a paper signed " by the Bishops assembled at Lambeth," the words " in Conference " being omitted; and it was signed in the same room, and during the continuance of the session, by *fifty-six* of the Bishops.[2] Nor was this all: for the same morning papers which published the Synodical Letter of the Lambeth Conference, published also the fact that a faithful and orthodox priest had been appointed to be consecrated in place of the deposed and excommunicated Colenso. The Committee on the Bishop of New Zealand's resolution, moreover, in their Report to the adjourned meeting of the Conference in December, covered pretty much the whole ground of the "substitute" that was ruled out in September; and it was received and published without a word of opposition.

On two other points my Father spoke in the September meeting of the Conference. One of the English Bishops made a well-meant but not a very happy allusion to the American

---

[1] The original is before me as I write. The Bishop of Capetown mentioning in his Letter of February 24, 1868, that the Bishop of Vermont's substitute did not appear on the Record at Lambeth, but that a blank had been left for its insertion, I forwarded a copy of it to the Archbishop of Canterbury, on the 27th of March, 1868, that the blank in the Record might be filled. The endorsement is photographed on the opposite page.

[2] The sole foundation for doing such a work in such a way, was the *fact* that the " private understanding with the Archbishop" excluded any more direct dealing with the subject: and courtesy towards him forbade the pushing of a decision over his head.

Bishops, as not enjoying the advantages of a union between Church and State. This brought out from the Bishop of Vermont a rejoinder which, without attacking the position of the Church Establishment in England, so pointedly put the case on the other side as to call forth the enthusiastic admiration of many of the American Bishops who afterwards spoke of it.

The other point was, as to the publication of the stenographic Report of the proceedings, which had been resolved on at the preliminary meeting. But the Colenso episode had made a change. The good Archbishop's blunder was a very uncomfortable blunder for him, and for many of the English Bishops: and the Colonial and American Bishops were courteously unwilling to add to his annoyance by publicity. But the trouble was, how to avoid it. The first alteration of the original resolution was, that the publication should be made, with such omissions as the President should deem judicious. It was soon seen, however, that to make clean work of this, the Report would be something like "the play of Hamlet, with the part of Hamlet left out." So, at the close, it was resolved that the stenographic Report should be written out in full, and laid up in the archives in Lambeth, to be consulted only by Bishops; and even by them, not for publication. In vain did my Father oppose this Resolution. Two American Bishops,—but, so far as known, only two,[1] —opposed him; and the amiable Archbishop was evidently so little desirous of full publication, that with few affirmative votes and still fewer in the negative, the resolution was carried. Before leaving England, my Father made a pressing application to the Archbishop for a transcript of the stenographic Report, to be made at the expense of the American Bishops and for their use. He urged this on the very reasonable ground that "Our absent brethren have a right to know what we said and did as representing them." But the reply was a polite and even kind refusal;— the Archbishop " could not, consistently with the expressed will and judgment of the Conference, comply with the request. He held out hopes, however, that something might be done about it at the adjourned meeting in December; and then, accordingly, a resolution was adopted:—

[1] The Bishops of Ohio and New York.

That his Grace be requested, if applied to by the House of Bishops in the Episcopal Church in the United States of America, to allow a copy of the Records of the Conference to be made for them, and to be lodged in the hands of such officer as shall be designated by the House of Bishops to receive it, for reference by Bishops only, but not for publication.

If any such request has ever been made by our House of Bishops, it has been so quietly done that nobody has ever heard of it. Such a copy here would be as useless as the original is in Lambeth.

The September session, it was thought, would be over at 2 o'clock in the afternoon of Friday: but it did not end until nearly three hours later. Those outside who had long been waiting the close, heard faintly the familiar tones of the *Gloria in Excelsis*, as led by the voice of an American Bishop: and, after the Archbishop's Blessing of Peace, all issued forth; but not at once to rest. Weary as they were with their protracted and exciting work, they were waylaid by photographers on reaching the gate, and were detained till they had been twice pictured by the sun. Once more the homeward way was resumed: but coaches urged by furious drivers rushed after them, chased them down in the open streets, captured them and carried them off in triumph to the *Conversazione* in St. James's Hall, where a patient crowd had been awaiting them for three hours. The indefatigable Archbishop was already in the chair, and after the presentation of an address of welcome to the American, Scottish and Colonial Bishops present, on the part of the Venerable Society for the Propagation of the Gospel, the American Presiding Bishop was first called on, and made a brief response. The Bishop of Capetown received a perfect tempest of applause. Many brief and telling speeches were made, the Bishop of Oxford happily saying that "they had not looked in the faces of their American brethren for nothing." After the speeches, and a Benediction, the Bishops mingled with the crowd of eager and interested Churchmen, the Archbishop leading the way, and taking with him the Bishop of Vermont, thus visibly exemplifying the fraternal unity of the Churches of England and America.

A large number of the Bishops and clergy dined that evening at Fulham, as the guests of the Bishop of London, the Presiding Bishop of the American Church being called to the right hand of his host. He was also one of the Bishops present at the concluding religious service of the Conference in the church of S. Mary, Lambeth, on Saturday morning, the service being full choral, with processional, a large surpliced choir of men and boys, a sermon by the Metropolitan of Montreal, and the Holy Eucharist: the Archbishop being celebrant, and the Hallelujah Chorus bursting forth triumphantly after the hush that followed the Blessing of Peace.

The exhaustion of this week's work was not a little felt by my Father. It was no great price to pay for the prominent position he had found himself compelled to take in the leading topics of debate;[1] but it made me anxious that he should have some immediate opportunity for repose. He therefore declined the kind and pressing invitations to attend the Church Congress which met at Wolverhampton the week after the adjournment of the Conference of Lambeth: but started at once, on Saturday after-

---

[1] This work is a Biography of the Bishop of Vermont, not a full history of the Lambeth Conference; and what is here said concerning my Father must not be interpreted as an intended disparagement of any other Bishop's share in that noble work. I have no wish to exaggerate that which is sufficiently honorable when stated with simple truth; but I prefer to state it in the words of others. Shortly after my Father's decease, the Bishop of New York—no enthusiastic admirer of him at any time—thus wrote: "In a good old age, in the highest position to which he could be raised in our Branch of the Church, carrying with him a distinguished reputation for learning and the gifts of speech, he had participated with signal credit to himself in an Ecclesiastical Council, certainly the most remarkable of his time, and in some respects, one of most remarkable of any age of the Christian Church. There can be no indelicacy in saying that on one or two occasions he spoke with such vigor and eloquence, and, in cases where there could have been no opportunity for special preparation, he brought his learning to bear with such readiness and force, that he received the thanks and congratulations of some of the most eminent members of the House." And the Bishop of Quebec, in his brief glowing address at the Burial, said: "One scene there is of his public life, concerning which I *can* speak as a competent witness. In that great assembly of Bishops, which was not long since convened at Lambeth, I saw him stand conspicuous—a Pillar of the Church. In that great assembly, where men so various in their gifts and acquirements, so various in their habits of mind, and in their habits of life—where the ripe Scholar emerging from his library, and the Missionary hastening from his toil and his travel—met face to face; . . . in that great assembly, when opened for counsel and debate, he bore himself as one in whom all might recognize a Master in Israel; as one in whom you might gladly recognize a representative man, the first Bishop of your Church. Replete with learning, ready of utterance, without fear and without favor, he contended earnestly for the faith once delivered to the Saints, and contributed in no slight measure to the prosperous issue of our deliberations. In how manful a manner he subsequently upheld the dignity of our insulted body—with how just a severity he administered rebuke, when rebuke was needed—is known to all."

noon, for Paris, spending the Sunday at Brighton, as the guest of the President of the English Church Union, who was a parishioner of S. Michael's.

It was the Feast of the Dedication of that parish church; and here my Father, for the first and only time in his life, saw a really high ritualistic service of the Anglican rite: though even here there was no incense used. At 8.30 P.M. that Saturday evening the procession entered the Church, the Cross carried aloft at the head of it being a genuine thirteenth century Crucifix newly gilded. The choristers and acolytes were in red cassocks with cottas; a number of priests followed in embroidered copes, some of which were of cloth of gold; two deacons in richly embroidered and apparelled dalmatics preceded the Bishop, one of them carrying a jewelled mitre before him; and last of all was the Bishop of Vermont, in his own robes,—the least ornate of the lengthened line. The procession moved all the way down the North aisle, then round and up the middle alley, singing all the way, "We march, we march to victory." The hymn was repeated over several times, the crowd being so dense that it was only with the greatest difficulty and long delays that the procession could make its way through at all: but it was sung with unflagging spirit and a true triumphal ring, owing to the success achieved for the Truth in the Conference at Lambeth, for which the Daily Sacrifice had been offered at the Altar of that Church, as at many hundreds of others in England and elsewhere, on each day of the Session. Nor was it the crowd alone that was remarkable: but the spirit of worship seemed to pervade every member of it, so that the processional Hymn was joined in by voices from every part of the Church. Apparently, there was not a single lounger, or mere sight-seer, present. Great numbers were of the working classes, yet taking so lively an interest in the services that though some wealthier persons in the other crowd outside the doors, who could not get in, offered as high as a guinea to any one inside who would give up his place for that service, no one inside was poor enough to accept the offer. The next day, Sunday, there were three early celebrations; and at the High Service at 11 o'clock, the Bishop of Vermont preached a brief sermon: and there were Altar lights, and flowers, and gorgeous vestments, and the solid unison of Gregorian Psalter and Canticles, with rich anthem and abundance of most elaborate music, far exceeding even what had given glory to the previous evening; while the full choral Vespers that day fell in no way behind. All the sermons preached at these services were extemporaneous in delivery.

The impression produced on my Father by this new experience was very deep and strong. He spoke of it, repeatedly, as "a new revelation to him of the reality and power of *worship*, such as he had never dreamed it possible that he should see in our Communion. Every individual of those crowds," he said, "seemed absorbed in devotion, as if all had but one heart and one soul." He openly expressed his delight, at the table of his host: but playfully rallied the clergy (the Rev. Thomas W. Perry is one of the clergy of that parish) on their inconsistency in not yet having had the courage to add incense to all the rest. His pressure on that point was taken very kindly.

On Monday evening we left for New Haven, crossing the Channel to Dieppe the next morning, and arriving about dusk at Rouen. Learning that there would be service at the Cathedral that evening, we went there in season. The vast nave was dark, except here and there a feeble taper to point the way: and through the deep and silent gloom, which echoed to every footfall, we paced the stone floor together till we reached the lighted Lady Chapel at the further end. There we found a little company of women and girls assembled, we being the only men except the priest and his acolyte. The service was mostly in French, and seemed to be a Litany of the Blessed Virgin, though we had no books, and were neither of us sufficiently familiar with spoken French to follow readily the rapid utterance of the priest. It was followed by the Benediction of the Host. We took *prie-dieus* at our entrance, and my Father remained on his knees until the end of the whole service. We could offer up our own devotions along with our fellow Catholics, even if we could not follow intelligently all the words in which they offered theirs.

At Rouen, my Father wished to purchase some small article as a personal present to my Mother—the only thing of the kind he ever did during his whole married life. He used to say,

"Where is the use of my making her any special present? Everything I have is hers, anyhow, and myself in the bargain." But for some reason he made an exception at Rouen, and bought a little Angel standing over a shell for the holding of Holy Water. He would have chosen in preference a beautiful Crucifix of carved ivory, which he long held in his hands and gazed at wishfully: its high price alone preventing his choosing it. The little Angel reached home safely, and has hung ever since over the bed of her for whom it was purchased. But it was in the constant yearning homage of the heart, ever felt though never allowed to interfere with duty to the Church, that his love for her was the most tenderly shown; and in comparison of this, the ordinary making of presents seems commonplace enough. As it was my first visit to Europe, I was naturally anxious to prolong our stay. Even one week more I should have been thankful for. And he was perfectly willing that I should remain as long as I pleased. But he insisted on going home himself, whether or no, in the steamer of the 15th. "My son," he said gently, "your dear Mother counts the days until my return, and I cannot consent to make her count a single day in vain."

On Wednesday afternoon we reached Paris, where my Father spent a very quiet week, the guest of Dr. and Mrs. Theodore Evans, whom he had united in marriage a few years before in Burlington. He went out little, and saw next to nothing of Paris, his main business being to rest. On Sunday, however, besides preaching twice,[1] he attended for the only time in his life, the Oriental Service at the Russian Church, with which he was exceedingly pleased. He was courteously invited within the Holy Doors during the Divine Liturgy: and testified on his return that there was no "superstition" in anything that he saw there.

On Friday morning, the 11th of October, we left our kind friends in Paris, arriving in London the same day in the evening; Monday afternoon brought us to Liverpool; and on Tuesday

[1] One English Clergyman, owing to his great admiration of "*The Law of Ritualism*," walked the whole length of the City on Sunday night through the rain, to hear my Father preach at the Anglo-American Chapel which was opened for service during the *Exposition Universelle*.

evening we took possession of our berths on the steamer *Minnesota*, the twin ship of the *Chicago*. To our agreeable surprise we found that, meanwhile, Capt. Price and all his officers had been transferred from the *Chicago* to the *Minnesota*, so that we were at home on board from the first. The lights of the city luridly streaming over the dark, rough water, while the moon dubiously struggled with heavy clouds above, were our farewell glimpse of dear Old England.

Our return voyage was very stormy, with obstinate gales dead ahead the whole way, except a day or two. The motion of the vessel interfered so grievously with my Father's sleep at night, that his ingenuity was stimulated to find a remedy. He made friends with the steward, and procured an extra mattress, which he placed upright, on edge, against the back of his berth; drawing the other mattress out a little, and turning part of it up as a protection against immediate contact with the board in front. Thus firmly wedged and cushioned on and between two mattresses, he slept as sweetly and as soundly as if there were neither winds nor waves on the outside.

The tedium of the stormy days was relieved by several *impromptu* evening concerts, in which a number of the passengers took their parts, aided by more than one recruit from among the ship's company; and my Father entered into the spirit of these pleasant acts of friendliness very heartily. Most of his time during the day was spent in reading: the Rev. Thomas W. Perry's work on the *Declaration on Kneeling* (given him by the Author) being perused with great care, and with entire conviction as to the soundness of its positions and the conclusiveness with which they are there demonstrated. On both the Sundays that we passed on shipboard he preached, though the motion of the vessel made it no very easy task. On the latter of the two, in the evening, as we were all expecting soon to reach port, he very beautifully alluded to the pleasantness of our brief companionship on board as interfering in no wise with the earnestness of our desire to reach our homes: and then showed that we were all, on earth, but travellers and pilgrims, and our hearts should be filled, even amidst the highest joys of this life, with an equal yearning after the infinitely greater and dearer happiness that awaits the faithful in their eternal Home in heaven.[1] So strong was the impression made by his gentle sweetness and cheerful patience during the voyage, that one after another of the lady passengers kissed the old man good-bye when they parted from him for ever in this world on the deck of the steamer in the harbor of New York.

The first act on shore, on Thursday, October 31, was to relieve the anxious hearts at Home by a telegraphic despatch; and on All Saints' day, in the afternoon, we reached Burlington in safety. There his faithful help-meet awaited him; and he found to his grateful surprise, that nearly half the Clergy of his Diocese had assembled to greet their Bishop. A little after six o'clock the procession entered the Church, chaunting the 122nd Psalm, *Lætatus sum*. The *Te Deum* was sung, and thanks were offered for a safe return from sea. An Address of affectionate welcome was then presented on the part of the Clergy. The Bishop, in response, gave at some length an account of the Conference and of the great work which it had accomplished, closing with words of thankful content with his own position in Vermont, and with that of the American Church as compared with the English. He also uttered hopeful anticipations concerning the "new era" that "had now opened in the history of the Church of England": for, as he understood it, "the closing resolution of the Conference not only recognized the importance of the meeting, but settled the certainty that there are to be similar meetings hereafter." The *Encyclical Letter* of the Conference was then read by one of the

---

[1] This thought found expression—as often before—in verse.

> Rolling, rolling, rolling
> On the restless sea :

thus the stanzas began : while the warmth of our longings for the dear ones at Home is contrasted with the coldness of our desires for a better world. This simple poem ended thus:—

> Alas ! the hope that rises
> Most fondly in the heart,
> Clings to our earthly prizes,
> Unwilling to depart !
> But yet, no more beguiling,
> When our last hour draws near,
> We'll leave those treasures smiling,
> Though smiling through a tear.

These were the last verses he ever wrote.

Clergy, all standing; the *Gloria in Excelsis* was sung by the whole congregation: and after the Benediction, the 150th Psalm, *Laudate Dominum*, was chaunted as the Bishop and Clergy retired. It was not until after thus giving thanks to God for his safe return, that my Father at length went out to his own house, and found himself once more safe and well at his beloved Rock Point.

Chapter XXIV.

AT HOME.

DURING my Father's absence abroad, the enlargement of S. Paul's Church, Burlington, in accordance with his designs, had been steadily carried on, under the energetic lay guidance to which allusion has already been made. And the satisfaction of the congregation with the services of the young priest whom he had called as an assistant, and who had taken the entire charge during his absence, was so general, that the Bishop of the Diocese soon found himself once more relieved from the pleasing burden of parish work. He wrote with his own hand the resolution calling his successor; and on the morning of the Sunday following, informed the congregation of the change, and transferred them to their new rector with an affectionate and cordial address which brought tears to the eyes of many. In their parting letter to him the vestry said:—

We shall never willingly forget the cheerful alacrity with which you came forward in our time of need, to undertake the charge of the parish, when the gravity of your other and higher duties might well have been offered as an excuse: nor the Christian courtesy and considerate regard for the feelings of all concerned that accompanied your retirement from the office, when time and circumstances enabled you to be relieved.

He was now free to devote himself once more wholly to the Diocese and to the Church at large. There were, of course, heavy arrearages of correspondence awaiting his attention on his return: and one of the delayed letters which soon reached him was from Dr. Stanley, Dean of Westminster, attempting to convey some sort of excuse for his refusal of the use of the Abbey for the closing service of the Lambeth Conference. The refusal was felt very deeply and keenly by the Bishops present at the Conference. But the whole story had better be told, as it was conversationally understood in London at the time.

The entire privacy of the opening service has been a mystery to many. One would naturally have supposed that the greatest possible *éclat* would have been gladly given to the opening of such an extraordinary meeting of Bishops. And the explanation of it is to be found in that same Colenso business, which, by that " honorable understanding " or " compact," was to be kept out of the Conference altogether, and which was, nevertheless, the controlling subject at the beginning, middle and end of the whole affair. The only Anglican Bishop in the world not expressly invited, was Bishop Colenso. But as he persisted in the claim that his condemnation, deposition and excommunication were all null and void, some people in England were firmly persuaded that he meant to come, and thrust himself upon the Lambeth Conference, uninvited. Moreover, Dean Stanley was well known to be a sympathizer with Colenso doctrinally, though no one could exactly say how far : and had again and again taken his part—or at least opposed Colenso's opponents—in every public discussion in which he had borne a part. If the opening service should be held in the Abbey, and Colenso, freshly arrived from Africa, should come forward and attempt to communicate at the Holy Eucharist, Dean Stanley, having the legal control of the building and its services, would, it was feared, communicate the excommunicated heretic as unscrupulously as he afterwards did Mr. Vance Smith, the Unitarian : and there would have been no possibility of avoiding an abominable scandal at the outset. Dean Milman, of S. Paul's Cathedral, was supposed to lean in the same direction, though not so mischievously aggressive as Dean Stanley. The monthly steamer from the Cape of Good Hope—on which alone it was probable that Colenso would come, if he came at all—was due at a time so near the day appointed for the Conference, that it was a simple necessity to complete the arrangements for the opening service before it was known whether he would come, or not. In Lambeth Chapel, the Archbishop was supreme; and the exclusion of the black sheep (or shepherd, rather) was a certainty. But, a few days before the Conference actually met, the Cape steamer had arrived. Colenso was not on board. It was certain that he could not arrive in England within a month. And, that being the case, overtures were made for the use of Westminster Abbey for the closing service, which would then have been of a character to atone for the quietness of the opening.

But now was Dean Stanley's turn. Whether he deserved suspicion or not, he knew that the Conference had not trusted him: and by his refusal of the use of the Abbey he showed how deep was his distrust of the Conference. He tried to avoid the palpable insult to the American and other Bishops who were then the invited guests of the Church of England, by parading them at some neutral-tinted service, while refusing them admittance as members of the Conference. He seemed to think that an American Bishop would be so glad to be seen, robed, in Westminster Abbey, that he would meekly accept any humiliation from the Dean who opened the door. But this unworthy dodge was unanimously rejected in the Conference, and a feeling was created which was hardly what the Dean expected or desired.[1] Hence his letter to the Bishop of Vermont, as Presiding Bishop, in the hope of covering or smoothing over the *faux pas* so far as the American Bishops were concerned.

This letter my Father heard of in England, but the divergences of travel so separated him from the American Bishop to whose hands it was confided, that it was not received until after his return to Burlington. He immediately sat down and wrote his reply, which he sent to me to be published in New York together with Dean Stanley's letter, "if," as he modestly wrote me, "you judge it advisable." The letter was printed at once, and was copied successively into nearly if not quite all the Church papers in the Anglican Communion,—even so far off as South Africa and Australia. And the satisfaction expressed was remarkably unanimous, except from a very small section. The old man's eye might be growing dim; but it was clear that the natural force of his mind and pen was by no means abated. Nothing that he had ever done had caused so universal a feeling of satisfaction, as this thorough setting-down administered to Dean Stanley.

[1] In spite of his repeated invitations, only *four* of the American Bishops ever made themselves known to him when visiting the Abbey. On the part of the rest "no response was made."

Copies of this letter have been so often asked for, and are now so difficult to procure, that the correspondence is reprinted in the *Appendix*,[1] together with an additional note from the Dean,[2] showing how deeply he regretted the slight apparently put upon the American Bishops, and how earnestly anxious he was to obliterate, if possible, all unpleasant traces of it. But it was too late. It was a bad business, and could not be mended. And the Dean, therefore, wisely left my Father's published letter unnoticed.

Immediately on finding himself free, the Bishop of Vermont resolved to undertake a winter visitation of his whole Diocese. This he had not attempted for many years; and on being earnestly remonstrated with by his family and others, against this reckless exposure of his health, his only reply was, "The night cometh, when no man can work." The appointments were sent out at once, bearing date only two days after his return from England. On Sunday the 1st of December—at the request of the new Rector, who had met with a domestic affliction—the Bishop preached, for the last time in S. Paul's Church, from the words, "So teach us to number our days that we may apply our hearts unto wisdom": and what he said concerning his long service among them, and the giving over of the work to younger hands, and the near approach of the time of his departure, was afterwards recalled by the people as bearing a deeper meaning than any of them dreamed at the time.

The next day a clergyman who had much conversation with him on the way from Burlington to Rutland, asked him, among other things, why he did not remain longer abroad after the Lambeth Conference: and his answer was, that "he felt that he must come home and set his house in order, for he was persuaded that his time was nearly spent, his work nearly done." And when further asked, how he had acquired such calm and cheerful fearlessness in prospect of death, he replied: "By contemplating the blessed change that awaits us,—the glory that lies beyond, the glory that shall be revealed." And as he ceased speaking,

---

[1] Pp. 472 *et seqq.*
[2] I have added in the *Appendix* the Dean's letter to the *Guardian* also, so that I believe every word that he has said for himself will be found there.

he gazed thoughtfully upon the distant mountains, within sight of which they were then passing. In this connection it may be added that the last book found open upon his table was one concerning the New Jerusalem.

The visitation began on the morrow, the 3d of December, with the meeting of his Convocation at Windsor. Every day thereafter, except Saturdays, an appointment was kept, in the Southern part of the Diocese, closing with the two parishes of Poultney and Wells on the Fourth Sunday in Advent. On Monday he returned Home with a severe cold,—his usual winter companion for many years previous: but it was accompanied by headache, which was a rare thing with him. He wrote me, on Tuesday, "If I do not feel better to-morrow, I shall postpone the rest of my parochial visits until Spring, for I know how anxious you are to have the old Presiding Bishop take care of himself, in the hope that it may please God to continue him to the Church a few years longer."

On Christmas-Day, Wednesday, finding himself a little better, he preached and celebrated in the Chapel of the Institute, his discourse being of "Peace, good-will towards men." One of the greatest comforts of his later years was to witness the steady growth of the Academic department of the Institute in success, both as to high reputation and numbers; and he was specially rejoiced at every ingathering of spiritual fruits from among the pupils. Most anxiously of all did he watch for indications, however slight, that some of those bright boys might hereafter prove worthy to be called to the sacred work of the Ministry of the Church. It was always a delight to him to worship and minister in that beautiful Chapel, which was more completely his own work than any other sanctuary on earth: and its dim religious light and quiet solemnity seemed always to communicate a thankful calmness to his spirit. He told his little flock on that Christmas morning, that he often preached to larger congregations, but to none that were so near and so dear to his heart as they.

On S. John's day he wrote the last letter I ever received from him. It said nothing about his health; but enclosed the last words which he ever sent for publication. These were, in reply, as Presiding Bishop, to a cordial *Address* from the London Society for Promoting Christian Knowledge to the American Bishops who attended the Lambeth Conference. In this reply, speaking of " our unity with our beloved Mother, the Church of England," he said :—

> The times in which we live demand the manifestation of this unity more and more. It was our conviction of this which induced us to accept so willingly the invitation of his Grace the Archbishop of Canterbury, and take our place among that great assembly of Bishops from every quarter of the world. We doubted not that it would be guided by the same Spirit who presided in the Primitive Councils. And we hailed the opportunity to give the best aid in our power to the sacred work of guarding the pure faith and promoting the saving influence of the Gospel of Christ, in accordance with the unerring Word of God and the Order of that Apostolic and " Holy Catholic Church " in which we profess to believe.

After describing the gratitude with which we American Churchmen look back to the nurturing care of the two venerable English Societies in our colonial days, he thus closes :—

> And we look forward with hope to the fruits of future effort, put forth in the vigor of active and primitive unity, with an humble dependence on that Divine Redeemer whose strength is made perfect in our weakness, in cordial sympathy with our beloved Mother Church, and in constant prayer that every member of her privileged Communion may be preserved by His grace from all false doctrine, heresy and schism, prospered in faith, in holiness, and charity, and finally united to Him in the perfect felicity of His heavenly and eternal Kingdom.

At the very moment when these words issued from the press in New York City, he who wrote them was struggling with death, and human skill confessed that it could do no more.

On the Sunday after Christmas, December 29, though his cold was still severe, he was at work again, in the Northern part of his Diocese, beginning at St. Alban's. During this last eight days of Episcopal labor, he visited eight parishes, preached nine times, and held eight confirmations, besides one in private. But almost all these parishes were off the railway lines, and could be reached in winter only by long drives in open sleighs; which, in the protracted term of bitterly cold weather that then prevailed, involved far too severe an exposure for one of his advanced years. At one time, on his way to Highgate, he was so severely chilled through, that it was more than an hour before he recovered his usual temperature. But he still persevered; and finding that they were not quite ready for him at Swanton and Fairfax, where he had expected to spend Sunday and Monday, he wrote to the Rev. William M. Ogden, rector of the parish at Plattsburgh, promising to spend the Sunday with him. Mr. Ogden had for some months been desiring greatly the visit of a Bishop, to confirm a large class. But the Bishop of New York (whose vast Diocese was then not yet divided) had been unable to come before leaving for Lambeth, and could not conveniently make a special visitation there after the winter had set in. At Mr. Ogden's instance, therefore, he requested the Bishop of Vermont to visit Plattsburgh and confirm for him. The Bishop of Vermont felt that his own Diocese had the first claim: but now that there was a vacant day,[1] it was cheerfully devoted in accordance with the Bishop of New York's request.

He arrived in Plattsburgh before noon on Saturday, in quite a flurry of snow, his cold being still oppressively severe. Though he had made an early start, and his journey had been tedious, he refused to lie down for rest, as he could never sleep in the daytime. He spent the afternoon in pleasant and cheerful conversation, leading the way to serious and important subjects, and yet with his usual good-humor and gentle raillery giving a freshness and ease to all he said. Among other things he ridiculed the wearing of the "bands," as "a foolish fashion" which originated "long subsequent to the time of the Reformation." He reasserted the principle for which he had fought so long, that the Church law of England was our Church law, unless we had legislated to the contrary: and claimed that we have now the same liberty in the use of Hymns that obtains in England. "If he could trust a candidate so as to ordain him," he said, "he would trust him to make his own selection of hymns." He expressed the pleasure given him by the Ritualistic services he had seen in

---

[1] He had made a previous appointment for S. Stephen's day, but was unwell enough then to send an apology. He thought himself better now.

England; but while he would allow a large liberty to others, he said it was not easy for an old man to change the habits of a lifetime, and he should continue his own usages pretty much the same to the end. Thus the afternoon and evening wore away. On Sunday morning he preached, and offered the Eucharistic Sacrifice for the last time. It was his *viaticum*. Confirmation was administered to a sick person in private during the afternoon. In the evening the Church was crowded, and twenty-one persons were confirmed, the Bishop preaching his last sermon on earth, on the words: *How shall we escape, if we neglect so great salvation?* The searching solemnity of that sermon deeply affected many who heard it, and is feelingly spoken of by them to this day. Thus closed his public ministry of forty-four years.

On Monday morning, the Feast of the Epiphany, he was at the early service, though having spent by no means a comfortable night. The next point was as to his return home. The intense cold weather still continued, and had already closed up with ice the narrower portions of the Lake. It was possible, however, that across the broad Lake, from Port Jackson to Burlington, a small steamer might still be running; and if so, he was very desirous to take that route, as it was only about one fourth as long as the other, and he could easily reach Home by daylight. The Sunday had been very severe, however, and his friends persuaded him that there was no reasonable chance that the boat could run, and that therefore he had better not expose himself in the bitter weather to the long drive in an open sleigh to Port Jackson, when it was so likely to be in vain. But when the sleigh drove to the door, with the cry, "Passengers for Port Jackson, to take the boat!" he suddenly changed his mind. The seven miles were traversed in vain. The boat did not run: and the seven miles were passed again in the same way. So much time was thus lost, that he had no opportunity either to warm himself or to dine, but barely caught the 3 P.M. train for Rouse's Point. With hardly any chance for refreshment, the slow hours wore away, bringing him through St. Alban's and towards Burlington some time after night-fall. At Winooski, about two miles from Burlington, the railway bridge across the river had lately been burned; and all the passengers were compelled to leave the train, and drive to Burlington in open sleighs. The sudden change from the overheated cars to the biting night wind with the thermometer 20° below zero, was too much for an endurance already so much overtaxed. On reaching Burlington, he was so benumbed with the cold, that he followed the kind suggestion of the driver, and went into the Central Hotel for awhile to warm himself. Before he was thoroughly comfortable, however, he was again in an open sleigh, facing the north wind over the two miles and a half that yet lay betwixt him and his Home. Arrived there at last, and thoroughly warmed, he enjoyed a late supper specially prepared for him. He seemed, indeed, in remarkably cheerful spirits, his heart being warmed by the evident growth of his Diocese. The Confirmations had been larger than ever before: and from present appearances, no less than *five* new parishes, he thought, would apply for admission to the next Diocesan Convention,—a thing unprecedented in the previous history of the Church in Vermont.

He retired late, but rose at his usual hour next morning, looking somewhat pale, but making no complaint. All the forenoon he worked at his correspondence, drawing cheques for some little bills that were due, and putting all his papers in order: and he continued this work heroically, though, from increasing pain, his handwriting became almost illegible. At one time, without informing any of the family, he attempted, by bathing his feet in hot water, to obtain some relief. But towards noon, he went down stairs, and informed my Mother that he believed he was about to be very ill;—that there were sharp pains all over his body, so that he was scarcely able to walk. He was soon made comfortable in bed: but the first few moments when he was alone, he rose, and without half clothing himself, walked out upon the porch in the open air, crying that he "was suffocating, he must have fresh air!" With such a beginning, and at his advanced age, there could have been little or no human chance of recovery from an attack of double pleura-pneumonia, which it proved to be. The oppression on the chest would not permit him long to lie down. The intense and constant pain, allowing him no real sleep until he slept to wake no more, was borne without a murmur, and with the utmost sweetness. The panting and gasping, with pain in every breath, made it almost impossible for him to utter a word that was not wrung from him by necessity. He said that he had all his life been praying "Thy Will be done": and it was time now that he should begin to suffer, if it were His will. His thankfulness for the past blessings of his whole life was often uttered, and the hopes of the life to come: but as to his sufferings there was only calm contentment, perfect resignation, and peace; his one anxiety being to avoid paining her who had for so many years been nearest and dearest to him on earth. It grieved him that he could say so little to her, nor even look his gratitude: and after some of her latest and tenderest ministerings, he slowly whispered in the midst of his agony, as if reproaching himself,— "And not even one smile in return for all your kindness!"[1] Everything that medical skill and affection could do was done, but without the slightest checking of an attack which seemed to have mastered the life from the moment it began. On Thursday morning, January 9th, he expressed his conviction that his work on earth was ended; and he spoke of death as calmly as he had done during the many years before it looked him in the face. Sitting, and in his library,—with the window open, to satisfy his one unappeasable craving for "fresh air"—he awaited the end. At nearly two o'clock in the afternoon, he feebly whispered, "I feel easier." Not long after, the oppressed breathing grew shorter and feebler. The hand fell helpless down at his side. He opened his eyes, and gazed for a moment intently upon vacancy, as if seeing there what no other eye could see,—perhaps the approaching angels: and then, while all were kneeling around him, and his son Theodore was offering up the Commendatory Prayer, the eyes fell, the head drooped gently, the breathing hushed softly: and he was at rest.

Of the outflow of public sympathy at so sudden a departure of such a man, extending not only through all our Church papers, but through the secular and sectarian press as well; of the letters of loving consolation from all manner of persons, from the Arch-

---

[1] With a spirit worthy of his, the first words of her widowhood were not uttered for herself: but "Oh! what a loss to the Church!" was the opening lamentation that passed her lips.

At Home. 439

bishop of Canterbury (who was so soon to follow him) down to the humble poor whom he had aided out of his own poverty in years gone by; of the tributes of the various bodies within the Church of which he had been a member; of the manifestations of admiration and love from abroad as well as at Home: this is not the place to speak in detail. Since the days of Bishop White, no Presiding Bishop had taken such hold on the popular heart of the Church. From Montreal to the uttermost parts of our own land, Churches were draped in mourning; sermons and addresses were made; and at some Altars the Holy Sacrifice was offered on the day and at the hour of his burial. And yet, in the midst of the grief, there was everywhere the nobler feeling of solemn joy that such an end had rounded and made perfect the story of such a life. To have fought his way through so many battles and storms; to have suffered so many disappointments and losses; to have endured so many years of obloquy and reproach: and at length to behold the success of that Diocesan School which was the darling of his old age; to see the reünion of his beloved country, and the more perfect reünion of his still more beloved Church; to aid in the growing revival of her truer and richer life and strength and beauty; to rejoice at the fulfilment of his own suggestions, and be present at the first free Council of the whole Anglican Communion, in such wise as to feel within it the germ of that which *may* bring about at last the reünion of all Christendom; to win, there, the deserved honor of being regarded as a chief pillar of truth and courage among all his brethren; and then to return and gather in—though it were in the frost of midwinter—richer spiritual harvests from his own hard tillage than he had ever reaped before: what better time than this could an old man find to die, even if a loving God had given him his own choice out of all the unknown future?

On the evening of Tuesday, January 14th, his Body was taken from the Episcopal residence, and conveyed more than two miles to the Church, accompanied by a number of the Diocesan clergy. It was placed in the tower porch. Under a solitary pendent light, the venerable face was seen, with its patriarchal beard, and the hands folded upon the breast over a cross of *arbor vitæ*--the Tree of Life. On the oaken coffin was a raised cross, extending the whole length and breadth of the lid, with the radiating crown at the intersection of the arms, and the foot resting upon a pyramid of eight steps, each step representing a decade of years.[1] Four of the younger clergy of the Diocese watched near by, in the nave of the Church, vested in surplice and stole, all the night long. At 9 o'clock on Wednesday morning the outer door was opened; and for three hours there was a constant stream of friends, high and low, rich and poor, one with another, who came to look for the last time upon those features placid in death, which they had known for so many years in the fulness of life and manly strength. Then the lid was closed. The pall spread over him was of deep purple silk, with a white cross extending the whole length and breadth, and was the same that was made for the burial of his old friend and colleague, Bishop Doane of New Jersey. On the pall lay his Pastoral Staff, wreathed with evergreen. And, notwithstanding the hardness of the winter, a cross and crown of the choicest flowers from the Church of the Advent in Boston, and wreaths of camellias from Albany, and of immortelles from Plattsburgh, were kept from the breath of the frost by the love of those who brought them, and covered the pall of death all over with the beauty and fragrance of life.

At noon, the procession of five Bishops and nearly fifty surpliced clergy from eight Dioceses moved down the broad alley of the Church towards the porch, and the Bishop of Quebec began the service, while eight of the leading laymen of the Diocese carried the Body in their hands, the pall bearers being eight of the older clergy. The Body was placed in the midst of the Choir, facing the Altar. That was the first day on which the newly enlarged Church was opened, and it was not even then quite finished. The Altar window had not received its stained glass,[2] and poured a flood of white light into the apsidal chancel, giving exquisite brilliance to the flowers and the green that rested

---

[1] He would have been 76 years of age on the 30th of that January.

[2] It has since been made a Memorial of the departed Bishop, and embraces a series of medallions illustrating the life of S. Paul:—1st. His sitting at the feet of Gamaliel; 2d. His Conversion; 3d. His Escape from Damascus in a basket; 4th. In the Council at Jerusalem; 5th. Striking Elymas blind; 6th. Preaching at Athens; 7th. Stoned by his brethren, the Jews; 8th. Shaking the Viper into the fire; 9th. His Martyrdom.

on the purple pall, and to the sweeping line of white-robed Bishops and Priests encircling the Altar and spreading down the choir on either side. There was no sign of mourning in the Chancel, except upon the empty Bishop's Chair at the crown of the apse. After the Lesson, the whole of the 212th Hymn was sung, to a melody composed by the Departed: [1]—

> Lo! what a cloud of witnesses
> Encompass us around;
> Men once like us with suffering tried,
> But now with glory crowned.

The Communion Service was then begun: and, after the Nicene Creed, the Bishops of Quebec and Connecticut delivered *Addresses* of deep feeling and loving appreciation of their Brother. The former, when consecrated, received the Holy Ghost partly through the laying on of the hands of the Bishop of Vermont, and could speak, with personal knowledge, of the work done by him at Lambeth.[2] His attendance, and that of so many of the Clergy of the Dioceses of Quebec and Montreal, was a tender and touching seal placed by them to the many mutual courtesies that had been so pleasing a feature of his whole Episcopate. The Bishop of Connecticut spoke from a long and intimate association in the most important spheres of Church activity, and as one who, having been the Assistant for many years of the previous Presiding Bishop, could measure better than any other, perhaps, the force of my Father's influence during his three years' tenure of the office. He was the celebrant in offering the Holy Eucharistic Sacrifice, which followed immediately; in the ministration of which he was assisted by the other Bishops present. Those blessed lines,

> Angels, and living saints, and dead,
> But one communion make,

were sung as the Communion hymn, to a melody by one of the Bishop's sons. The whole body of the Bishops and Clergy then received, followed by the family of the Departed, and then by the bearers. Of all that family, not one who was within three

---

[1] Originally written by him for the 48th Hymn, "Time hastens on, ye longing saints."

[2] See *Note*, on page 422.

hundred miles was absent, from Church or Altar; and not one of their voices, even of the nearest and dearest, was silent when the praises of God were sung that day in the great congregation. But as they kneeled on either side of the Body, some felt, as they never felt before, how truly darkness and mourning are the portion of those who yet live, while glory and brightness and beauty rest in their fulness only upon the Departed.

After the Blessing of Peace, the Procession formed once more; and, as the Body was lifted, the strains of the triumphant Hymn, "*Jesus lives*,"[1] were heard, every verse ending with an *Alleluia*. Out of doors the day was comparatively mild, but cloudy; and a thin feathery snow was falling, as the white-robed train passed on its winding way to the snow-clad cemetery, followed by the vast crowd which had remained in the Church to the end of the solemn service, and now lengthened the line that followed the bier. At the grave, one of the younger clergy took up the Pastoral Staff, to be delivered to the next Bishop, its evergreen wreath being untwined and buried with him who bore it first; and another, as a mark of reverent affection, cast the earth upon the Body with his naked hands. After the last *Amen*, the light snow fell for a moment in perfect silence: and all was over.

For a long time the idea had been entertained of setting apart a portion of the Rock Point farm on which my Father resided, as a cemetery. Nothing, however, had yet been done about it, nor could be at the season of the year when he so suddenly left us. It was therefore a simple necessity that he should first be laid in the family plot in the general cemetery of the town. But several acres have since been set apart, within sight of the waters of the Lake, at that end of Hemlock Hill which looks towards the Institute. In the centre of this portion a Home has been prepared for his remains, the walls of it being of the stone quarried on the spot; and they are surmounted by a carved cross of marble, resting on its three steps of granite.[2] There, nearly midway

---

[1] Hymn 117 of *Hymns Ancient and Modern*.

[2] The marble and the granite are both from Vermont, the former from Pittsford and the latter from Barre. Only the coping-stone of the wall is from outside the State, and that was brought from the other side of the Lake, where the capstone was placed upon his life's work. The plan of the monument was made at Rock Point; the workman who carved it is a Vermonter, and a communicant of the Church, con-

between the house that he lived in and the Church School that he founded, a place is reserved beside him for her who was nearest to his heart on earth during life, and who fain would not be far from him in death. And there, in consecrated ground, under the shadow of the Cross, among the trees he loved so well, and surrounded on every side with the memorials of his life's work,—there may he sleep in peace, until that morning when all the just shall awake in triumph!

S. MARK'S DAY, April 25, 1872.

THE BISHOP OF VERMONT.

In Memoriam.

ENTERED INTO LIFE, JANUARY 9, 1868.

The Vigil.

In Church Porch a Bishop sleepeth,
White-robed watch a Vigil keepeth;
Household band in sorrow weepeth:—
    Grant him rest, dear Lord!

Light eternal to his spirit;—
Bliss immortal to inherit
For sweet JESU'S precious merit,
    At the dreadful day.

Kindly looks he in his rest;
Hands calm folded o'er his breast;
By Cross beneath, his Faith confessed,—
    Cross of living green.

Lonely light above that brow
White-haired halo shews us now;
Night-winds chant, with gentle flow,
    Life's Recessional.

In Church Porch;—symbolic spot!
Heaven as yet attained not;
Deepest doctrine hereby taught,—
    Paradise the Portal.

Compline past;—the watch still kneel,
Lauds and Matins onward steal,
Prime at last doth Day reveal;
    Tierce,—his friends behold him.

The Celebration.

Sexts! The long procession see
Sweeping on in majesty:—
At their head no longer he,
    In the Church's van.

Grieve we not for loving leader,
Gone elsewhere to be our pleader
Stronger as our interceder,
    In his Middle Home.

Kneel we now at Holy Altar
With a faith that cannot falter,
With a trust that cannot alter,
    To receive our GOD.

Noble form in solemn state
'Earth to earth' doth still await.
To speed the soul, we celebrate:
    JESU, hear our prayer!

The Committal.

Forth the aged Saint they bear,
'Neath a pall of beauty rare:
Alleluia fills the air,—
    'Tis no hour for grief.

In Paradise his place is set,
With those grand souls, already met,
Keble and Neale and Philaret,
    And Saints on earth unknown.

Apostolic tones breathe low ;—
Loving hand last earth doth throw ;—
Nunc dimittis saith the snow :
    With his GOD we leave him.

[These verses were received, without name, not long after my Father's departure, and with only a modest pencilled memorandum, "*Not meant for publication.*"]

APPENDIX.

I.

COMPLETE LIST OF THE PUBLICATIONS OF BISHOP HOPKINS.

[Titles of bound volumes are printed in SMALL CAPITALS.]

1820. Address delivered before the Young Men's Auxiliary Bible Society, Nov. 2, 1819. Pittsburgh: Butler & Lambdin. 1820. Pp. 21.

1831. Religion the only Safeguard of National Prosperity. Thanksgiving Sermon, Dec. 1, 1831. Pp. 24.

1832. Sermon before the Howard Benevolent Society, Jan. 20, 1832. Pp. 20.

Religious Education, the safest means of Ministerial Increase, Christ Church, Hartford, Sept. 26, 1832. Pp. 32.

Defence of the Convention of the Diocese of Massachusetts, against certain Editorial Statements of "The Banner of the Church." 1832. Pp. 44.

1833. CHRISTIANITY VINDICATED, in Seven Discourses on the External Evidences of the New Testament; with a concluding Dissertation. Burlington: Edward Smith. 1833. Pp. 174.

1834. THE PRIMITIVE CREED, Examined and Explained. Burlington: Edward Smith. 1834. Pp. 415.

1835. THE PRIMITIVE CHURCH, compared with the Protestant Episcopal Church of the present day, etc.; with a Dissertation on sundry points of Theology and Practice, etc. Burlington: Smith & Harrington. 1835. Pp. 380. *Two Editions.*

Two Sermons on the Religious Education of the Poor, preached in the Cathedral Church of Quebec, Oct. 25, 1835. Pp. 30.

1836. ESSAY ON GOTHIC ARCHITECTURE, with various Plans and Drawings, etc. Burlington: Smith & Harrington. 1836. 4to. Pp. 46. 13 Pages of Plates.

1837. THE CHURCH OF ROME in her Primitive Purity, compared with the Church of Rome at the Present Day: being a Candid Examination of her Claims to Universal Dominion. Burlington: Vernon Harrington. 1837. Pp. 406.

Reprinted in London, 1839, by J. G. and F. Rivington, Revised and corrected by the Author, with an Introduction by the Rev. Henry Melvill, B.D. Pp. 396.

1838. Statement of the Studies, Terms and General Principles of The Vermont Episcopal Institute. Philadelphia: William Stavely. 1838. Pp. 16.

1839. Twelve Canzonets, words and music. London; and Firth and Hall, New York.

1841. The Sacrifice of Atonement, a Sermon preached in S. Paul's Church, Burlington, June 6. Chauncey Goodrich. 1841. Pp. 23.

Scripture and Tradition, preached at the Ordination of Ten Candidates for the Diaconate, in S. Paul's Chapel, New York. 1841. Pp. 24.

1842. Primary Charge, on the Missionary Constitution, the Oxford Tracts, and Nestorianism. Sept. 21, 1842. Pp. 40.

A Letter to the Rt. Rev. Francis Patrick Kenrick, Roman Bishop of Arath, etc. Burlington: Chauncey Goodrich. Dec. 26, 1842. Pp. 10.

1843. A Second Letter to the Rt. Rev. Francis Patrick Kenrick, Roman Catholic Bishop of Philadelphia. Burlington: Chauncey Goodrich. May 26, 1843. Pp. 64. *Two Editions.*

Two Discourses on the Second Advent of the Redeemer, with special reference to the year 1843. Burlington: C. Goodrich. 1843. Pp. 32. *Four Editions.*

1844. THE NOVELTIES WHICH DISTURB OUR PEACE. Four Letters addressed to the Bishops, Clergy and Laity, etc. H. Hooker, Philadelphia. 1844. Pp. 71, 80, 84, and 71. *Two Editions.*

SIXTEEN LECTURES ON THE CAUSES, PRINCIPLES, AND RESULTS OF THE BRITISH REFORMATION. Philadelphia: James M. Campbell & Co. 1844. Pp. 387.

1845. Episcopal Government. A Sermon preached at the Consecration of the Rev. Alonzo Potter, D.D., as Bishop of Pennsylvania. 1845. Pp. 24.

1846. Pastoral Letter, addressed by the Bishop to the people of his Diocese, on the subject of his Correspondence with the Rev. William Henry Hoit. Burlington: C. Goodrich. 1846. Pp. 47.

An Humble but Earnest Address to the Bishops, Clergy and Laity, etc., on the Tolerating among our Ministry of the Doctrines of the Church of Rome. New York: Harper & Brothers. 1846. Pp. 23.

Letter to the Rev. Samuel Seabury, D.D., Editor of the *Churchman*. 1846. Pp. 16.

1847. The Unity of the Church consistent with the Divisions of Party. Sermon before the General Convention of 1847. New York: Daniel Dana, Jr. 1847. Pp. 24.

1849. Defect of the Principle of Religious Authority in Modern Education. Address before the American Institute of Instruction, Aug. 14, 1849. Pp. 26.

    The Case of the Rev. Mr. Gorham against the Bishop of Exeter considered. Nov., 1849. Pp. 40.

1850. THE HISTORY OF THE CONFESSIONAL. New York: Harper & Brothers. 1850. Pp. 334.

    Address on the Death of Gen. Z. Taylor, delivered at St. Alban's, Aug 2, 1850. Pp. 26.

    Fraternal Unity in the Church of God. Triennial Sermon before the Board of Missions, in Cincinnati. 1850. Pp. 15.

1851. Hoffman on American Canon Law. Article in the *Church Review* of January, 1851. Pp. 26.

    Slavery: Its Religious Sanction, its Political Dangers, and the best mode of doing it away. A Lecture, delivered in Buffalo and Lockport. Jan., 1851. Pp. 32.

    The Divine Law for the Support of the Ministry. A Sermon, in Grace Church, Boston. March, 1851. Pp. 20.

    Address at the First Annual Meeting of the P. E. Historical Society. June, 1851. Pp. 19.

1852. A Pastoral Letter, on the Support of the Clergy. 1852. Pp. 15.

1854. A Defence of the Constitution of the Diocese of Vermont, in reply to the Strictures of the *Episcopal Recorder*. 1854. Pp. 26.

    A Pastoral Letter on the Support of the Clergy. 1854. Pp. 8.

    "THE END OF CONTROVERSY" CONTROVERTED. A Refutation of Milner's "End of Controversy," in a series of letters addressed to the Most Rev. Francis Patrick Kenrick, R.C. Archbishop of Baltimore. New York: Pudney & Russell. 1854. 2 vols. Pp. 468, 398. *Three Editions.*

    A Tract for the Church in Jerusalem: A Letter of Friendly Remonstrance to the Editors of *The Church Journal*. 1854. Pp. 38.

    The True Principles of Restoration to the Episcopal Office. 1854. Pp. 39.

    Address before the House of Convocation of Trinity College. 1854. Pp. 30.

1854. The Historical Evidences of Christianity. XIVth Essay. Pp. 363-383 in a vol. Pp. 20.

1855. "To the Friends of Sound Doctrine, Piety and Education," in behalf of the Vermont Episcopal Institute. Oct., 1855. Pp. 4.

A Pastoral Letter on the Subject of the Church Institute. 1855.

1857. THE AMERICAN CITIZEN: His Rights and Duties, according to the Spirit of the Constitution of the United States. New York: Pudney & Russell. 1857. Pp. 459. *Three Editions.*

1861. Letter on the Bible View of Slavery. Jan., 1861. Pp. 12.

A Letter to the Bishops and Delegates of the Church, now assembled at Montgomery. June, 1861.

1862. Protest, and Draft of a Pastoral Letter. Oct., 1862. Pp. 16.

1864. A SCRIPTURAL, ECCLESIASTICAL AND HISTORICAL VIEW OF SLAVERY, from the Days of the Patriarch Abraham to the Nineteenth Century. New York: W. I. Pooley & Co. 1864. Pp. 376. *Seven Editions.*

1866. THE LAW OF RITUALISM, examined in its relation to the Word of God, to the Primitive Church, to the Church of England, and to the P. E. Church in the United States. New York: Hurd & Houghton. 1866. Pp. 98. *Four Editions.*

DITTO, English Edition. Joseph Masters, Aldersgate St. 1867. Pp. 83.

[Private.] AUTOBIOGRAPHY in Verse. 1866. Pp. 121.

1867. THE HISTORY OF THE CHURCH IN VERSE. New York: W. I. Pooley. 1867. Pp. 256.

1868. [Posthumous.] A CANDID EXAMINATION OF THE QUESTION WHETHER THE POPE OF ROME IS THE GREAT ANTICHRIST OF SCRIPTURE. New York: Hurd & Houghton. 1868. Pp. 150.

[No Memorandum is here made of Communications to the Daily or Weekly Press; or of works left in Manuscript, or incomplete; or of unprinted Sermons, of which the number left is very great.]

II.

CONVERSATION COMPARISONS.

[My Father and another gentleman—who either was not or pretended not to be an admirer of the fair sex—one evening had a conversation, in the presence of a lady, upon the relative merits of the two sexes. My Father's share of the argument crystallized, before retiring that night, in the following verses, which appeared in the *Pittsburgh Gazette* of Oct. 2. 1818. They afterwards were inserted (not quite correctly) in the *Sheffield Iris*, an English Annual ; and were thence transplanted into a little work published in Philadelphia, called, *The Spirit of Foreign Annuals*.]

Man is the rugged, lofty pine,
    That frowns on many a wave-beat shore :
Woman, the slender, graceful vine,
Whose curling tendrils round it twine,
    And deck its rough bark sweetly o'er.

Man is the rock, whose towering crest
    Nods o'er the mountain's barren side :
Woman the soft and mossy vest,
That loves to clasp its sterile breast,
    And wreathe its brow in verdant pride.

Man is the cloud of coming storm,
    Dark as the raven's murky plume :
Save where the sunbeam, light and warm,
Of woman's soul and woman's form,
    Gleams brightly o'er the gathering gloom.

Yes, lovely sex ! to you 'tis given
    To rule our hearts with angel sway,
Blend with each woe a blissful leaven,
Change earth into an embryon heaven,
    And sweetly smile our cares away.

1818.

Appendix.

THE BELL OF S. JOHN'S.

[WRITTEN on a sleepless Sunday night passed at the house of Bishop Hobart, next door to S. John's Chapel, New York City, in November, 1825.]

The bell of S. John's told *one*.
Awake on my couch I lay ;
Sleep from my eyelids had flown,
Though I knew not what chased it away.
The evening prayer had been said,
The evening hymn was done,
The vows of the heart were paid
To the blessed Redeemer's throne ;
And the Sabbath had flown on the wings of love
To the Father of Spirits in heaven above.

I thought of my home the while ;
I thought of that wife, so dear,
Who could cheer my breast with a smile,
Or sadden it with a tear.
I thought of my children too,
So far and so long away ;
And what could a parent do,
But lift up his soul, and pray
That He, Whose eye marks the sparrow fall,
Might tenderly keep and watch o'er them all?

I saw the mild moon-beam,
As it shone on the chamber floor,
And I thought how it silvered the stream
In sight of my own loved door.
I heard the swelling breeze,
As it swept o'er the churchyard wall,
And I thought of the willow trees
Which grew near my humble hall,
And the grove of oaks, whose leaves fell fast
In the breath of that chill and wintry blast.

The bell of S. John's told *two ;*
And still did poor memory dwell,
In sweet though sad review,
On the home she loved so well.

Though the stranger's smile was bright,
Though his welcome was warm and kind,
Yet my thoughts would wing their flight
To the dear ones I left behind ;
And the wish still throbbed through my busy brain,
" Oh, would I could fly to their arms again !"

Ah, when will my bosom feel
As warm a longing given,—
As lively and true a zeal,
For my far-off home in Heaven !
Oh, when will my Saviour's love
Possess my reluctant soul,—
Draw my first thoughts above,
Inspire and guide the whole !
When, O my God, when shall I see
This fond, foolish heart more full of Thee !

Like the flash of the Northern Light,—
Like flowers which bloom, to die,—
Like gleams of sunshine bright
O'er the gloom of a stormy sky,—
Like the snow-flake which falls, to melt,—
Like all things that charm, and flee,
Are the longings my soul has felt
For the Home that dwells with Thee.
One moment I rise,—alas ! in vain !
'Tis gone ;—and I sink to the earth again.
The gifts of Thy love round my heart entwine,
And usurp the best portion, which should be *Thine*.

Oh teach me, while yet on this mortal shore,
Not to love them less,—but to love Thee more !

III.

BISHOP RAVENSCROFT'S OPPOSITION TO THE CONSECRATION OF BISHOP MEADE.

THERE never was a more conscientious effort made than this of Bishop Ravenscroft's, though his object seems to have been, at last, rather to obtain if possible some assurance that would enable him to give his own consent to the Consecration. In the earlier stage of the movement—begun when there was a prospect of Mr. Meade's being elected Assistant Bishop of Pennsylvania—the object certainly was to stop the Consecration of Mr. Meade, or any one of like opinions.

Among the Ravenscroft Papers in the hands of the Rev. Wm. Stevens Perry, D.D., there is, in the handwriting of that Bishop, the following

" MEMORANDUM.

" At the General Convention of 1826, the following was submitted to
" the Bishops who were present at the close of the Convention, by the
" subscriber, the youngest of the then Bishops of the Protestant Episcopal
" Church in America.

" The case supposed is, the election to the Episcopate of a person
" unqualified in any respect ; but especially of a person who is considered
" lax and unsettled on the cardinal points of the Orders in the Ministry,
" and irregular in practice as to the Forms and Services of the Church, as
" contained in the Liturgy and Rubricks.

" In such a case, can Consecration follow ? or is it to be understood,
" by the Bishops, that it shall be unanimously refused ?

" In such a case, is previous conduct to be considered as overruling
" any profession of future conformity ?

" In such a case, is it to be relied upon, that no Consecration will be
" proceeded in, without full communication with each other ; and with a
" deep sense of the high obligation we are conceived to be under, to
" maintain unity of sentiment and practice ?

" On the private application by the subscriber for the opinion of the
" Bishops on the cases, as stated,

" The Presiding Bishop concurs.
" Bishop Hobart   do.
" Bishop Kemp   do.
" Bishop Croes   do.
" Bishop Chase requires time to consider.
" Bishop Griswold   do.   do.

"Bishops Brownell and Bowen had obtained leave of absence, and had left the city.

"Bishop Moore did not attend the Convention.

"JNO. S. RAVENSCROFT, Bishop of the P. E. Church and of the Diocese of No. Carolina."

Among the same Papers is a first draft of the above with an additional paragraph at the beginning and at the end, both crossed out with pencil-marks. The former of the two begins thus :—" In the present ominous aspect of things for the Peace of the Church, presented by the late occurrences in the Diocese of Pennsylvania," etc. And the latter runs thus :— " The Reasons which suggest this application are not detailed, but they are felt to be imperious, and that some such measure is called for on the part of the Bishops for their own satisfaction and for the Peace of the Church. Philadelphia, Nov. 15, 1826." This draft is endorsed :—"Original of the Cases put to the other Bishops present, by the Bishop of North Carolina, on the Consecration of an improper person elected to the Episcopate, corrected by Bishop Hobart."

Two years after, with the prospect of Mr. Meade's election as Assistant Bishop of Virginia, Bishop Ravenscroft's anxiety of mind on this subject returned, and he wrote to Bishop Hobart (November 13, 1828) :—" I learn from a source entitled to credit, that the change proposed in the Ecclesiastical Constitution of that Diocese [it previously permitted but one Bishop] will be carried, though not without opposition ; and if so, Mr. Meade will be elected the Assistant Bishop. What in such an event is likely to be the course pursued by the House of Bishops ? What ought to be their course, under existing circumstances ? And what the probability that the real interests of the Church and true religion will prevail against the specious but fallacious pretense of maintaining peace by yielding to innovation ?

" These are subjects which haunt me, I may almost say ; and which even the anxiety consequent on the daily decline of my poor wife's health, cannot shut out. . . . I need not say, I trust, that I shall rejoice to hear from you, to receive the benefit of your greater experience, more extended range of observation, and knowledge of character, and that I shall most readily impart that information which a knowledge of the principles and views of the leaders in Virginia, acquired by a service of six years as their fellow-presbyter, has given me. It was my part, during that period,—and, I now see, not without design,—to stand between Bishop Moore and every assault made upon him, by the very men into whose arms he has now cast himself. But that is all forgotten. I pray God he may awake to his danger, and the danger to the Church, before the spell become indissoluble."

At the General Convention of 1829, Bishop Ravenscroft requested a personal interview with Mr. Meade, through the Rev. William M. Green (now Bishop of Mississippi), in the hope that it might enable the Bishop of North Carolina to consent to the Consecration of Mr. Meade. Nothing could exceed the kindly personal courtesy on both sides: but the interview was declined, for perfectly satisfactory reasons, and such as would apply in every similar case. Mr. Meade declared that his theological opinions had undergone no change since Bishop Ravenscroft had left Virginia; and the Bishop's consent to the Consecration of Mr. Meade was, in writing, refused.

IV.

O PEACE, O HEAVENLY PEACE.

[WRITTEN in October, 1845, when public opinion was rapidly ripening towards the outbreak of the Mexican war.]

O Peace, O heavenly Peace,
When shall we see the hour
When wars in all the earth shall cease,
Through thy celestial power ;—
When swords shall plough the soil,
And spears shall prune the tree,
And trumpets, formed for deadly broil,
Shall sound the jubilee !

O Peace, O heavenly Peace,
When shall thine influence move
All hearts from hate and bitterness,
By thy sweet law of love ;—
When shall the bigot's zeal
To scorn and shame be hurled,
And pure Religion's light reveal
The conquest of the world !

O Peace, O heavenly Peace,
Thy kingdom yet shall shine
In truth and joy and righteousness,
And love and power divine.
A subject of that reign
Seek thou, my heart, to be ;
That He, the Prince of Peace, may deign
To be at peace with thee !

1845.

LINES

[WRITTEN on returning from his Northern Visitation, August 12th, 1854.]

" Having a desire to depart, and to be with Christ, which is far better."—PHIL. i. 23.

Oh ! how the spirit
Looks to the sky,
Longing for glory
Promised on high ;

Toil-sick and care-worn
In the world's strife,
Bound down with sorrow,
Weary of life.

Sadly we wander,
Compassed with sin ;
Warring with troubles
Without and within ;
Pleasures so fleeting,
Hopes all so vain,
Earth's fondest greeting
Ending in vain.

Nought but the Gospel
Lightens the gloom ;
None but the Saviour
Conquers the tomb ;
By His great triumph
Victory is given,
And the bright future
Crowns us in Heaven!

1854.

V.

THE BISHOP OF VERMONT'S PROTEST AGAINST THE POLITICAL TONE OF THE PASTORAL LETTER OF 1862.

To the House of Bishops in General Convention assembled:

RIGHT REVEREND BRETHREN,—It is with much regret that I find myself obliged to enter my solemn protest against the political aspect of the Pastoral Letter which your venerable Body has adopted, and to withdraw from the final act of its public delivery. On minor topics of opinion, during my Episcopate of thirty years, I have never departed from my obligation to preserve the unity of this House, to the utmost of my small ability. But this action, in my judgment, involves a fundamental principle in our ecclesiastical position. We stand opposed, in this country, to any union between Church and State. In our individual capacity, as citizens, we are bound by the plain precepts of the inspired Apostles, to bear true allegiance to "the powers that be"—the earthly government under which the Providence of God has placed us. For *that*, our system sets forth an ample arrangement, in the Homily against Rebellion, in the Catechism appointed for the instruction of youth, in the Lessons of Scripture, in our Litany, and in the Prayers for the President and Congress, to say nothing of the special supplications set forth for the present national troubles, all uniting in the most positive testimony to the duty of Christian loyalty. But beyond this, I cannot allow that this House of Bishops, assembled in our official relations to the Church of God, has a right to go, by expressing any judgment on the measures of secular government. Under the American Constitution, the State has no right to declare its sentence on the legislation of the Church, so long as we do nothing to impair this duty of loyalty. And, under our Apostolic Constitution, the Church has no right to utter her sentence upon the legislation of the State, so long as it forbears to assail our Christian liberty. Their respective functions are distinct. The Almighty Ruler of the world has committed to the State the wide sphere of temporal interest, and He has committed to the Church the far higher sphere which embraces the interests of eternity. Each has its own allotted orbit, and I cannot comprehend how any reflecting and intelligent man in our Communion should desire that those orbits, in the present condition of mankind, should come together. I know, indeed, that this conjunction was attempted, though in different forms, by Popery and Puritanism. I know that it exists, to some extent, in the Establishment of England. But I also know that the primitive Church spread her triumphs throughout the earth in total independence of the State, and that all our clergy have been educated to regard the union of Church and State as a mistake and a calamity.

Maintaining this as a fundamental principle of our ecclesiastical position, from which I cannot justify any departure, I proceed to show how the Church has acted with relation to the policy of war, along the main track of her history, even under the disadvantages of her secular connections.

From the period when Christianity became established in the old Roman empire, there were many insurrections, and intestine as well as foreign wars, but I can call to mind no instance, in all the Councils, where the justice or the injustice of those wars was made a topic for ecclesiastical consideration. In the civil wars of England, which were numerous before the Reformation, I think it will not be found that the Church committed herself, by any formal and united action, either to the one side or to the other. In the great rebellion against Charles I., I am not aware that the Bishops were assembled to set forth any sentence on the political right or wrong involved in the conflict, although it threatened, and, for a season, accomplished, their own official downfall. And when the American Colonies revolted, and the Rev. William White became the first Chaplain to the revolutionary Congress, I do not see the slightest movement in our Mother Church to condemn his course, or that of the ministers who acted with him. The Bishop of London was the Diocesan of all the clergy in the Colonies, and had the undoubted right to suspend or to depose them, if the act of secular rebellion had been a proper ground for ecclesiastical denunciation. But that, in every age, has been regarded as a subject for the action of the State, and I doubt whether an instance can be found, in the whole range of the Church's history, where an ecclesiastical Court has tried a man for secular rebellion. If the Church of England had held it to be her duty to adopt the principle which this House of Bishops has laid down in the Pastoral Address, the Rev. William White and his colleagues could hardly have been accepted as fit subjects for Episcopal consecration, and the whole character of our ministerial succession would most probably have passed away, forever.

It is due to the solemn responsibility under which I present this protest, that I should enforce its positions by the citation of some high authorities.

Thus the general principle is set forth by the learned Palmer (London edition of 1839, vol. 2, p. 96):—

" In maintaining the right of the Church," saith he, " to judge in controversies, it is necessary to limit her authority to its proper object. It is not, then, supposed by any one, that the Church is authorized to determine questions relating to philosophy, science, legislation, or any other subjects beyond the doctrine of revelation. Her office relates entirely to the truth once revealed by Jesus Christ."

Appendix. 463

I need hardly remind my respected brethren of our XXth Article, in which it is declared that "the Church hath authority in controversies of faith": excluding by fair implication, controversies of secular policy.

The proper objects to be secured by the meetings of ecclesiastical Councils are thus set forth by Field, in his well known Treatise (p. 643):—

"The causes why General Councils assemble," saith he, "are three: 1st, the suppressing of heresies; 2d, a general and uniform reformation of abuses crept into the Church; and 3d, the taking away of schisms about the election of pastors and the rejection of intruders. And the causes that were wont to be examined in the meetings of the Bishops of the province (p. 514) were, the ordinations of Bishops when any Churches were void, and the depriving and rejecting all such as were found unworthy—and, in a word, any complaint or wrong done in any church was then to be heard."

To these I shall only add some interesting statements of the faithful and laborious Bingham (B. xvi. ch. 2, vol. 2, p. 880, of Bohn's London edition):—

"The power of the Church originally," saith this author, "was a mere spiritual power, her sword only a spiritual sword, as Cyprian terms it, to affect the soul and not the body. Hence the ancient Bishops were accustomed to plead with the magistrates and the emperors, to save the lives of those who were condemned to death by law."

The writer proceeds to quote S. Augustine's language to an African judge, as follows:—

"I know the Apostle says 'ye bear not the sword in vain, but are ministers of God to execute wrath upon them that do evil.' But the cause of the State is one thing, and the cause of the Church is another. The administration of the State is to be carried on by terror, but the meekness of the Church is to be commended by her clemency. These men, with the sword of unrighteousness, shed Christian blood: do you withhold even the lawful sword of judgment from being imbrued in their blood."

"It was also thought some cruelty," saith Bingham elsewhere (vol. 2 p. 1055), "or at least a very improper and unbecoming thing, for any clergyman to be concerned in judging or giving sentence in cases of blood. The laws allowed them to be chosen arbitrators of men's differences in civil causes, but they had no power at all in criminal causes except such as were purely ecclesiastical, and least of all in such criminal causes where life and death were concerned. Therefore there are many Canons forbidding this under the highest censure of deprivation. The Council of Tarragon universally forbids the clergy to sit as judges in any criminal causes. The Council of Auxerre more particularly enjoins presbyters not to sit in judgment when any man is to be condemned to die. The fourth Council of Toledo allows not priests to sit judges in cases of treason, even at the command of the prince, except the prince promised beforehand upon oath that he would pardon the offence, and remit the punishment. If they did otherwise, they were to be held guilty of bloodshed before Christ, and to lose their order and degree in the Church. And the eleventh Council of Toledo goes even further, refusing them lay-communion, until they were at the point of death."

These quotations might be greatly multiplied, but they must surely be sufficient to prove the broad distinction between the duty of the State and the office of the Church, at all times, but especially when wars and rebellions, which demand so large and awful an amount of bloodshed, are concerned. The great and glorious object of the divine Head of the Church was "not to destroy men's lives but to save them." And if the voice of His Church is to be lifted up at all, with reference to the avenging sword of earthly government, it would seem to be only when she is prepared to urge, for Christ's sake, the blessed work of peace and conciliation. If she may not, with propriety, do this, under the existing condition of our country, she is at least bound to abstain from any act which would make her a party in the mournful work of slaughter.

On the whole view, therefore, which I have been able to take of this deeply important question, I am constrained, however reluctantly, to stand entirely aloof from the novel movement, which pledges the Church to the State in its merely political administration. To that, as individual citizens, we owe all lawful obedience and support. But here, acting as Bishops in the Church of Christ, we have no right to pass beyond the circle of our spiritual functions, nor to express any opinion, direct or indirect, upon the measures of our secular government. In the world, we are all ready to render unto Cæsar the things that are Cæsar's. In the Church, we must confine ourselves unto our higher duty of rendering unto God the things that are God's.

The adoption of any other principle, in my humble judgment, can only lead to strife and confusion. For, if we claim the right to applaud the course of our secular government when it pleases us, we must also claim the right to condemn its measures when they may happen to be unacceptable. And the inevitable result must be that the clergy would have the warrant of our example to discuss every political movement in the House of God, and thus degrade our high and spiritual standing to the temporal uses of party and popular excitement.

In conclusion, I desire to say that I yield to no man in my loyalty as a citizen, in my attachment to the Federal Union of the States, or in my deep sorrow that any event should have occurred by which that Union could be endangered or destroyed. But my duty as a citizen is one thing, and my duty as a Bishop is another. By the first, I hold a relation to the State, under the laws and the Constitution. By the second, I hold, however unworthy, a high office in the kingdom of Christ, which is not of this world. And while I maintain a just allegiance to the State, I am bound to maintain the infinitely more solemn and sublime allegiance to my omnipotent Lord and Master in such wise, that I may not confound the lines of demarcation which He has placed between them. I claim no influence, however, for my humble judgment over any other mind, and am perfectly aware that I am personally of too little importance to expect it. But I am compelled to act on my own conclusions of duty, knowing, as I do, that they have been formed on the widest examination in my power, against my personal sympathies and interest, and solely from my conviction of their truth. I deny not the same claim to conscientious sincerity, on the part of my respected brethren from whom I differ. I shall withdraw myself from any participation in the Pastoral Letter, with the kindliest feelings of fraternal affection towards all my colleagues without exception. And I trust, by the mercy of God, that I shall be allowed to meet them at a future day, under happier circumstances, when we may assemble together again in a true union of sentiment and action.

JOHN H. HOPKINS,
Bishop of Vermont.

New York, House of Bishops, Oct. 15, 1862.

VI.

REFLECTIONS ON THE STATE OF THE CHURCH OF ENGLAND.

[WRITTEN in England, in 1867.]

PART I.

'Tis York Cathedral, venerable pile!
    Adorned with Gothic art to charm the eye
Beneath this noble arch I'll rest a while,
    And mark the sculptured forms that round me lie.

But hark! the solemn chimes proclaim the hour
    Which calls me to the Choir, for praise and prayer.
How floats that music from the lofty tower!
    The nave, the chancel, O how wondrous fair!

The surpliced choristers in bright array,
    While boyish beauty shines in every face,
Followed by white-robed men, now take their way,
    To raise the chant, with reverential grace.

No mode of worship to the Church is given,
    In these degenerate days, more dear than this:
It brings to mind the angel choir of heaven,
    And yields a foretaste of celestial bliss.

Yet far more glorious was the psalm of praise
    When ancient Israel raised her choral song,
In the wise Solomon's triumphant days,
    With well-trained voices, near three hundred strong,

While shawms and timbrels gave their solemn sound,
    With harps and psalteries interposed between,
And incense breathed its grateful odor round,
    And gorgeous garments graced the splendid scene.

Here was the model by the Word divine
    Given for the earthly worship of the Lord:
But where does England's best Cathedral shrine
    The same impressive majesty afford?

The Eastern Churches reach a loftier aim,
    And Russia makes a far more grand display :
While Rome preserves her old historic fame,
    And guards with pomp sublime her priestly sway.

Compared with these our modes of worship shrink
    As if we were afraid to show our zeal :
For so, at least, our travellers often think,
    Though few the thought are willing to reveal.

No incense rolls its fragrant cloud on high,
    No lights upon those sacred Altars shine,
No gorgeous robes attract the gazing eye,
    No ardor warms the words of life divine.

The doctrine's pure, but uttered in a style
    So cold and formal that it sounds like art ;
The mind is freed from superstition's guile,
    But where's the fervid glow that wins the heart?

Doubtless our clergy are a faithful band,
    Who preach the truth and know its saving power,
Yet rarely venture to assume the stand
    Of earnest feeling, in devotion's hour.

With calm monotony the prayers they read,
    With calm monotony they warn the soul,
With sermons dry the hungry flock they feed,
    But shun emotion's warm and strong control.

It was not thus the prophets of the Lord
    Rebuked with trumpet voice old Israel's sin ;
Not thus did John the Baptist preach the Word,
    In mercy sent, that stubborn race to win.

Not thus S. Paul fulfilled his zealous course,
    Beseeching men, with tears, their souls to save,
And urging them, with love's constraining force,
    To seek the life that lies beyond the grave.

Think how the faithful round the Apostle hung,
    Weeping upon his neck with anguished heart !
What modern Bishop, from old England sprung,
    Would from his grieving people thus depart ?

Official dignity would bar the way,
    And etiquette would almost deem it sin,
For feeling here avoids its frank display,
    However much the soul may yearn within.

Yet English hearts are earnest, warm and true ;
 And English senses gaze with fond delight
When forms of beauty open to the view,
 And claim the grateful homage of the sight.

Why should religion lay her light aside?
 Why should her Altars dark and dull be found,
While near the Throne such wealth and pomp abide,
 And lavish grandeur sheds its radiance round?

Why do her priesthood, when they should rejoice
 Before the Table of their heavenly King,
Pour forth no hymn with high and grateful voice,
 Nor splendid robes, nor lights, nor incense bring?

Is this to give due honor to their Lord?
 Is this the sacrifice of love to pay?
Is this in fair accordance with His Word
 So plainly kept in Israel's palmy day?

The grand Cathedrals haply still remain,
 Erected by the piety of yore ;
The choral service, too, we yet retain :
 But when will loving zeal the rest restore?

York, England, August 29, 1867.

PART II.

The Church, in union with the State, appears
 In honor. So esteems the English mind :
And hence her welfare, through all future years,
 To that connection seems to be confined.

Yet many deem this notion a mistake,
 Believing that her energies are bound
In fetters, which her real friends must break,
 Before her true position can be found.

For now her power of government is lost ;
 She has no voice that she can call her own ;
Her judgment may by Parliament be crossed,
 Or rendered vain and futile by the Throne.

She cannot choose her prelates by her vote,—
 That choice is still dictated by the Crown.
She has no discipline, and all may note
 How few there are who fear their Bishop's frown.

Her House of Convocation used to be
    The Church's Parliament; with wisdom's skill,
And calm authority, from bondage free,
    She there could promulgate her sacred will.

But this was silenced by the Sovereign's word,
    Through many reigns, and only now of late
Has partly been permitted to afford
    Some prospect of its old efficient state.

'Tis true, the Bishops occupy a place
    Amongst the peers, in robes of office fair;
While the lay lords, with no respectful grace,
    Sit covered, in their common garments, there.

And so "the Church is represented"! How?
    What power have they to guard her holy claim?
Their small minority is forced to bow,
    And yield the substance for a shadow's name.

For "Parliament's omnipotent," they say:
    The Lord's own Kingdom bends to earthly rule;
The Church, once held her Bishops to obey,
    Is governed by the legal laymen's school.

Nor are they always Churchmen. With a view
    To "liberal progress," men together stand,—
The infidel, the Papist, and the Jew,—
    To make the laws which rule throughout the land.

Thus men of hostile creed, or none at all,
    Are placed in trust to guard the Church of God:
Men who would gladly aid to work her fall,
    And cast her patrimonial wealth abroad.

Such is her present state. When shall we see
    Her ancient flag of *Liberty* unfurled?
When will it please the Lord to set her free
    From this Erastian bondage to the world?

When will her Bishops leave their lordly seat
    In Parliament, and consecrate their time
With prayer and blessings oft their flock to greet,
    And aid their Clergy in their task sublime?

When will they wake their own long dormant power
    Of discipline, the Church's ills to cure,
And give with missionary zeal each hour
    To gather in the outcast and the poor?

When will the priests and people all unite
 To have for Bishop their elected man,
Instead of yielding to the Throne their right,
 Against the true and Apostolic plan?

When will the Church lift up her potent voice
 In her Provincial Synods, as of yore,
Learn in her ancient freedom to rejoice,
 And be the organ of her Lord once more?

Alas! There's little hope of such a change.
 The yoke of bondage is too old and strong.
Most men would deem it foolish, wild, and strange,
 To alter what has now endured so long.

It needs the courage of a martyr's soul
 In him who such a mighty task would dare.
Who now inclines to brave the world's control?
 Or view the contest save with sad despair?

But though the age of martyrdom has passed,
 Its zeal may yet inspire the favored few
The fear of mortal strife away to cast,
 And in the strength of God the truth pursue.

Men may arise, whose hearts resolved shall be
 To burst the bondage which they now obey,
No longer satisfied with grief to see
 Each bold schismatic sect more free than they.

The Church's doctrine pure, by Scripture tried;
 Her government, from the Apostles ta'en;
Holy and Catholic in all beside:
 Why should this dark Erastian blot remain?

And yet 'tis hard to contemplate the strife
 Which such a change seems likely to attend;
Hard to disturb the Church's peaceful life,
 In doubtful hope of victory in the end.

May not this bondage, now three centuries old,
 Have been ordained by the Redeemer's will,
To be the safeguard of His favored fold,
 Protecting it from every other ill?

Without its aid, could England's Church have kept
 Her foothold, after Cromwell's mighty sway,
With puritanic violence, had swept
 Her fair and honored fabric all away?

Do we not pray for unity and peace?
  And shall we seek our union to destroy?
Or should we, were the present ills to cease,
  A better state of privilege enjoy?

These are grave questions, which no mortal mind
  Can now determine. Be it still our part
To leave them to the Lord, with will resigned,
  With patient hopefulness and faithful heart.

Meanwhile, we may with gratitude rejoice
  To see how far our Mother Church has gone;
To East and West and North and South, her voice
  Has called the Nations to the Saviour's throne.

Long may she prosper, by His power divine,
  In all the graces by His Spirit given!
Long may her light with growing brightness shine,
  And show the world the safest path to heaven!

London, Sept. 4, 1867.

VII.

THE WESTMINSTER ABBEY CORRESPONDENCE.

In order to present this whole case in such wise as to give Dean Stanley the benefit of all that he has written on his side of the question, his own letter to the *Guardian* is here inserted first, including the three letters —two from him to the Archbishop, and one from the latter in reply—forwarded by him to that paper for publication.

From the *Guardian* of October 9, 1867.
THE CONFERENCE IN WESTMINSTER ABBEY.

The Dean of Westminster presents his compliments to the Editor of the *Guardian*, and requests the publication of the following correspondence.

It will be seen that whilst, as guardian of Westminster Abbey, he could not allow it to be used for the purpose of giving sanction to the Conference, he was anxious to give any such facilities as were compatible with this duty.

The allusions in his letter to the intentions of the Primate refer to expressions used by his Grace in previous communications, assuring him that all party questions would be avoided.

From the Dean of Westminster to the Archbishop of Canterbury.

Deanery, Westminster, September 21,[1] 1867.

"My Dear Lord Archbishop—I have been honored with a communication from your Grace through the Bishop of London, requesting the use of Westminster Abbey for a special service to be held for the English, American, and Scottish Bishops now assembled in England, to be held, as I understood, on September 28th.

"On all occasions it is my earnest desire to render the Abbey and the Precincts of Westminster available for purposes of general utility and edification, and this desire is increased when the request comes from your Grace.

"You will kindly allow me to state the difficulty which I feel in the present instance. I have endeavored to act in such matters on the rule

[1] It will be noticed that this refusal was made *before the Conference opened.* It was evidently gathered, from the debates in the preliminary meeting of the 17th, that the Colenso question could not be so entirely excluded as was intended: so that the amiable Archbishop, after all, satisfied neither party.

of granting the use of the Abbey to such purposes, and such only, as are either coextensive with the Church of England, or have a definite object of usefulness or charity, apart from party or polemical considerations.

"Your Grace will, I am sure, see that however much your Grace's intentions would have brought the proposed Conference at Lambeth within this sphere, in fact it can hardly so be considered. The absence of the Primate and the larger part of the Bishops of the Northern Province, not to speak of the Bishops of India and Australia and of other important colonial or missionary sees, must, even irrespectively of other indications, cause it to present a partial aspect of the English Church, whilst the appearance of other prelates not belonging to our Church places it on a different footing from the institutions which are confined to the Church of England.[1] And, further, the absence of any fixed information as to the objects to be discussed and promoted by the Conference leaves me, in common with all who stand outside, in uncertainty as to what would be the proposals or measures which would receive, by implication, the sanction given by the use of the Abbey,—a sanction which, in the case of a church so venerable and national in its character, ought, I conceive, to be lent only to public objects of well-defined or acknowledged beneficence.

"These are the grounds why I hesitate to take upon myself the responsibility suggested. But, when stating this difficulty, I feel so strongly the value of the friendly intercourse to promote which has been the chief intention of your Grace, and of, I doubt not, many of the prelates who have concurred in this Conference—and I am so desirous that the Abbey shall be made to minister to the edification of large sections of our Church, even when not representing the whole, and of those outside our own immediate pale (especially our brethren from America) who are willing to coöperate with us in all things lawful and good,—that I would gladly, if possible, join in advancing such a purpose.

"It has occurred to me that, as the service indicated by your Grace is to be held after the Conference is finished, the Abbey might be granted for it, without any relation to the Conference itself; but either for some specific object, such as the Society for the Propagation of the Gospel, or for other Home or Foreign Missions of unquestioned importance, or else (in those general terms which, as I apprehend, express your Grace's wishes) for the promotion of brotherly good-will and mutual edification amongst all members of the Anglican communion.

"Under these circumstances, and on this understanding, which I

---

[1] Here, the *presence* of the American Bishops is given as one reason for excluding the Conference: while afterwards he labors very hard to show himself "so desirous that the Abbey shall be made to minister to the edification of . . . *especially our brethren from America*." In subsequent passages it is a little more considerately put, as "*mutual* edification of all members of the Anglican communion."

should wish to be made as public as the announcement of the service itself, I should have great pleasure in permitting the use of the Abbey for such a service, to be held in the morning or afternoon of September 28th (as may be deemed most convenient); and I trust that, if this meets your Grace's wishes, your Grace will undertake to preach on the occasion.

" I beg to remain, my dear Lord Archbishop,

" Yours faithfully and respectfully

" A. P. STANLEY."

From the Archbishop of Canterbury to the Dean of Westminster.

" ADDINGTON PARK, CROYDON, September 25, 1867.

" MY DEAR DEAN—I laid your note before the Conference yesterday, but it will probably not close its sittings on Friday evening, as there is reason to believe that committees will be appointed to report at a future date. Under these circumstances, it is obvious from the tenor of your letter that the Abbey is not open us. I regret, therefore, that we shall not be able to avail ourselves of your kind offer under the specified conditions.

" Believe me, my dear Dean, yours very truly,

" C. T. CANTUAR."

From the Dean of Westminster to the Archbishop of Canterbury.

" DEANERY, WESTMINSTER, September 27, 1867.

" MY DEAR LORD ARCHBISHOP—I have to acknowledge with thanks your Grace's letter of the 25th, and to express my regret that your Grace and the Bishops assembled should have felt themselves precluded from accepting my proposal—in reply to your Grace's request—to meet in the Abbey for 'some specific object' of charity or usefulness, 'or for the purpose of promoting brotherly good-will and mutual edification amongst all members of the Anglican communion.'

" I beg, however, that you will assure the prelates assembled, especially those of our American brethren, for whose sake, as I stated in my former letter, I especially proposed to grant the use of the Abbey as before mentioned, that if they or any of them should wish to attend the services in the Abbey on Sunday next (at 10 A.M. or at 3 P.M.) every accommodation and welcome shall be afforded.

" I beg to remain, my dear Lord Archbishop,

" Yours faithfully and respectfully,

" A. P. STANLEY."

Appendix.

This last offer was so entirely unmeaning that it is no wonder that when it was read in the Conference "no response was made." It was not long before the Dean began to suspect that he had made a mistake. The note to the Bishop of Vermont was penned some days after (it has no more precise date than "Oct.," but it was certainly on or before the 13th of October); and it was confided to the charge of the Bishop of Pittsburgh. It was not received by my Father until after his return to Burlington.

Meanwhile, late in the evening of the 13th of October, my Father received the following note[1]:—

From the Dean of Westminster to the Bishop of Vermont.

DEANERY, WESTMINSTER, Oct. 13, '67.

The Dean of Westminster presents his compliments to the Bishop of Vermont, and begs to say that he has addressed a letter to him through the Bishop of Pittsburgh, which he hopes that the Bishop of Vermont may by this time have received. But he takes the liberty of mentioning it, because the letter may possibly have failed of its destination, owing to the uncertainty of the Bishop's movements.

The Dean also begs to say that if he can be of any use in showing the Abbey to the Bishop of Vermont, he will be at home during the morning of to-morrow (Tuesday) till 1, and shall be very glad to do so.

From the Bishop of Vermont to the Dean of Westminster.

WESTMINSTER PALACE HOTEL, Oct. 14, 1867.

The Bishop of Vermont presents his compliments to the Dean of Westminster, and begs to say, in answer to the note received last night, that the letter addressed to him by the Dean, through the Bishop of Pittsburgh, has not yet reached its destination.

The Bishop leaves London for Liverpool to-day, and expects to sail to-morrow on his return to the United States. He thanks the Dean for his offer to show him the Abbey; but that matter was attended to, through the courtesy of the Ven. Archdeacon Wordsworth, during the week which preceded the Conference at Lambeth.

It was certainly anticipated by the Bishop that he should have seen more of the dignified Clergy of the Church of England during his visit,—undertaken, as it was, solely on the invitation of their Ecclesiastical Head, the Archbishop of Canterbury. But he is aware of the causes which have existed, and probably still exist, to bar the ordinary avenues of Christian urbanity; and doubts not that his respected brethren thought themselves fully justified in their course on the occasion.

[1] The three notes here next ensuing have never before been printed.

From the Dean of Westminster to the Bishop of Vermont.

DEANERY, WESTMINSTER, Oct. 16, '67.

The Dean of Westminster presents his compliments to the Bishop of Vermont, and begs to thank him for his note, and to enclose to him a copy of the letter which he had already forwarded to him thro' the Bishop of Pittsburgh, and which he will thank him to communicate to the other American Bishops.

The Dean is not surprised that the American Bishops should have misapprehended the complicated circumstances which imposed on the Dean the painful but necessary duty of acting as was incumbent on himself and others in like position.[1] But he must confess that he was surprised to find that in answer to his offer, twice repeated, of a special service in the Abbey, with a special view to the American Prelates, for any specific or general purpose of Christian charity or usefulness,—and again to his offers, more than twice repeated, of receiving in the Abbey any American Prelates who wished to avail themselves of his services and his attentions,—no response was made,[2] except in four instances which he will remember with pleasure in connection with the visits of the American Bishops to England.

He begs also to repeat to the Bishop of Vermont, what he has already expressed to all the Bishops with whom he had the power of communicating, his regret that the severe domestic affliction, under which he has received no more cordial sympathy than from the Bishop's own countrymen in the United States, should have prevented him from showing that hospitality, the want of which he could have hoped might have been ascribed to this its only cause,[3] and not, as the Bishop in his note sug-

---

[1] Referring, doubtless, to the Dean of S. Paul's.

[2] The Dean's "surprise" that "no response was made" to such offers under such circumstances is hardly complimentary to the American Bishops. He might as well have said that he was surprised to find that they had the sensibilities of gentlemen. The open affront having been put upon the whole Conference, of which they were members, and which they came to England specially to attend, it was not for them alone to condone it in return for offers which were aimed to separate their case from that of the English, Scottish, and Colonial Bishops. Nor was it much to invite them to receive, in duplicate, from the Dean those attentions in the Abbey which had already been rendered three or four weeks previous by somebody else. If the offer reached other Bishops, as it did the Bishop of Vermont, only the day before sailing for Home, it would be another sufficient reason why "no response was made."

[3] This was not the cause why the Abbey was refused to the Conference, while it was offered freely for any meaningless service: which was the only cause of offence. Social hospitality no one expected, when the existence of domestic affliction was known: but probably very few of the Americans, travelling as they had been for weeks, were aware of the death of Sir Frederick Bruce; and still fewer would have known, until they were told, that Sir Frederick Bruce was the brother-in-law of the Dean of Westminster. It may be our republican ignorance, it is true: but to an American Churchman, a Dean in the Church of England is a much greater man than one who is only the son of an Earl. The social hospitality of Dean Stanley in his own

gests, to any absence of urbanity towards those whom else he would have been delighted to see and receive.

The Dean hopes that this communication will entirely remove from the Bishop's mind the misapprehension under which he appears to labor, and that on any future visit to England, the Dean may have the pleasure of receiving the Bishop under his roof, and within the walls of the venerable Abbey.

Enclosed in the foregoing note was the following copy of the letter originally confided to the Bishop of Pittsburgh for my Father, but not previously received:—

From the Dean of Westminster to the Bishop of Vermont.

DEANERY, WESTMINSTER, Oct., 1867.

MY LORD BISHOP—Understanding that some misapprehension exists on the part of the American Bishops as to their invitation to a service in Westminster Abbey, I beg that you will do me the favor of communicating the following statement, in as public a way as you think fit, to your Episcopal brethren.

It was impossible for me as guardian of a building like the Abbey, which belongs to the whole Church and people of England, to take the responsibility of giving its sanction to a Meeting that included only a portion of the English Bishops, and of which the objects were undefined, the issues unknown, and the discussions secret. But I was so anxious to show every courtesy to the Bishops from the United States, that chiefly on their account, as I particularly specified in my letter to the Archbishop, I deviated so far from the usual rules which guide the services in the Abbey, as to propose the use of the Abbey for a service which should gather them there, either for some specific object of charity or usefulness, or for the general promotion of good-will and mutual edification of all members of the Anglican communion. I was encouraged the more to make this offer, by the pledge which I had received, that no questions exciting party differences should be introduced into the Meeting, and I was therefore in hopes that his Grace would have felt himself able to accept a proposal which I had reason to believe would have been gratifying to our American brethren.

The proposal was, however, declined: and I must therefore, through you, beg to express my regret that such an opportunity was lost, of cultivating that feeling of amity between the two countries which is at all times so welcome. The circumstance of the severe domestic affliction which has recently befallen us, whilst it prevented me from showing that

house is well known, and is one of the chief means by which he has gained and retained an influence which the obliquity of his theological views would, of itself, have rendered impossible.

hospitality which I should otherwise have offered to you, makes me doubly anxious that in a country, from which we have received expressions of such sincere sympathy, there should be no misunderstanding as to the cordial desire which I entertain to welcome Americans on all occasions to our great national sanctuary.

I remain, etc., etc., etc.,

ARTHUR P. STANLEY.

From the Bishop of Vermont to the Dean of Westminster.

BURLINGTON, VT., Nov. 9, 1867.

VERY REV. AND DEAR SIR—Your letter of October, addressed through me to all the American Bishops, reached me last night, and I have sent it for publication to the Editor of *The Church Journal*, New York.

The high reputation which you enjoy as an author of acknowledged ability concurs with your elevated position as the Dean of Westminster to give importance to your course, in withholding the use of the venerable Abbey from the Pan-Anglican Council. How far your explanation will be satisfactory to my respected colleagues, it is not for me to say. But with regard to myself, I frankly confess that I do not understand it.

You state, as the reason for your decision, that you are the guardian of the Abbey, which belongs to the whole Church and people of England, and that you could not give its sanction to a meeting which included a portion only of the English Bishops, and of which the objects were undefined, the issues unknown, and the discussions secret.

Here are several points to which I cannot assent, in accordance with true Church principle.

In a certain sense, it may be said that the Abbey, and every Cathedral, —nay, even every parish church, belongs to the whole Church of England. But in the strict and proper sense of jurisdiction, the Abbey belongs to the Diocese of London[1] and the Province of Canterbury. You are, indeed, the Dean, and, so far, the guardian of the edifice; but I do not comprehend how this can discharge the vows of ordination which bound you to "obey your Bishop" and Archbishop, and "follow, with a glad mind and will, their godly admonitions." Nor do I perceive on what ground of ecclesiastical law you thought fit to take a course directly contrary to what you knew to be their design in holding this important Conference of Bishops from every quarter of the world. The call was given by your own Archbishop, to whom you owe respect and deference. The Council was attended by your own Bishop, to whom you owe canonical obedience. It was fully sanctioned by the great majority

---

[1] By Act of Parliament, Westminster Abbey is "a Royal Peculiar," although united to the Diocese of London.

of the other English Bishops. It had the express approval of the Convocation of Canterbury, to which you belong. It had the cordial concurrence of the Archbishops and Bishops of Ireland, the Metropolitans and Bishops of the Colonies, the Bishops of Scotland, and those of the United States. And its proceedings were marked by the unanimous consent of the whole. Are you, on any ground of true Church principle, or even of common sense, to be regarded as the representative of "the whole Church and people of England," in withholding the use of the venerable Abbey from an assembly like this? What previous meeting of Bishops has ever been held within its walls which would bear a comparison in numbers and in dignity? And are you, by virtue of your office as the Dean, an absolute Autocrat, to deny, in opposition to your own Archbishop and Bishop, and all the other prelates of the English Communion, the use of the Abbey by the Council of Lambeth, on the sole pretext that some three or four of the Bishops, who have no authority whatever over the Diocese of London, thought fit to dissent from the judgment of all their brethren?

You disapproved the Council because "its objects were undefined, and its issues unknown." I pray you to remember, if you can, any Council of the Church, whose action could be known beforehand. Was it not enough to be assured that an assembly called by your own Archbishop, and consisting of the Bishops of the Church, could not possibly be supposed to have any object, or arrive at any issue, inconsistent with truth and duty? Could not the Dean of Westminster trust seventy-six prelates of the Church with the care of her sacred interests? Or was he really justified in regarding them as a band of conspirators against her honor and dignity, so that he was conscientiously compelled, in despite of all real canonical principle, to shut his Abbey doors against them?

This, my dear sir, is the position in which your strange course has placed you, in my humble judgment. You will pardon me, I trust, for speaking plainly. I cannot do otherwise, on a question in which the honor of the Church is concerned. I have no hesitation in saying that I think you made a great mistake, and that, as a justification of it seems altogether impossible, it would be more frank and candid on your part to call it by its proper name, and let it be forgotten as soon as possible, since the remembrance of it can only be attended by mortification.

Your allusion to your offer to receive our Bishops, provided they came in their official capacity and without any connection with the Council, renders it proper for me to say that the invitation, thus limited, was unanimously declined, as being, indeed, an assault upon the Council, and upon ourselves for coming to attend it. I am very willing to suppose that you did not so intend it; but it could hardly admit of any other fair construction.

And your reference to your own domestic affliction, of which I had heard nothing at the time, while it certainly calls on me for sympathy, and furnishes a sufficient apology for the absence of any social hospitality, would have been better made when we were on the spot, since then we could not have been led to suppose that your antipathy to the Council was the cause of your seeming discourtesy.

But this, being merely a private and personal matter, is easily explained, and could not be the ground of any unpleasant feeling. I am persuaded that the kind and cordial attention which our Bishops received from other quarters was quite as great as we could have expected or desired. And we had certainly no reason to complain of any failure in English hospitality.

The only question of any real importance is the very serious one, whether the Dean of Westminster has a right, on true Church principles, to withhold the Abbey from the meeting of a Council called by his Archbishop, and sanctioned by his own Bishop of London. This question extends itself to S. Paul's Cathedral, as it was openly stated in Council that the Bishop had no power to tender either of those buildings for the closing service of the great assembly, though no one doubted that one of these sacred edifices would have been the proper place for that solemn occasion.

If the Dean possesses such a right,—if the Bishop of London has no power over the use of the Cathedral of S. Paul or Westminster Abbey,— I must distinctly aver that I regard the fact as a serious blot upon the ecclesiastical system of our venerable Mother Church of England, entirely inconsistent with primitive practice, and existing nowhere else in Christendom. The Bishop is the Rector-in-Chief of all the churches in the Diocese, and hence the promise of obedience to his godly judgment is an essential part of the vows made in ordination. But especially is he the Rector-in-Chief of his own Cathedral, which is the place containing his official seat, and called *Cathedral* for that very reason, because the Bishop's *Chair* is there.

It was understood in the Council that the Dean of S. Paul's, like the Dean of Westminster, was hostile to our assembly, and that they had the legal authority to close, against their own Bishop and Archbishop, so far as the Conference at Lambeth was concerned, the doors of both the Cathedral and the Abbey. And this is what I stated, in the beginning, that I could not understand. Believing that our Mother Church is truly Catholic in all her essential principles, I certainly do not understand how she could have fallen into so flagrant an inconsistency, and so gross a departure from Ecclesiastical law and order as they existed universally in the purest ages of the Christian dispensation.

I trust that your own part in the late case may have the good result of turning the attention of the Church of England to this anomaly, and restoring to the Bishops those ancient rights in their own Cathedrals and quasi-Cathedrals which have been so long withheld. It is this hope which has led me to write so much at large upon the subject, because it is one which deserves the serious attention of all concerned. For it must be remembered that the affront was not offered so much to the American Bishops, as to your own.

With all personal respect and regard,

Your faithful brother in Christ,

JOHN H. HOPKINS,

Bishop of Vermont.

To the Very Rev. the Dean of Westminster.

From the innumerable comments of the press on this correspondence, in various shapes of prose and verse, the following *jeu d'esprit* from the London *Churchman* may be selected as a specimen of the way in which the whole thing struck the minds of others.

THE DEAN'S MISTAKE.

Archbishop.

SEVENTY-SIX Prelates to Lambeth have gone,
Not from England, and Scotland, and Ireland alone,
But from all round the world ; and in concord most kind,
The American Bishops are all of our mind.
So in Westminster Abbey we'll all join in praise,
If you, Mr. Dean, no objection will raise.

Dean.

In Westminster Abbey the Synod sha'n't pray ;
Don't suppose you're the Church :—so I, the Dean, say.
For what is Archbishop or Bishop to me,
Or a few score of Prelates from over the sea,—
To me, Dean of Westminster, Arthur Stanley
For indeed some have not come, although they were bid,
And your objects you know not, discussions are hid.
Would you only fix something for *me* to approve.
I'd receive you all here in affection and love.

Bishop of Vermont.

By the laws of the Church a Dean's but a Dean,
Not a Bishop, Archbishop, or Pope, as I ween :
He is bound to obey, and his province is small :—
You've mistaken the rank, Mr. Dean, of us all.

M. E.

Milton Keynes UK
Ingram Content Group UK Ltd.
UKHW040735260224
438379UK00007BA/920